Philosophy as a Way of Life

Philosophy as a Way of Life

Spiritual Exercises from Socrates to Foucault

Pierre Hadot

Edited with an introduction by
Arnold I. Davidson

Translated by
Michael Chase

Blackwell
Publishing

© 1995 by Pierre Hadot
English translation © 1995 by Blackwell Publishing Ltd

BLACKWELL PUBLISHING
350 Main Street, Malden, MA 02148-5020, USA
9600 Garsington Road, Oxford OX4 2DQ, UK
550 Swanston Street, Carlton, Victoria 3053, Australia

Parts of this work first published as *Exercices spirituels et philosophie antique*
by Etudes Augustiniennes, Paris 1987 (2nd edition)

English edition first published 1995

28   2016

Library of Congress Cataloging-in-Publication Data
Hadot, Pierre.
[Exercices spirituels et philosophie antique. English]
Philosophy as a way of life: spiritual exercises from Socrates to Foucault/Pierre Hadot;
edited by Arnold Davidson; translated by Michael Chase.
p. cm.
Includes bibliographical references and index.
ISBN 978-0-631-18032-6 (hbk. : alk. paper)—ISBN 978-0-631-18033-3 (pbk.: alk. paper)
1. Philosophy.   2. Spiritual exercises - History.   I. Davidson, Arnold Ira.
II. Title
B105.S66H3313   1995
100—dc20   94-28788   CIP

A catalogue record for this title is available from the British Library.

Set in 10.5 on 12 pt Ehrhardt
by Pure Tech Corporation, Pondicherry, India
Printed and bound in Singapore
by C.O.S. Printers Pte Ltd

For further information on Blackwell Publishing, visit our website:
www.blackwellpublishing.com

Contents

Translator's Note   vi
List of Abbreviations   ix
Introduction: Pierre Hadot and the Spiritual Phenomenon of
Ancient Philosophy   Arnold I. Davidson   1

Part I   Method   47
  1   Forms of Life and Forms of Discourse in Ancient Philosophy   49
  2   Philosophy, Exegesis, and Creative Mistakes   71

Part II   Spiritual Exercises   79
  3   Spiritual Exercises   81
  4   Ancient Spiritual Exercises and "Christian Philosophy"   126

Part III   Figures   145
  5   The Figure of Socrates   147
  6   Marcus Aurelius   179
  7   Reflections on the Idea of the "Cultivation of the Self"   206

Part IV   Themes   215
  8   "Only the Present is our Happiness": The Value of the Present
    Instant in Goethe and in Ancient Philosophy   217
  9   The View from Above   238
10   The Sage and the World   251
11   Philosophy as a Way of Life   264

Postscript: An Interview with Pierre Hadot   277
Select Bibliography   287
Index   301

Translator's Note

The thought of Pierre Hadot is based on a lifetime's study of, and meditation upon, ancient Greek and Latin philosophical texts. In the course of this long period, he has, of course, developed his own methodology for the study of such texts. Based as it is on the methods of his own teachers, such as Paul Henry and Pierre Courcelle,[1] this method is distinctly his own, and he has transmitted it to a whole generation of French scholars in the field of late antique thought.

The first stage of Hadot's method is a scrupulous, textually critical reading of the original texts, followed by an equally exacting translation of these texts into French.[2] Only on the foundation of the intense, detailed confrontation with the text which real translation demands, Hadot feels, can one begin the processes of exegesis, interpretation, and, perhaps, criticism. Thus, Hadot's thought is, at least to a large extent, based on his methods of translation. This being the case, it is impossible to understand the former without understanding the latter.

Such a situation presents obvious difficulties for Hadot's translators. Given the importance he accords to the study of ancient texts, Hadot tends to quote them frequently and extensively, in his own translations from the Greek, the Latin, and the German. Now, a translator's normal procedure would be to dig up the already existing English translations of the respective texts, and insert them where Hadot's own translations had stood in the original. After much consultation, we have found this method inadequate, for the following reasons:

1 Many existing English translations are themselves inadequate; some are old and outdated; others based on different textual readings from those adopted by Hadot. In the case of still others, finally, no English translation exists at all.

2 There is no such thing as an "objective translation." All translators base their work on their own conception of what their author was trying to say. Naturally, Hadot has often arrived at views of what his authors meant which differ from those of the various other translators; his own translations consequently differ, sometimes fundamentally, from the existing English versions.[3]

3 The use of existing English translations would often make Hadot's thought impossible to understand. If we were to insert, for example, a 60-year-old English translation of, say, Marcus Aurelius into the text, and then follow it with Hadot's explanation of the passage, the result would be ludicrously incoherent. Most importantly, it would make it impossible for the reader to gain any notion of the genesis and development of Hadot's thought – which is, after all, the goal of this publication. As I have said, the origin of Hadot's thought is to be sought in his interpretation of ancient texts, and his translations of these texts are both the result and an integral part of his hermeneutical method. Deprived of his translations, we could simply not see how Hadot had arrived at his particular interpretations of particular ancient texts, and consequently we would be at a loss to understand the conclusions he has based on these interpretations.

This being the case, the method I have chosen to follow in the translation of *Spiritual Exercises* is the following: in the case of each of Hadot's quotations of passages in Greek, Latin, or German, I have begun by a simple English translation of Hadot's French version. I have then checked the result against the original Greek, Latin, or German. If the English translation of Hadot's version, read on its own, then seemed to me to be a good translation of the original text, I let it stand; if not, I modified it slightly, with two goals in mind: first, to bring it into accord with modern English usage; secondly, to make sure the English transmitted, as far as possible, all the nuances of the original languages. In cases of particular difficulty, I have benefited from Hadot's thoughtful advice and comments, partly by correspondence, and partly during the course of a memorable stay at the Hadot's home in the summer of 1991.[4]

The resulting translations therefore often bear little resemblance to existing English translation; this is especially so in the case of authors like Plato, Marcus Aurelius, and Plotinus, to whom M. Hadot has devoted a lifetime of study. Nevertheless, we have decided to include references to the most accessible – not necessarily the best – extant English translations, in case the interested reader should care to consult the ancient authors cited in this book.

Such a method is, obviously, more time-consuming than the usual slapdash method of translation. My hope is that the result justifies the delays incurred: I would like to think the result is a scholarly and above all faithful version of Hadot's thought.

NOTES

1 Cf. above
2 Among the results of his work on this stage of his method are Hadot's projects

for completely new translations of those thinkers who have particularly occupied his attention: Plotinus, Marcus Aurelius, Marius Victorinus, etc.

3 This is so even in the case of so eminent a student of Plotinus, and so conscientious a translator, as A.H. Armstrong. Although he, too, has devoted a lifetime of careful study to Plotinus, he often reaches conclusions in the interpretation of particular Plotinian passages which differ from those of Hadot. The reason for this is not hard to seek: Plotinus is an extremely difficult author, and his writings are susceptible of many different interpretations.

4 Here I should like to express, on behalf of my wife Isabel and myself, our deep gratitude for the Hadots' wonderful hospitality.

Abbreviations

ACW: *Ancient Christian Writers, The Works of the Fathers in Translation*, eds Johannes Quasten and Joseph C. Plumpe, Westminster MD/London.

ANF: *The Ante-Nicene Fathers, Translations of the Writings of the Fathers down to A.D. 325*, eds Rev. Alexander Roberts and James Donaldson, American Reprint of the Edinburgh Edition, revised and chronologically arranged, with brief prefaces and occasional notes, by A. Cleveland Coxe, Buffalo.

FC: *The Fathers of the Church. A New Translation*, Washington DC.

GCS: *Die Griechischen Christlichen Scriftsteller der Ersten Jahrhunderte*, ed. Kommission für Spätantike Religionsgeschichte der Deutschen Akademie der Wissenschaften zu Berlin.

GW: *Gesammelte Werke*, Søren Kierkegaard, Düsseldorf/Cologne 1961.

LCL: Loeb Classical Library, London/Cambridge MA.

PG: *Patrologia Graeca*, ed. J.P. Migne, Paris 1844–55.

PL: *Patrologia Latina*, ed. J.P. Migne, Paris 1857–66.

SC: *Sources chrétiennes*, Paris 1940ff.

SVF: *Stoicorum Vetenum Fragmenta*, ed. H. Von Arnim, 4 vols, Leipzig 1903.

Introduction: *Pierre Hadot and the Spiritual Phenomenon of Ancient Philosophy*

I believe it was in 1982 that Michel Foucault first mentioned Pierre Hadot to me. Struck by Foucault's enthusiasm, I photocopied a number of Hadot's articles, but, to my regret, never got around to reading them until several years after Foucault's death. I immediately understood, and shared, Foucault's excitement, for Hadot's work exhibits that rare combination of prodigious historical scholarship and rigorous philosophical argumentation that upsets any preconceived distinction between the history of philosophy and philosophy proper. Expressed in a lucid prose whose clarity and precision are remarkable, Hadot's work stands as a model for how to write the history of philosophy. This collection of essays will, I hope, help to make his work better known in the English-speaking world; the depth and richness of his writing contain lessons not only for specialists in ancient philosophy, but for all of us interested in the history of philosophical thought.

Pierre Hadot has spent most of his academic career at the École pratique des Hautes Études and at the Collège de France. Appointed a *directeur d'études* of the fifth section of the École in 1964, Hadot occupied a chair in Latin Patristics, where he gave extraordinary lectures, many of which remain unpublished, on, among other topics, the works of Ambrose and Augustine. In 1972, in response to Hadot's interest in and work on non-Christian thought, the title of his chair was changed to "Theologies and Mysticisms of Hellenistic Greece and the End of Antiquity." Hadot gave courses on Plotinus and Marcus Aurelius, but also began to devote increased attention to more general themes in the history of ancient philosophical and theological thought. In February 1983 he assumed the chair of the History of Hellenistic and Roman Thought at the Collège de France. He has published translations of and commentaries on Marius Victorinus, Porphyry, Ambrose, Plotinus, and Marcus Aurelius. His essays on ancient philosophy range over virtually every topic of major significance, and constitute nothing less than a general perspective, both methodologically and substantively, on how to approach and understand the development of the entire history of ancient thought. A reading of Hadot's complete corpus of writings reveals, as one might expect, important essays on the history of medieval philosophy, but also, perhaps more surprisingly, brilliant contributions to our understanding of Goethe, Nietzsche, and Wittgenstein. Hadot has also been increasingly preoccupied with the pertinence of ancient thought for philosophy today, recognizing that ancient experience raises questions that *we* cannot and should not overlook or ignore.

This collection of essays is based on the second edition of *Exercices spirituels et philosophie antique*, originally published in 1987 and now out of print.[1] But it also includes a number of essays that were written subsequent to the book, essays that take up, develop, and extend the themes of *Exercices spirituels*. Moreover, Hadot has made revisions in some of the chapters for their inclusion in this volume, and he has rewritten his discussion of Marcus Aurelius in light of his commentary on the *Meditations*.[2] Thus this collection represents an expanded discussion of the topics of spiritual exercises and ancient philosophy.

In my introduction, I shall not summarize the individual essays. Rather, I shall try to indicate the general orientation of Hadot's thought, as well as relate these essays to other questions and problems – methodological, historical, and philosophical – treated elsewhere by Hadot. Instead of concentrating on questions of detail, I shall try to highlight some of the philosophical lessons and insights offered to us by Hadot's work.

1   Method and Practices of Interpretation in the History of Ancient Philosophy and Theology

In the summary of his work prepared for his candidacy at the Collège de France, Hadot wrote:

> The problems, the themes, the symbols from which Western thought has developed were not all born, quite obviously, in the period that we have studied. But the West has received them for the most part in the form that was given to them either by Hellenistic thought, or by the adaptation of this thought to the Roman world, or by the encounter between Hellenism and Christianity.[3]

The historical period he has studied has led Hadot to be especially sensitive to the ways in which different systems of thought – Jewish, Greek, Roman, and Christian – have interacted with one another. At the end of antiquity, one is faced with a vast phenomenon of transposition, a gigantic *meta-phora* in which all the forms of structures, political, juridical, literary, philosophical, artistic, have crossed over into new environments, have contaminated themselves with other forms or structures, thus modifying, more or less profoundly, their original meaning, or losing their meaning, or receiving a new meaning (which sometimes is a "mistranslation") [*contresens*].[4]

For example, the development of a Latin philosophical language required the adaptation of Greek models, so that to each term of this technical Latin language corresponded a quite specific Greek term; but "on the occasion of this translation many slippages of meaning, if not misinterpretations," were produced.[5] Furthermore, when it was a question of the philosophical and theological exegesis by Latin Christian writers of biblical texts, additional problems were posed by the presence of Latin versions of Greek versions of the original Hebrew. Along with the misinterpretations brought about by these translations, Christian writers added their own lack of understanding of Hebraic ideas. Hadot gives the wonderful example of Augustine, who read in the Latin version of Psalm IV: 9 the expression *in idipsum*. Although the Hebrew text contains wording that simply means "at this very moment" or "immediately," Augustine, prompted by Neoplatonist metaphysics, discovers in this *in idipsum* a name of God, "the selfsame." He thus discovers here a metaphysics of identity and divine immutability, interpreting the expression as meaning "in him who is identical with himself."[6] Both a Latin translation and a Neoplatonist metaphysics come between his reading and the text.

To take another example, in Ambrose's sermon *De Isaac vel anima*, we find undeniable borrowings, indeed literal translations, from Plotinus; more specifically, the use of texts from Plotinus that relate to the detachment from the body and to the withdrawal from the sensible as a condition of contemplation. These texts of Plotinian mysticism are joined to texts of Origenean mysticism that derive from Origen's commentary on the *Song of Songs*. But in this encounter between Plotinian and Origenean mysticism, Plotinian mysticism loses its specificity. One does not find in Ambrose any important trace of what is essential to Plotinus' thought, namely the surpassing of the intelligible in order to attain the One in ecstasy. Such texts concerning the mysticism of the One are translated by Ambrose in such a way that they lose this meaning and are related to the union of the soul with the Logos. So Hadot speaks of "a Plotinian ascesis put in the service of an Origenean mysticism that is a mysticism of Jesus."[7] Thus Ambrose can identify the Good and Christ, since with respect to the Good he brings in Paul's Colossians I: 20, which does indeed concern Christ. Yet, as Hadot remarks, "this identification is absolutely foreign to the whole economy of the Plotinian system."[8] Borrowings, *contresens*, the introduction of a logic into texts that had a different logic[9] – this whole phenomenon is central to the development of ancient thought, and, as Hadot makes clear, not to ancient thought alone.

In his essay "La fin du paganisme" Hadot examines the struggles, contaminations, and symbioses between paganism and Christianity at the end of antiquity. We can relatively straightforwardly reconstruct the philosophical struggles and divergences; for instance, the claim on the part of pagan polemicists that at the time of his trial and death Jesus did not behave like a sage, the pagan philosophy of history that charged Christians with lacking historical roots and that denied them the right to claim that their tradition was the sole possessor of the truth, the pagan argument that the Christians imagined God as a tyrant with unforeseeable whims who carries out completely arbitrary and irrational actions, such as the creation of the world at a specific moment of time, the election and then rejection of the Jewish people, the incarnation, the resurrection, and, finally, the destruction of the world.[10] We can also discover in the pagan world certain attempts to assimilate Christian elements, and even, in certain epochs, the phenomenon of symbiosis between pagan and Christian thought. Thus, for example, the emperor Alexander Severus used to render honor to certain portraits (*effigies*) of men who, thanks to their exceptional virtue, had entered the sphere of divinity. Among these men were Orpheus, Appollonius of Tyana, Abraham, and Christ, and so the emperor made a place for Christ in his pantheon.[11] In the case of some individuals one could legitimately wonder whether they were pagans or Christians. The *Hymns* of Synesius could be considered as having been inspired by the Christian trinitarian doctrine or, on the contrary, as a representative of a pagan theology that one could link to the tradition of Porphyry.[12]

More historically subtle is the process that Hadot has labeled "contamination," that is, "the process according to which paganism or Christianity were lead to adopt the ideas or the behaviors characteristic of their adversary."[13] Such contamination, which could operate with different degrees of awareness, extended from specific doctrines and behaviors to very general ideas and institutions. Eusebius of Caesarea could bring together the doctrines of Plotinus and Numenius on the First and Second God with the Christian doctrine of the Father and the Son and their relations.[14] And the emperor Julian could wish to impose the organization of the Christian church on paganism, wanting the pagan church to imitate the Christian church's activities.[15]

Most important from a philosophical point of view, Christianity borrowed the very idea of theology, its methods and principles, from paganism. As Hadot has shown, both pagans and Christians had an analogous conception of truth; truth was an historical reality of divine origin, a revelation given by God to humanity at a particular time. As a consequence, their conceptions of philosophy and theology were identical – "human thought could only be exegetical, that is, it must try to interpret an initial datum: the revelation contained in myths, traditions, the most ancient laws."[16] Not only was

Christianity contaminated by the pagan idea of theology, but the ancient Christian idea of hierarchical monotheism, so central to early Christianity, could be found within the evolution of paganism itself, especially under the influence of the imperial ideology. The conceptions of monotheism and hierarchy that served to define the Byzantine Christian world were thus also contaminations from the pagan world; indeed, these ideas could be said to sum up the entire essence of late paganism.[17] These contaminations inevitably led to distortions, deformations, misunderstandings of all kinds, but the overlap and intersections brought about by these contaminations also led to the evolution of thought, the development of fresh ideas, the creation, by way of creative misinterpretations, of new concepts, categories, arguments, and conclusions.

In the first century BC, as a consequence of the destruction of most of the permanent philosophical institutions in Athens (which had existed from the fourth to the first century BC), the four great philosophical schools – Platonism, Aristotelianism, Epicureanism, and Stoicism – could no longer be supported by the Athenian institutions created by their founders.

> In order to affirm their fidelity to the founder, the four philosophical schools, scattered in different cities of the Orient and Occident, can no longer depend on the institution that he had created, nor on the oral tradition internal to the school, but solely on the texts of the founder. The classes of philosophy will therefore consist above all in commentaries on the text.[18]

The exegetical phase of the history of ancient philosophy was characterized by the fact that the principal scholarly exercise was the explication of a text. Exegetical philosophy conceived of the philosopher not as a "solitary thinker who would invent and construct his system and his truth in an autonomous way. The philosopher thinks in a tradition." [19] For the philosopher during this period, truth is founded on the authority of this tradition, and it is given in the texts of the founders of the tradition.

Perhaps the most extraordinary instance of the weight and pressures of exegetical thought is to be found in the example, extensively discussed by Hadot, of the appearance of the distinction between "being" as an infinitive (*to einai*) and "being" as a participle (*to on*). In a series of articles Hadot has shown that this distinction arose as a result of the need to give a coherent exegesis of Plato's second hypothesis in the *Parmenides*, "If the one *is*, how is it possible that it should not participate in being [*ousia*]?" [20] The Neoplatonist exegesis of the *Parmenides* required that each of Plato's hypotheses correspond to a different hypostasis; thus, this second hypothesis corresponded to the second One. Since this second One must participate in *ousia*, and since by "participation" the Neoplatonists meant "receiving a form from a superior and transcendent Form," the second One's participation in *ousia* is understood to be participation in an *ousia* in itself which transcends the participating subject. However, according to good Neoplatonist doctrine, above the second One there is only the first One, and this first One, absolutely simple, cannot be an *ousia*. The first *ousia* must be the second One. So how could Plato have spoken of an *ousia* that precedes the second One? An anonymous Neoplatonist commentator on the *Parmenides*, whom Hadot has identified as Porphyry, squarely confronted these difficulties: "influenced by the exegetical tradition characteristic of his school, the words of Plato evoked for him the entities of a rigid system, and the literal text became reconcilable only with difficulty with what he believed to be Plato's meaning."[21] Porphyry's solution to this difficulty would consist in presenting an exegesis according to which Plato had employed the word *ousia* in an enigmatic way, instead of another word whose meaning is close to the word *ousia*, namely the word *einai*. If Plato speaks of an *ousia* in which the second One participates, he wants it to be understood that the second One receives the property of being a "being" (*to on*) and of being "*ousia*" from the first One, because the first One is itself "being" (*to einai*) "not in the sense of a subject but in the sense of an activity of being, considered as pure and without subject."[22] Thus, as Hadot shows, we can see appear for the first time in the history of onto-theology a remarkable distinction between being as an infinitive and being as a participle. Being as an infinitive characterizes the first One, pure absolutely indeterminate activity, while being as a participle is a property of the second One, the first substance and first determination that participates in this pure activity. This distinction arises from the formulation used by Plato at the beginning of the second hypothesis of the *Parmenides*, joined to the Neoplatonist exegesis of the *Parmenides* and the need for Porphyry to try to explain, from within this system of exegesis, why Plato said what he did.[23] The result, according to Hadot, was "certainly a misinterpretation, but a creative misinterpretation, sprung from the very difficulties of the exegetical method."[24] This creative misunderstanding was to have a profound influence on the development of a negative theology of being, and, by way of Boethius' distinction between *esse* and *id quod est*, was decisively to affect the history of Western philosophical thought.[25]

As early as 1959, Hadot described a phenomenon, constant in the history of philosophy,

> that stems from the evolution of the philosophical consciousness: it is impossible to remain faithful to a tradition without taking up again the formulas of the creator of this tradition; but it is also impossible to use these formulas without giving them a meaning that the previous philosopher could not even have suspected. One then sincerely believes

that this new meaning corresponds to the deep intention of this philosopher. In fact, this new meaning corresponds to a kind of possibility of evolution of the original doctrine.[26]

Not all such bestowals of new meaning are creative misunderstandings, as Hadot well realizes. But some of them have led to new ideas of great philosophical significance. We must study the history of these exegeses, discover how these misunderstandings have been used, what philosophical consequences and what paths of evolution have resulted from them, in order to determine whether they have indeed been creative. In the most interesting of cases, we may find that a history of misinterpretation and a history of philosophical creativity are intimately linked.[27]

In his inaugural lecture to the Collège de France, Hadot writes:

> It seems to me, indeed, that in order to understand the works of the philosophers of antiquity we must take account of all the concrete conditions in which they wrote, all the constraints that weighed upon them: the framework of the school, the very nature of *philosophia*, literary genres, rhetorical rules, dogmatic imperatives, and traditional modes of reasoning. One cannot read an ancient author the way one does a contemporary author (which does not mean that contemporary authors are easier to understand than those of antiquity). In fact, the works of antiquity are produced under entirely different conditions than those of their modern counterparts.[28]

Hadot's studies of the history of ancient philosophy and theology have always included the analysis of "the rules, the forms, the models of discourse," the framework of the literary genre whose rules are often rigorously codified, in which the thoughts of the ancient author are expressed.[29] Such analysis is necessary in order to understand both the details of the work, the exact import of particular statements, as well as the general meaning of the work as a whole. Literary structure and conceptual structure must never be separated.[30] Describing his method of study for Latin Patristics, Hadot has invoked an exceptionally illuminating analogy, comparing what happens in these studies to what takes place in those curious paintings where

> one sees at first sight a landscape that seems to be composed normally. One thinks that if there is, in such and such a place in the picture, a house or a tree it depends solely on the imagination of the artist. But if one looks at the whole painting from a certain angle the landscape transforms itself into a hidden figure, a face or a human body, and one understands then that the house or the tree was not there out of pure

fancy, but was necessary because it made up part of the hidden figure. When one discovers the structure or the fundamental form of a text, one has an analogous experience: certain details that seemed to be there only in an arbitrary way become necessary, because they make up an integral part of the traditional figure used. And just as one can contrast or compare the sense of the face and the sense of the countryside, one can compare the meaning of the traditional form or structure, considered in themselves, and that of the text which has borrowed them . . . We often have the impression when we read ancient authors that they write badly, that the sequence of ideas lacks coherence and connection. But it is precisely because the true figure escapes us that we do not perceive the form that renders all the details necessary . . . once discovered, the hidden form will make necessary all of the details that one often believed arbitrary or without importance.[31]

This description brilliantly captures the significance of placing the work studied in the framework of its literary genre, the transformation in understanding brought about when one moves from the insignificant and arbitrary to the meaningful and necessary. Hadot's methodological prescriptions can be fruitfully applied at virtually every level in the analysis of ancient thought.

I want to consider briefly a series of examples not taken up by Hadot in order to emphasize the depth and accuracy of his analogy. I have in mind the extraordinary work on mystical cryptography undertaken by Margherita Guarducci. By carefully delineating the historical and geographical context and by discovering "a *coherent and rational system*,"[32] Guarducci was able to show that certain ancient graffiti, both pagan and Christian, contained hidden and almost dissimulated thoughts of a philosophical and religious character.[33] The situation that results is precisely one in which phenomena that were neglected or unacknowledged now assume a profound significance. So, for example, she has demonstrated that the letters *PE*, the two initial letters of the name *Petrus*, sometimes take on the form of the characteristic monogram $\frac{P}{E}$ or $\frac{P}{E}$, that this monogram represents the keys of the first vicar of Christ, and that the monogram sometimes even visually resembles, with the three teeth of the *E* adjoined to the *P*, a key – $\frac{P}{E}$.[34] Peter's monogram can also be adjoined to a monogram for Christ ($\cancel{P}$), so that we find on wall g of the Vatican this kind of graffiti, $\cancel{P}E$, expressing the indissoluble union of Peter and Christ.[35] By unraveling the rational and coherent system formed by this mystical cryptography she can show that an inscription that previously found no plausible explanation can be clearly and convincingly explained. Thus the inscription found on a tomb (and shown in plate I.1) wishes life in Christ and Peter to the deceased. The bivalence of the Greek *rho* and the Latin *pi* is used to superpose the monogram of Christ ($\cancel{P}$) with the letters *PE* thus forming,

Ɏ which is inserted within the preposition *in*.[36] Just as Hadot has described it, these are cases where "once discovered, the hidden form will make necessary all of the details that one often believed arbitrary or without significance."[37]

This mystical cryptography can also be found in the pagan world, where a form that can seem to be intrinsically insignificant is transformed, once the hidden figure is discovered, into the expression of a philosophical doctrine. Thus not only did the Pythagoreans recognize in the letter *Y* the initial letter of the word ὑγίεια and therefore the concept of "salvation"; they also used this letter to represent graphically the ancient concept of the divergent paths of virtue and vice, the doctrine that life presented a forking path and that one must choose between the path of virtue on the right, which will lead to peace, and the path of vice on the left, where one will fall into misery.[38] A funereal stele, datable from the first century AD, of a deceased man named "Pythagoras" exhibits a large *Y* that divides the stone into five sections (shown in plate I.2). Each section contains various scenes inspired by Pythagorean doctrine. In the center is an image of the deceased (or perhaps of his homonym, Pythagoras of Samo); to the right are scenes personifying virtue, to the left are scenes personifying dissoluteness. Guarducci concludes that it is "easy to recognize in the succession of these scenes that which the literary sources have handed down to us . . . : the Pythagorean *Y*, symbol of the divergent paths of virtue and of vice, one of which brings . . . eternal pleasure, the other . . . definitive ruin."[39] It is indeed easy to come to this recognition, once one has uncovered and deciphered the genre of mystical cryptography. But if one fails to perceive the rigorously codified rules, one will see nothing of importance, one will be forced to resort to lapidary error and accident to explain away various features, one will find no coherence in many of the inscriptions.[40] The difference between recognizing profound significance and trivial error or arbitrariness will depend on whether the true form has escaped us or has transformed our understanding.[41]

One might well imagine that the endeavor to hide religious and philosophical thoughts within inscriptions and graffiti would require that we discover the hidden form necessary to give coherence and sense to these graffiti. But one might also assume that when we are confronted with extended philosophical writing, ancient texts, like many modern ones, will exhibit their structure more or less on the surface. And then when we fail to discern this structure, we conclude, as Hadot remarks, that ancient authors "write badly, that the sequence of ideas lacks coherence and connection."[42] That the assumption on which this conclusion is based is false, that the structure of even extended ancient philosophical texts may not lie easily open to view, is clearly shown by Hadot's own discovery of the underlying structure or fundamental form of Marcus Aurelius' *Meditations*. Indeed, Hadot's description of the experience of seeing a text transform itself once one has discovered its hidden form very compellingly represents, years before the fact, his own discovery about Marcus Aurelius' text.

The first printed edition of Marcus Aurelius' *Meditations* appeared in 1559, accompanied by a Latin translation. The editor, "Xylander" (Wilhelm Holzmann), faced with what he saw as the total disorder of the text, conjectured that the *Meditations*, as presented in the manuscript he edited, were only disconnected extracts from the work of Marcus Aurelius, that Marcus' book had reached us in a mutilated, incomplete, disordered state.[43] This conjecture was taken up again in 1624 by Caspar Barth, who, recognizing that one could detect traces of organization and sometimes lengthy reasoning in the *Meditations*, claimed that the text that had reached us consisted only of extracts from a vast, systematic treatise of ethics that the emperor had written.[44] Such conjectures, and their variations, have accompanied the *Meditations* throughout its history, always trying to account for the disorder and haphazardousness of this work.[45] The contemporary reader may find individual aphorisms that seem to speak for themselves, but will be left with the basic impression that, as Hadot puts it, "these sentences seem to follow one another without order, with the randomness of the impressions and states of soul of the emperor-philosopher."[46]

Hadot has recognized that Marcus Aurelius' *Meditations* belong to the type of writing known as *hypomnemata*, personal notes and reflections written day to day. This kind of writing existed throughout antiquity, and at least two of Marcus' seventeenth-century editors and translators also recognized his work

as consisting of personal notes.[47] Marcus wrote day to day without trying to compose a work intended for the public; his *Meditations* are for the most part exhortations to himself, a dialogue with himself.[48] Moreover, his thoughts and reflections were written down according to "a very refined literary form, because it was precisely the perfection of the formulas that could assure them their psychological efficacy, their power of persuasion."[49] Thus, although Marcus' work belongs to the literary genre of personal notes written day to day (*hypomnemata*), they are also quite distinct from other examples of such notes. As Hadot concludes, "it appears indeed that unlike other *hypomnemata*, the *Meditations* of Marcus Aurelius are 'spiritual exercises,' practiced according to a certain method."[50]

Spiritual exercises are practiced in the *Meditations* according to a method, Hadot has written, "as rigorous, as codified, as systematic as the famous *Spiritual Exercises* of Saint Ignatius."[51] And the key to this method, and thus to the *Meditations*, is to be found in the three philosophical *topoi* distinguished by Epictetus. Epictetus distinguished three acts or functions of the soul – judgment, desire, and inclination or impulsion. Since each of these activities of the soul depends on us, we can discipline them, we can choose to judge or not to judge and to judge in a particular way, we can choose to desire or not to desire, to will or not to will. And so to each of these activities corresponds a spiritual exercise, a discipline of representation and judgment, a discipline of desire, and a discipline of inclinations or impulses to action.[52] Moreover,

Hadot has shown that Epictetus identified the three disciplines with the three parts of philosophy – the discipline of assent with logic, the discipline of desire with physics, and the discipline of inclinations with ethics.[53] And he used the word *topos* "to designate the three lived exercises that . . . are in a certain way the putting into practice of the three parts of philosophical discourse."[54] Thus Epictetus' three *topoi* are three lived spiritual exercises.

Marcus Aurelius took up these three *topoi* and employed them as the underlying structure of his *Meditations*. They are the key to the interpretation of virtually the entire work, and our recognition of their role allows the surface disorder of the *Meditations* to transform itself, so that we see beneath this apparent lack of order a rigorous underlying form or structure:

> beneath this apparent disorder hides a rigorous law that explains the content of the *Meditations*. This law is, moreover, expressed clearly in a ternary schema that reappears often in certain maxims. But this schema was not invented by Marcus Aurelius: in fact it corresponds exactly to the three philosophical *topoi* that Epictetus distinguishes in his *Discourses*. It is this ternary schema that inspires the whole composition of the *Meditations* of the emperor. Each maxim develops either one of these very characteristics *topoi*, or two of them, or three of them.[55]

> These three disciplines of life are truly the key to the *Meditations* of Marcus Aurelius. It is in fact around each of them that the different dogmas . . . are organized, are crystallized. To the discipline of judgment are linked the dogmas that affirm the freedom of judgment, the possibility that man has to criticize and modify his own thought; around the discipline that directs our attitude with regard to external events are gathered all the theorems on the causality of universal Nature; lastly, the discipline of action is nourished by all the theoretical propositions relative to the mutual attraction that unites reasonable beings.
>
>   Finally, one discovers that behind an apparent disorder, one can uncover, in the *Meditations*, an extremely rigorous conceptual system.[56]

Each maxim, aphorism, sentence of the *Meditations* is an exercise of actualization and assimilation of one or more of the three disciplines of life.[57] Thus Hadot, discovering the form "that renders all the details necessary," allows us to read the *Meditations* coherently, transforms our experience from that of reading a disconnected journal to one of reading a rigorously structured philosophical work.[58]

Hadot's discovery of the ternary schema underlying the *Meditations* not only allows us to give structure to its merely apparent disorder. It also allows us to keep from falling into misplaced psychological judgments about the author of these spiritual exercises. Precisely because the *Meditations* are traditional Stoic spiritual exercises, we must be very prudent about drawing conclusions concerning the personal psychological states of Marcus. As Hadot has said, we are all too ready to project our own attitudes and intentions on ancient works, to see the *Meditations* as the spontaneous effusion of Marcus' everyday feelings, to see Lucretius' *On the Nature of Things* as the work of an anxious man attempting to combat his anxiety, or to understand Augustine's *Confessions* as the expression of his desire to confess and so to give us an autobiographical account of his life.[59] But in antiquity,

> the rules of discourse were rigorously codified: in order to say what one wanted to say, an author had to say it in a certain way, according to traditional models, according to rules prescribed by rhetoric and philosophy . . . [the *Meditations*] are an exercise realized according to definite rules; they imply . . . a pre-existent outline which the emperor-philosopher can only amplify. Often, he only says certain things because he *must* say them in virtue of the models and precepts that impose themselves on him. One will therefore only be able to understand the sense of this work when one has discovered, among other things, the prefabricated schemata that were imposed on it.[60]

Hadot has charted all of the supposed psychological portraits of Marcus drawn from the *Meditations*, which see him as suffering from gloomy resignation, extreme skepticism, despair. Some modern authors have claimed to find in the *Meditations* evidence of a gastric ulcer and its psychological consequences, or of the psychological effects of Marcus' abuse of opium.[61] But all of these attempts at historical psychology ignore the mechanisms of literary composition in antiquity, and fail to take into account Marcus' modes of thought, the fact that he was practicing spiritual exercises, derived from Stoicism, more particularly from Epictetus, whose essential goal is to influence himself, to produce an effect in himself.[62]

Take, for example, the repeated claims that the *Meditations* show us that Marcus was a pessimist. After all, he does write things such as the following:

> Just like your bath-water appears to you – oil, sweat, filth, dirty water, all kinds of loathsome stuff – such is each portion of life, and every substance.[63]

> These foods and dishes . . . are only dead fish, birds and pigs; this Falernian wine is a bit of grape-juice; this purple-edged toga is some sheep's hairs dipped in the blood of shellfish; as for sex, it is the rubbing together of pieces of gut, followed by the spasmodic secretion of a little bit of slime.[64]

What are these remarks, if not the expression of Marcus' characteristic pessimism? In each of these cases of supposed pessimism, Hadot has been able to show specifically that Marcus was not giving us his personal impressions, that he was not expressing a negative experience that he had lived, but was rather "exercising himself, spiritually and literarily." [65] Marcus is, first of all, practicing the Stoic discipline of giving physical definitions which, adhering to the objective representation of the phenomenon, are employed "to dispel the false conventional judgements of value that people express concerning objects." [66] Marcus writes:

> always make a definition or description of the object that occurs in your representation, so as to be able to see it as it is in its essence, both as a whole and as divided into its constituent parts, and say to yourself its proper name and the names of those things out of which it is composed, and into which it will be dissolved. [67]

This kind of definition is intended to strip representations of "all subjective and anthropomorphic considerations, from all relations to the human point of view," thus defining objects, in a certain way, scientifically and physically. [68] Such definitions belong both to the discipline of judgment, or logic, and to the discipline of desire, or physics. The critique of representations and the pursuit of the objective representation are, obviously enough, part of the domain of logic; but these definitions can only be realized if one places oneself in "the point of view of physics, by situating events and objects in the perspective of universal Nature." [69]

Marcus is not giving us his personal perception of reality, from which we may then deduce conclusions about his sensibility or characteristic dispositions. He is rather employing various means to transform himself, to acquire a certain inner state of freedom and peace. To do so he must overcome "solidly rooted prejudices, irrational terrors," employing all the means available to him. [70] Here is how Hadot describes the ultimate goal of these physical definitions:

> This spiritual exercise of "physical" definition has exactly the effect of rendering us indifferent before indifferent things, that is, of making us renounce making differences among things that do not depend on us, but which depend on the will of universal Nature. No longer to make differences is therefore, first of all, to renounce attributing to certain things a false value, measured only according to human scale. This is the meaning of the apparently pessimistic declarations. But to no longer make differences is to discover that all things, even those which seem disgusting to us, have an equal value if one measures them according to the scale of universal Nature, that is, looks at things with the same vision

that Nature looks at them. . . . This inner attitude by which the soul does not make differences, but remains indifferent before things, corresponds to magnanimity of the soul [*grandeur d'âme*].[71]

Thus with respect to the issue of Marcus' pessimism, we see the importance of placing the *Meditations* in its literary and philosophical context. Abstracting from this context leads to an improper psychology, and to an uncreative misreading of the force of the *Meditations*, ignoring its basic philosophical aims and procedures. Hadot diagnoses, with great insight, the dangers of historical psychology:

We have here a fine example of the dangers of historical psychology applied to ancient texts. Before presenting the interpretation of a text, one should first begin by trying to distinguish between, on the one hand, the traditional elements, one could say prefabricated, that the author employs and, on the other hand, what he wants to do with them. Failing to make this distinction, one will consider as symptomatic formulas or attitudes which are not at all such, because they do not emanate from the personality of the author, but are imposed on him by tradition. One must search for what the author wishes to say, but also for what he can or cannot say, what he must or must not say, as a function of the traditions and the circumstances that are imposed on him.[72]

That the temptation to read ancient texts as expressions of their author's psychological states and character is extremely difficult to overcome is shown by the development of Hadot's own interpretation of Augustine's *Confessions*. In a widely cited paper, originally delivered in 1960, Hadot concludes his discussion of the development of the notion of the person with the claim that in Augustine's *Confessions*, "the modern self rises into view in history."[73] Citing various passages from Augustine on the mystery of the self, and following Groethuysen's interpretation, Hadot is led to conclude, on the basis of these passages, that "With Augustine the 'I' makes its entry into philosophical reasoning in a way that implies a radical change of inner perspective."[74] Hadot came little by little to realize, however, that one must not be misled by Augustine's use of "I," that "the autobiographical part of the *Confessions* is not as important as one might believe."[75] The "I" of Augustine's *Confessions* continues the "I" of Job, David, or Paul, that is, Augustine "identifies himself with the *self* who speaks in the Scriptures. Ultimately the human *self* who speaks in the Bible is Adam, a sinner without doubt, but converted by God and renewed in Christ."[76] Thus, following Pierre Courcelle, Hadot recognizes that the *Confessions* is essentially a theological work, in which each scene may assume a symbolic meaning. So "in this literary genre . . . it is extremely difficult to distinguish between a symbolic enactment and an account of a historical event."[77]

Hadot therefore insists on the theological significance, in the first part of Book II of the *Confessions*, of the images used by Augustine in order to describe his inner state.[78] And in the second part of Book II, when Augustine recounts at length his adolescent theft of pears, we are in fact confronted with a theological account concerning original sin. The "psychology of Augustine the sinner is reconstructed from the ideal psychology of Adam, disobedient to God in order to imitate, in a perverse way, the divine freedom."[79] Rather than using this scene to draw a psychological portrait of Augustine the individual, Hadot understands it as part of an anti-Manichean theological polemic. Here is his interpretation, which is a model of how to avoid the excesses of historical psychology when reading ancient texts:

> the psychological and theological problem of original sin is posed on the occasion of Augustine's theft, and we find ourselves once again in an anti-Manichean problematic: in stealing the pears, as Adam stealing the forbidden fruit, Augustine did not desire the fruit itself, that is, an existing reality; rather he desired evil itself, that is, something that doesn't have any substance. How is this possible? After having posed the problem at length (4, 9–6, 13), Augustine responds by showing that he had loved something "positive" in the evil: to imitate the freedom of God, but in a perverse way. Every sin appears thus as an upside-down imitation of the divine reality.[80]

Instead of engaging in a psychological interpretation of Augustine's adolescence, Hadot's reading allows us to see that we are in the presence of a theological discussion of the nature of sin, and that Augustine's lengthy recounting of his theft is not autobiographically motivated, but is necessary in order for us to see the way in which sin is a perverse imitation of divine reality.

Moreover, by placing the *Confessions* within the Christian exegetical tradition, Hadot is able to show that the last three books of the *Confessions*, in which Augustine seems to abandon autobiography to devote himself to exegesis, far from being foreign to the rest of the work, do not ultimately have "a different object from the account that is narrated in the biographical part."[81] Hadot demonstrates that Augustine very often brings together the two states of his soul – obscurity, then light – with the two states of the earth at the beginning of the account of Genesis. In its first state the earth was *invisibilis* and *incomposita*, and in its second state it received the illumination of the *Fiat lux*.[82] In Book II, Augustine presents his adolescence as a state of obscurity and bubbling fluidity, and Hadot has shown that in this description one can recognize "the vocabulary employed in Book XIII of the *Confessions* to describe the chaos of *Gen* 1, 2."[83] Furthermore, in Book XIII the images of darkness and fluctuation serve precisely to describe "the state of the soul still 'formless,' before its conversion to God." [84] Thus Hadot can claim that "the idea of the passage of the creature from a formless state to a state of formation and of conversion dominates the whole work." [85] In Book XIII the biblical account of creation becomes the description of the phases and stages of the salvation of humanity. [86] Putting together Augustine's autobiographical and exegetical descriptions, Hadot can demonstrate the inner unity of the work, the fact that for Augustine "Genesis is . . . the account produced by the Holy Spirit of the conversion of the soul, as the *Confessions* is the account that he himself produces of his own conversion." [87] Hadot therefore warns us that we must interpret this text in light of the literary genre to which it belongs, the tradition of exegesis of Ambrose and Origen, and that we will commit a misunderstanding if we believe we have discovered the *self* "already" in the *Confessions*. [88] We find in Hadot's own interpretation of Augustine the initial outline of a kind of historical psychology, one that discovers in the *Confessions* the beginnings of the modern self. However, this is followed by a more detailed attention to the mechanisms of literary composition and to the theological genre of the *Confessions*, an attention that both prevents the apparent autobiography from becoming the philosophical center of the work and permits us to see the unity between the first ten books and the last three. There is, of course, a self to be found in the *Confessions*, but "it must not be understood as the incommunicable singularity of the man Augustine, but, on the contrary, as universal humanity of which the events of the life of Augustine are only the symbols." [89]

Hadot's insistence on not separating conceptual structure from literary structure also played a significant role in his interpretation of Wittgenstein's work. As far as I have been able to determine, Hadot presented the first detailed discussions in French of Wittgenstein's books, reviewing everything from the *Tractatus Logico-Philosophicus* to the *Philosophical Investigations* and *Remarks on the Foundations of Mathematics*. [90] In his 1959 discussion of the later Wittgenstein, Hadot argues, quite remarkably, that the goal of *Philosophical Investigations* requires a certain literary genre, that one cannot dissociate the form of the *Investigations* from Wittgenstein's conception of philosophy.

It is a therapeutics that is offered to us. Philosophy is an illness of language . . . The true philosophy will therefore consist in curing itself of philosophy, in making every philosophical problem completely and definitively disappear . . . Wittgenstein continues [from the *Tractatus* to the *Investigations*] . . . to devote himself to the same mission: to bring a radical and definitive peace to metaphysical worry. Such a purpose imposes a certain literary genre: the work cannot be the exposition of a system, a doctrine, a philosophy in the traditional sense . . . [*Philosophical Investigations*] wishes to act little by little on our spirit, like a cure, like a medical treatment. The work therefore does not have a systematic structure, strictly speaking [*pas de plan, à proprement parler*].[91]

At the time Hadot was writing about Wittgenstein, and even today, so many philosophers ignored the way *Philosophical Investigations* is written that it is astonishing, at first sight, to see an historian of ancient philosophy clearly understanding the import of this aspect of Wittgenstein's work. But Hadot has long emphasized that ancient philosophy presented itself as a therapeutics and that this goal profoundly affected the philosophical writing of antiquity.[92] As early as 1960 Hadot wrote that in ancient philosophy "more than theses, one teaches ways, methods, spiritual exercises," that "dogmas" have only a secondary aspect.[93] No doubt it was precisely Hadot's understanding of the history of ancient philosophy that made it possible for him to see central, but still neglected, characteristics of Wittgenstein's work.

In "Jeux de langage et philosophie," Hadot was to employ Wittgenstein's notion of a language game in an historical perspective that, as he recognized, went well beyond anything with which Wittgenstein was preoccupied. Hadot argued that we must "break with the idea that philosophical language functions in a uniform way" and that "it is impossible to give a meaning to the positions of philosophers without situating them in their language game."[94] Aware of the different philosophical language games of antiquity, Hadot could well insist that an ancient formula be placed in the concrete context of its determinate language game, that its meaning could change as a function of a change in language game.[95] Thus Hadot could draw the general historiographical conclusion that we must "consider as very different language games those literary genres, so profoundly diverse, represented by the dialogue, the exhortation or protreptic, the hymn or prayer . . . the manual, the dogmatic treatise, the meditation."[96] And we must also distinguish between the attitudes represented by dialectic, rhetorical argumentation, logical reasoning, and didactic exposition, since we will often be able to establish that "the very fact of situating oneself in one of these traditions predetermines the very content of the doctrine that is expressed in this language game."[97] By overcoming the temptation to see philosophical language as always functioning in the same way, Hadot could take account of the conceptual and literary specificity of different philosophical attitudes. Whether reading Plotinus, Marcus Aurelius, or Augustine, Hadot has made detailed use of his methodological prescriptions, not allowing the surface pronouncements of the texts to obscure the underlying structure, the literary genre and modes of thought that confer a determinate meaning on these pronouncements. Employing all of their resources, Hadot has used these practices of interpretation to try to reconstruct the fundamental meaning (*sens de base*), the meaning "intended" by the author (*le sens "voulu" par l'auteur*), of these ancient texts.[98] More often than not, as is evident from the examples

I have given, this meaning will not be apparent. And if Hadot's practices of interpretation are most often employed with respect to ancient philosophical and theological writing, his discussion of Wittgenstein makes clear the need, throughout the history of philosophy, for such practices. To restrict the importance of Hadot's lessons to one period in the history of thought would be radically to misunderstand the techniques and procedures of human thought.

2 Spiritual Exercises

Hadot has written that he was led to become aware of the importance of what he has called "spiritual exercises" by his work of interpretation of ancient philosophical texts.[99] On the one hand, like his predecessors and contemporaries, Hadot encountered the well-known phenomenon of the incoherences, even contradictions, in the works of ancient philosophical authors. On the other hand, many modern historians of ancient philosophy have begun from the assumption that ancient philosophers were attempting, in the same way as modern philosophers, to construct systems, that ancient philosophy was essentially a philosophical discourse consisting of a "certain type of organization of language, comprised of propositions having as their object the universe, human society, and language itself."[100] Thus the essential task of the historian of philosophy was thought to consist in "the analysis of the genesis and the structures of the literary works that were written by the philosophers, especially in the study of the rational connection and the internal coherence of these systematic expositions."[101] Under these interpretive constraints, modern historians of ancient philosophy could not but deplore the awkward expositions, defects of composition, and outright incoherences in the ancient authors they studied.[102]

Hadot, however, rather than deploring these ancient authors' failures to measure up to the modern standard of the systematic philosophical treatise, realized that in order to understand and explain these apparent defects, one must not only analyze the structure of these ancient philosophical texts, but one must also situate them in the "living praxis from which they emanated."[103] An essential aspect of this living praxis was the oral dimension of ancient philosophy, and the written philosophical works of Greco-Roman antiquity were "never completely free of the constraints imposed by oral transmission."[104] Hadot has described this written work as only a material support for a spoken word intended to become spoken word again, "like a modern record or cassette which are only an intermediary between two events: the recording and the rehearing."[105] All of ancient philosophy believed in what Hadot once called, thinking of Plato's *Phaedrus*, the "ontological value of the spoken word"; this living and animated discourse was not principally intended to transmit information, but "to produce a certain psychic effect in the reader or listener." [106] Thus the "propositional element" was not the most important element of ancient philosophical teaching, and Hadot has frequently cited Victor Goldschmitt's formula, originally applied to the Platonic dialogues but used by Hadot to characterize ancient philosophy more generally, that ancient philosophical discourse intended "to form more than to inform." [107]

Hadot claims that it is probably a mistake about the nature of ancient philosophy to consider abstraction, made possible by writing, its most important characteristic:

> For ancient philosophy, at least beginning from the sophists and Socrates, intended, in the first instance, to form people and to transform souls. That is why, in Antiquity, philosophical teaching is given above all in oral form, because only the living word, in dialogues, in conversations pursued for a long time, can accomplish such an action. The written work, considerable as it is, is therefore most of the time only an echo or a complement of this oral teaching. [108]

This is one reason why, for Hadot, to philosophize is to learn how to dialogue. [109] A Socratic dialogue is a spiritual exercise practiced in common, and it incites one to give attention to oneself, to take care of oneself, to know oneself. The Socratic maxim "know thyself" requires a relation of the self to itself that "constitutes the basis of all spiritual exercises." [110] Every spiritual exercise is dialogical insofar as it is an "exercise of authentic presence" of the self to itself, and of the self to others. [111] The Socratic and Platonic dialogues exhibit this authentic presence in the way that they show that what is most important is not the solution to a particular problem, but the path traversed together in arriving at this solution. Hence, we can understand the critical significance of the dimension of the interlocutor, with all of its starts and stops, hesitations, detours, and digressions. This essential dimension

> prevents the dialogue from being a theoretical and dogmatic account and forces it to be a concrete and practical exercise, because, to be precise, it is not concerned with the exposition of a doctrine, but with guiding an interlocutor to a certain settled mental attitude: it is a combat, amicable but real. We should note that this is what takes place in every spiritual exercise; it is necessary to make oneself change one's point of view, attitude, set of convictions, therefore to dialogue with oneself, therefore to struggle with oneself. [112]

Although Hadot recognizes that some ancient philosophical works are so to speak "more written" than others, he insists that even these works "are closely linked to the activity of teaching" and must "be understood from the perspective of dialectical and exegetical scholarly exercises." [113] The task of the philosopher was not primarily one of communicating "an encyclopedic knowledge in the form of a system of propositions and of concepts that would reflect, more or less well, the system of the world." [114] Therefore, even definitions were nothing by themselves, independently of the road traveled to reach them. The philosophers of antiquity were concerned not with ready-made knowledge, but with imparting that training and education that would allow their disciples to "orient themselves in thought, in the life of the city, or in the world." [115] If this is most obviously true of the Platonic dialogues, Hadot has reminded us that it is also true of the methods of Aristotle and the treatises of Plotinus: "the written philosophical work, precisely because it is a direct or indirect echo of oral teaching, now appears to us as a *set of exercises*, intended to make one practice a method, rather than as a doctrinal exposition." [116]

Moreover, these exercises were not conceived of as purely intellectual, as merely theoretical and formal exercises of discourse totally separated from life. Throughout the history of ancient philosophy, we can find criticisms of those philosophers who went no further than to develop a beautiful style of discourse or dialectical subtlety, who wished to stand out by making an ostentatious display of their philosophical discourse, but did not exercise themselves in the things of life. [117] Rather than aiming at the acquisition of a purely abstract knowledge, these exercises aimed at realizing a transformation of one's vision of the world and a metamorphosis of one's personality. The philosopher needed to be trained not only to know how to speak and debate, but also to know how to live. The exercise of philosophy "was therefore not only intellectual, but could also be spiritual." [118] Hence, the teaching and training of philosophy were intended not simply to develop the intelligence of the disciple, but to transform all aspects of his being – intellect, imagination, sensibility, and will. Its goal was nothing less than an art of living, and so spiritual exercises were exercises in learning to live the philosophical life. [119] Spiritual exercises were *exercises* because they were practical, required effort and training, and were lived; they were *spiritual* because they involved the entire spirit, one's whole way of being. [120] The art of living demanded by philosophy was a lived exercise exhibited in every aspect of one's existence.

Since the ultimate goal of the theoretical discourse of philosophy was to produce an effect in the soul of the listener or reader, this discourse had to bear in mind not only pedagogical constraints, but "the needs of psychagogy, of the direction of souls." [121] Rhetorical resources were abundantly made use of by the philosopher, and in attempting to influence himself and others all means were good. [122] In order "to rectify distorted opinions, tenacious prejudices, irrational terrors," the philosopher might have "to twist them in the other direction, to exaggerate in order to compensate." [123] In ancient texts, we discover that "one slides rapidly from theoretical exposition to exhortation," as often happens in Plotinus' treatises;[124] we even find at the end of the *Nicomachean Ethics* an accentuated protreptic and exhortative character, as Aristotle is recommending to others a certain kind of life, a specific conception of the good life.[125] The "presentation, literary form and content" of philosophical discourse were modified by "the intention to influence the disciples."[126] It is from this perspective that Hadot believes we must understand "the effort of systematization of the Stoics and Epicureans."[127] He has argued that the systematic discourse of these schools did not have for its chief goal

> to procure a total and exhaustive explanation of all reality, but to link, in an unshakable way, a small group of principles, vigorously articulated together, which, on the one hand, on the basis of this systematization, possess a greater persuasive force, a better psychological efficacy and which, on the other hand, enable the philosopher to orient himself in the world.[128]

This systematization thus allows the philosopher to bring together and focus the fundamental rules of life so that he can "keep them ready to hand at each instant of his life."[129] As Hadot says, "their systematic presentation produces assurance [*la certitude*] in the soul, therefore peace and serenity."[130]

In studying the literary genre of the ancient consolation, Ilsetraut Hadot has clearly demonstrated the intimate connection between the practice of spiritual exercises, the use of rhetoric and psychagogy, and literary form and content. Since, beginning with Plato, ancient philosophy represented itself as an exercise and training for death, the consolation is an ideal genre in which to observe the ancient practice of philosophy.[131] Noting that in all the written consolations of antiquity, we encounter nearly always the same arguments, she remarks that new and original arguments were not what the ancients sought after; in the best instances, the consolations had as their goal "to recall well-known things, to reactivate them in the soul."[132] These consolations were one important place where ancient philosophers tried to provide their followers with the spiritual means to maintain their psychic equilibrium, a goal that was especially acute and difficult in situations that were precarious and painful.

> In order to obtain this result, they had, on the one hand, to develop and teach their philosophical doctrines, but, on the other hand, they were perfectly conscious of the fact that the simple knowledge of a doctrine, beneficial as it was, did not guarantee its being put into practice. To have learned theoretically that death is not an evil does not suffice to no longer fear it. In order for this truth to be able to penetrate to the depths of one's being, so that it is not believed only for a brief moment, but

becomes an unshakable conviction, so that it is always "ready," "at hand," "present to mind," so that it is a "habitus of the soul" as the Ancients said, one must exercise oneself constantly and without respite – "night and day," as Cicero said. To this is joined a simple mode of life, in order not to be accustomed to what is superfluous the day it will be necessary to separate oneself from it.

These exercises are certainly exercises of meditation, but they do not only concern reason; in order to be efficacious, they must link the imagination and affectivity to the work of reason, and therefore all the psychagogical means of rhetoric . . .[133]

Hence we also find recommended, especially by the Stoics, the practice of premeditation on future evils that may occur, and the need to keep present and available in one's memory "all the edifying examples that history, epic poetry and tragedy" entrust to us.[134]

The central place accorded to spiritual exercises in ancient philosophy determines how we should situate and understand the writings of ancient philosophers, their philosophical discourse. The significance and aims of this discourse were conditioned by the ultimate goal of transforming the lives of individuals, of providing them with a philosophical art of living that required nothing less than spiritual metamorphosis. We must not forget that in the philosophy of this period, "theory is never considered an end in itself, it is clearly and decidedly put in the service of practice," a practice so radical and all-encompassing as to make the philosopher *atopos*, unclassifiable, since he is in love with wisdom, which makes him strange, and foreign to the world of most mortals.[135] Hadot pointedly captures the relation between philosophical writing, the oral tradition, and an art of living when he writes that ancient philosophy "always endeavored to be more a living voice than writing and still more a life than a voice."[136] The animated words of the philosopher are at the service of the philosopher's way of life, and his writing is an echo of these words. We might think here of Socrates, of his constant dialogue with himself and others. This dialogue is never closed in on itself, separate and isolated, but is part of, and in service to, Socrates' way of living and way of dying. According to Xenophon, when Hippias demanded the definition of justice from Socrates, he finally responded with these words: "Instead of speaking of it, I make it understood by my acts."[137] If spiritual exercises were the core of ancient philosophy, that is because philosophy was essentially a way of life.

In order to understand the centrality of spiritual exercises to ancient philosophy, it is crucial not to limit or reduce them to ethical exercises. As I have said, spiritual exercises involved all aspects of one's existence; they did not attempt only to insure behavior in accordance with a code of good conduct; they had, as Hadot says, not only a moral value, but an existential value.[138] More specifically, if we recall the traditional distinction between the three parts of philosophy – dialectic or logic, physics, and ethics – we must not place the practice of spiritual exercises simply in the ethical part of philosophy.[139] We must not represent logic and physics as being those parts of philosophy where theoretical discourse is located, presenting ethics as the practical part where spiritual exercises are enacted. As Hadot has argued at length, the distinction between theory and practice is located within each of the parts of philosophy; there is a theoretical discourse concerning logic, physics and ethics, but there is also a practical or lived logic, a lived physics, and a lived ethics.[140]

Ethics itself contains a theoretical discourse that sets forth principles, definitions, distinctions, and analyses of the virtues and vices. But, more importantly for the philosopher, there is also a lived ethics that puts into practice the fundamental rules of life.[141] Similarly, there is a theory of logic, which includes a conception of the proposition, and explains different forms of syllogisms, and different ways of refuting sophisms; in addition, the theory of logic was comprised of scholarly exercises in which one learned to apply the abstract rules. These rules of logic were also employed in the theoretical discourses of physics and ethics, the two other parts of philosophy. Yet, again, there was also an everyday practice of logic that had to be carried out in the domain of judgment and assent. This lived logic consisted in "not giving one's consent to what is false or doubtful." [142] Finally, the discipline of physics included not only a theory, but a lived physics, a true spiritual exercise, which involved a way of seeing the world, a cosmic consciousness, and procured pleasure and joy for the soul.[143] The spiritual exercises of ethics, logic, and physics meant that the practice of philosophy did not ultimately consist in "producing the theory of logic, that is the theory of speaking well and thinking well, nor in producing the theory of physics, that is of the cosmos, nor in producing the theory of acting well, but it concerned actually speaking well, thinking well, acting well, being truly conscious of one's place in the cosmos." [144]

The significance of locating spiritual exercises within *each* of the parts of philosophy can be seen clearly in Hadot's criticisms of Michel Foucault. One way of describing Hadot's misgivings about Foucault's interpretation of ancient spiritual exercises is to say that Foucault not only gave a too narrow construal of ancient ethics, but that he limited the "care of the self" to ethics alone.[145] Foucault made no place for that cosmic consciousness, for physics as a spiritual exercise, that was so important to the way in which the ancient philosopher viewed his relation to the world. By not attending to that aspect of the care of the self that places the self within a cosmic dimension, whereby the self, in becoming aware of its belonging to the cosmic Whole, thus transforms itself, Foucault was not able to see the full scope of spiritual exercises, that physics (and logic), as much as ethics, aimed at self-transformation. Indeed, in a very different context, Paul Veyne has reported the following exchange with Foucault: "One day when I asked Foucault: 'The care of the self, that is very nice, but what do you do with logic, what do you do with physics?', he responded: 'Oh, these are enormous excrescences!' "[146] Nothing could be further from Hadot's own attitude, since for him logic and physics, as lived spiritual exercises, are as central to the nature of philosophy as is ethics. Far from being excrescences, disfiguring and superfluous, the practices of logic and physics were a necessary part of the ancient philosopher's way of life, were crucial to his experience of himself as a philosopher, a lover of wisdom.

In recent writings, Hadot has focused on the Stoic doctrine that logic, physics, and ethics are not parts of philosophy itself, but are parts of philosophical discourse (*logos kata philosophian*), of the discourse relating to philosophy.[147] The Stoics held that "these parts could only appear distinct and separate in the discourse of teaching and of exposition of the philosophical dogmas," and that philosophy, strictly speaking, was not divided into parts.[148] Although expository, didactic, and pedagogical requirements made it necessary "to cut up" philosophy into parts, philosophy proper, as an exercise of wisdom, was considered a "single act, renewed at every instant, that one can describe, without breaking its unity, as being the exercise of logic as well as of physics or of ethics, according to the directions in which it is exercised."[149] That is to say, in the lived singular act of philosophy, logic, physics, and ethics are but "aspects of the very same virtue and very same wisdom"; they are not really distinguished with respect to one another, but only by "the different relations that relate them to different objects, the world, people, thought itself."[150] As Hadot summarizes this view, "logic, physics and ethics distinguish themselves from one another when one *speaks* of philosophy, but not when one *lives* it."[151]

For the Stoics the dynamic unity of reality, the coherence of reason with itself, meant that

> It is the same Logos that produces the world, enlightens the human being in his faculty of reasoning and expresses itself in human discourse, while remaining completely identical with itself at all stages of reality. Therefore, physics has for its object the Logos of universal nature, ethics the Logos of reasonable human nature, logic this same Logos expressing itself in human discourse. From start to finish, it is therefore the same force and the same reality that is at the same time creative Nature, Norm of conduct and Rule of discourse.[152]

This fundamental intuition of the Stoics, according to which the Logos is the common object of logic, physics, and ethics, is continued by those early

Christian thinkers who present God as the common object of the three parts of philosophy.[153] So, according to Augustine, the object of physics is God as cause of being, the object of logic is God as norm of thought and the object of ethics is God as rule of life. Moreover, this order – physics, logic, ethics – corresponds to the order of the divine persons in the Trinity: the Father is the Principle of being, the Son is Intellect and the Holy Spirit is Love. Thus, as Hadot writes, "the systematic unity of the parts of philosophy reflects here the reciprocal interiority of the divine Persons."[154]

When the Stoic philosopher, such as Epictetus or Marcus Aurelius, acts according to the Logos, he puts into practice spiritual exercises, that is, he disciplines his judgments, his desire, his inclinations, he enacts a lived logic, a lived physics, a lived ethics. These three acts of the soul exhibit the coherence and harmony of reason with itself, and from this perspective "the three parts of philosophy are no longer anything but three aspects of the fundamental spiritual attitude of the Stoic."[155] Although emphasizing that the parts of philosophy are required by and located within philosophical discourse and that philosophy itself is the site of spiritual exercises, Hadot also insists on the central role that discourse plays in the philosophical life. The philosopher can "only act on himself and others through discourse," and philosophy is thus "a mode of life that includes as an integral part a certain mode of discourse."[156] The theoretical discourse of the school to which he belongs is inwardly repeated and assimilated by the philosopher so that he can master his own inner discourse, so that his discourse will be ordered according to the fundamental choices and principles that were the starting point and basis for the theoretical discourse of his school.[157]

Recently, Hadot has distinguished between two senses of the word "discourse" in ancient philosophy.

> On the one hand, discourse insofar as it is addressed to a disciple or to oneself, that is to say, the discourse linked to an existential context, to a concrete praxis, discourse that is actually spiritual exercise; on the other hand, discourse considered abstractly in its formal structure, in its intelligible content. It is the latter that the Stoics would consider different from philosophy, but which is precisely what is usually made the object of most of the modern studies of the history of philosophy. But in the eyes of the ancient philosophers, if one contents oneself with this discourse, one does not do philosophy.[158]

Although discourse, both inner and outer, is essential to the philosopher, and although it can even take on the dimensions of a spiritual exercise, it is not the unique component of the philosophical life, and this life must not be reduced to discourse.

The essential element [of philosophical life] is in fact, one could say, non-discursive, insofar as it represents a choice of life, a wish to live in such and such a way, with all the concrete consequences that that implies in everyday life.[159]

In Antiquity the philosopher regards himself as a philosopher, not because he develops a philosophical discourse, but because he lives philosophically.[160]

We find this essential element, this orientation and point of view, in the remark of Epicurus' that "Our only occupation should be the cure of ourselves," or in the sentence attributed to him, "Empty is the discourse of that philosopher by which no human passion is attended to."[161] Or we find Epictetus saying,

A carpenter does not come up to you and say "Listen to me discourse about the art of carpentry," but he makes a contract for a house and builds it . . . Do the same thing yourself. Eat like a man, drink like a man . . . get married, have children, take part in civic life, learn how to put up with insults, and tolerate other people . . .[162]

Epictetus elsewhere rebukes the person who, in the discipline of judgment, is presented with representations some of which are adequate and others not, yet who refuses to differentiate between them, but "would prefer to read theoretical treatises on the understanding."[163] And in commenting on Epictetus' *Manual*, Simplicius writes,

One must produce the actions that are taught by discourses. The goal of discourse is actually actions. It is for the sake of them that the discourses were uttered (or written) . . . In fact, Chrysippus did not write on this subject [the nature of man] with the goal of being interpreted and understood, but so that one makes use of his writings in life. If therefore I make use of his writings in life, at that very moment I participate in the good they contain. But if I admire the exegete because he provides good explanations, and if I can understand and myself interpret the text and if, quite frankly, everything falls to my lot except the fact of making use of these writings in life, would I have become anything other than a grammarian instead of a philosopher? . . . the fact of just simply reading the writings of Chrysippus or of explaining them on the request of somebody else, and of not making use of them in life, is reprehensible. In fact, he should rightly be ashamed who, being ill, would find some writings containing cures for his illness, would read them with insight and, distinguishing clearly (the different parts), would explain them if need be to others, but would not make use of these cures for his illness.[164]

Philosophy is an art of living that cures us of our illnesses by teaching us a radically new way of life.

Hadot recognizes that it is only in Hellenistic philosophy that one finds a distinction between philosophy and philosophical discourse explicitly formulated. But he has also argued that "this distinction was clearly implicit in the previous period in Plato and Aristotle." [165] Indeed, recalling the importance of the mysteries of Eleusis in the history of ancient thought, Hadot reminds us of the famous sentence attributed to Aristotle that the initiates of Eleusis do not *learn* anything, but they *experience* a certain impression or emotion.[166] The initiate did not learn his other-worldly fate at Eleusis, but lived this supra-individual life of the other world.[167] The "true secret of Eleusis is therefore *this very experience*, this moment when one plunges into the completely other, this discovery of an unknown dimension of existence." [168]

Hadot also finds an implicit distinction between philosophy and philosophical discourse in Plato's definition of philosophy (*Phaedo*, 67 c–d) as a training for death. The purification of the soul, its separation as far as possible from the body and its gathering itself together within itself, is the true practice of philosophy. Hence philosophy consists of a lived concrete exercise and not of a theory or a conceptual edifice: "The theoretical philosophical discourse is completely different from the lived exercises by which the soul purifies itself of its passions and spiritually separates itself from the body." [169] Plotinus continues this tradition when in *Ennead*, IV, 7, 10, he argues that the soul cannot become aware of its own immateriality if it does not perform a moral purification that liberates it from its passions, that strips away everything that is not truly itself.[170] It is this purification that allows us to gain knowledge of the immateriality of our soul. More generally, in *Ennead*, VI, 7, 36, Plotinus distinguishes carefully between the methods of rational theology that teach us about the Good, and the spiritual exercises that lead us to the Good. The four methods of rational theology, the method of analogy, the negative method, the affirmative method drawn from the knowledge of the things that come from the Good, and the method of stages or degrees (*anabasmoi*; *Symposium*, 211c) all give us *knowledge* about the Good. However, only the spiritual exercises of purification, of the practice of the virtues, of putting ourselves in order, allow us to *touch* the Good, to *experience* it.[171] Plotinus' philosophy does not wish only

> to be a discourse about objects, be they even the highest, but it wishes actually to lead the soul to a living, concrete union with the Intellect and the Good . . . Reason, by theological methods, can raise itself to the

notion of the Good but only life according to Intellect can lead to the *reality* of the Good.[172]

Furthermore, as Hadot writes, "it is mystical experience that founds negative theology, and not the reverse."[173] This mystical experience, like the mysteries of Eleusis, does not consist in learning something, but in "living another life" where the self "*becomes* the absolutely Other."[174]

It is perhaps Aristotle whom we are most tempted to think of as a pure theoretician. Although it is true that Aristotle's philosophy is a philosophy of *theoria*, "this Aristotelian *theoria* is nevertheless not purely theoretical in the modern sense of the word."[175] For Aristotle, to dedicate oneself to philosophy is to chose a *bios*, a way of life, that is the best realization of those capacities that are essential to being human. The *bios theoretikos*, the life of contemplation, is a way of life that is also the realization of our supreme happiness, an activity that contains the purest pleasures.[176] Even scientific research on the entities of nature is not proposed by Aristotle as an end in itself, but as "a particular way of carrying out 'the philosophical life', one of the possible practical realizations of the aristotelian prescription for happiness, the life devoted to the activity of the intellect."[177] Moreover, the life of the intellect is a participation in the divine way of life, it is the actualization of the divine in the human, and it requires inner transformation and personal *askesis*.[178] And it is a way of life that is, in one sense of the term, practical, since Aristotle says that those thoughts are practical not only that calculate the results of action, but which are "contemplation and reasoning, that have their end in themselves and take themselves as object."[179] This life of *theoria* is thus not opposed to the practical, since it is a life of philosophy lived and practiced; it is precisely the "*exercise* of a *life*."[180]

Hadot has distinguished two senses of the term "theoretical," for which he has employed the terms *théorique* and *théorétique*. The first meaning of "theoretical" is opposed to "practical," since it designates theoretical discourse as opposed to lived philosophy. But the adjective *théorétique* which characterizes the life of contemplation, the life according to the intellect, is not opposed by Aristotle to philosophy as practiced and lived. In Aristotle this "theoretical life [*vie théorétique*] is not a pure abstraction, but a life of the intellect, which, no doubt, can use a theoretical discourse [*discours théorique*], but nonetheless remains a life and a praxis, and which can even make room for a nondiscursive activity of thought, when it is a question of perceiving indivisible objects and God himself by noetic intuition."[181] Thus to think of Aristotle as a pure theoretician is to focus exclusively on his theoretical discourse without bearing in mind that it is a way of life, however intellectualized, that he is recommending, and which is the ultimate basis of his philosophy.

The idea of philosophy as a way of life, and not just as philosophical discourse, was also exhibited in antiquity by the designation of individuals as philosophers who were neither scholars, professors, nor authors, but who were honored as philosophers because of their way of life. As Hadot says, the extension of the concept of philosopher was quite different from that of our modern concept. In antiquity, the philosopher was not necessarily "a professor or a writer. He was first of all a person having a certain style of life, which he willingly chose, even if he had neither taught nor written."[182] Thus we find philosophical figures not only such as Diogenes the Cynic and Pyrrho, but also women who did not write, and celebrated statesmen who were considered true philosophers by their contemporaries.[183] It was not only Chrysippus or Epicurus who were considered philosophers, because they had developed a philosophical discourse, but also every person who lived according to the precepts of Chrysippus or Epicurus.[184]

True philosophers lived in society with their fellow citizens, and yet they lived in a different way from other people. They distinguished themselves from others by "their moral conduct, by speaking their mind [*leur franc parler*], by their way of nourishing themselves or dressing themselves, by their attitude with respect to wealth and to conventional values."[185] Although they did not live a cloistered life, as in Christian monasticism, philosophy was nevertheless analogous to the monastic movement in requiring that one convert oneself so as to fervently adhere to a philosophical school: the philosopher had to "make a choice that obliged him to transform his whole way of living in the world."[186] Hence the felt rupture of the philosophical life with the conduct and perceptions of everyday life.[187] The significance of philosophy as a way of life can also be seen in the importance given to biographies in ancient philosophical work. As Giuseppe Cambiano has emphasized, a philosophical biography was not predominantly a narrative intended to allow one to understand an author and his doctrines; it was not just a report of what the author said and believed. Rather, "it was, in the first place, a tool of philosophical battle," since one could defend or condemn a philosophy by way of the characteristics of the mode of life of those who supported it.[188]

The philosopher was a philosopher because of his *existential attitude*, an attitude that was the foundation of his philosophy and that required that he undergo a real conversion, in the strongest sense of the word, that he radically change the direction of his life.[189] All six schools of philosophy in the Hellenistic period present themselves

> as choices of life, they demand an existential choice, and whoever adheres to one of these schools must accept this choice and this option. One too often represents Stoicism or Epicureanism as a set of abstract theories about the world invented by Zeno or Chrysippus or Epicurus. From these theories would spring, as if by accident one could say, a morality. But it is the reverse that is true. It is the abstract theories that are intended to justify the existential attitude. One could say, to express

it otherwise, that every existential attitude implies a representation of the world that must necessarily be expressed in a discourse. But this discourse alone is not the philosophy, it is only an element of it, for the philosophy is first of all the existential attitude itself, accompanied by inner and outer discourses: the latter have as their role to express the representation of the world that is implied in such and such an existential attitude, and these discourses allow one at the same time to rationally justify the attitude and to communicate it to others.[190]

Hence we begin with a fundamental existential choice on behalf of a style of life that consists of certain practices, activities, and conduct that are precisely what Hadot calls "spiritual exercises." This style of life is given concrete form

> either in the order of inner discourse and of spiritual activity: meditation, dialogue with oneself, examination of conscience, exercises of the imagination, such as the view from above on the cosmos or the earth, or in the order of action and of daily behavior, like the mastery of oneself, indifference towards indifferent things, the fulfilment of the duties of social life in Stoicism, the discipline of desires in Epicureanism.[191]

Philosophical discourse, of oneself with oneself and of oneself with others, will, of course, be needed to justify and communicate these spiritual exercises, to represent the fundamental existential attitude, but philosophy itself consists primarily in choosing and living the attitude.

Hadot recognizes that this ancient understanding of philosophy can appear very far removed from the way in which we now understand the nature of philosophy. He has pointed to three aspects of the evolution of the representation of philosophy that have contributed to our current understanding of it as a purely theoretical, abstract activity, and to our identification of it with philosophical discourse alone. The first aspect, which Hadot has called "a natural inclination of the philosophical mind" and "connatural to the philosopher," is the "constant tendency that the philosopher always has, even in Antiquity, to satisfy himself with discourse, with the conceptual architecture that he has constructed, without putting into question his own life."[192] This tendency, which was already criticized in antiquity, has been said by Hadot to be "the perpetual danger of philosophy" – the philosopher is always tempted to take refuge in, to shut himself up in, the "reassuring universe of concepts and of discourse instead of going beyond discourse in order to take upon himself the risk of the radical transformation of himself."[193] To this tendency is opposed the equally natural inclination of the philosophical mind to want to examine itself, to want to learn how to live the philosophical life.

Faced with the overwhelming reality of life, with worries, anxiety, suffering, death, philosophical discourse can appear to be nothing but "empty chattering and a derisive luxury," mere words when what is needed is a new attitude towards life, one which will produce inner freedom, tranquillity, happiness.[194] It is at these moments that our contrary natural inclinations will be felt to be most acutely opposed to one another. We will then be forced to ask, "What is finally most beneficial to the human being as a human being? Is it to discourse on language, or on being and non-being? Or is it not rather to learn how to live a human life?"[195] Yet despite our "elementary need" for this philosophical consciousness and way of life, the history of philosophy also testifies unambiguously to the powerful tendency of our "self-satisfaction with theoretical discourse."[196]

A second aspect that helps to account for the changed understanding and representation of philosophy in the modern world has to do with the historical evolution of philosophy, especially with the relation between philosophy and Christianity. Although in early Christianity, especially the monastic movements, Christianity itself was presented as a *philosophia*, a way of life in conformity with the divine Logos, as the Middle Ages developed, one witnessed a "total separation" of ancient spiritual exercises, which were no longer considered a part of philosophy but were integrated into Christian spirituality, and philosophy itself, which became a "simple theoretical tool" at the service of theology, an *ancilla theologiae*.[197] Philosophy's role was now to provide theology with the "conceptual, logical, physical and metaphysical materials it needed," and the "Faculty of Arts became no more than a preparation for the Faculty of Theology."[198] Philosophical speculation thus became a purely abstract and theoretical activity, which was set strictly apart from theological thought and religious practice and spirituality.[199] No longer a way of life, philosophy became a conceptual construction, a servant of theology, and the idea of philosophy as a system began to appear.[200]

A third aspect underlying our modern representation of philosophy is of a sociological nature, and can be traced back to the functioning of the university, as it was created by the medieval church. One central feature of the university is that it is an institution made up of professors who train other professors, of specialists who learn how to train other specialists. Unlike in antiquity, when philosophical teaching was directed towards the human being so as to form him as a human being, the modern university forms professionals who teach future professionals, and thus philosophy, rather than proposing an art of living, is presented above all as a "technical language reserved for specialists."[201] As Hadot says, in "modern university philosophy, philosophy is obviously no longer a way of life, a kind of life, unless it is the kind of life of the professor of philosophy."[202] This sociological requirement of professionalism, this situation of scholasticism, facilitates and reinforces the tendency to take refuge in the "comfortable universe of concepts and of discourses";[203] it gives this natural tendency a social basis and impetus, encouraging the display of a specialized technical language, as if philosophical depth were exhausted by one's ability to make use of conceptual abstractions and by one's skill at demonstrating the truth and falsity of various propositions.

Thus Hadot has provided three reasons, which one could think of as, respectively, philosophical, historical, and sociological, that help to account for the representation of philosophy as a purely theoretical activity, and for the reduction of philosophy to philosophical discourse. But he has not overlooked the fact that one can find elements of the ancient representation of philosophy throughout the history of philosophy, that certain of the "existential aspects of ancient philosophy" have been constantly rediscovered.[204] Among the philosophers he has named as exhibiting this ancient representation are Abelard and the Renaissance humanists, such as Petrarch and Erasmus. We might think here of the latter's remark with respect to his *Enchiridion Militis Christiani:* "Let this book lead to a theological life rather than theological disputation."[205] Hadot has repeatedly pointed to Montaigne's *Essays*, especially "That to Philosophise is to Learn How to Die," as embodying the ancient exercise of philosophy, referring to the *Essays* as "the breviary of ancient philosophy, the manual of the art of living."[206] Among modern philosophers, Hadot has singled out certain aspects of Descartes' *Meditations*, particularly Descartes' advice that one invest some months or at least weeks meditating on his first and second *Meditations*, which Hadot says ultimately shows that for Descartes "evidence can only be perceived thanks to a spiritual exercise."[207] Hadot also mentions Spinoza's *Ethics*, and its emphasis on teaching us how to radically transform ourselves, to accede to beatitude, to approach the ideal of the sage, as well as Shaftesbury's remarkable *Exercises*, inspired by the spiritual exercises of Epictetus and Marcus Aurelius.[208] He has indicated, too, the continuation of the ancient idea of philosophy in the French *philosophes* of the eighteenth century, and in Kant's ideas of the interest of reason and the primacy of the practical.[209] In more recent times, we can find the spirit of the ancient philosopher's demand that we radically change our way of living and of seeing the world in Goethe, Schopenhauer, Nietzsche, and Kierkegaard, and, in different ways, in the young Hegelians and Marx.[210] In the twentieth century, Hadot points to Bergson, to Wittgenstein, to Foucault, and to certain aspects of phenomenology and existentialism as embodying the ancient attitude, practices, and sense of what philosophy means.[211] And recently, Hadot has taken up Thoreau's *Walden*, finding in his decision to live in the woods Thoreau's undertaking of a philosophical act.[212] This constant reoccurrence of the ancient experience of philosophy, side by side with the tendency to understand philosophy as a conceptual structure, an abstract discourse, shows how complex and even contradictory philosophy's own self-understanding has been. Hadot's work calls for a detailed historical account of philosophy's representations of itself, of the various ways in which philosophy imagines itself and exercises its ideals, and of the factors that contribute to its changing evaluations of itself, to how it views and reviews its own purposes and ultimate goals.

The permanence of the existential aspects of ancient philosophy has been highlighted by Hadot in his most recent discussions of what he has called "the fundamental and universal attitudes of the human being when he searches for wisdom."[213] From this point of view, Hadot has discerned a universal Stoicism, Epicureanism, Platonism, Aristotelianism, Cynicism, and Pyrrhonism, each of which corresponds to a permanent possibility of the human spirit, and which are independent of the particular "philosophical or mythical discourses that have claimed or claim to justify them definitively."[214] Hadot, obviously enough, does not believe that we can adopt any of these attitudes wholly and unmodified, as if we could totally convert to the dogmas and practices of these schools of ancient philosophy.[215] But he does believe that detached from their outmoded elements and reduced to their essence, to the extent that "we try to give a meaning to our life, they call upon us to discover the transformation that could be brought about in our life, if we realized (in the strongest sense of the term) certain values" that constitute the spirit of each of these attitudes.[216]

With respect to Stoicism, Hadot has described four features that constitute the universal Stoic attitude. They are, first, the Stoic consciousness of "the fact that no being is alone, but that we make up part of a Whole, constituted by the totality of human beings as well as by the totality of the cosmos"; second, the Stoic "feels absolutely serene, free, and invulnerable to the extent that he has become aware that there is no other evil but moral evil and that the only thing that counts is the purity of moral consciousness"; third, the Stoic "believes in the absolute value of the human person," a belief that is "at the origin of the modern notion of the 'rights of man' "; finally, the Stoic exercises his concentration "on the present instant, which consists, on the one hand, in living as if we were seeing the world for the first and for the last time, and, on the other hand, in being conscious that, in this lived presence of the instant, we have access to the totality of time and of the world."[217] Thus, for Hadot, cosmic consciousness, the purity of moral consciousness, the recognition of the equality and absolute value of human beings, and the concentration on the present instant represent the universal Stoic attitude. The universal Epicurean attitude essentially consists, by way of "a certain discipline and reduction of desires, in returning from pleasures mixed with pain and suffering to the simple and pure pleasure of existing."[218] Platonism, Aristotelianism, Cynicism, and Pyrrhonism also each have a universal character, and one of the historical and philosophical tasks called forth by Hadot's work is precisely to provide a description of each of these universal existential attitudes, each of the styles of life that they propose.

Moreover, Hadot has insisted that we do not have to choose between these different universal attitudes, opting for one to the exclusion of all of the others. The plurality of ancient schools allows us to compare the consequences of the different possible fundamental attitudes of reason, thus offering us "a privileged field of experimentation." [219] And we should not be surprised to find, for example, that there are certain people who are half Stoic and half Epicurean, who accept and combine "Epicurean sensualism" and "Stoic communion with nature," who practice both Stoic spiritual exercises of vigilance and Epicurean spiritual exercises aimed at the true pleasure of existing. [220] That is precisely how Hadot characterizes Goethe, Rousseau, and Thoreau. [221] Indeed, Hadot has said that Stoicism and Epicureanism seem to correspond to "two opposite but inseparable poles of our inner life: tension and relaxation, duty and serenity, moral consciousness and the joy of existing." [222] To these poles of our inner life, we must add the experiences of Platonic love and the ascent of the soul as well as of Plotinian unity, Aristotelian contemplation, Cynic criticism of conventional values and the effort to endure every test and ordeal we face, Pyrrhonic suspension of judgment and absolute indifference. [223] It is these experiences and ideals, more than any concepts, that are the legacy of ancient philosophy to Western civilization. [224] The study of ancient philosophy has taught Hadot that "human reality is so complex that one can only live it by using simultaneously or successively the most different methods: tension and relaxation, engagement and detachment, enthusiasm and reserve, certainty and criticism, passion and indifference." [225] Lessons in how to live human reality, with all that that implies – those are the enduring lessons of ancient philosophy.

In his preface to the monumental *Dictionnaire des philosophes antiques*, Hadot surveys all of the insufficiently exploited resources that are available to the historian of ancient philosophy. He shows how the lists of titles of philosophical works as well as iconography, papyruses, and inscriptions can all be used to characterize more fully and accurately the phenomena of philosophy. But even this vast historical undertaking would not fulfill Hadot's own ultimate aims:

> for the historian of philosophy the task will not be finished for all that: or more exactly, it should cede place to the philosopher, to the philosopher who should always remain alive in the historian of philosophy. This final task will consist in asking oneself, with an increased lucidity, the decisive question: "What is it to philosophize?" [226]

Pierre Hadot's own work itself provokes us to reask the question of what it means to philosophize, and he provides a response as relevant, profound, and unsettling today as it was centuries ago. In the last analysis, that is what makes Pierre Hadot not just a consummate historian of philosophy, but also a philosopher for our own times.

Arnold I. Davidson

NOTES

1 Pierre Hadot, *Exercices spirituels et philosophie antique*, 2nd edn, Paris 1987.
2 Pierre Hadot, *La Citadelle intérieure. Introduction aux Pensées de Marc Aurèle*, Paris 1992.
3 Pierre Hadot, *Titres et travaux de Pierre Hadot*, privately printed for the Collège de France, p. 9.
4 Pierre Hadot, "Patristique Latine," *Problèmes et méthodes d'histoire des religions, Mélanges publiés par la Section des Sciences religieuses à l'occasion du centenaire de l'École pratique des Hautes Études*, Paris 1968, pp. 211–13. *Contresens* is a central concept in Hadot's interpretation of the history of exegetical thought. It covers strict cases of mistranslation as well as more general phenomena of misunderstanding and misinterpretation. I return to this aspect of Hadot's thought in what follows.
5 Hadot, *Titres et travaux*, p. 8.
6 Hadot, "Patristique Latine," p. 212, and Pierre Hadot, "Patristique," in *Encyclopedia Universalis*, vol. 12, p. 608, Paris, 1972. Among other texts of Augustine, see *Confessions*, IX, 4, 11.
7 Pierre Hadot, *Comptes rendus des conférences données a l'École pratique des Hautes Études de 1964 a 1980*, privately printed. I have paraphrased the *compte rendu* from 1964–1965. The quotation is from pp. 2–3.
8 Pierre Hadot, "Platon et Plotin dans trois sermons de saint Ambrose," *Revue des études latines* XXXIV (1956), p. 209, n. 5.
9 Hadot, "Patristique," p. 608.
10 Pierre Hadot, "La fin du paganisme," in H.-Ch. Peuch, ed., *Histoire des religions*, vol. II, pp. 101–7, Paris 1972.
11 Ibid, p. 109. See also Margherita Guarducci, *Il primato della Chiesa di Roma. Documenti, riflessioni, conferme*, Milan 1991, pp. 85–7.
12 Hadot, "La fin du paganisme," p. 110.
13 Ibid, pp. 107–8.
14 Ibid, p. 108. See also Édouard des Places, "Numenius et Eusèbe de Césarée," in *Études platoniciennes 1929–1979*, Leiden 1981, esp. pp. 322–5.
15 Hadot, "La fin du paganisme," p. 111.
16 Ibid, pp. 108 and 105. Also, Pierre Hadot, "Théologie, exégèse, révélation, écriture, dans la philosophie grecque," in Michel Tardieu, ed., *Les règles de l'interprétation*, Paris 1987.
17 Hadot, "La fin du paganisme," pp. 83–4, 109.
18 Hadot, "Théologie, exégèse, révélation," p. 14.
19 Ibid, p. 22.

20 In trying to summarize Hadot's very complex discussion, without distorting it, I have mainly followed "L'être et l'étant dans le néoplatonisme," in *Études neoplatoniciennes*, Neuchâtel 1973; "Théologie, exégèse, révélation," esp. pp. 19–20; and "Philosophy, Exegesis, and Creative Mistakes," this volume. See also Pierre Hadot, *Porphyre et Victorinus*, 2 vols, Paris 1968.

21 Hadot, "Théologie, exégèse, révélation," p. 20.

22 Ibid.

23 Hadot, "L'être et l'étant dans le néoplatonisme," pp. 34–5.

24 Hadot, "Théologie, exégèse, révélation," p. 20.

25 Hadot, "L'être et l'étant dans le néoplatonisme," pp. 34–5; Pierre Hadot, "La distinction de l'être et de l'étant dans le 'De Hebdomadibus' de Boèce," in *Miscellanea Mediaevalia*, vol. 2, Berlin 1963; and Pierre Hadot, "*Forma essendi.* Interprétation philologique et interprétation philosophique d'une formule de Boèce," *Les Études classiques* XXXVII (1970), pp. 143–56. Hadot also explicitly relates this distinction to Heidegger's writings; see Hadot, "L'être et l'étant dans le néoplatonisme," p. 27.

26 Pierre Hadot, "Heidegger et Plotin," *Critique* 145 (1959), p. 542.

27 See Hadot's discussion in "Forms of Life and Forms of Discourse in Ancient Philosophy," this volume, especially pp. 65–6.

28 Ibid, pp. 61–2.

29 For the quoted phrase, see Hadot, *Titres et travaux*, p. 23.

30 Hadot, "Patristique Latine," p. 218.

31 Ibid, pp. 216–17.

32 Margherita Guarducci, "La Crittografia mistica e i graffiti vaticani," *Archeologia Classica* XIII (1961), p. 236, my emphasis.

33 Margherita Guarducci, "Dal Gioco letterale alla crittografia mistica," in *Scritti scelti sulla religione greca e romana e sul cristianesimo*, Leiden 1983, pp. 421–2.

34 Ibid, p. 441. On the relationship between the three teeth of the *E* and the symbol of the key see also Margherita Guarducci, "Ancora sul misterioso *E* di Delfi," in *Scritti scelti*.

35 Margherita Guarducci, "La Crittografia mistica," p. 219.

36 Guarducci, *Il primato della Chiesa di Roma*, pp. 126–7.

37 Quoted above, p. 8.

38 Guarducci, "Dal Gioco letterale alla crittografia mistica," p. 427.

39 Ibid, p. 428.

40 On the resort to lapidary error and accident, see Guarducci, "La Crittografia mistica," pp. 203–10.

41 For a superb example, see ibid, p. 206.

42 Quoted above, p. 8.

43 Hadot, *La Citadelle intérieure*, pp. 39–40. See also Pierre Hadot, "Les Pensées de Marc Aurèle," *Bulletin de l'Association Guillame Budé* (June 1981), pp. 183–4.

44 Hadot, *La Citadelle intérieure*, p. 41.

45 Ibid, pp. 39–42.

46 Pierre Hadot, "Une clé des *Pensées* de Marc Aurèle: les trois *Topoi* philosophiques

selon Épictète," in *Exercices spirituels*, p. 135. This essay was originally published in 1978.

47 Hadot, *La Citadelle intérieure*, pp. 40–1, 46–7. See also Hadot, "Les *Pensées* de Marc Aurèle," pp. 183–4.

48 Hadot, *La Citadelle intérieure*, pp. 47, 49.

49 Ibid, p. 49.

50 Ibid.

51 Hadot, "Les *Pensées* de Marc Aurèle," p. 185. See also Hadot, *Titres et travaux*, p. 29.

52 Hadot, *La Citadelle intérieure*, pp. 85–6, 98–106. See also "Marcus Aurelius," this volume. Hadot has argued that, before Marcus, Epictetus was the *only* Stoic to have distinguished between three activities or functions of the soul. See Hadot, *La Citadelle intérieure*, pp. 85, 99, 145.

53 Ibid, pp. 106–15. See also Pierre Hadot, "Philosophie, discours philosophique, et divisions de la philosophie chez les stoiciens," *Revue internationale de la philosophie* 178 (1991), pp. 205–19.

54 Hadot, *La Citadelle intérieure*, p. 106. I will return to Hadot's discussion of the distinction between philosophical discourse and philosophy.

55 Hadot, "Une clé des *Pensées* de Marc Aurèle," p. 135.

56 Hadot, *La Citadelle intérieure*, p. 62.

57 Hadot, "Les *Pensées* de Marc Aurèle," p. 187. See also Hadot, "Une clé des *Pensées* de Marc Aurèle," p. 150.

58 The words quoted are from the quotation above, p. 8.

59 Hadot, *Titres et travaux*, p. 12. See also "Marcus Aurelius," this volume, p. 186.

60 Hadot, *La Citadelle intérieure*, p. 10. Hadot has applied these remarks to other ancient works. See Hadot, *Titres et travaux*, p. 13; and "Forms of Life and Forms of Discourse in Ancient Philosophy," this volume, pp. 65–6.

61 Hadot, *La Citadelle intérieure*, pp. 262–75. See also Pierre Hadot, "Marc Aurèle était-il opiomane?," in E. Lucchesi and H.D. Saffrey, eds, *Memorial André-Jean Festugière*, Geneva 1984.

62 Hadot, *La Citadelle intérieure*, pp. 261–2, 274.

63 Marcus Aurelius, *Meditations*, VIII, 24. Cited in "Marcus Aurelius," this volume, p. 184.

64 Marcus Aurelius, *Meditations*, VI, 13. Cited in "Marcus Aurelius," this volume, p. 185.

65 Hadot, *La Citadelle intérieure*, p. 194.

66 Ibid, p. 181. On physical definitions, see also pp. 122–3; and Hadot, "Les *Pensées* de Marc Aurèle," pp. 188–9.

67 Marcus Aurelius, *Meditations*, III, 11. Cited in "Marcus Aurelius," this volume, p. 187.

68 Hadot, *La Citadelle intérieure*, p. 123.

69 Ibid.

70 Hadot, "Les *Pensées* de Marc Aurèle," p. 189.

71 Pierre Hadot, "La Physique comme exercice spirituel ou pessimisme et optimisme chez Marc Aurèle," in *Exercices spirituels*, pp. 132–3. This article was

originally published in 1972. For Hadot's argument that this inner attitude is not one of fatalist resignation, see Hadot, *La Citadelle intérieure*, pp. 224–6.

72 Hadot, *La Citadelle intérieure*, p. 268. See also Hadot, *Titres et travaux*, p. 12. For other methodological limitations of this kind of psychological interpretation, see Hadot's remarkable discussion of the *Passio Perpetuae* in his *compte rendu* from 1967–8, in Hadot, *Comptes rendus des conférences*, pp. 19–23. Of course, Hadot does not believe that Marcus is totally absent from the *Meditations*. See Hadot, *La Citadelle intérieure*, pp. 261–2, 275–314. See also "Marcus Aurelius," this volume, pp. 196–9.

73 Pierre Hadot, "De Tertullien à Boèce. Le développement de la notion de personne dans les controverses théologiques," in I. Myerson, ed., *Problèmes de la personne, Colloque du Centre de recherches de Psychologie comparative*, Paris/La Haye 1973, p. 132.

74 Ibid, p. 133. These claims of Hadot continue to be cited with approval. See, for example, Jean-Pierre Vernant, "L'individu dans la cité," in *Sur l'individu*, Paris 1987, p. 37. For another expression of this early view of Hadot, see Hadot, "L'image de la Trinité dans l'âme chez Victorinus et chez saint Augustin," in *Studia Patristica*, vol. VI, part IV, Berlin 1962. See esp. p. 440 where Hadot writes, "From Victorinus to Augustine, there is all of the distance that separates the ancient soul from the modern self."

75 Hadot, "Patristique Latine," p. 215.

76 Ibid.

77 Hadot, "Forms of Life and Forms of Discourse in Ancient Philosophy," this volume, p. 52. For Pierre Courcelle, see *Recherches sur les "Confessions" de saint Augustin* (Paris: Études Augustiniennes, 1950).

78 Hadot, *Comptes rendus des conférences*, p. 8. This is the *compte rendu* from 1965–6.

79 Hadot, "Patristique Latine," p. 215.

80 Hadot, *Comptes rendus des conférences*, p. 9. For a good discussion of the literature on Book II of the *Confessions*, see Franco De Capitani, "Il libro II delle *Confessioni* di sant'Agostino," in *"Le Confessioni" di Agostino d'Ippona, Libri I–II*, Palermo 1984.

81 Hadot, "Patristique Latine," pp. 215–16, together with Hadot, *Comptes rendus des conférences*, p. 9.

82 Hadot, "Patristique Latine," p. 215.

83 Hadot, *Comptes rendus des conférences*, p. 8.

84 Ibid.

85 Ibid, p. 9.

86 *Compte rendu* from 1970–71, in ibid, pp. 45–8.

87 Hadot, "Patristique Latine," p. 215.

88 Ibid, p. 216, together with "Forms of Life and Forms of Discourse in Ancient Philosophy," this volume, p. 52. I have quoted extensively from Hadot's various discussions of Augustine, since many of them are not easily available. Hadot had once intended to publish a translation and commentary on the *Confessions*, a project he never completed.

89 Hadot, "Patristique Latine," p. 215.

90 See, among other essays, Pierre Hadot, "Wittgenstein, philosophe du langage (I)," *Critique* 149 (October 1959), pp. 866–81; and "Wittgenstein, philosophe du langage (II)," *Critique* 150 (November 1959), pp. 972–83.

91 Hadot, "Wittgenstein, philosophe du langage (II)," p. 973. The importance of the connection between Wittgenstein's literary style and his thought has been a constant theme of Stanley Cavell's writing. For an early statement, see Cavell, "The availability of Wittgenstein's later philosophy," in *Must We Mean What We Say?*, New York 1969, pp. 70–3. I bring together Hadot and Cavell's work in "La découverte de Thoreau et d'Emerson par Stanley Cavell ou les exercices spirtuels de la philosophie" (forthcoming in Sandra Laugier, ed., *Lire Cavell*).

92 Hadot has highlighted these claims in the overview of his work that he presented to the Collège International de Philosophie in May, 1993. I will refer to the unpublished typescript of his presentation as "Présentation au Collège International de Philosophie." See, for example, pp. 2–3.

93 Pierre Hadot, "Jeux de langage et philosophie," *Revue de Métaphysique et de Morale* LXIV (1960), p. 341.

94 Ibid, p. 340.

95 Ibid, pp. 339–43.

96 Ibid, pp. 342–3.

97 Ibid, p. 343.

98 Hadot, *La Citadelle intérieure*, p. 9. See also Hadot, *Titres et travaux*, p. 12.

99 Pierre Hadot, "La philosophie antique: une éthique ou une pratique?," in Paul Demont, ed., *Problèmes de la morale antique*, Amiens 1993, pp. 7–8. See also the section "Learning How to Read" in "Spiritual Exercises," this volume, pp. 101–9.

100 Hadot, "Philosophie, discours philosophique, et divisions de la philosophie chez les stoiciens," p. 205.

101 Pierre Hadot, "Préface," in Richard Goulet, ed., *Dictionnaire des philosophes antiques*, Paris 1989, p. 12.

102 Hadot, "La philosophie antique: une éthique ou une pratique?," p. 8. See also Hadot, "Présentation au Collège International de Philosophie," pp. 1–2.

103 Hadot, "La philosophie antique: une éthique ou une pratique?," p. 10.

104 "Forms of Life and Forms of Discourse in Ancient Philosophy," this volume, p. 62.

105 Hadot, "La philosophie antique: une éthique ou une pratique?," p. 9. See also Pierre Hadot, "Préface," in M.D. Richard, *L'Enseignement oral de Platon*, Paris 1986, pp. 9–10.

106 Reading together Hadot, "Jeux de langage et philosophie," p. 341, and Hadot, "Présentation au Collège International de Philosophie," p. 2.

107 Hadot, "Présentation au Collège International de Philosophie," p. 2. To the best of my knowledge, Hadot first invoked this formula of Goldschmitt in "Jeux de langage et philosophie," p. 341.

108 Hadot, "Préface," in *L'Enseignement oral de Platon*, p. 11.

109 See the section "Learning to Dialogue" in "Spiritual Exercises," this volume, pp. 89–93.

110 "Spiritual Exercises," this volume, pp. 19–20.

111 Ibid, p. 21.

112 Ibid, pp. 21–2. (I have modified the translation.)

113 "Forms of Life and Forms of Discourse in Ancient Philosophy," this volume, pp. 63–4.

114 Hadot, "La philosophie antique: une éthique ou une pratique?," p. 11.

115 Ibid.

116 Ibid, my emphasis.

117 Ibid, pp. 11–12.

118 Ibid, p. 12. See also "Spiritual Exercises," this volume.

119 See the section "Learning to Live" in "Spiritual Exercises," this volume, pp. 82–9. Also see Hadot, "La philosophie antique: une éthique ou une pratique?," pp. 12–14.

120 See esp. the opening pages of "Ancient Spiritual Exercises and 'Christian Philosophy'," this volume.

121 Hadot, "La philosophie antique: une éthique ou une pratique?," p. 13. On the direction of souls in Seneca, see Ilsetraut Hadot, *Seneca und die griechisch-römische Tradition der Seelenleitung*, Berlin, 1969. In antiquity, the philosopher was not the only kind of spiritual guide; for other figures of spiritual guidance, see Ilsetraut Hadot, "The spiritual guide," in A.H. Armstrong, ed., *Classical Mediterranean Spirituality*, New York 1986.

122 Hadot, "La philosophie antique: une éthique ou une pratique?," pp. 17–18.

123 Ibid, p. 118, speaking of Marcus Aurelius' *Meditations*.

124 Ibid, p. 17.

125 Carlo Natali, *Bios Theoretikos. La vita d'Aristotele e l'organizzazione della sua scuola*, Bologna 1991, p. 98.

126 Hadot, "La philosophie antique: une éthique ou une pratique?," pp. 16–17.

127 Ibid, p. 15.

128 Hadot, "Philosophie, discours philosophique, et divisions de la philosophie chez les stoiciens," p. 216, and Hadot, "La philosophie antique: une éthique ou une pratique?," p. 16.

129 Hadot, "La philosophie antique: une éthique ou une pratique?," p. 16.

130 Ibid.

131 See the section "Learning to Die" in "Spiritual Exercises," this volume, pp. 93–101.

132 Ilsetraut Hadot, "Préface," in Seneca, *Consolations*, Paris 1992, p. 17.

133 Ibid, pp. 18–19.

134 Ibid, p. 19.

135 "Forms of Life and Forms of Discourse in Ancient Philosophy," this volume, pp. 58–60. On the unclassifiability of the philosopher, see pp. 55–60.

136 Hadot, "Préface," in *Dictionnaire des philosophes antiques*, p. 12.

137 Xenophon, *Memorabilia*, IV, 4, 10. Hadot offers two slightly different translations of this remark. One can be found in the essay "The Figure of Socrates," this volume. I have cited the one from "La philosophie antique: une éthique ou une pratique?," p. 36.

138 See the opening pages of both "Spiritual Exercises" and "Ancient Spiritual Exercises and 'Christian Philosophy'," this volume.

139 On the ancient doctrine of the division of the parts of philosophy, see Pierre Hadot, "Les divisions des parties de la philosophie," *Museum Helveticum* 36 (1979), pp. 201–23.
140 Hadot, "La philosophie antique: une éthique ou une pratique?," pp. 18–29; Hadot, "Philosophie, discours philosophique, et divisions de la philosophie chez les stoiciens"; and Hadot, *La Citadelle intérieure*, ch. 5.
141 Hadot, "La philosophie antique: une éthique ou une pratique?," pp. 19–20.
142 Ibid, pp. 20–1.
143 Ibid, pp. 21–4.
144 Hadot, "Philosophie, discours philosophique, et divisions de la philosophie chez les stoiciens," p. 212. See also Hadot, *La Citadelle intérieure*, p. 98, and "Philosophy as a Way of Life," this volume.
145 See ch. 7, this volume. I have discussed Hadot's criticisms of Foucault at length in "Ethics as ascetics: Foucault, the history of ethics and ancient thought," in Jan Goldstein, ed., *Foucault and the Writing of History*, Oxford 1994.
146 See Veyne's remarks in *Les Grecs, les Romains et nous. L'Antiquité est-elle moderne?*, ed. Roger Pol-Droit, Paris 1991, pp. 57–8.
147 See Hadot, "Philosophie, discours philosophique, et divisions de la philosophie chez les stoiciens"; Hadot, "La philosophie antique: une éthique ou une pratique?," pp. 25–6; and Hadot, *La Citadelle intérieure*, pp. 94–8. Zeno of Tarsus was an exception to this doctrine; see Diogenes Laertius, *Lives of Eminent Philosophers*, VII, 39 and 41.
148 Hadot, "Philosophie, discours philosophique, et divisions de la philosophie chez les stoiciens," p. 211.
149 Reading together Hadot, "La philosophie antique: une éthique ou une pratique?," p. 26, and Hadot, "Philosophie, discours philosophique, et divisions de la philosophie chez les stoiciens," p. 212.
150 Reading together Hadot, "Philosophie, discours philosophique, et divisions de la philosophie chez les stoiciens," p. 212, and Hadot, "La philosophie antique: une éthique ou une pratique?," p. 26.
151 Hadot, *La Citadelle intérieure*, p. 98. See also Hadot, "Philosophie, discours philosophique, et divisions de la philosophie chez les stoiciens," p. 212.
152 Hadot, "Les divisions des parties de la philosophie," p. 211.
153 Ibid, p. 212.
154 Ibid. For Augustine, see *The City of God*, book 8, ch. 4, and book 2, ch. 25.
155 Hadot, "Les divisions des parties de la philosophie," p. 211. See also Hadot, "Philosophie, discours philosophique, et divisions de la philosophie chez les stoiciens," pp. 218–19, and Hadot, *La Citadelle intérieure*, pp. 99–115. I have not presented here Hadot's discussion of those classifications of the parts of philosophy based essentially on the notion of spiritual progress. See Hadot, "Les divisions des parties de la philosophie," pp. 218–21.
156 Hadot, "La philosophie antique: une éthique ou une pratique?," p. 27.
157 Ibid, p. 28.
158 Hadot, "Présentation au Collège International de Philosophie," p. 4.
159 Hadot, "La philosophie antique: une éthique ou une pratique?," p. 28.
160 Hadot, "Présentation au Collège International de Philosophie," p. 4. See

also "Philosophy as a Way of Life," this volume. Hadot also develops this theme at the conclusion of his unpublished paper on Thoreau's *Walden*, "Réflexions sur Walden," delivered at the École Normale Supérieure, June 1993.

161 Cited by Hadot in "La philosophie antique: une éthique ou une pratique?," pp. 13–14.

162 Cited in "Philosophy as a Way of Life," this volume, p. 267.

163 Epictetus, *Discourses*, IV, 4, 13. Cited in Hadot, "La philosophie antique: une éthique ou une pratique?," p. 21.

164 Cited by Ilsetraut Hadot, "Aristote dans l'enseignement philosophique néo-platonicien. Les préfaces des commentaires sur les *Catégories*," *Revue de théologie et de philosophie* 124 (1992), p. 419, n. 38.

165 Hadot, "La philosophie antique: une éthique ou une pratique?," pp. 28–9.

166 Pierre Hadot, "Le Génie du lieu dans la Grèce antique," in Michel Crépu, Richard Figuier, and René Louis, eds, *Hauts Lieux*, Paris 1990, p. 150. For a discussion of the role of this fragment, especially in the mysticism of Pseudo-Dionysius, see Ysabel de Andia, "παθὼν τὰ βεια", in Stephen Gersh and Charles Kannengiesser, eds, *Platonism in Late Antiquity*, Notre Dame 1992.

167 Hadot, "Le Génie du lieu dans la Grèce antique," p. 150. Hadot is following the interpretation of D. Sabbatucci, *Essai sur le mysticisme grec*, Paris 1982.

168 Hadot, "Le Génie du lieu dans la Grèce antique," p. 150, my emphasis.

169 Hadot, "La philosophie antique: une éthique ou une pratique?," p. 34.

170 Ibid.

171 Ibid. p. 35. For extensive discussion, see Pierre Hadot, *Plotin. Traité 38*, Paris 1988, pp. 44–52 and 347–51.

172 Hadot, *Plotin. Traité 38*, reading together p. 45 and p. 349.

173 Pierre Hadot, "Apophatisme et théologie négative," in *Exercices spirituels*, p. 193.

174 Hadot, "Le Génie du lieu dans la Grèce antique," p. 152, my emphasis. For a discussion of Hadot's interpretation of Plotinus' mysticism, see my "Reading Hadot reading Plotinus," intro. in Pierre Hadot, *Plotinus or the Simplicity of Vision*, Chicago 1993.

175 Pierre Hadot, "Postface à la seconde édition," in *Exercices spirituels*, p. 236.

176 Ibid.

177 Natali, *Bios Theoretikos*, pp. 137–8. Natali's remark is made with particular reference to *On the Parts of Animals*, 645a 7–10. For the dangers of viewing Aristotle as if he were a modern university professor, and as if the life of *theoria* were purely abstract, or the career of a modern scientist, see Natali, *Bios Theoretikos*, pp. 67–74 and 129–38.

178 Pierre Hadot, "Les modèles de bonheur proposés par les philosophes antiques," *La Vie spirituelle* (Jan.–Feb. 1992), pp. 34–6. See also Hadot, "Postface à la seconde édition," p. 236. Hadot has in mind primarily *Nicomachean Ethics*, X, 7, and *Metaphysics*, 1072b 28.

179 Aristotle, *Politics*, VII, 3, 8, 1325b. Cited by Hadot in "La philosophie antique: une éthique ou une pratique?," pp. 31–2.

180 Hadot, "La philosophie antique: une éthique ou une pratique?," p. 31, my emphasis.

181 Ibid, p. 32.

182 Hadot, "Préface," in *Dictionnaire des philosophes antiques*, pp. 11–12.
183 Ibid.
184 "Philosophy as a Way of Life," this volume, pp. 272–3.
185 Hadot, "Préface," in *Dictionnaire des philosophes antiques*, p. 13.
186 Ibid.
187 Ibid. See also "Forms of Life and Forms of Discourse in Ancient Philosophy," this volume, pp. 55–8.
188 Giuseppe Cambiano, "La figura del filosofo e le altre forme del sapere," *Quaderni di Storia* XIX, 37 (Jan.–June 1993), p. 81.
189 On the importance of the act of conversion, see Pierre Hadot, "Epistrophè et metanoia dans l'histoire de la philosophie," in *Actes du XIᵉᵐᵉ congrès international de philosophie*, XII, Amsterdam 1953, and Pierre Hadot, "Conversion," in *Exercices spirituels*.
190 Pierre Hadot, "La philosophie hellénistique," in *Histoire de la philosophie. 1. Les pensées fondatrices*, Paris 1993, pp. 69–70. See also Hadot, "Présentation au Collège International de Philosophie," pp. 3–4.
191 Hadot, "Présentation au Collège International de Philosophie," p. 3.
192 Ibid, reading together p. 7 and p. 6.
193 Ibid, p. 5.
194 Pierre Hadot, "La philosophie est-elle un luxe?," *Le Monde de l'éducation* (Mar. 1992), p. 91.
195 Ibid.
196 Reading together ibid p. 92, and Hadot, "Présentation au Collège International de Philosophie," p. 9.
197 On early Christianity as a philosophy, see "Ancient Spiritual Exercises and 'Christian Philosophy'" and "Philosophy as a Way of Life," this volume. The quoted words come from Hadot, "Présentation au Collège International de Philosophie," p. 7.
198 "Philosophy as a Way of Life," this volume, p. 270.
199 Hadot, "Présentation au Collège International de Philosophie," p. 7.
200 Hadot says that it is with Suarez that the idea of systematic philosophy would appear for the first time. See ibid.
201 "Philosophy as a Way of Life," this volume, pp. 270 and 272–3. (I have slightly modified the translation.) See also Hadot, "Présentation au Collège International de Philosophie," p. 7.
202 "Philosophy as a Way of Life," this volume, p. 271. (I have slightly modified the translation.)
203 Hadot, "Présentation au Collège International de Philosophie," p. 7.
204 "Philosophy as a Way of Life," this volume, pp. 271–2.
205 Hadot, "Présentation au Collège International de Philosophie," pp. 7–8. The quotation from Erasmus is taken from a letter he wrote to Abbot Voltz in 1518. See *The Essential Erasmus*, ed. John P. Dolan, New York 1964, p. 28.
206 Pierre Hadot, "Émerveillements," in *La Bibliothèque imaginaire du Collège de France*, Paris 1990, p. 122.
207 Pierre Hadot, "Un dialogue interrompu avec Michel Foucault. Convergences et

divergences," in *Exercices spirituels*, p. 232. See also "Philosophy as a Way of Life," this volume, pp. 271–2.

208 "Philosophy as a Way of Life," this volume, pp. 271–2, and Hadot, "Présentation au Collège International de Philosophie," p. 8.

209 Hadot, "Présentation au Collège International de Philosophie," pp. 8–9.

210 On Schopenhauer, the young Hegelians and Marx, see "Philosophy as a Way of Life," this volume, pp. 271–2. On Goethe's relation to ancient philosophy, see especially "'Only the Present is our Happiness': The Value of the Present Instant in Goethe and in Ancient Philosophy," this volume. On Nietzsche and Kierkegaard, see especially "The Figure of Socrates," this volume.

211 On twentieth-century philosophy, see, among other essays, "Philosophy as a Way of Life," "The Sage and the World," and "Reflections on the Idea of the 'Cultivation of the Self'," all in this volume.

212 Hadot, "Réflexions sur Walden."

213 Hadot, "Présentation au Collège International de Philosophie," p. 9. See also Hadot, *La Citadelle Intérieure*, p. 330.

214 Hadot, "Présentation au Collège International de Philosophie," p. 9.

215 Hadot, *La Citadelle intérieure*, p. 329.

216 Reading together ibid, pp. 329–30, and "Philosophy as a Way of Life," this volume, pp. 272–3. The quoted words are used with respect to Stoicism, but it is clear that Hadot would apply them to the other universal attitudes as well.

217 Hadot, *La Citadelle intérieure*, pp. 331–2.

218 Hadot, "Réflexions sur Walden," p. 6.

219 "Philosophy as a Way of Life," this volume, pp. 272–3.

220 Hadot, "Réflexions sur Walden," pp. 7–8.

221 Ibid.

222 "Spiritual Exercises," this volume, p. 108 (translation slightly modified). See also "Philosophy as a Way of Life," this volume, pp. 272–3.

223 On Cynicism and Pyrrhonism, see Hadot, "La philosophie hellénistique," pp. 70, 77–8.

224 Ibid, p. 79.

225 Hadot, "Émerveillements," p. 122.

226 Hadot, "Préface," in *Dictionnaire des philosophes antiques*, p. 16.

Part I
Method

Part I

Methods

1

Forms of Life and Forms of Discourse in Ancient Philosophy

Mr Administrator,
Dear colleagues,
Ladies and Gentlemen,

"Each one of you expects two things from me on the occasion of this inaugural lecture: first of all, that I express my thanks to those who made my presence here possible and second, that I present the method that I will use to carry out the task entrusted to me." [1] Petrus Ramus, who held the chair in rhetoric and philosophy at the Collège Royal, opened his inaugural lecture, delivered in Latin, with words to this effect on August 24, 1551, only twenty years after the founding of this institution. We see that the practice of giving this lecture dates back more than four hundred years and that even at that time its major themes were already set. And I in turn will remain faithful to this venerable tradition today.

More than a year has gone by already, dear colleagues, since you decided to create a chair in the History of Hellenistic and Roman Thought. Shortly thereafter you honored me by entrusting it to me. How, without being awkward or superficial, can I express the extent of my gratitude and my joy at the confidence you have shown toward me?

I am able to see in your decision a reflection of that freedom and independence of mind that have traditionally characterized the great institution into which you have welcomed me. For, despite my election, I possess few of the qualities that would usually attract notice, and the discipline I represent is not among those in fashion today. In a way I am what the Romans called a *homo nouus*, as I do not belong to that intellectual nobility one of whose principal titles is traditionally that of "former student of the Ecole Normale Supérieure." Moreover, you certainly noticed during my visits to you that I lack that tranquil authority conferred by the use and mastery of the idioms currently spoken in the Republic of Letters. My language, as you will again ascertain today, is not graced with those mannerisms that now seem to be required when one ventures to speak of the human sciences. However, several of you encouraged me to present my candidacy, and during the traditional visits, which so enriched me, I was extremely touched to find so much sympathy and interest, particularly among those of you who are specialists in the exact sciences, for the field of research I have come before you to defend. In other words, I believe I did not have to convince you – you were persuaded already – of the need for the Collège to ensure a way to maintain the close bonds between areas of teaching and research that are too often artificially separated: Latin and Greek, philology and philosophy, Hellenism and Christianity. I thus marveled to discover that at the end of the twentieth century, when many of you on a daily basis employ technical procedures, modes of reasoning, and representations of the universe of almost superhuman complexity that open a future to humanity we could not even conceive of earlier, the ideal of humanism, which inspired the foundation of the Collège de France, continues to retain for you, undoubtedly in a more conscious and critical but also more vast, intense, and profound form, all of its value and significance.

I spoke of a close connection between Greek and Latin, philology and philosophy, Hellenism and Christianity. I believe that this formulation corresponds exactly to the inspiration found in the teaching of Pierre Courcelle, who was my colleague at the Fifth Section of the École Pratique des Hautes Études and to whom I wish to render homage today, indeed, whom I succeed, if I may say so, in an indirect line, via the appointment of Rolf Stein. I believe that Pierre Courcelle, who was so brutally taken from us, is intensely present in the hearts of many of us tonight. For me he was a teacher who taught me much, but he was also a friend who showed great concern for me. I will speak now only of the scholar, to recall his immense output of truly great books, innumerable articles, and hundreds of reviews. I do not know if the scope of this gigantic labor has been sufficiently measured. The first lines of his great work *Lettres grecques en Occident de Macrobe à Cassiodore* give a clear idea of the revolutionary direction his work had for his time. "A substantial book on Hellenistic literature in the West from the death of Theodosius up to the time of the Justinian reconquest may seem surprising," wrote Courcelle. First of all, it was surprising for a Latinist to be interested in Greek literature. However, as Courcelle noted, this Greek literature made possible the flowering of Latin literature and produced Cicero, who represented the most complete development of Greco-Roman culture at its apex, and it was this literature that nearly became a substitute for Latin when during the second century AD Latin was overshadowed by Greek as a literary language. However, it still must be stated and deplored that, despite Courcelle's initiative and example and owing to a prejudice that has not been totally overcome and that maintains the disastrous break made in French scholarship between Greek and Latin, what he had to say in 1943, forty years ago, is unfortunately still true today: "I know of no synthetic work that examines the Greek influence on the thought and culture of the Roman Empire." Once again it was surprising to see a Latinist devote such an important study to a later period and show that in the fifth and sixth centuries, a time of so-called decadence, Greek literature had undergone a remarkable renaissance, which, thanks to Augustine, Macrobius, Boethius, Martianus Capella, and Cassiodorus, was to make it possible for the European Middle Ages to maintain contact with Greek thought until the Arab translations made possible its rediscovery in richer sources. Again, it was surprising to see a philologist attack problems in the history of philosophy, showing the key influence exercised on Latin Christian thought by Greek and pagan Neoplatonism, not only by Plotinus but – this was an important detail – by his disciple Porphyry as well. Even more surprising, this philologist based his conclusions on a rigorously philological method. I mean that he was not content merely to reveal vague analogies between Neoplatonic and Christian doctrines or to evaluate influences and originalities in a purely subjective way – in a word, to rely on rhetoric and inspiration to establish his conclusions. No, following the example of Paul Henry, the learned editor of Plotinus who has also been a model of scientific method for me, Courcelle compared the texts. He discovered what anyone could have seen but no one had seen before him, that a certain text of Ambrose had been literally translated from Plotinus, that one of Boethius had been literally translated from a Greek Neoplatonic commentator on Aristotle. This method made it possible to establish indisputable facts, to bring the history of thought out of the vagueness and artistic indistinctness into which certain historians, even contemporaries of Courcelle, tended to relegate it.

If *Les Lettres grecques en Occident* provoked surprise, the *Recherches sur les "Confessions" de saint Augustin*, the first edition of which appeared in 1950, almost caused a scandal, particularly because of the interpretation Courcelle proposed for Augustine's account of his own conversion. Augustine recounts that as he was weeping beneath a fig tree, overcome with pressing questions and heaping bitter reproaches upon himself for his indecision, he heard a child's voice repeating, "Take it ip and read." He then opened Paul's Epistles at random, as if he were drawing a lot, and read the passage that converted him. Alerted by his profound knowledge of Augustine's literary procedures and the traditions of Christian allegory, Courcelle dared to write that the fig tree could well have a purely symbolic value, representing the "mortal shadow of sin," and that the child's voice could also have been introduced in a purely literary way to indicate allegorically the divine response to Augustine's questioning. Courcelle did not suspect the uproar his interpretation would unleash. It lasted almost twenty years. The greatest names in international patristics entered the fray. Obviously I do not wish to rekindle the flames here. But I would like to stress how interesting his position was from a methodological point of view. Indeed it began with the very simple principle that a text should be interpreted in light of the literary genre to which it belongs. Most of Courcelle's opponents were victims of the modern, anachronistic prejudice that consists in believing that Augustine's *Confessions* is primarily an autobiographical account. Courcelle on the contrary had understood that the *Confessions* is essentially a theological work, in which each scene may take on a symbolic meaning. One is always surprised, for example, by the length of Augustine's account of his stealing pears while he was an adolescent. But this is explained by the fact that these fruits stolen from a garden become symbolically, for Augustine, the forbidden fruit stolen from the Garden of Eden, and the episode gives him the opportunity to develop a theological reflection on the nature of sin. In this literary genre, then, it is extremely difficult to distinguish between a symbolic enactment and an account of a historical event.

A very large part of Courcelle's work was devoted to tracing the fortunes of great themes such as "Know thyself" or great works such as Augustine's *Confessions* or Boethius' *Consolation of Philosophy* in the history of Western thought. Not the least original of his contributions, appearing in several of the major works he wrote from this perspective, was his association of literary study and iconographical inquiry, pertaining, for example, to illustrations produced throughout the ages for the *Confessions* or the *Consolation*. These iconographical studies, which are fundamental in reconstructing the history of religious mentalities and imagination, were all undertaken in collaboration with Mrs Jeanne Courcelle, whose great knowledge of the techniques of art history and iconographic description greatly enriched her husband's work.

This all-too-brief recollection permits a glimpse, I hope, of the general development, the itinerary, of Courcelle's research. Starting from late antiquity, he was led to go back in time, especially in his book on the theme of "Know thyself," toward the philosophy of the imperial and Hellenistic period, and, on the other hand, to follow, across the years, ancient works, themes, and images as they evolved in the Western tradition. Finally, it is my hope that this history of Hellenistic and Roman thought I am now going to present to you reflects the spirit and the profound orientation of Courcelle's teaching and work.

According to the scheme given by Petrus Ramus, I have just spoken of what he himself called the *ratio muneris officiique nostri*: the object and method of the teaching entrusted to me. In the title of my chair, the word *thought* can seem very vague; indeed it can be applied to an immense and undefined domain ranging from politics to art, from poetry to science and philosophy, or religion and magic. In any event, the term invites one to make breathtaking excursions into the vast world of wondrous and fascinating works produced during the great period of the history of humanity that I propose to study. Perhaps we will accept this invitation from time to time, but our intention is to turn to the essential, to recognize the typical or the significant, to attempt to grasp the *Urphänomene*, as Goethe would say. And specifically, *philosophia*, the way the term was understood then, is one of the typical and significant phenomena of the Greco-Roman world. It is this above all which engages our attention. Nevertheless, we have preferred to speak of "Hellenistic and Roman thought" to reserve the right to follow this *philosophia* in its most varied manifestations and above all to eliminate the preconceptions the word *philosophy* may evoke in the modern mind.

"Hellenistic and Roman": these words themselves open an immense period before us. Our history begins with the highly symbolic event represented by Alexander's fantastic expedition and with the emergence of the world called Hellenistic, that is, with the emergence of this new form of Greek civilization beginning from the moment when Alexander's conquests and, in their wake, the rise of kingdoms extended this civilization into the barbarian world from Egypt to the borders of India, and then brought it into contact with the most diverse nations and civilizations. The result is a kind of distance, a historical distance, between Hellenistic thought and the Greek tradition preceding it. Our history then covers the rise of Rome, which will lead to the destruction of the Hellenistic kingdoms, brought to completion in 30 BC with Cleopatra's death. After that will come the expansion of the Roman empire, the rise and triumph of Christianity, the barbarian invasions, and the end of the Western empire.

We have just traversed a millennium. But from the standpoint of the history of thought, this long period must be treated as a whole. Indeed it is impossible to know Hellenistic thought without recourse to later documents, those of the imperial era and late antiquity, which reveal it to us; and it is equally impossible to understand Roman thought without taking its Greek background into account.

We need to recognize from the outset that almost all of Hellenistic literature, principally its philosophical productions, has disappeared. The Stoic philosopher Chrysippus, to cite only one example, among many, wrote seven hundred works, all of which are lost; only a few fragments have come down to us. We would undoubtedly have a very different idea of Hellenistic philosophy if this gigantic catastrophe had not occurred. How can we hope to compensate in some way for this irreparable loss? Obviously, there is the chance that discoveries might sometimes bring unknown texts to light. For example, in the mid-eighteenth century, an Epicurean library was found at Herculaneum. It contained texts of remarkable interest, not only for the knowledge it provided of that school but also regarding Stoicism and Platonism. Even today the Institute of Papyrology in Naples continues to mine, in an exemplary manner, these precious documents, endlessly improving both the texts and the commentaries. Another example: during the excavations, led for fifteen years by our colleague Paul Bernard in Aï Khanoun, near the border between Afghanistan and the USSR, to find the remains of a Hellenistic town of the kingdom of Bactrian, a philosophical text, unfortunately terribly mutilated, was discovered. The presence of such a document in such a place suffices, furthermore, to make one recognize the extraordinary expansion of Hellenism brought on by the Alexandrian conquests. Most likely it dates from the third or second century BC and represents a fragment, unfortunately very difficult to read, of a dialogue in which it is possible to recognize a passage inspired by the Aristotelian tradition.[2]

Except for finds of this type, which are extremely rare, one is obliged to exploit existing texts to their fullest, which often are of a much later date, in order to find information about the Hellenistic period. Obviously, it is necessary to begin with the Greek texts. Despite many excellent studies, much remains to be done in this area. For example, the collections of philosophical fragments that have come down to us need to be completed or updated. Hans von Arnim's collection of fragments from the earliest Stoics is exactly eighty years old and requires serious revision. Moreover, there exists no collection of fragments for the Academicians from the period that runs from Arcesilas to Philo of Larissa. On the other hand, mines of information, such as the works of Philo of Alexandria, Galen, Athenaeus, and Lucian, or the commentaries on Plato and Aristotle written at the end of antiquity, have never been systematically made use of. But the Latin writers are also indispensable to this line of inquiry. For although the Latinists do not always agree, one has to admit that Latin literature, except for the historians (and even there!), is comprised largely of either translations, paraphrases, or imitations of Greek texts. Sometimes this is completely evident, for one can compare line by line and word for word the Greek originals that were translated or paraphrased by the Latin writers; sometimes the Latin writers themselves also quote their Greek sources; sometimes, finally, one can legitimately speculate about these influences with the help of reliable evidence. Thanks to the Latin writers, a large part of Hellenistic thought was preserved. Without Cicero, Lucretius, Seneca, or Aulus Gellius, many aspects of the philosophy of the Epicureans, Stoics, and Academicians would be irretrievably lost. The Latins of the Christian period are moreover just as precious: without Marius Victorinus, Augustine, Ambrose of Milan, Macrobius, Boethius, or Martianus Capella, how many Greek sources would be completely unknown to us! Two projects are thus inseparable: on the one hand, to explain Latin thought in light of its Greek background, and, on the other hand, to rediscover Greek thought, which has been lost to us, in the works of Latin writers. If both these tasks are to be carried out, any separation of Greek and Latin scholarship is totally impossible.

Here we are witness to the great cultural event of the West, the emergence of a Latin philosophical language translated from the Greek. Once again, it would be necessary to make a systematic study of the formation of this technical vocabulary that, thanks to Cicero, Seneca, Tertullian, Victorinus, Calcidius, Augustine, and Boethius, would leave its mark, by way of the Middle Ages, on the birth of modern thought. Can it be hoped that one day, with current technical means, it will be possible to compile a complete lexicon of the correspondences of philosophical terminology in Greek and Latin? Furthermore, lengthy commentaries would be needed, for the most interesting task would be to analyze the shifts in meaning that take place in the movement from one language to another. In the case of the ontological vocabulary the translation of *ousia* by *substantia*, for example, is justly famous and has again recently inspired some remarkable studies. This brings us once more to a phenomenon we discretely alluded to earlier with the word *philosophia*, and which we will encounter throughout the present discussion: the misunderstandings, shifts or losses in meaning, the reinterpretations, sometimes even to the point of misreadings, that arise once tradition, translation, and exegesis coexist. So our history of Hellenistic and Roman thought will consist above all in recognizing and analyzing the evolution of meanings and significance.

It is precisely the need to explain this evolution that justifies our intention to study this period as a whole. Translations from the Greek into Latin are indeed only a particular aspect of this vast process of unification, that is, of Hellenization, of the different cultures of the Mediterranean world, Europe, and Asia Minor that took place progressively from the fourth century BC up until the end of the ancient world. Hellenic thought had the strange capacity to absorb the most diverse mythical and conceptual themes. All the cultures of the Mediterranean world thus eventually expressed themselves in the categories of Hellenic thought, but at the price of important shifts in meaning that distorted the content of the myths, the values, and the wisdom of each culture, as well as the content of the Hellenic tradition itself. First the Romans, who were able to retain their language, then the Jews, and then the Christians fell into this sort of trap. Such was the price for the creation of the remarkable linguistic and cultural community that characterizes the Greco-Roman world. This process of unification also ensured a surprising continuity at the heart of philosophical and religious literary traditions.

This evolutionary continuity and progressive unification can be seen most remarkably in the area of philosophy. At the beginning of the Hellenistic period an extraordinary proliferation of schools emerged in the wake of the Sophist movement and the Socratic experience. But beginning with the third century BC a kind of sorting out occurred. In Athens the only schools to survive were those whose founders had thought to establish them as well-organized institutions: the school of Plato, the school of Aristotle and Theophrastus, the school of Epicurus, and that of Zeno and Chrysippus. In addition to these four schools there were two movements that are primarily spiritual traditions: Skepticism and Cynicism. After the institutional foundations of the schools in Athens collapsed at the end of the Hellenistic period, private schools and even officially subsidized teaching posts continued to be established throughout the empire, and here the spiritual traditions of their founders were their reference points. Thus, for six centuries, from the third century BC until the third century AD, we witness a surprising stability among the six traditions we have just mentioned. However, beginning with the third century AD, Platonism, in the culmination of a movement underway since the first century, yet again at the price of subtle shifts in meaning and numerous reinterpretations, came to absorb both Stoicism and Aristotelianism in an original synthesis, while all the other traditions were to become marginal. This unifying phenomenon is of major historical importance. Thanks to the writers of lesser antiquity but also to the Arab translations and the Byzantine tradition, this Neoplatonist synthesis was to dominate all the thought of the Middle Ages and Renaissance and was to provide, in some fashion, the common denominator among Jewish, Christian, and Moslem theologies and mysticisms.

We have just given a very brief outline of the main paths of the history of the philosophical schools of antiquity. But as a history of ancient *philosophia*, our history of Hellenistic and Roman thought is less focused on studying the doctrinal diversities and particularities of these different schools than it is on attempting to describe the very essence of the phenomenon of *philosophia* and finding the traits shared by the "philosopher" or by "philosophizing" in antiquity. We must try to recognize in some way the strangeness of this phenomenon, in order then to try to understand better the strangeness of its permanence throughout the whole history of Western thought. Why, you may ask, speak of strangeness when *philosophia* is a very general and common thing? Doesn't a philosophical quality color all of Hellenistic and Roman thought? Weren't the generalization and popularization of philosophy characteristics of the time? Philosophy is found everywhere – in speeches, novels, poetry, science, art. However, we must not be deceived. These general ideas, these commonplaces that may adorn a literary work, and true "philosophizing" are separated by an abyss. Indeed, to be a philosopher implies a rupture with what the skeptics called *bios*, that is, daily life, when they criticized other philosophers for not observing the common conduct of life, the usual manner of seeing and acting, which for the Skeptics consisted in respecting customs and laws, practicing a craft or plying a trade, satisfying bodily needs, and having the faith in appearances indispensable to action. It is true that even while the Skeptics chose to conform to the common conduct of life, they remained philosophers, since they practiced an exercise demanding something rather strange, the suspension of judgment, and aiming at a goal, uninterrupted tranquillity and serenity of the soul, that the common conduct of life hardly knew.

This very rupture between the philosopher and the conduct of everyday life is strongly felt by non-philosophers. In the works of comic and satiric authors, philosophers were portrayed as bizarre, if not dangerous characters. It is true, moreover, that throughout all of antiquity the number of charlatans who passed themselves off as philosophers must have been considerable, and Lucian, for example, freely exercised his wit at their expense. Jurists too considered philosophers a race apart. According to Ulpian, in the litigation between professors and their debtors the authorities did not need to concern themselves with philosophers, for these people professed to despise money. A regulation made by the emperor Antoninus Pious on salaries and compensations notes that if a philosopher haggles over his possessions, he shows he is no philosopher. Thus philosophers are strange, a race apart. Strange indeed are those Epicureans, who lead a frugal life, practicing a total equality between the men and women inside their philosophical circle – and even between married women and courtesans; strange, too, those Roman Stoics who disinterestedly administer the provinces of the empire entrusted to them and are the only ones to take seriously the laws promulgated against excess; strange as well this Roman Platonist, the Senator Rogatianus, a disciple of Plotinus, who on the very day he is to assume his functions as praetor gives up his responsibilities, abandons all his possessions, frees his slaves, and eats only every other day. Strange indeed all those philosophers whose behavior, without being inspired by religion, nonetheless completely breaks with the customs and habits of most mortals.

By the time of the Platonic dialogues Socrates was called *atopos*, that is, "unclassifiable." What makes him *atopos* is precisely the fact that he is a "philo-sopher" in the etymological sense of the word; that is, he is in love with wisdom. For wisdom, says Diotima in Plato's *Symposium*, is not a human state, it is a state of perfection of being and knowledge that can only be divine. It is the love of this wisdom, which is foreign to the world, that makes the philosopher a stranger in it.

So each school will elaborate its rational depiction of this state of perfection in the person of the sage, and each will make an effort to portray him. It is true that this transcendent ideal will be deemed almost inaccessible; according to some schools there never was a wise man, while others say that perhaps there were one or two of them, such as Epicurus, this god among men, and still others maintain that man can only attain this state during rare, fleeting moments. In this transcendent norm established by reason, each school will express its own vision of the world, its own style of life, and its idea of the perfect man. This is why in every school the description of this transcendent norm ultimately coincides with the rational idea of God. Michelet remarked very profoundly, "Greek religion culminated with its true god, the sage." We can interpret this remark, which Michelet does not develop, by noting that the moment philosophers achieve a rational conception of God based on the model of the sage, Greece surpasses its mythical representation of its gods. Of course, classical descriptions of the sage depict the circumstances of human life and take pleasure in describing how the sage would respond to this or that situation, but the beatitude the wise man resolutely maintains throughout his difficulties is that of God himself. Seneca asks what the sage's life would be in solitude, if he were in prison or exile, or cast upon the shores of a desert island. And he answers that it would be the life of Zeus (that is, for the Stoics, the life of universal Reason), when, at the end of each cosmic period, after the activity of nature has ceased, he devotes himself freely to his thoughts; like Zeus the sage would enjoy the happiness of being self-sufficient. Thus the thoughts and will of the Stoic wise man completely coincide with the thoughts, will, and development of Reason immanent to the evolution of the Cosmos. As for the Epicurean sage, he, like the gods, watches the infinity of worlds arising out of atoms in the infinite void; nature is sufficient for his needs, and nothing ever disturbs the peace of his soul. For their part, the Platonic and Aristotelian sages raise themselves in subtly different ways, by their life of the mind, to the realm of the divine Mind itself.

Now we have a better understanding of *atopia*, the strangeness of the philosopher in the human world. One does not know how to classify him, for he is neither a sage nor a man like other men. He knows that the normal, natural state of men should be wisdom, for wisdom is nothing more than the vision of things as they are, the vision of the cosmos as it is in the light of reason, and wisdom is also nothing more than the mode of being and living that should correspond to this vision. But the philosopher also knows that this wisdom is an ideal state, almost inaccessible. For such a man, daily life, as it is organized and lived by other men, must necessarily appear abnormal, like a state of madness, unconsciousness, and ignorance of reality. And nonetheless he must live this life every day, in this world in which he feels himself a stranger and in which others perceive him to be one as well. And it is precisely in this daily life that he must seek to attain that way of life which is utterly foreign to the everyday world. The result is a perpetual conflict between the philosopher's effort to see things as they are from the standpoint of universal nature and the conventional vision of things underlying human society, a conflict between the life one should live and the customs and conventions of daily life. This conflict can never be totally resolved. The Cynics, in their refusal of the world of social convention, opt for a total break. On the contrary, others, such as the Skeptics, fully accept social convention, while keeping their inner peace. Others, the Epicureans, for example, attempt to recreate among themselves a daily life that conforms to the ideal of wisdom. Others still, such as the Platonists and the Stoics, strive, at the cost of the greatest difficulties, to live their everyday and even their public lives in a "philosophical" manner. In any event, for all of them, the philosophical life will be an effort to live and think according to the norm of wisdom, it will be a movement, a progression, though a never-ending one, toward this transcendent state.

Each school, then, represents a form of life defined by an ideal of wisdom. The result is that each one has its corresponding fundamental inner attitude – for example, tension for the Stoics or relaxation for the Epicureans – and its own manner of speaking, such as the Stoic use of percussive dialectic or the abundant rhetoric of the Academicians. But above all every school practices exercises designed to ensure spiritual progress toward the ideal state of wisdom, exercises of reason that will be, for the soul, analagous to the athlete's training or to the application of a medical cure. Generally, they consist, above all, of self-control and meditation. Self-control is fundamentally being attentive to oneself: an unrelaxing vigilance for the Stoics, the renunciation of unnecessary desires for the Epicureans. It always involves an effort of will, thus faith in moral freedom and the possibility of self-improvement; an acute moral consciousness honed by spiritual direction and the practice of examining one's conscience; and lastly, the kind of practical exercises described with such remarkable precision particularly by Plutarch: controlling one's anger, curiosity, speech, or love of riches, beginning by working on what is easiest in order gradually to acquire a firm and stable character.

Of first importance is "meditation," which is the "exercise" of reason; moreover, the two words are synonymous from an etymological point of view. Unlike the Buddhist meditation practices of the Far East, Greco-Roman philosophical meditation is not linked to a corporeal attitude but is a purely rational, imaginative, or intuitive exercise that can take extremely varied forms. First of all it is the memorization and assimilation of the fundamental dogmas and rules of life of the school. Thanks to this exercise, the vision of the world of the person who strives for spiritual progress will be completely transformed. In particular, philosophical meditation on the essential dogmas of physics, for example the Epicurean contemplation of the genesis of worlds in the infinite void or the Stoic contemplation of the rational and necessary unfolding of cosmic events, can lead to an exercise of the imagination in which human things appear of little importance in the immensity of space and time. It is necessary to try to have these dogmas and rules for living "ready to hand" if one is to be able to conduct oneself like a philosopher under all of life's circumstances. Moreover, one has to be able to imagine these circumstances in advance in order to be ready for the shock of events. In all the schools, for various reasons, philosophy will be especially a meditation upon death and an attentive concentration on the present moment in order to enjoy it or live it in full consciousness. In all these exercises, all the means obtainable by dialectic and rhetoric will be utilized to obtain the maximum effect. In particular, this consciously willed application of rhetoric explains the impression of pessimism that some readers believe they discern in the *Meditations* of Marcus Aurelius. All images are suitable for him if they strike the imagination and make the reader conscious of the illusions and conventions of mankind.

The relationship between theory and practice in the philosophy of this period must be understood from the perspective of these exercises of meditation. Theory is never considered an end in itself; it is clearly and decidedly put in the service of practice. Epicurus is explicit on this point: the goal of the science of nature is to obtain the soul's serenity. Or else, as among the Aristotelians, one is more attached to theoretical activity considered as a way of life that brings an almost divine pleasure and happiness than to the theories themselves. Or, as in the Academicians' school or for the skeptics, theoretical activity is a critical activity. Or, as among the Platonists, abstract theory is not considered to be true knowledge: as Porphyry says, "Beatific contemplation does not consist of the accumulation of arguments or a storehouse of learned knowledge, but in us theory must become nature and life itself." And, according to Plotinus, one cannot know the soul if one does not purify oneself of one's passions in order to experience in oneself the transcendence of the soul with respect to the body, and one cannot know the principle of all things if one has not had the experience of union with it.

To make possible these exercises in meditation, beginners are exposed to maxims or summaries of the principal dogmas of the school. Epicurus' *Letters*, which Diogenes Laertius preserved for us, are intended to play this role. To ensure that these dogmas have a great spiritual effectiveness, they must be presented in the form of short, striking formulae, as in Epicurus' *Principal Doctrines*, or in a rigorously systematic form, such as the *Letter to Herodotus* by the same author, which permitted the disciple to grasp in a kind of single intuition the essentials of the doctrine in order to have it more easily at hand. In this case the concern for systematic coherence was subordinated to spiritual effectiveness.

The dogmas and methodological principles of each school are not open to discussion. In this period, to philosophize is to choose a school, convert to its way of life, and accept its dogmas. This is why the core of the fundamental dogmas and rules of life for Platonism, Aristotelianism, Stoicism, and Epicureanism remained unchanged throughout antiquity. Even the scientists of antiquity always were affiliated with a philosophical school: the development of their mathematical and astronomical theorems changed nothing of the fundamental principles of the school to which they claimed allegiance.

This does not mean that theoretical reflection and elaboration are absent from the philosophical life. However, this activity never extended to the dogmas themselves or the methodological principles but rather to the ways of demonstrating and systematizing these dogmas and to secondary, doctrinal points issuing from them on which there was not unanimity in the school. This type of investigation is always reserved for the more advanced students, for whom it is an exercise of reason that strengthens them in their philosophical life. Chrysippus, for example, felt himself capable of finding the arguments justifying the Stoic dogmas established by Zeno and Cleanthes, which led him, moreover, to disagree with them not concerning these dogmas but on the way of establishing them. Epicurus, too, leaves the discussion and study of points of detail to the more advanced students, and much later the same attitude will be found in Origen, who assigns the "spiritual ones" the task of seeking, as he himself says, by way of exercise, the "hows" and "whys" and of discussing these obscure and secondary questions. This effort of theoretical reflection can result in the composition of enormous works.

Obviously, these systematic treaties and scholarly commentaries, such as Origen's treatise on *Principles* or Proclus' *Elements of Theology*, very legitimately attract the attention of the historian of philosophy. The study of the progress of thought in these great texts must be one of the principal tasks in a reflection on the phenomenon of philosophy. However, it must be recognized that generally speaking the philosophical works of Greco-Roman antiquity almost always perplex the contemporary reader. I do not refer only to the general public, but even to specialists in the field. One could compile a whole anthology of complaints made against ancient authors by modern commentators, who reproach them for their bad writing, contradictions, and lack of rigor and coherence. Indeed, it is my astonishment both at these critics and at the universality and persistence of the phenomenon they condemn that inspires the reflections I have just presented, as well as those I wish to turn to now.

It seems to me, indeed, that in order to understand the works of the philosophers of antiquity we must take account of all the concrete conditions in which they wrote, all the constraints that weighed upon them: the framework of the school, the very nature of *philosophia*, literary genres, rhetorical rules, dogmatic imperatives, and traditional modes of reasoning. One cannot read an ancient author the way one does a contemporary author (which does not mean that contemporary authors are easier to understand than those of antiquity). In fact, the works of antiquity are produced under entirely different conditions than those of their modern counterparts. I will not discuss the problem of material support: the *volumen* or *codex*, each of which has its own constraints. But I do want to stress the fact that written works in the period we study are never completely free of the constraints imposed by oral transmission. In fact, it is an exaggeration to assert, as has still been done recently, that Greco-Roman civilization early on became a civilization of writing and that one can thus treat, methodologically, the philosophical works of antiquity like any other written work.

For the written works of this period remain closely tied to oral conduct. Often they were dictated to a scribe. And they were intended to be read aloud, either by a slave reading to his master or by the reader himself, since in antiquity reading customarily meant reading aloud, emphasizing the rhythm of the phrase and the sounds of the words, which the author himself had already experienced when he dictated his work. The ancients were extremely sensitive to these effects of sound. Few philosophers of the period we study resisted this magic of the spoken word, not even the Stoics, not even Plotinus. So if oral literature before the practice of writing imposed rigorous constraints on expression and obliged one to use certain rhythmic, stereotypic, and traditional formulae conveying images and thoughts independent, if one may say so, of the author's will, this phenomenon is not foreign to written literature to the degree that it too must concern itself with rhythm and sound. To take an extreme but very revealing example, the use of poetic meter in *De rerum natura* dictates the recourse to certain somewhat stereotypical formulae and keeps Lucretius from freely using the technical vocabulary of Epicureanism that he should have employed.

This relationship between the written and the spoken word thus explains certain aspects of the works of antiquity. Quite often the work proceeds by the associations of ideas, without systematic rigor. The work retains the starts and stops, the hesitations, and the repetitions of spoken discourse. Or else, after re-reading what he has written, the author introduces a somewhat forced systematization by adding transitions, introductions, or conclusions to different parts of the work.

More than other literature, philosophical works are linked to oral transmission because ancient philosophy itself is above all oral in character. Doubtless there are occasions when someone was converted by reading a book, but one would then hasten to the philosopher to hear him speak, question him, and carry on discussions with him and other disciples in a community that always serves as a place of discussion. In matters of philosophical teaching, writing is only an aid to memory, a last resort that will never replace the living word.

True education is always oral because only the spoken word makes dialogue possible, that is, it makes it possible for the disciple to discover the truth himself amid the interplay of questions and answers and also for the master to adapt his teaching to the needs of the disciple. A number of philosophers, and not the least among them, did not wish to write, thinking, as did Plato and without doubt correctly, that what is inscribed in the soul by the spoken word is more real and lasting than letters drawn on papyrus or parchment.

Thus for the most part the literary productions of the philosophers are a preparation, extension, or echo of their spoken lessons and are marked by the limitations and constraints imposed by such a situation.

Some of these works, moreover, are directly related to the activity of teaching. They may be either a summary the teacher drafted in preparing his course or notes taken by students during the course, or else they may be texts written with care but intended to be read during the course by the professor or a student. In all these cases, the general movement of thought, its unfolding, what could be called its own temporality, is regulated by the temporality of speech. It is a very heavy constraint, whose full rigor I am experiencing today.

Even texts that were written in and for themselves are closely linked to the activity of teaching, and their literary genre reflects the methods of the schools. One of the exercises esteemed in the schools consists of discussing, either dialectically, that is, in the form of questions and answers, or rhetorically, that is, in a continuous discourse, what were called "theses," that is, theoretical positions presented in the form of questions: Is death an evil? Is the wise man ever angry? This provides both training in the mastery of the spoken word and a properly philosophical exercise. The largest portion of the philosophical works of antiquity, for example those of Cicero, Plutarch, Seneca, Plotinus, and more generally those classified by the moderns as belonging to what they called the genre of diatribe, correspond to this exercise. They discuss a specific question, which is posed at the outset of the work and which normally requires a yes or no answer. In these works, the course of thought consists in going back to general principles that have been accepted in the school and are capable of resolving the problem in question. This search to find principles to solve a given problem thus encloses thought within narrowly defined limits. Different works written by the same author and guided according to this "zetetic" method, "one that seeks," will not necessarily be coherent on all points because the details of the argument in each work will be a function of the question asked.

Another school exercise is the reading and exegesis of the authoritative texts of each school. Many literary works, particularly the long commentaries from the end of antiquity, are the result of this exercise. More generally, a large number of the philosophical works from that time utilize a mode of exegetical thinking. Most of the time, discussing a "thesis" consists in discussing not the problem in itself but the meaning that one should give to Plato's or Aristotle's statements concerning this problem. Once this convention has been taken into account, one does in fact discuss the question in some depth, but this is done by skillfully giving Platonic or Aristotelian statements the meanings that support the very solution one wishes to give to the problem under consideration. Any possible meaning is true provided it coheres with the truth one believes one has discovered in the text. In this way there slowly emerges, in the spiritual tradition of each school, but in Platonism above all, a scholasticism which, relying on argument from authority, builds up gigantic doctrinal edifices by means of an extraordinary rational reflection on the fundamental dogmas. It is precisely the third philosophical literary genre, the systematic treatise, that proposes a rational ordering of the whole of doctrine, which sometimes is presented, as in the case of Proclus, as a *more geometrico*, that is, according to the model of Euclid's *Elements*. In this case one no longer returns to the principles necessary to resolve a specific question but sets down the principles directly and deduces their consequences. These works are, so to speak, "more written" than the others. They often comprise a long sequence of books and are marked by a vast, overarching design. But, like the *Summae theologicae* of the Middle-Ages that they prefigure, these works must themselves also be understood from the perspective of dialectical and exegetical scholarly exercises.

Unlike their modern counterparts, none of these philosophical productions, even the systematic works, is addressed to everyone, to a general audience, but they are intended first of all for the group formed by the members of the school; often they echo problems raised by the oral teaching. Only works of propaganda are addressed to a wider audience.

Moreover, while he writes the philosopher often extends his activity as spiritual director that he exercises in his school. In such cases the work may be addressed to a particular disciple who needs encouragement or who finds himself in a special difficulty. Or else the work may be adapted to the spiritual level of the addressees. Not all the details of the system can be explained to beginners; many details can be revealed only to those further along the path. Above all, the work, even if it is apparently theoretical and systematic, is written not so much to inform the reader of a doctrinal content but to form him, to make him traverse a certain itinerary in the course of which he will make spiritual progress. This procedure is clear in the works of Plotinus and Augustine, in which all the detours, starts and stops, and digressions of the work are formative elements. One must always approach a philosophical work of antiquity with this idea of spiritual progress in mind. For the Platonists, for example, even mathematics is used to train the soul to raise itself from the sensible to the intelligible. The overall organization of a work and its mode of exposition may always answer to such preoccupations.

Such then are the many constraints that are exercised on the ancient author and that often perplex the modern reader with respect to both what is said and the way in which it is said. Understanding a work of antiquity requires placing it in the group from which it emanates, in the tradition of its dogmas, its literary genre, and requires understanding its goals. One must attempt to distinguish what the author was required to say, what he could or could not say, and, above all, what he meant to say. For the ancient author's art consists in his skillfully using, in order to arrive at his goals, all of the constraints that weigh upon him as well as the models furnished by the tradition. Most of the time, furthermore, he uses not only ideas, images, and patterns of argument in this way but also texts or at least pre-existing formulae. From plagiarism pure and simple to quotation or paraphrase, this practice includes – and this is the most characteristic example – the literal use of formulae or words employed by the earlier tradition to which the author often gives a new meaning adapted to what he wants to say. This is the way that Philo, a Jew, uses Platonic formulae to comment on the Bible, or Ambrose, a Christian, translates Philo's text to present Christian doctrines, the way that Plotinus uses words and whole sentences from Plato to convey his experience. What matters first of all is the prestige of the ancient and traditional formula, and not the exact meaning it originally had. The idea itself holds less interest than the prefabricated elements in which the writer believes he recognizes his own thought, elements that take on an unexpected meaning and purpose when they are integrated into a literary whole. This sometimes brilliant reuse of prefabricated elements gives an impression of "bricolage," to take up a word currently in fashion, not only among anthropologists but among biologists. Thought evolves by incorporating prefabricated and pre-existing elements, which are given new meaning as they become integrated into a rational system. It is difficult to say what is most extraordinary about this process of integration: contingency, chance, irrationality, the very absurdity resulting from the elements used, or, on the contrary, the strange power of reason to integrate and systematize these disparate elements and to give them a new meaning.

An extremely significant example of this conferring of a new meaning can be seen in the final lines of Edmund Husserl's *Cartesian Meditations*. Summing up his own theory, Husserl writes, "The Delphic oracle $\gamma v \tilde{\omega} \theta \iota$ $\sigma \varepsilon \alpha v \tau \acute{o} v$ [know thyself] has acquired a new meaning. . . . One must first lose the world by the $\grave{\varepsilon} \pi o \chi \acute{\eta}$ [for Husserl, the 'phenomenological bracketing' of the world], in order to regain it in a universal self-consciousness. *Noli foras ire*, says St Augustine, *in te redi, in interiore homine habitat veritas*." This sentence of Augustine's, "Do not lose your way from without, return to yourself, it is in the inner man that truth dwells," offers Husserl a convenient formula for expressing and summarizing his own conception of consciousness. It is true that Husserl gives this sentence a new meaning. Augustine's "inner man" becomes the "transcendental ego" for Husserl, a knowing subject who regains the world in "a universal self-consciousness." Augustine never could have conceived of his "inner man" in these terms. And nonetheless one understands why Husserl was tempted to use this formula. For Augustine's sentence admirably summarizes the whole spirit of Greco-Roman philosophy that prepares the way for both Descartes' *Meditations* and Husserl's *Cartesian Meditations*. And by the same procedure of taking up such a formula again, we ourselves can apply to ancient philosophy what Husserl says of his own philosophy: the Delphic oracle "Know thyself" has acquired a new meaning. For all the philosophy of which we have spoken also gives a new meaning to the Delphic formula. This new meaning already appeared among the Stoics, for whom the philosopher recognizes the presence of divine reason in the human self and who opposes his moral consciousness, which depends on him alone, to the rest of the universe. This new meaning appeared even more clearly among the Neoplatonists, who identify what they call the true self with the founding intellect of the world and even with the transcendent unity that founds all thought and all reality. In Hellenistic and Roman thought this movement, of which Husserl speaks, is thus already outlined, according to which one loses the world in order to find it again in universal self-consciousness. Thus Husserl consciously and explicitly presents himself as the heir to the tradition of "Know thyself" that runs from Socrates to Augustine to Descartes. But that is not all. This example, borrowed from Husserl, better enables us to understand concretely how these conferrals of new meaning can be realized in antiquity as well. Indeed, the expression *in interiore homine habitat veritas*, as my friend and colleague Goulven Madec has pointed out to me, is an allusion to a group of words borrowed from chapter 3, verses 16 and 17, of Paul's letter to the Ephesians, from an ancient Latin version, to be exact, in which the text appears as *in interiore homine Christum habitare*. But these words are merely a purely material conjunction that exists only in this Latin version and do not correspond to the contents of Paul's thought, for they belong to two different clauses of the sentence. On the one hand, Paul wishes for *Christ to dwell in the heart* of his disciples through faith, and, on the other hand, in the preceding clause, he wishes for God to allow his disciples *to be strengthened* by the divine Spirit *in the inner man, in interiorem hominem*, as the Vulgate has it. So the earlier Latin version, by combining *in interiore homine* and *Christum habitare*, was either a mistranslation or was miscopied. The Augustinian formula, *in interiore homine habitat veritas*, is thus created from a group of words that do not represent a unified meaning in St Paul's text; but taken in itself, this group of words has a meaning for Augustine, and he explains it in the context of *De vera religione* where he uses it: the inner man, that is, the human spirit, discovers that what permits him to think and reason is the truth, that is, divine reason – that is, for Augustine, Christ, who dwells in, who is present within, the human spirit. In this way the formula takes on a Platonic meaning. We see how, from St Paul to Husserl, by way of Augustine, a group of words whose unity was originally only purely material, or which was a misunderstanding of the Latin translator, was given a new meaning by Augustine, and then by Husserl, thus taking its place in the vast tradition of the deepening of the idea of self-consciousness.

This example borrowed from Husserl allows us to touch on the importance of what in Western thought is called the *topos*. Literary theories use the term to refer to the formulae, images, and metaphors that forcibly impose themselves on the writer and the thinker in such a way that the use of these prefabricated models seems indispensable to them in order to be able to express their own thoughts.

Our Western thought has been nourished in this way and still lives off a relatively limited number of formulae and metaphors borrowed from the various traditions of which it is the result. For example, there are maxims that encourage a certain inner attitude such as "Know thyself"; those which have long guided our view of nature: "Nature makes no leaps," "Nature delights in diversity." There are metaphors such as "The force of truth," "The world as a book" (which is perhaps extended in the conception of the genetic code as a text). There are biblical formulae such as "I am who I am," which have profoundly marked the idea of God. The point I strongly wish to emphasize here is the following: these prefabricated models, of which I have just given some examples, were known during the Renaissance and in the modern world in the very form that they had in the Hellenistic and Roman tradition, and they were originally understood during the Renaissance and in the modern world with the very meaning these models of thought had during the Greco-Roman period, especially at the end of antiquity. So these models continue to explain many aspects of our contemporary thought and even the very significance, sometimes unexpected, that we find in antiquity. For example, the classical prejudice, which has done so much damage to the study of late Greek and Latin literatures, is an invention of the Greco-Roman period, which created the model of a canon of classical authors as a reaction against mannerism and the baroque, which, at that time, were called "Asianism." But if the classical prejudice already existed during the Hellenistic and especially imperial eras, this is precisely because the distance we feel with respect to classical Greece also appeared at that time. It is precisely this Hellenistic spirit, this distance, in some ways modern, through which, for example, the traditional myths become the objects of scholarship or of philosophical and moral interpretations. It is through Hellenistic and Roman thought, particularly that of late antiquity, that the Renaissance was to perceive Greek tradition. This fact was to be of decisive importance for the birth of modern European thought and art. In another respect contemporary hermeneutic theories that, proclaiming the autonomy of the written text, have constructed a veritable tower of Babel of interpretations where all meanings become possible, come straight out of the practices of ancient exegesis, about which I spoke earlier. Another example: for our late colleague Roland Barthes, "many features of our literature, of our teaching, of our institutions of language . . . would be elucidated and understood differently if we fully knew . . . the rhetorical code that gave its language to our culture." This is completely true, and we could add that this knowledge would perhaps enable us to be conscious of the fact that in their methods and modes of expression our human sciences often operate in a way completely analogous to the models of ancient rhetoric.

Our history of Hellenistic and Roman thought should therefore not only analyze the movement of thought in philosophical works, but it should also be a historical topics that will study the evolution of the meaning of the *topoi*, the models of which we have spoken, and the role they have played in the formation of Western thought. This historical topics should work hard at discerning the original meanings of the formulae and models and the different significances that successive reinterpretations have given them.

At first, this historical topics will take for its object of study those works that were founding models and the literary genres that they created. Euclid's *Elements*, for example, served as a model for Proclus's *Elements of Theology* but also for Spinoza's *Ethics*. Plato's *Timaeus*, itself inspired by pre-Socratic cosmic poems, served as a model for Lucretius' *De rerum natura*, and the eighteenth century, in turn, was to dream of a new cosmic poem that would exhibit the latest discoveries of science. Augustine's *Confessions*, as it was misinterpreted, moreover, inspired an enormous literature up to Rousseau and the romantics.

This topics could also be a topics of aphorisms: for example, of the maxims about nature that dominated the scientific imagination until the nineteenth century. This year [at the Collège de France], we will study in this way the aphorism of Heraclitus that is usually phrased as "Nature loves to hide herself," although this is certainly not the original meaning of the three Greek words so translated. We will examine the significance this formula takes on throughout antiquity and later on, as a function of the evolution of the idea of nature, the very interpretation proposed by Martin Heidegger.

Above all, this historical topics will be a topics about the themes of meditations of which we spoke a few minutes ago, which have dominated and still dominate our Western thought. Plato, for example, had defined philosophy as an exercise for death, understood as the separation of the soul from the body. For Epicurus this exercise for death takes on a new meaning; it becomes the consciousness of the finitude of existence that gives an infinite value to each instant: "Persuade yourself that every new day that dawns will be your last one. And then you will receive each unhoped for hour with gratitude." In the perspective of Stoicism, the exercise for death takes on a different character; it invites immediate conversion and makes inner freedom possible: "Let death be before your eyes each day and you will not have any base thoughts or excessive desires." A mosaic at the Roman National Museum is inspired, perhaps ironically, by this meditation, as it depicts a skeleton with a scythe accompanied by the inscription *Gnothi seauton*, "Know thyself." Be that as it may, Christianity will make abundant use of this theme of meditation. There it can be treated in a manner close to Stoicism, as in this monk's reflection: "Since the beginning of our conversation, we have come closer to death. Let us be vigilant while we still have the time." But it changes radically when it is combined with the properly Christian theme of participation in Christ's death. Leaving aside all of the rich Western literary tradition, so well illustrated by Montaigne's chapter "That to philosophize is to learn to die," we can go straight to Heidegger in order to rediscover this fundamental philosophical exercise in his definition of the authenticity of existence as a lucid anticipation of death.

Linked to the meditation upon death, the theme of the value of the present instant plays a fundamental role in all the philosophical schools. In short it is a consciousness of inner freedom. It can be summarized in a formula of this kind: you need only yourself in order immediately to find inner peace by ceasing to worry about the past and the future. You can be happy right now, or you will never be happy. Stoicism will insist on the effort needed to pay attention to oneself, the joyous acceptance of the present moment imposed on us by fate. The Epicurean will conceive of this liberation from cares about the past and the future as a relaxation, a pure joy of existing: "While we are speaking, jealous time has flown; seize today without placing your trust in tomorrow." This is Horace's famous *laetus in praesens*, this "enjoyment of the pure present," to use André Chastel's fine expression about Marsilio Ficino, who had taken this very formula of Horace's for his motto. Here again the history of this theme in Western thought is fascinating. I cannot resist the pleasure of evoking the dialogue between Faust and Helena, the climax of part two of Goethe's *Faust*: "Nun schaut der Geist nicht vorwärts, nicht zurück, / Die Gegenwart allein ist unser Glück" ["And so the spirit looks neither ahead nor behind. The present alone is our joy . . . Do not think about your destiny. Being here is a duty, even though it only be an instant"].

I have come to the end of this inaugural address, which means that I have just completed what in antiquity was called an *epideixis*, a set speech. It is in a direct line with those that professors in the time of Libanius, for example, had to give in order to recruit an audience while at the same time trying to demonstrate the incomparable worth of their speciality and to display their eloquence. It would be interesting to investigate the historic paths by which this ancient practice was transmitted to the first professors at the Collège de France. In any case, at this very moment, we are in the process of fully living a Greco-Roman tradition. Philo of Alexandria said of these set speeches that the lecturer "brought into broad daylight the fruit of long efforts pursued in private, as painters and sculptors seek, in realizing their works, the applause of the public." And he opposed this behavior to the true philosophical instruction in which the teacher adapts his speech to the state of his listeners and brings them the cures they need in order to be healed.

The concern with individual destiny and spiritual progress, the intransigent assertion of moral requirements, the call for meditation, the invitation to seek this inner peace that all the schools, even those of the skeptics, propose as the aim of philosophy, the feeling for the seriousness and grandeur of existence – this seems to me to be what has never been surpassed in ancient philosophy and what always remains alive. Perhaps some people will see in these attitudes an escape or evasion that is incompatible with the consciousness we should have of human suffering and misery, and they will think that the philosopher thereby shows himself to be irremediably foreign to the world. I would answer simply by quoting this beautiful text by Georges Friedmann, from 1942, which offers a glimpse of the possibility of reconciling the concern for justice and spiritual effort; it could have been written by a Stoic of antiquity:

> Take flight each day! At least for a moment, however brief, as long as it is intense. Every day a "spiritual exercise," alone or in the company of a man who also wishes to better himself. . . . Leave ordinary time behind. Make an effort to rid yourself of your own passions. . . . Become eternal by surpassing yourself. This inner effort is necessary, this ambition, just. Many are those who are entirely absorbed in militant politics, in the preparation for the social revolution. Rare, very rare, are those who, in order to prepare for the revolution, wish to become worthy of it.[3]

NOTES

Delivered as the inaugural lecture to the chair of the History of Hellenistic and Roman Thought, Collège de France, 18 February 1983. © 1983 by The Collège de France, Trans. Arnold I. Davidson and Paula Wissing. First published in English in *Critical Inquiry* 16 (spring 1990)

1 Petrus Ramus, *Regii Eloquentiae Philosophiaeque Professoris, Oratio Initio Suae Professionis Habita*, Paris 1551. See Walter J. Ong, *Ramus and Talon Inventory: A Short-Title Inventory of the Published Works of Peter Ramus (1515–1572) and of Omer Talon (ca. 1510–1562) in Their Original and in Their Variously Altered Forms*, Cambridge MA 1958, p. 158.

2 See Pierre Hadot and Claude Rapin, "Les Textes littéraires grecs de la Trésorerie d'Aï Khanoun," pt. 1, *Études, Bulletin de Correspondance Hellénique* 111 (1987): 225–

3 Georges Friedmann, *La Puissance de la sagesse*, Paris 1970, p. 359.

2

Philosophy, Exegesis, and Creative Mistakes

Everyone is familiar with Whitehead's remark: "Western philosophy is nothing but a series of footnotes to Plato's dialogues." This statement could be interpreted in two ways: we could take it to mean that Plato's problematics have made a definitive mark upon Western philosophy, and this would be true. Alternatively, it could be taken to mean that, in a concrete sense, Western philosophy has assumed the form of commentaries – be they on Plato or on other philosophers – and that, more generally speaking, it has taken the form of exegesis. This, too, is to a very large extent true. It is important to realize that, for almost two thousand years – from the mid-fourth century BC to the end of the sixteenth century AD – philosophy was conceived of, above all, as the exegesis of a small number of texts deriving from "authorities," chief among whom were Plato and Aristotle. We are, moreover, justified in asking ourselves if, even after the Cartesian revolution, philosophy does not still bear traces of its lengthy past, and if, even today, at least to a certain extent, it has not remained exegesis.

The long period of "exegetical" philosophy is linked to a sociological phenomenon: the existence of philosophical schools, in which the thought, life-style, and writings of a master were religiously preserved. This phenomenon seems already to have existed among the Presocratics, but we are best able to observe it from Plato on.

Plato had given his Academy an extremely solid material and juridical organization. The leaders of the school succeeded one another[1] in a continuous chain until Justinian's closure of the school of Athens in 529, and throughout this entire period, scholarly activity was carried out according to fixed, traditional methods. The other great schools, whether Peripatetic, Stoic, or Epicurean, were organized along similar lines. The writings of each school's founder served as the basis for its instruction, and it was determined in which order the student should read these writings, in order to acquire the best possible education. We still have some of the writings in which Platonists gave advice on the order in which Plato's dialogues were to be read. Thus, we can tell that from the fourth century BC on, Aristotle's logical writings were arranged in a definite scholastic order – the *Organon* – which would not change until modern times.

Instruction consisted above all in commenting on Plato and Aristotle, using previous commentaries and adding a new interpretation here and there. In this regard, we have an interesting testimony from Porphyry about the lessons of Plotinus:

> During his classes, he used to have the commentaries read, perhaps of Severus or of Cronius or of Numenius or Gaius or Atticus, or of Peripatetics like Aspasius, Alexander, or whichever other came to hand. Yet he never repeated anything from these commentaries word for word, restricted himself to these readings alone. Rather, he himself used to give a general explanation [*theoria*] of (Plato's or Aristotle's) text in his own personal way, which was different from current opinion. In his investigations, moreover, he brought to bear the spirit of Ammonius.[2]

The first commentator on Plato's *Timaeus* seems to have been Crantor (ca. 330 BC), and Platonic commentators continued their activity until the end of the Athenian school in the sixth century. From this point, the tradition was continued, both in the Arab world and in the Latin West, up until the Renaissance (Marsilio Ficino). As for Aristotle, he was first commented upon by Andronicus of Rhodes (first century BC), who was the first in a series extending through the end of the Renaissance, in the person of Zabardella. In addition to commentaries *stricto sensu*, the exegetical activity of the philosophical schools took the form of dogmatic treatises, devoted to particular points of exegesis, and manuals designed to serve as introductions to the study of the masters. Moreover, the end of antiquity witnessed the appearance of other authorities, in addition to Plato and Aristotle: the authority of Revelations. For Christians and Jews, this meant primarily the Bible, and for pagan philosophers, the *Chaldaean Oracles*. Both Judaism and Christianity sought to present themselves to the Greek world as philosophies; they thus developed, in the persons of Philo and Origen respectively, a biblical exegesis analogous to the traditional pagan exegesis of Plato. For their part, such pagan commentators on the *Chaldaean Oracles* as Porphyry, Iamblichus, and Proclus did their best to show that the teachings of the "gods" coincided with Plato's doctrines. If we understand by "theology" the rational exegesis of a sacred text, then we can say that during this period philosophy was transformed into theology, and it was to stay that way throughout the Middle Ages. From this perspective, medieval Scholastics appears as the logical continuation of the ancient exegetical tradition. M.-D. Chenu[3] has defined the specific character of Scholastics as "dialectics applied to the comprehension of a text: either a *continuous* text, in which case the goal is the writing of a commentary, or of a *series* of texts, which are selected to serve as bases and proofs for a given speculative construction."[4] For this scholar, Scholastics is "a rational form of thought which is consciously and deliberately elaborated, taking as its starting-point a text considered as authoritative."[5] If we accent these definitions, we can assert that Scholastic thought did nothing other than adopt thought-processes already traditionally used in the majority of ancient philosophical schools. Conversely, we could also say that these schools were already engaging in Scholastic thought. Throughout the Middle Ages, instruction consisted essentially in textual commentary, whether of the Bible, Aristotle, Boethius, or the *Sentences* of Peter Lombard.

These facts have important consequences for the general interpretation of the history of philosophy, especially during its pre-Cartesian period. Insofar as philosophy was considered exegesis, the search for truth, throughout this period, was confounded with the search for the meaning of "authentic" texts; that is, of those texts considered as authoritative. Truth was contained *within these texts*; it was the property of their authors, as it was also the property of those groups who recognized the authority of these authors, and who were consequently the "heirs" of this original truth.

Philosophical problems were expressed in exegetical terms. For example, we find Plotinus writing the following in the course of his investigation of the problem of evil: "We must try to find out in what sense Plato says that evils shall not pass away, and that their existence is necessary."[6] Typically, the rest of Plotinus' inquiry consists in a discussion of the terminology used by Plato in his *Theaetetus*.[7] The famous battle over universals, which divided the Middle Ages, was based on the exegesis of a single phrase from Porphyry's *Isagoge*. It would be possible to make a list of all the texts which, upon being discussed, formed the basis of all ancient and medieval problematics. The list would not be long: it might contain a few passages from Plato (especially the *Timaeus*), Aristotle, Boethius, the first chapter of *Genesis*, and the prologue to the *Gospel of John*.

The fact that authentic texts raise questions is not due to any inherent defect. On the contrary: their obscurity, it was thought, was only the result of a technique used by a master, who wished to hint at a great many things at once, and therefore enclosed the "truth" in his formulations. Any potential meaning, as long as it was coherent with what was considered to be the master's doctrine, was consequently held to be true. Charles Thurot's remark[8] about the commentators on the grammarian Priscianus is applicable to all the philosopher exegetes:

> In their explanations of a text, the glossators did not seek to understand the author's thought; but rather to teach the doctrine itself which they

supposed to be contained in it. What they termed an "authentic" author could neither be mistaken, nor contradict himself, nor develop his arguments poorly, nor disagree with any other authentic author. The most forced exegesis was used in order to accommodate the letter of the text to what was considered the truth.[9]

It was believed that the truth had been "given" in the master's texts, and that all that had to be done was to bring it to light and explicate it. Plotinus, for example, writes: "These statements are not new; they do not belong to the present time, but were made long ago, although not explicitly, and what we have said in this discussion has been an interpretation of them, relying on Plato's own writings for evidence that these views are ancient."[10] Here we encounter another aspect of the conception of truth implied by "exegetical" philosophy. Each philosophical or religious school or group believed itself to be in possession of a traditional truth, communicated from the beginning by the divinity to a few wise men. Each therefore laid claim to being the legitimate depositary of the truth.

From this perspective, the conflict between pagans and Christians, from the second century AD on, is highly instructive. As both pagans and Christians recognized affinities between their respective doctrines, they accused each other of theft. Some claimed Plato plagiarized Moses, while others affirmed the contrary; the result was a series of chronological arguments destined to prove which of the two was historically prior. For Clement of Alexandria, the theft dated back even before the creation of humanity. It had been some wicked angel who, having discovered some traces of the divine truth, revealed philosophy to the wise of this world.[11]

Pagans and Christians explained in the same way the differences which, despite certain analogies, persisted between their doctrines. They were the result of misunderstandings and mistranslations – in other words, bad exegesis – of stolen texts. For Celsus, the Christian conception of humility was nothing but a poor interpretation of a passage in Plato's *Laws*;[12] the idea of the kingdom of God only a misreading of a passage in Plato's text on the king of all things,[13] and the notion of the resurrection only a misunderstanding of the idea of transmigration. On the Christian side, Justin asserted that some of Plato's statements showed that he had misunderstood the text of Moses.[14]

In this intellectual atmosphere, error was the result of bad exegesis, mistranslation, and faulty understanding. Nowadays, however, historians seem to consider *all* exegetical thought as the result of mistakes or misunderstandings. We can briefly enumerate the forms these alleged mistakes and deformations are thought to assume: in the first place, the exegetes make arbitrary systematizations. For instance, they take out of context passages originally widely separated from each other, and analyze them in a purely formal way, in order to reduce the texts to be explained to a body of coherent doctrine. In this way, for instance, a four- or five-tiered hierarchy of being was extracted from various dialogues of Plato.

Nor is this the most serious abuse. Whether consciously or not, systematization amalgamates the most disparate notions, which had originated in different or even contradictory doctrines. Thus we find the commentators on Aristotle using Stoic and Platonic ideas in their exegesis of Aristotelian texts. It is fairly frequent, especially in the case of translated texts, to find commentators trying to explain notions which simply do not exist in the original. In *Psalm* 113: 16, for example, we read: "The heaven is the heaven of the Lord." Augustine, however, started out from the Greek translation of the Bible, and understood: "The heaven of heavens is of [i.e. belongs to] the Lord." Augustine is thus led to imagine a cosmological reality, which he identifies with the intelligible world, which he then goes on to try and locate with relation to the "heaven" mentioned in the first verse of *Genesis*. From the point of view of the actual text of the Bible, this whole construction is based on thin air.

Cases of misunderstanding are not always this extreme. Nevertheless, it frequently occurs that exegeses construct entire edifices of interpretation on the basis of a banal or misunderstood phrase. The whole of Neoplatonic exegesis of the *Parmenides* seems to be an example of such a phenomenon.

The modern historian may be somewhat disconcerted on coming across such modes of thought, so far removed from his usual manner of reasoning. He is, however, forced to admit one fact: very often, mistakes and misunderstandings have brought about important evolutions in the history of philosophy. In particular, they have caused new ideas to appear. The most interesting example of this seems to me to be the appearance of the distinction between "being" as an infinitive and "being" as a participle,[15] which, as I have shown elsewhere,[16] was thought up by Porphyry in order to solve a problem posed by a passage in Plato. In the *Parmenides*,[17] Plato had asked: "If the One *is*, is it possible that it should not participate in being [*ousia*]?" For the Neoplatonist Porphyry, the One in question here is the second One. If this second One participates in *ousia*, he reasons, we must assume that *ousia* is prior to the second One. Now, the only thing prior to the second One is the first One, and this latter is not in any sense *ousia*. Thus, Porphyry concludes that, in this passage, the word *ousia* designates the first One in an enigmatic, symbolical way. The first One is not *ousia* in the sense of "substance"; rather, it is being (*être*) in the sense of a pure, transcendent act, prior to being as a substantial object (*étant*). *L'étant*, then, is the first substance and the first determination of *l'être*.

The history of the notion of being is, moreover, marked by a whole series of such creative mistakes. If we consider the series formed by *ousia* in Plato, *ousia* in Aristotle, *ousia* in the Stoics, *ousia* in the Neoplatonists, and *substantia* or *essentia* in the church Fathers and the Scholastics, we shall find that the idea of *ousia* or essence is amongst the most confused and confusing of notions. I have tried to show elsewhere[18] that the distinction, established by Boethius, between *esse* and *quod est*[19] did not originally have the meaning that the Middle Ages was later to attribute to it.

It is clear that historians of philosophy must use the greatest caution in applying the idea of "system" for the comprehension of the philosophical works of antiquity and the Middle Ages. It is not the case that every properly philosophical endeavor is "systematic" in the Kantian or Hegelian sense. For two thousand years, philosophical thought utilized a methodology which condemned it to accept incoherences and far-fetched associations, precisely to the extent that it wanted to be systematic. But to study the actual progress of exegetical thought is to begin to realize that thought can function rationally in many different ways, which are not necessarily the same as those of mathematical logic or Hegelian dialectic.

Philosophers of the modern era, from the seventeenth to the beginning of the nineteenth centuries, refused the argument from authority and abandoned the exegetical mode of thinking. They began to consider that the truth was not a ready-made given, but was rather the result of a process of elaboration, carried out by a reason grounded in itself. After an initial period of optimism, however, in which people believed it was possible for thought to postulate *itself* in an absolute way, philosophy began to become more and more aware, from the nineteenth century on, of its historical and especially linguistic conditioning.

This was a legitimate reaction, but it could be that its result has been that philosophers have let themselves be hypnotized by philosophical discourse taken in and for itself. In the last analysis, philosophical discourse now tends to have as its object nothing but more philosophical discourse. In a sense, contemporary philosophical discourse has once again become exegetical, and, sad to say, it often interprets its texts with the same violence used by ancient practitioners of allegory.

NOTES

1 Even if, from a juridical point of view, the succession of Platonic *diadochoi* was interrupted in the first century BC, the successors of Plato nevertheless always considered themselves heirs of an unbroken *spiritual* tradition.
2 Porphyry, *Life of Plotinus*, 14, 11.
3 M.-D. Chenu, *Introduction à l'étude de saint Thomas d'Aquin*, Paris 1954.
4 Ibid, p. 55.
5 Ibid.
6 Plotinus, *Enneads*, I, 8, 6, 1.
7 Plato, *Theaetetus*, 176a5–8.
8 Charles Thurot, *Extraits de . . . manuscrits latins pour servir à l'histoire des doctrines grammaticales*, Paris 1869.

9 Ibid, p. 103.

10 Plotinus, *Enneads*, 5 1, 8, 11–14.

11 Clement of Alexandria, *Stromata*, I, 17, 81, 4.

12 Plato, *Laws*, 716a.

13 Plato, *Second Letter*, 312a.

14 For the texts from Celsus and Justin, cf. C. Andresen, *Logos und Nomos*, Berlin 1955, pp. 146 ff. On the idea of the "ownership of the truth," cf. Hans Blumenberg, *Die Legitimität der Neuzeit*, Frankfurt 1966, p. 47.

15 [The distinction alluded to here is that between the French words *être* – 'to be' or 'being' – and the participle *étant*, 'a being' (the corresponding Greek terms are *to einai* and *to on*.) Porphyry conceived of the infinitive 'being' as pure activity; while 'being' as a noun was an emanation from, and substantification of, this being *qua* pure activity. – Trans.]

16 Pierre Hadot, *Porphyre et Victorinus*, 2 vols, Paris 1968, vol. I, pp. 129–32.

17 Plato, *Parmenides*, 142b.

18 Pierre Hadot, "La distinction de l'être et l'étant dans le 'De Hebdomadibus' de Boèce," in *Miscellania Mediaevalia*, vol. 2, Berlin 1963, pp. 147–53.

19 ["Being" / "to be," and "that which is." – Trans.]

Part II

Spiritual Exercises

3

Spiritual Exercises

To take flight every day! At least for a moment, which may be brief, as long as it is intense. A "spiritual exercise" every day – either alone, or in the company of someone who also wishes to better himself. Spiritual exercises. Step out of duration . . . try to get rid of your own passions, vanities, and the itch for talk about your own name, which sometimes burns you like a chronic disease. Avoid backbiting. Get rid of pity and hatred. Love all free human beings. Become eternal by transcending yourself.

This work on yourself is necessary; this ambition justified. Lots of people let themselves be wholly absorbed by militant politics and the preparation for social revolution. Rare, much more rare, are they who, in order to prepare for the revolution, are willing to make themselves worthy of it.

With the exception of the last few lines, doesn't this text look like a pastiche of Marcus Aurelius? It is by Georges Friedmann,[1] and it is quite possible that, when he wrote it, the author was not aware of the resemblance. Moreover, in the rest of his book, in which he seeks a place "to re-source himself",[2] he comes to the conclusion that there is no tradition – be it Jewish, Christian, or Oriental – compatible with contemporary spiritual demands. Curiously, however, he does not ask himself about the value of the philosophical tradition of Greco-Roman antiquity, although the lines we have just quoted show to just what extent ancient tradition continues – albeit unconsciously – to live within him, as it does within each of us.

"Spiritual exercises." The expression is a bit disconcerting for the contemporary reader. In the first place, it is no longer quite fashionable these days to use the word "spiritual." It is nevertheless necessary to use this term, I believe, because none of the other adjectives we could use – "psychic," "moral," "ethical," "intellectual," "of thought," "of the soul" – covers all the aspects of the reality we want to describe. Since, in these exercises, it is thought which, as it were, takes itself as its own subject-matter,[3] and seeks to modify itself, it would be possible for us to speak in terms of "thought exercises." Yet the word "thought" does not indicate clearly enough that imagination and sensibility play a very important role in these exercises. For the same reason, we cannot be satisfied with "intellectual exercises," although such intellectual factors as definition, division, ratiocination, reading, invest-igation, and rhetorical amplification play a large role in them. "Ethical exercises" is a rather tempting expression, since, as we shall see, the exercises in question contribute in a powerful way to the therapeutics of the passions, and have to do with the conduct of life. Yet, here again, this would be too limited a view of things. As we can glimpse through Friedmann's text, these exercises in fact correspond to a transformation of our vision of the world, and to a metamorphosis of our personality. The word "spiritual" is quite apt to make us understand that these exercises are the result, not merely of thought, but of the individual's entire psychism. Above all, the word "spiritual" reveals the true dimensions of these exercises. By means of them, the individual raises himself up to the life of the objective Spirit; that is to say, he re-places himself within the perspective of the Whole ("Become eternal by transcending yourself").

Here our reader may say, "All right, we'll accept the expression 'spiritual exercises'. But are we talking about Ignatius of Loyola's *Exercitia spiritualia?*[4] What relationship is there between Ignatian meditations and Friedmann's program of "stepping out of duration . . . becoming eternal by transcending oneself?" Our reply, quite simply, is that Ignatius' *Exercitia spiritualia* are nothing but a Christian version of a Greco-Roman tradition, the extent of which we hope to demonstrate in what follows. In the first place, both the idea and the terminology of *exercitium spirituale* are attested in early Latin Christianity, well before Ignatius of Loyola, and they correspond to the Greek Christian term *askesis*.[5] In turn, *askesis* – which must be understood not as asceticism, but as the practice of spiritual exercises – already existed within the philosophical tradition of antiquity.[6] In the final analysis, it is to antiquity that we must return in order to explain the origin and significance of this idea of spiritual exercises, which, as Friedmann's example shows, is still alive in contemporary consciousness.

The goal of the present chapter is not merely to draw attention to the existence of spiritual exercises in Greco-Latin antiquity, but above all to delimit the scope and importance of the phenomenon, and to show the consequences which it entails for the understanding not only of ancient thought, but of philosophy itself.[7]

1 Learning to Live

Spiritual exercises can be best observed in the context of Hellenistic and Roman schools of philosophy. The Stoics, for instance, declared explicitly that philosophy, for them, was an "exercise."[8] In their view, philosophy did not consist in teaching an abstract theory[9] – much less in the exegesis of texts[10] – but rather in the art of living.[11] It is a concrete attitude and determinate life-style, which engages the whole of existence. The philosophical act is not situated merely on the cognitive level, but on that of the self and of being. It is a progress which causes us to *be* more fully, and makes us better.[12] It is a conversion[13] which turns our entire life upside down, changing the life of the person who goes through it.[14] It raises the individual from an inauthentic condition of life, darkened by unconsciousness and harassed by worry, to an authentic state of life, in which he attains self-consciousness, an exact vision of the world, inner peace, and freedom.

In the view of all philosophical schools, mankind's principal cause of suffering, disorder, and unconsciousness were the passions: that is, unregulated desires and exaggerated fears. People are prevented from truly living, it was taught, because they are dominated by worries. Philosophy thus appears, in the first place, as a therapeutic of the passions[15] (in the words of Friedmann: "Try to get rid of your own passions"). Each school had its own therapeutic method,[16] but all of them linked their therapeutics to a profound transformation of the individual's mode of seeing and being. The object of spiritual exercises is precisely to bring about this transformation.

To begin with, let us consider the example of the Stoics. For them, all mankind's woes derive from the fact that he seeks to acquire or to keep possessions that he may either lose or fail to obtain, and from the fact that he tries to avoid misfortunes which are often inevitable. The task of philosophy, then, is to educate people, so that they seek only the goods they are able to obtain, and try to avoid only those evils which it is possible to avoid. In order for something good to be always obtainable, or an evil always avoidable, they must depend exclusively on man's freedom; but the only things which fulfill these conditions are *moral* good and evil. They alone depend on us; everything else does *not* depend on us. Here, "everything else," which does not depend on us, refers to the necessary linkage of cause and effect, which is not subject to our freedom. It must be indifferent to us: that is, we must not introduce any differences into it, but accept it in its entirety, as willed by fate. This is the domain of nature.

We have here a complete reversal of our usual way of looking at things. We are to switch from our "human" vision of reality, in which our values depend on our passions, to a "natural" vision of things, which replaces each event within the perspective of universal nature.[17]

Such a transformation of vision is not easy, and it is precisely here that spiritual exercises come in. Little by little, they make possible the indispensable metamorphosis of our inner self.

No systematic treatise codifying the instructions and techniques for spiritual exercises has come down to us.[18] However, allusions to one or the other of such inner activities are very frequent in the writings of the Roman and Hellenistic periods. It thus appears that these exercises were well known, and that it was enough to allude to them, since they were a part of daily life in the philosophical schools. They took their place within a traditional course of oral instruction.

Thanks to Philo of Alexandria, however, we do possess two lists of spiritual exercises. They do not completely overlap, but they do have the merit of giving us a fairly complete panorama of Stoico-Platonic inspired philosophical therapeutics. One of these lists[19] enumerates the following elements: research (*zetesis*), thorough investigation (*skepsis*), reading (*anagnosis*), listening (*akroasis*), attention (*prosoche*), self-mastery (*enkrateia*), and indifference to indifferent things. The other[20] names successively: reading, meditations (*meletai*), therapies[21] of the passions, remembrance of good things,[22] self-mastery (*enkrateia*), and the accomplishment of duties. With the help of these lists, we shall be able to give a brief description of Stoic spiritual exercises. We shall study the following groups in succession: first attention, then meditations and "remembrances of good things," then the more intellectual exercises: reading, listening, research, and investigation, and finally the more active exercises: self-mastery, accomplishment of duties, and indifference to indifferent things.

Attention (*prosoche*) is the fundamental Stoic spiritual attitude.[23] It is a continuous vigilance and presence of mind, self consciousness which never sleeps, and a constant tension of the spirit.[24] Thanks to this attitude, the philosopher is fully aware of what he does at each instant, and he *wills* his actions fully. Thanks to his spiritual vigilance, the Stoic always has "at hand" (*procheiron*) the fundamental rule of life: that is, the distinction between what depends on us and what does not. As in Epicureanism, so for Stoicism: it is essential that the adepts be supplied with a fundamental principle which is formulable in a few words, and extremely clear and simple, precisely so that it may remain easily accessible to the mind, and be applicable with the sureness and constancy of a reflex. "You must not separate yourself from these general principles; don't sleep, eat, drink, or converse with other men without them." [25] It is this vigilance of the spirit which lets us apply the fundamental rule to each of life's particular situations, and always to do what we do "appropriately." [26] We could also define this attitude as "concentration on the present moment": [27]

> Everywhere and at all times, it is up to you to rejoice piously at what is occurring *at the present moment*, to conduct yourself with justice towards the people who are *present here and now*, and to apply rules of discernment to your *present* representations, so that nothing slips in that is not objective.[28]

Attention to the present moment is, in a sense, the key to spiritual exercises. It frees us from the passions, which are always caused by the past or the future[29] – two areas which do *not* depend on us. By encouraging concentration on the minuscule present moment, which, in its exiguity, is always bearable and controllable,[30] attention increases our vigilance. Finally, attention to the present moment allows us to accede to cosmic consciousness, by making us attentive to the infinite value of each instant,[31] and causing us to accept each moment of existence from the viewpoint of the universal law of the *cosmos*.

Attention (*prosoche*) allows us to respond immediately to events, as if they were questions asked of us all of a sudden.[32] In order for this to be possible, we must always have the fundamental principles "at hand" (*procheiron*).[33] We are to steep ourselves in the rule of life (*kanon*),[34] by mentally applying it to all life's possible different situations, just as we assimilate a grammatical or mathematical rule through practice, by applying it to individual cases. In this case, however, we are not dealing with mere knowledge, but with the transformation of our personality.

We must also associate our imagination and affectivity with the training of our thought. Here, we must bring into play all the psychagogic techniques and rhetorical methods of amplification.[35] We must formulate the rule of life to ourselves in the most striking and concrete way. We must keep life's events "before our eyes," [36] and see them in the light of the fundamental rule. This is known as the exercise of memorization (*mneme*)[37] and meditation (*melete*)[38] on the rule of life.

The exercise of meditation[39] allows us to be ready at the moment when an unexpected – and perhaps dramatic – circumstance occurs. In the exercise called *praemeditatio malorum*,[40] we are to represent to ourselves poverty, suffering, and death. We must confront life's difficulties face to face, remembering that they are not evils, since they do not depend on us. This is why we must engrave striking maxims in our memory,[41] so that, when the time comes, they can help us accept such events, which are, after all, part of the course of nature; we will thus have these maxims and sentences "at hand." [42] What we need are persuasive formulae or arguments (*epilogismoi*),[43] which we can repeat to ourselves in difficult circumstances, so as to check movements of fear, anger, or sadness.

First thing in the morning, we should go over in advance what we have to do during the course of the day, and decide on the principles which will guide and inspire our actions.[44] In the evening, we should examine ourselves again, so as to be aware of the faults we have committed or the progress we have made.[45] We should also examine our dreams.[46]

As we can see, the exercise of meditation is an attempt to control inner discourse, in an effort to render it coherent. The goal is to arrange it around a simple, universal principle: the distinction between what does and does not depend on us, or between freedom and nature. Whoever wishes to make progress strives, by means of dialogue with himself[47] or with others,[48] as well as by writing,[49] to "carry on his reflections in due order" [50] and finally to arrive at a complete transformation of his representation of the world, his inner climate, and his outer behavior. These methods testify to a deep knowledge of the therapeutic powers of the world.[51]

The exercise of meditation and memorization requires nourishment. This is where the more specifically intellectual exercises, as enumerated by Philo, come in: reading, listening, research, and investigation. It is a relatively simple matter to provide food for meditation: one could read the sayings of the poets and philosophers, for instance, or the *apophthegmata*.[52] "Reading," however, could also include the explanation of specifically philosophical texts, works written by teachers in philosophical schools. Such texts could be read or heard within the framework of the philosophical instruction given by a professor.[53] Fortified by such instruction, the disciple would be able to study with precision the entire speculative edifice which sustained and justified the fundamental rule, as well as all the physical and logical research of which this rule was the summary.[54] "Research" and "investigation" were the result of putting instruction into practice. For example, we are to get used to defining objects and events from a physical point of view, that is, we must picture them as they are when situated within the cosmic Whole.[55] Alternatively, we can divide or dissect events in order to recognize the elements into which they can be reduced.[56]

Finally, we come to the practical exercises, intended to create habits. Some of these are very much "interior," and very close to the thought exercises we have just discussed. "Indifference to indifferent things," for example, was nothing other than the application of the fundamental rule.[57] Other exercises, such as self-mastery and fulfilling the duties of social life, entailed practical forms of behavior. Here again, we encounter Friedmann's themes: "Try to get rid of your own passions, vanities, and the itch for talk about your own name . . . Avoid backbiting. Get rid of pity and hatred. Love all free human beings."

There are a large number of treatises relating to these exercises in Plutarch: *On Restraining Anger, On Peace of Mind, On Brotherly Love, On the Love of Children, On Garrulity, On the Love of Wealth, On False Shame, On Envy and Hatred*. Seneca also composed works of the same genre: *On Anger, On Benefits, On Peace of Mind, On Leisure*. In this kind of exercise, one very simple principle is always recommended: begin practicing on easier things, so as gradually to acquire a stable, solid habit.[58]

For the Stoic, then, doing philosophy meant practicing how to "live": that is, how to live freely and consciously. Consciously, in that we pass beyond the limits of individuality, to recognize ourselves as a part of the reason-animated *cosmos*. Freely, in that we give up desiring that which does not depend on us and is beyond our control, so as to attach ourselves only to what depends on us: actions which are just and in conformity with reason.

It is easy to understand that a philosophy like Stoicism, which requires vigilance, energy, and psychic tension, should consist essentially in spiritual exercises. But it will perhaps come as a surprise to learn than Epicureanism, usually considered the philosophy of pleasure, gives just as prominent a place as Stoicism to precise practices which are nothing other than spiritual exercises. The reason for this is that, for Epicurus just as much as for the Stoics, philosophy is a therapeutics: "We must concern ourselves with the healing of our own lives." [59] In this context, healing consists in bringing one's soul back from the worries of life to the simple joy of existing. People's unhappiness, for the Epicureans, comes from the fact that they are afraid of things which are not to be feared, and desire things which it is not necessary to desire, and which are beyond their control. Consequently, their life is consumed in worries over unjustified fears and unsatisfied desires. As a result, they are deprived of the only genuine pleasure there is: the pleasure of existing. This is why Epicurean physics can liberate us from fear: it can show us that the gods have no effect on the progress of the world and that death, being complete dissolution, is not a part of life.[60] Epicurean ethics: Epicurean, as deliverance from desires can deliver us from our insatiable desires, by distinguishing between desires which are both natural and necessary, desires which are natural but not necessary, and desires which are neither natural nor necessary. It is enough to satisfy the first category of desires, and give up the last – and eventually the second as well – in order to ensure the absence of worries,[61] and to reveal the sheer joy of existing: "The cries of the flesh are: 'Not to be hungry', 'not to be thirsty', 'not to be cold'. For if one enjoys the possession of this, and the hope of continuing to possess it, he might rival even Zeus in happiness." [62] This is the source of the feeling of gratitude, which one would hardly have expected, which illuminates what one might call Epicurean piety towards all things: "Thanks be to blessed Nature, that she has made what is necessary easy to obtain, and what is not easy unnecessary." [63]

Spiritual exercises are required for the healing of the soul. Like the Stoics, the Epicureans advise us to meditate upon and assimilate, "day and night," brief aphorisms or summaries which will allow us to keep the fundamental dogmas "at hand." [64] For instance, there is the well-known *tetrapharmakos*, or four-fold healing formula: "God presents no fears, death no worries. And while good is readily attainable, evil is readily endurable." [65] The abundance of collections of Epicurean aphorisms is a response to the demands of the spiritual exercise of meditation.[66] As with the Stoics, however, the study of the dogmatic treatises of the school's great founders was also an exercise intended to provide material for meditation,[67] so as more thoroughly to impregnate the soul with the fundamental intuitions of Epicureanism.

The study of physics is a particularly important spiritual exercise: "we should not think that any other end is served by knowledge of celestial phenomena . . . than freedom from disturbance and firm confidence, just as in the other fields of study." [68] Contemplation of the physical world and imagination of the infinite are important elements of Epicurean physics. Both can bring about a complete change in our way of looking at things. The closed universe is infinitely dilated, and we derive from this spectacle a unique spiritual pleasure:

> the walls of the world open out, I see action going on throughout the whole void, . . . Thereupon from all these things a sort of divine delight gets hold upon me and a shuddering, because nature thus by your power (i.e. Epicurus') has been so manifestly laid open and unveiled in every part.[69]

Meditation, however, be it simple or erudite, is not the only Epicurean spiritual exercise. To cure the soul, it is not necessary, as the Stoics would have it, to train it to stretch itself tight, but rather to train it to relax. Instead of picturing misfortunes in advance, so as to be prepared to bear them, we must rather, say the Epicureans, detach our thought from the vision of painful things, and fix our eyes on pleasurable ones. We are to relive memories of past pleasures, and enjoy the pleasures of the present, recognizing how intense and agreeable these present pleasures are.[70] We have here a quite distinctive spiritual exercise, different from the constant vigilance of the Stoic, with his constant readiness to safeguard his moral liberty at each instant. Instead, Epicureanism preaches the deliberate, continually renewed choice of relaxation and serenity, combined with a profound gratitude[71] toward nature and life,[72] which constantly offer us joy and pleasure, if only we know how to find them.

By the same token, the spiritual exercise of trying to live in the present moment is very different for Stoics and Epicureans. For the former, it means mental tension and constant wakefulness of the moral conscience; for the latter, it is, as we have seen, an invitation to relaxation and serenity. Worry, which tears us in the direction of the future, hides from us the incomparable value of the simple fact of existing: "We are born once, and cannot be born twice, but for all time must be no more. But you, who are not master of tomorrow, postpone your happiness: life is wasted in procrastination and each one of us dies overwhelmed with cares."[73] This is the doctrine contained in Horace's famous saying: *carpe diem.*

> Life ebbs as I speak:
> so seize each day, and grant the next no credit.[74]

For the Epicureans, in the last analysis, pleasure is a spiritual exercise. Not pleasure in the form of mere sensual gratification, but the intellectual pleasure derived from contemplating nature, the thought of pleasures past and present, and lastly the pleasure of friendship. In Epicurean communities, friendship[75] also had its spiritual exercises, carried out in a joyous, relaxed atmosphere. These include the public confession of one's faults;[76] mutual correction, carried out in a fraternal spirit; and examining one's conscience.[77] Above all, friendship itself was, as it were, the spiritual exercise *par excellence*: "Each person was to tend towards creating the atmosphere in which hearts could flourish. The main goal was to be happy, and mutual affection and the confidence with which they relied upon each other contributed more than anything else to this happiness." [78]

2 Learning to Dialogue

The practice of spiritual exercises is likely to be rooted in traditions going back to immemorial times.[79] It is, however, the figure of Socrates that causes them to emerge into Western consciousness, for this figure was, and has remained, the living call to awaken our moral consciousness.[80] We ought not to forget that this call sounded forth within a specific form: that of dialogue.

In the "Socratic"[81] dialogue, the question truly at stake is not *what* is being talked about, but *who* is doing the talking.

> anyone who is close to Socrates and enters into conversation with him is liable to be drawn into an argument, and whatever subject he may start, he will be continually carried round and round by him, until at last he finds that he has to give an account both of his present and past life, and when he is once entangled, Socrates will not let him go until he has completely and thoroughly sifted him . . . And I think there is no harm in being reminded of any wrong thing which we are, or have been, doing; he who does not run away from criticism will be sure to take more heed of his afterlife.[82]

In a "Socratic" dialogue, Socrates' interlocutor does not learn anything, and Socrates has no intention of teaching him anything. He repeats, moreover, to all who are willing to listen, that the only thing he knows is that he does not know anything.[83] Yet, like an indefatigable horsefly,[84] Socrates harassed his interlocutors with questions which put *themselves* into question, forcing them to pay attention to and take care of themselves.[85]

> My very good friend, you are an Athenian, and belong to a city which is the greatest and most famous in the world for its wisdom and strength. Are you not ashamed that you give your attention to acquiring as much money as possible, and similarly with reputation and honour, and give no attention or thought to truth [*aletheia*] or thought [*phronesis*] or the perfection of your soul [*psyche*]?[86]

Socrates' mission consisted in inviting his contemporaries to examine their conscience, and to take care for their inner progress:

> I did not care for the things that most people care about – making money, having a comfortable home, high military or civil rank, and all the other activities, political appointments, secret societies, party organizations, which go on in our city . . . I set myself to do you – each one of you, individually and in private – what I hold to be the greatest possible service. I tried to persuade each one of you to *concern himself less with what he has than with what he is*, so as to render himself as excellent and as rational as possible.[87]

In Plato's *Symposium*, Alcibiades describes the effect made on him by dialogues with Socrates in the following terms: "this latter-day Marsyas, here, has often left me in such a state of mind that I've felt I simply couldn't go on living the way I did . . . He makes me admit that while I'm spending my time on politics, I am neglecting all the things that are crying for attention in myself."[88]

Thus, the Socratic dialogue turns out to be a kind of communal spiritual exercise. In it, the interlocutors are invited[89] to participate in such inner spiritual exercises as examination of conscience and attention to oneself; in other words, they are urged to comply with the famous dictum, "Know thyself." Although it is difficult to be sure of the original meaning of this formula, this much is clear: it invites us to establish a relationship of the self to the self, which constitutes the foundation of every spiritual exercise. To know oneself means, among other things, to know oneself *qua* non-sage: that is, not as a *sophos*, but as a *philo-sophos*, someone *on the way toward* wisdom. Alternatively, it can mean to know oneself in one's essential being; this entails separating that which we *are not* from that which we *are*. Finally, it can mean to know oneself in one's true moral state: that is, to examine one's conscience.[90]

If we can trust the portrait sketched by Plato and Aristophanes, Socrates, master of dialogue with others, was also a master of dialogue with himself, and, therefore, a master of the practice of spiritual exercises. He is portrayed as capable of extraordinary mental concentration. He arrives late at Agathon's banquet, for example, because "as we went along the road, Socrates directed his intellect towards himself, and began to fall behind."[91] Alcibiades tells the story of how, during the expedition against Poteidaia, Socrates remained standing all day and all night, "lost in thought."[92] In his *Clouds*, Aristophanes seems to allude to these same Socratic habits:

> Now, think hard and cogitate; spin round in every way as you concentrate. If you come up against an insoluble point, jump to another

. . . Now don't keep your mind always spinning around itself, but let your thoughts out into the air a bit, like a may-beetle tied by its foot.[93]

Meditation – the practice of dialogue with oneself – seems to have held a place of honor among Socrates' disciples. When Antisthenes was asked what profit he had derived from philosophy, he replied: "The ability to converse with myself."[94] The intimate connection between dialogue with others and dialogue with oneself is profoundly significant. Only he who is capable of a genuine encounter with the other is capable of an authentic encounter with himself, and the converse is equally true. Dialogue can be genuine only within the framework of presence to others and to oneself. From this perspective, every spiritual exercise is a dialogue, insofar as it is an exercise of authentic presence, to oneself and to others.[95]

The borderline between "Socratic" and "Platonic" dialogue is impossible to delimit. Yet the Platonic dialogue is always "Socratic" in inspiration, because it is an intellectual, and, in the last analysis, a "spiritual" exercise. This characteristic of the Platonic dialogue needs to be emphasized.

Platonic dialogues are model exercises. They are models, in that they are not transcriptions of real dialogues, but literary compositions which present an ideal dialogue. And they are exercises precisely insofar as they are dialogues: we have already seen, *apropos* of Socrates, the dialectical character of all spiritual exercises. A dialogue is an itinerary of the thought, whose route is traced by the constantly maintained accord between questioner and respondent. In opposing his method to that of eristics, Plato strongly emphasizes this point:

> When two friends, like you and I, feel like talking, we have to go about it in a gentler and more dialectical way. "More dialectical," it seems to me, means that we must not merely give true responses, but that we must base our replies only on that which our interlocutor admits that he himself knows.[96]

The dimension of the interlocutor is, as we can see, of capital importance. It is what prevents the dialogue from becoming a theoretical, dogmatic exposé, and forces it to be a concrete, practical exercise. For the point is not to set forth a doctrine, but rather to guide the interlocutor towards a determinate mental attitude. It is a combat, amicable but real.

The point is worth stressing, for the same thing happens in every spiritual exercise: we must *let* ourselves be changed, in our point of view, attitudes, and convictions. This means that we must dialogue with ourselves, and hence we must do battle with ourselves. This is why, from this perspective, the methodology of the Platonic dialogue is of such crucial interest:

Despite what may have been said, Platonic thought bears no resemblance to a light-winged dove, who needs no effort to take off from earth to soar away into the pure spaces of utopia . . . at every moment, the dove has to fight against the soul of the interlocutor, which is filled with lead. Each degree of elevation must be fought for and won.[97]

To emerge victorious from this battle, it is not enough to disclose the truth. It is not even enough to demonstrate it. What is needed is *persuasion*, and for that one must use psychagogy, the art of seducing souls. Even at that, it is not enough to use only rhetoric, which, as it were, tries to persuade from a distance, by means of a continuous discourse. What is needed above all is *dialectic*, which demands the explicit consent of the interlocutor at every moment. Dialectic must skillfully choose a tortuous path – or rather, a series of apparently divergent, but nevertheless convergent, paths[98] – in order to bring the interlocutor to discover the contradictions of his own position, or to admit an unforeseen conclusion. All the circles, detours, endless divisions, digressions, and subtleties which make the modern reader of Plato's *Dialogues* so uncomfortable are destined to make ancient readers and interlocutors travel a specific path. Thanks to these detours, "with a great deal of effort, one rubs names, definitions, visions and sensations against one another"; one "spends a long time in the company of these questions"; one "lives with them"[99] until the light blazes forth. Yet one keeps on practicing, since "for reasonable people, the measure of listening to such discussions is the whole of life." [100]

What counts is not the solution of a particular problem, but the road travelled to reach it; a road along which the interlocutor, the disciple, and the reader form their thought, and make it more apt to discover the truth by itself:[101]

> *Stranger:*   Suppose someone asked us this question about our class of elementary school-children learning to read. "When a child is asked what letters spell a word – it can be any word you please – are we to regard this exercise as undertaken to discover the correct spelling of the particular word the teacher assigned, or as designed rather to make the child better able to deal with all words he may be asked to spell?"
>
> *Young Socrates:*   Surely we reply that the purpose is to teach him to read them all.
>
> *Stranger:*   How does this principle apply to our present search for the statesman? Why did we set ourselves the problem? Is our chief purpose to find the statesman, or have we the larger aim of becoming better dialecticians, more able to tackle all questions?
>
> *Young Socrates:*   Here, too, the answer is clear; we aim to become better dialecticians with regard to all possible subjects.[102]

As we see, the subject-matter of the dialogue counts less than the method applied in it, and the solution of a problem has less value than the road travelled in common in order to resolve it. The point is not to find the answer to a problem before anyone else, but to practice, as effectively as possible, the application of a method:

> ease and speed in reaching the answer to the problem propounded are most commendable, but the *logos* requires that this be only a secondary, not a primary reason for commending an argument. What we must value first and foremost, above all else, is the philosophical method itself, and this consists in ability to divide according to forms. If, therefore, either a lengthy *logos* or an unusually brief one leaves the hearer more able to find the forms, it is this presentation of the *logos* which must be diligently carried through.[103]

As a dialectical exercise, the Platonic dialogue corresponds exactly to a spiritual exercise. There are two reasons for this. In the first place, discreetly but genuinely, the dialogue guides the interlocutor – and the reader – towards conversion. Dialogue is only possible if the interlocutor has a real *desire* to dialogue: that is, if he truly wants to discover the truth, desires the Good from the depths of his soul, and agrees to submit to the rational demands of the Logos.[104] His act of faith must correspond to that of Socrates: "It is because I am convinced of its truth that I am ready, with your help, to inquire into the nature of virtue."[105]

In fact, the dialectical effort is an ascent in common towards the truth and towards the Good, "which every soul pursues."[106] Furthermore, in Plato's view, every dialectical exercise, precisely because it is an exercise of pure thought, subject to the demands of the Logos, turns the soul away from the sensible world, and allows it to convert itself towards the Good.[107] It is the spirit's itinerary towards the divine.

3 Learning to Die

There is a mysterious connection between language and death. This was one of the favorite themes of the late Brice Parain, who wrote: "Language develops only upon the death of individuals."[108] For the Logos represents a demand for universal rationality, and presupposes a world of immutable norms, which are opposed to the perpetual state of becoming and changing appetites characteristic of individual, corporeal life. In this opposition, he who remains faithful to the Logos risks losing his life. This was the case with Socrates, who died for his faithfulness to the Logos.

Socrates' death was the radical event which founded Platonism. After all, the essence of Platonism consists in the affirmation that the Good is the ultimate cause of all beings. In the words of a fourth-century Neoplatonist:

> If all beings are beings only by virtue of goodness, and if they participate in the Good, then the first must necessarily be a good which transcends being. Here is an eminent proof of this: souls of value despise being for the sake of the Good, whenever they voluntarily place themselves in danger, for their country, their loved ones, or for virtue.[109]

Socrates exposed himself to death for the sake of virtue. He preferred to die rather than renounce the demands of his conscience,[110] thus preferring the Good above being, and thought and conscience above the life of his body. This is nothing other than *the* fundamental philosophical choice. If it is true that philosophy subjugates the body's will to live to the higher demands of thought, it can rightly be said that philosophy is the training and apprenticeship for death. As Socrates puts it in the *Phaedo*: "it is a fact, Simmias, that those who go about philosophizing correctly are in training for death, and that to them of all men death is least alarming." [111]

The death in question here is the spiritual separation of the soul and the body:

> separating the soul as much as possible from the body, and accustoming it to gather itself together from every part of the body and concentrate itself until it is completely independent, and to have its dwelling, so far as it can, both now and in the future, alone and by itself, freed from the shackles of the body.[112]

Such is the Platonic spiritual exercise. But we must be wary of misinterpreting it. In particular, we must not isolate it from the philosophical death of Socrates, whose presence dominates the whole of the *Phaedo*. The separation between soul and body under discussion here – whatever its prehistory – bears absolutely no resemblance to any state of trance or catalepsy. In the latter, the body loses consciousness, while the soul is in a supernatural visionary state.[113] All the arguments in the *Phaedo*, both preceding and following the passage we have quoted above, show that the goal of this philosophical separation is for the soul to liberate itself, shedding the passions linked to the corporeal senses, so as to attain to the autonomy of thought.[114]

We can perhaps get a better idea of this spiritual exercise if we understand it as an attempt to liberate ourselves from a partial, passionate point of view – linked to the senses and the body – so as to rise to the universal, normative viewpoint of thought, submitting ourselves to the demands of the Logos and the norm of the Good. Training for death is training to die *to one's individuality and passions*, in order to look at things from the perspective of universality and objectivity.

Such an exercise requires the concentration of thought upon itself, by means of meditation and an inner dialogue. Plato alludes to this process in the *Republic*, once again in the context of the tyranny of individual passions. The tyranny of desire, he tells us, shows itself particularly clearly in dreams:

> The savage part of the soul . . . does not hesitate, in thought, to try to have sex with its mother, or with anyone else, man, god, or animal. It is ready to commit any bloody crime; there is no food it would not eat; and, in a word, it does not stop short of any madness or shamelessness.[115]

To liberate ourselves from this tyranny, we are to have recourse to a spiritual exercise of the same type as that described in the *Phaedo*:

> When, however, a man does not go to sleep before he has awakened his rational faculty, and regaled it with excellent discourses and investigations, concentrating himself on himself, having also appeased the appetitive part . . . and calmed the irascible part . . . once he has calmed these two parts of the soul, and stimulated the third, in which reason resides . . . it is then that the soul best attains to truth.[116]

Here we shall ask the reader's indulgence to embark on a brief digression. To present philosophy as "training for death" was a decision of paramount importance. As Socrates' interlocutor in the *Phaedo* was quick to remark, such a characterization seems somewhat laughable, and the common man would be right in calling philosophers moribund mopers who, if they are put to death, will have earned their punishment well.[117] For anyone who takes philosophy seriously, however, this Platonic dictum is profoundly true. It has had an enormous influence on Western philosophy, and has been taken up even by such adversaries of Platonism as Epicurus and Heidegger. Compared to this formulation, the philosophical verbiage both of the past and of the present seems empty indeed. In the words of La Rochefoucauld, "Neither the sun nor death can be looked at directly." [118]

Indeed, the only ones even to *attempt* to do so are philosophers. Beneath all their diverse conceptions of death, one common virtue recurs again and again: lucidity. For Plato, he who has already tasted of the immortality of thought cannot be frightened by the idea of being snatched away from sensible life. For the Epicurean, the thought of death is the same as the consciousness of the finite nature of existence, and it is this which gives an infinite value to each instant. Each of life's moments surges forth laden with incommensurable value: "Believe that each day that has dawned will be your last; then you will receive each unexpected hour with gratitude." [119]

In the apprenticeship of death, the Stoic discovers the apprenticeship of freedom. Montaigne, in one of his best-known essays, *That Philosophizing is Learning how to Die*, plagiarizes Seneca: "He who has learned how to die, has un-learned how to serve." [120] The thought of death transforms the the tone and level of inner life: "Keep death before your eyes every day . . . and then you will never have any abject thought nor any excessive desire." [121] This philosophical theme, in turn, is connected with that of the infinite value of the present moment, which we must live as if it were, simultaneously, both the first moment and the last. [122]

Philosophy is still "a training for death" for a modern thinker such as Heidegger. For him, the authenticity of existence consists in the lucid anticipation of death, and it is up to each of us to choose between lucidity and diversion. [123]

For Plato, training for death is a spiritual exercise which consists in changing one's point of view. We are to change from a vision of things dominated by individual passions to a representation of the world governed by the universality and objectivity of thought. This constitutes a conversion (*metastrophe*) brought about with the totality of the soul. [124] From the perspective of pure thought, things which are "human, all too human" seem awfully puny. This is one of the fundamental themes of Platonic spiritual exercises, and it is this which will allow us to maintain serenity in misfortunes:

> The rational law declares that it is best to keep quiet as far as possible in misfortune, and not to complain, because we cannot know what is really good and evil in such things, and it does us no good for the future to take them hard, and nothing in human life is worthy of great concern, and our grieving is an obstacle to the very thing we need to come to our aid as quickly as possible in such cases.
> What do you mean?
> To deliberate, I said, about what has happened to us, and, as in dice-games, to re-establish our position according to whatever numbers turn up, however reason indicates would be best, and . . . always accustom the soul to come as quickly as possible to cure the ailing part and raise up what has fallen, making lamentations disappear by means of its therapy. [125]

One could say that this spiritual exercise is already Stoic, [126] since in it we can see the utilization of maxims and principles intended to "accustom the soul," and liberate it from the passions. Among these maxims, the one affirming the unimportance of human affairs plays an important role. Yet, in its turn, this maxim is only the consequence of the movement described in the *Phaedo*, whereby the soul, moving from individuality to universality, rises to the level of pure thought.

The three key concepts of the insignificance of human affairs, contempt for death, and the universal vision characteristic of pure thought are quite plainly linked in the following passage:

> there is this further point to be considered in distinguishing the philosophical from the unphilosophical nature . . . the soul must not contain any hint of servility. For nothing can be more contrary than such pettiness to the quality of a soul which must constantly strive to embrace the *universal totality* of things divine and human . . . But that soul to which pertain grandeur of thought and the *contemplation of the totality* of time and of being, do you think that it can consider human life to be a matter of great importance? Hence such a man will not suppose death to be terrible.[127]

Here, "training for death" is linked to the contemplation of the Whole and elevation of thought, which rises from individual, passionate subjectivity to the universal perspective. In other words, it attains to the exercise of pure thought. In this passage, for the first time, this characteristic of the philosopher receives the appellation it will maintain throughout ancient tradition: greatness of soul.[128] Greatness of soul is the fruit of the universality of thought. Thus, the whole of the philosopher's speculative and contemplative effort becomes a spiritual exercise, insofar as he raises his thought up to the perspective of the Whole, and liberates it from the illusions of individuality (in the words of Friedmann: "Step out of duration . . . become eternal by transcending yourself").

From such a perspective, even physics becomes a spiritual exercise, which is situated on three levels. In the first place, physics can be a contemplative activity, which has its end in itself, providing joy and serenity to the soul, and liberating it from day-to-day worries. This is the spirit of Aristotelian physics: "nature, which fashioned creatures, gives amazing pleasure in their study to all who can trace links of causation, and are naturally philosophers."[129] As we have seen, it was in the contemplation of nature that the Epicurean Lucretius found "a divine delight."[130] For the Stoic Epictetus, the meaning of our existence resides in this contemplation: we have been placed on earth in order to contemplate divine creation, and we must not die before we have witnessed its marvels and lived in harmony with nature.[131]

Clearly, the precise meaning of the contemplation of nature varies widely from one philosophy to another. There is a great deal of difference between Aristotelian physics, for example, and the feeling for nature as we find it in Philo of Alexandria and Plutarch. It is nevertheless interesting to note with what enthusiasm these two authors speak about their imaginative physics:

Those who practice wisdom . . . are excellent contemplators of nature
and everything she contains. They examine the earth, the sea, the sky,
the heavens, and all their inhabitants; they are joined in thought to the
sun, the moon, and all the other stars, both fixed and wandering, in their
courses; and although they are attached to the earth by their bodies, they
provide their souls with wings, so that they may walk on the ether and
contemplate the powers that live there, as is fitting for true citizens of the
world . . . and so, filled with excellence, accustomed to take no notice of
ills of the body or of exterior things . . . it goes without saying that such
men, rejoicing in their virtues, make of their whole lives a festival.[132]

These last lines are an allusion to an aphorism of Diogenes the Cynic, which
is also quoted by Plutarch: "Does not a good man consider every day a
festival?" "And a very splendid one, to be sure," continues Plutarch,

if we are virtuous. For the world is the most sacred and divine of
temples, and the one most fitting for the gods. Man is introduced into
it by birth to be a spectator: not of artificial, immobile statues, but of
the perceptible images of intelligible essences . . . such as the sun, the
moon, the stars, the rivers whose water always flows afresh, and the
earth, which sends forth food for plants and animals alike. A life which
is a perfect revelation, and an initiation into these mysteries, should be
filled with tranquillity and joy.[133]

Physics as a spiritual exercise can also take on the form of an imaginative
"overflight," which causes human affairs to be regarded as of little importance.[134] We encounter this theme in Marcus Aurelius:

Suppose you found yourself all of a sudden raised up to the heavens,
and that you were to look down upon human affairs in all their motley
diversity. You would hold them in contempt if you were to see, in the
same glance, how great is the number of beings of the ether and the air,
living round about you.[135]

The same theme occurs in Seneca:

The soul has attained the culmination of happiness when, having
crushed underfoot all that is evil, it takes flight and penetrates the inner
recesses of nature. It is then, while wandering amongst the very stars,
that it likes to laugh at the costly pavements of the rich . . . But the soul
cannot despise [all these riches] before it has been all around the world,
and casting a contemptuous glance at the narrow globe of the earth from
above, says to itself: "So this is the pin-point which so many nations

divide among themselves with fire and sword? How ridiculous are the boundaries of men!"[136]

In this spiritual exercise of the vision of totality, and elevation of thought to the level of universal thought, we can distinguish a third degree, in which we come closer to the Platonic theme from which we started out. In the words of Marcus Aurelius:

> Don't limit yourself to breathing along with the air that surrounds you; from now on, think along with the Thought which embraces all things. For the intellective power is no less universally diffused, and does not penetrate any the less into each being capable of receiving it, than the air in the case of one capable of breathing it . . . you will make a large room at once for yourself by embracing in your thought the whole Universe, and grasping ever-continuing Time.[137]

At this stage, it is as though we die to our individuality; in so doing, we accede, on the one hand, to the interiority of our consciousness, and on the other, to the universality of thought of the All.

> You were already the All, but because something else besides the All came to be added on to you, you have become less than the All, by the very fact of this addition. For the addition did not come about from being – what could be added to the All? – but rather from not-being. When one becomes "someone" out of not-being, one is no longer the All, until one leaves the not-being behind. Moreover, you increase yourself when you reject everything other than the All, and when you have rejected it, the All will be present to you . . . The All had no need to *come* in order to be present. If it is *not* present, the reason is that it is *you* who have distanced yourself from it. "Distancing yourself" does not mean leaving it to go someplace else – for it would be there, too. Rather, it means turning away from the All, despite the fact that it is there.[138]

With Plotinus, we now return to Platonism. The Platonic tradition remained faithful to Plato's spiritual exercises. We need only add that, in Neoplatonism, the idea of spiritual progress plays a much more explicit role than in Plato's writings. In Neoplatonism, the stages of spiritual progress corresponded to different degrees of virtue. The hierarchy of these stages is described in many Neoplatonic texts,[139] serving in particular as the framework for Marinus' *Life of Proclus*.[140] Porphyry, editor of Plotinus' *Enneads*, systematically arranged his master's work according to the stages of this spiritual progress. First, the soul was purified by its gradual detachment from the body; then came the knowledge of, and subsequent passing beyond, the sensible world; finally, the soul achieved conversion toward the Intellect and the One.[141]

Spiritual exercises are a prerequisite for spiritual progress. In his treatise *On Abstinence from Animate Beings*, Porphyry sums up the Platonic tradition quite well. We must, he tells us, undertake two exercises (*meletai*): in the first place, we must turn our thought away from all that is mortal and material. Secondly, we must return toward the activity of the Intellect.[142] The first stage of these Neoplatonic exercises includes aspects which are highly ascetic, in the modern sense of the word: a vegetarian diet, among other things. In the same context, Porphyry insists strongly on the importance of spiritual exercises. The contemplation (*theoria*) which brings happiness, he tells us, does not consist in the accumulation of discourse and abstract teachings, even if their subject is true Being. Rather, we must make sure our studies are accompanied by an effort to make these teachings become "nature and life" within us.[143]

In the philosophy of Plotinus, spiritual exercises are of fundamental importance. Perhaps the best example can be found in the way Plotinus defines the essence of the soul and its immateriality. If we have doubts about the immortality and immateriality of the soul, says Plotinus, this is because we are accustomed to see it filled with irrational desires and violent sentiments and passions.

> If one wants to know the nature of a thing, one must examine it in its pure state, since every addition to a thing is an obstacle to the knowledge of that thing. When you examine it, then, remove from it everything that is not itself; better still *remove all your stains from yourself and examine yourself*, and you will have faith in your immortality.[144]

> If you do not yet see your own beauty, do as the sculptor does with a statue which must become beautiful: he removes one part, scrapes another, makes one area smooth, and cleans the other, until he causes the beautiful face in the statue to appear. In the same way, you too must remove everything that is superfluous, straighten that which is crooked, and purify all that is dark until you make it brilliant. Never stop sculpting your own statue, until the divine splendor of virtue shines in you . . . If you have become this . . . and have nothing alien inside you mixed with yourself . . . when you see that you have become this . . . concentrate your gaze and see. For it is only an eye such as this that can look on the great Beauty.[145]

Here we can see how the the demonstration of the soul's immateriality has been transformed into experience. Only he who liberates himself and purifies himself from the passions, which conceal the true reality of the soul, can understand that the soul is immaterial and immortal. Here, knowledge *is* a spiritual exercise.[146] We must first undergo moral purification, in order to become capable of understanding.

When the object of our knowledge is no longer the soul, but the Intellect[147] and above all the One, principle of all things, we must once again have recourse to spiritual exercises. In the case of the One, Plotinus makes a clear distinction between, on the one hand, "instruction," which speaks about its object in an exterior way, and, on the other, the "path," which truly leads to concrete knowledge of the Good: "We are *instructed about it* by analogies, negations, and the knowledge of things which come from it . . . we are *led towards it* by purifications, virtues, inner settings in order, and ascents into the intelligible world." [148] Plotinus' writings are full of passages describing such spiritual exercises, the goal of which was not merely to *know* the Good, but to *become identical with it*, in a complete annihilation of individuality. To achieve this goal, he tells us, we must avoid thinking of any determinate form,[149] strip the soul of all particular shape,[150] and set aside all things other than the One.[151] It is then that, in a fleeting blaze of light, there takes place the metamorphosis of the self:

> Then the seer no longer sees his object, for in that instant he no longer distinguishes himself from it; he no longer has the impression of two separate things, but *he has, in a sense, become another*. He is no longer himself, nor does he belong to himself, but he is one with the One, as the centre of one circle coincides with the centre of another.[152]

4 Learning How to Read

In the preceding pages, we have tried to describe – albeit too briefly – the richness and variety of the practice of spiritual exercises in antiquity. We have seen that, at first glance, they appear to vary widely. Some, like Plutarch's *ethismoi*, designed to curb curiosity, anger or gossip, were only practices intended to ensure good moral habits. Others, particularly the meditations of the Platonic tradition, demanded a high degree of mental concentration. Some, like the contemplation of nature as practiced in all philosophical schools, turned the soul toward the cosmos, while still others – rare and exceptional – led to a transfiguration of the personality, as in the experiences of Plotinus. We also saw that the emotional tone and notional content of these exercises varied widely from one philosophical school to another: from the mobilization of energy and consent to destiny of the Stoics, to the relaxation and detachment of the Epicureans, to mental concentration and renunciation of the sensible world among the Platonists.

Beneath this apparent diversity, however, there is a profound unity, both in the means employed and in the ends pursued. The means employed are the rhetorical and dialectical techniques of persuasion, the attempts at mastering one's inner dialogue, and mental concentration. In all philosophical schools, the goal pursued in these exercises is self-realization and improvement. All schools agree that man, before his philosophical conversion, is in a state of unhappy disquiet. Consumed by worries, torn by passions, he does not live a genuine life, nor is he truly himself. All schools also agree that man can be delivered from this state. He can accede to genuine life, improve himself, transform himself, and attain a state of perfection. It is precisely for this that spiritual exercises are intended. Their goal is a kind of self-formation, or *paideia*, which is to teach us to live, not in conformity with human prejudices and social conventions – for social life is itself a product of the passions – but in conformity with the nature of man, which is none other than reason. Each in its own way, all schools believed in the freedom of the will, thanks to which man has the possibility to modify, improve, and realize himself. Underlying this conviction is the parallelism between physical and spiritual exercises: just as, by dint of repeated physical exercises, athletes give new form and strength to their bodies, so the philosopher develops his strength of soul, modifies his inner climate, transforms his vision of the world, and, finally, his entire being.[153] The analogy seems all the more self-evident in that the *gymnasion*, the place where physical exercises were practiced, was the same place where philosophy lessons were given; in other words, it was also the place for training in *spiritual* gymnastics.[154]

The quest for self-realization, final goal of spiritual exercises, is well symbolized by the Plotinian image of sculpting one's own statue.[155] It is often misunderstood, since people imagine that this expression corresponds to a kind of moral aestheticism. On this interpretation, its meaning would be to adopt a pose, to select an attitude, or to fabricate a personality for oneself. In fact, it is nothing of the sort. For the ancients, sculpture was an art which "took away," as opposed to painting, an art which "added on." The statue pre-existed in the marble block, and it was enough to take away what was superfluous in order to cause it to appear.[156]

One conception was common to all the philosophical schools: people are unhappy because they are the slave of their passions. In other words, they are unhappy because they desire things they may not be able to obtain, since they are exterior, alien, and superfluous to them. It follows that happiness consists in independence, freedom, and autonomy. In other words, happiness is the return to the essential: that which is truly "ourselves," and which depends on us.

This is obviously true in Platonism, where we find the famous image of Glaucos, the god who lives in the depths of the sea. Covered as he is with mud, seaweed, seashells, and pebbles, Glaucos is unrecognizable, and the same holds true for the soul: the body is a kind of thick, coarse crust, covering and completely disfiguring it, and the soul's true nature would appear only if it rose up out of the sea, throwing off everything alien to it.[157] The spiritual exercise of apprenticeship for death, which consists in separating oneself from the body, its passions, and its desires, purifies the soul from all these superfluous additions. It is enough to practice this exercise in order for the soul to return to its true nature, and devote itself exclusively to the exercise of pure thought.

Much the same thing can be said for Stoicism. With the help of the distinction between what does and does not depend on us; we can reject all that is alien to us, and return to our true selves. In other words, we can achieve moral freedom.

Finally, the same also holds true for Epicureanism. By ignoring unnatural and unnecessary desires, we can return to our original nucleus of freedom and independence, which may be defined by the satisfaction of natural and necessary desires.

Thus, all spiritual exercises are, fundamentally, a return to the self, in which the self is liberated from the state of alienation into which it has been plunged by worries, passions, and desires. The "self" liberated in this way is no longer merely our egoistic, passionate individuality: it is our *moral* person, open to universality and objectivity, and participating in universal nature or thought.

With the help of these exercises, we should be able to attain to wisdom; that is, to a state of complete liberation from the passions, utter lucidity, knowledge of ourselves and of the world. In fact, for Plato, Aristotle, the Epicureans, and the Stoics, such an ideal of human perfection serves to define *divine* perfection, a state by definition inaccessible to man.[158] With the possible exception of the Epicurean school,[159] wisdom was conceived as an ideal after which one strives without the hope of ever attaining it. Under normal circumstances, the only state accessible to man is *philo-sophia*: the love of, or progress toward, wisdom. For this reason, spiritual exercises must be taken up again and again, in an ever-renewed effort.

The philosopher lives in an intermediate state. He is not a sage, but he is not a non-sage, either.[160] He is therefore constantly torn between the non-philosophical and the philosophical life, between the domain of the habitual and the everyday, on the one hand, and, on the other, the domain of consciousness and lucidity.[161] To the same extent that the philosophical life is equivalent to the practice of spiritual exercises, it is also a tearing away from everyday life. It is a conversion,[162] a total transformation of one's vision, life-style, and behavior.

Among the Cynics, champions of *askesis*, this engagement amounted to a total break with the profane world, analogous to the monastic calling in Christianity. The rupture took the form of a way of living, and even of dress, completely foreign to that of the rest of mankind. This is why it was sometimes said that Cynicism was not a philosophy in the proper sense of the term, but a state of life (*enstasis*).[163] In fact, however, all philosophical schools engaged their disciples upon a new way of life, albeit in a more moderate way. The practice of spiritual exercises implied a complete reversal of received ideas: one was to renounce the false values of wealth, honors, and pleasures, and turn towards the true values of virtue, contemplation, a simple life-style, and the simple happiness of existing. This radical opposition explains the reaction of non-philosophers, which ranged from the mockery we find expressed in the comic poets, to the outright hostility which went so far as to cause the death of Socrates.

The individual was to be torn away from his habits and social prejudices, his way of life totally changed, and his way of looking at the world radically metamorphosed into a cosmic-"physical" perspective. We ought not to underestimate the depth and amplitude of the shock that these changes could cause, changes which might seem fantastic and senseless to healthy, everyday common sense. It was impossible to maintain oneself at such heights continuously; this was a conversion that needed always to be reconquered. It was probably because of such difficulties that, as we learn in Damascius' *Life of Isidorus*, the philosopher Sallustius used to declare that philosophy was impossible for man.[164] He probably meant by this that philosophers were not capable of remaining philosophers at every instant of their lives. Rather, even though they kept the title of "philosophers," they would be sure to fall back into the habits of everyday life. The Skeptics, for instance, refused outright to live philosophically, deliberately choosing to "live like everybody else," [165] although not until *after* having made a philosophical detour so intense that it is hard to believe that their "everyday life" was quite so "everyday" as they seem to have pretended.

Our claim has been, then, that philosophy in antiquity was a spiritual exercise. As for philosophical theories: they were either placed explicitly in the service of spiritual practice, as was the case in Stoicism and Epicureanism, or else they were taken as the objects of intellectual exercises, that is, of a practice of the contemplative life which, in the last analysis, was itself nothing other than a spiritual exercise. It is impossible to understand the philosophical theories of antiquity without taking into account this concrete perspective, since this is what gives them their true meaning.

When we read the works of ancient philosophers, the perspective we have described should cause us to give increased attention to the existential attitudes underlying the dogmatic edifices we encounter. Whether we have to do with dialogues as in the case of Plato, class notes as in the case of Aristotle, treatises like those of Plotinus, or commentaries like those of Proclus, a philosopher's works cannot be interpreted without taking into consideration the concrete situation which gave birth to them. They are the products of a philosophical school, in the most concrete sense of the term, in which a master forms his disciples, trying to guide them to self-transformation and

-realization. Thus, the written work is a reflection of pedagogical, psycha-gogic, and methodological preoccupations.

Although every written work is a monologue, the philosophical work is always implicitly a dialogue. The dimension of the possible interlocutor is always present within it. This explains the incoherencies and contradictions which modern historians discover with astonishment in the works of ancient philosophers.[166] In philosophical works such as these, thought cannot be expressed according to the pure, absolute necessity of a systematic order. Rather, it must take into account the level of the interlocutor, and the concrete tempo of the *logos* in which it is expressed. It is the economy proper to a given written *logos* which conditions its thought content, and it is the *logos* that constitutes a living system which, in the words of Plato, "ought to have its own body . . . it must not lack either head or feet: it must have a middle and extremities so composed as to suit each other and the whole work." [167]

Each *logos* is a "system," but the totality of *logoi* written by an author does *not* constitute a system. This is obviously true in the case of Plato's dialogues, but it is equally true in the case of the lectures of Aristotle. For Aristotle's writings are indeed neither more nor less than lecture-notes; and the error of many Aristotelian scholars has been that they have forgotten this fact, and imagined instead that they were manuals or systematic treatises, intended to propose a complete exposition of a systematic doctrine. Consequently, they have been astonished at the inconsistencies, and even contradictions, they discovered between one writing and another. As Düring[168] has convincingly shown, Aristotle's various *logoi* correspond to the concrete situations created by specific academic debates. Each lesson corresponds to different conditions and a specific problematic. It has inner unity, but its notional content does not overlap precisely with that of any other lesson. Moreover, Aristotle had no intention of setting forth a complete system of reality.[169] Rather, he wished to train his students in the technique of using correct methods in logic, the natural sciences, and ethics. Düring gives an excellent description of the Aristotelian method:

> the most characteristic feature in Aristotle is his incessant discussion of problems. Almost every important assertion is an answer to a question put in a certain way, and is valid only as an answer to this particular question. That which is really interesting in Aristotle is his framing of the problems, not his answers. It is part of his method of inquiry to approach a problem or a group of problems again and again from different angles. His own words are ἄλλην ἀρχὴν ποιησάμενοι ["now, taking a different starting-point . . ."] . . . From different starting-points, ἀρχαὶ he strikes off into different lines of thought and ultimately reaches inconsistent answers. Take as example his discussion

of the soul . . . in each case the answer is the consequence of the manner in which he posits the problem. In short, it is possible to explain this type of inconsistencies as natural results of the method he applies.[170]

In the Aristotelian method of "different starting-points," we can recognize the method Aristophanes attributed to Socrates, and we have seen to what extent all antiquity remained faithful to this method.[171] For this reason, Düring's description can in fact apply, *mutatis mutandis*, to almost all the philosophers of antiquity. Such a method, consisting not in setting forth a system, but in giving precise responses to precisely limited questions, is the heritage – lasting throughout antiquity – of the dialectical method; that is to say, of the dialectical *exercise*.

To return to Aristotle: there is a profound truth in the fact that he himself used to call his courses *methodoi*.[172] On this point, moreover, the Aristotelian spirit corresponds to the spirit of the Platonic Academy, which was, above all, a school which formed its pupils for an eventual political role, and a research institute where investigations were carried out in a spirit of free discussion.[173]

It may be of interest to compare Aristotle's methodology with that of Plotinus. We learn from Porphyry that Plotinus took the themes for his writings from the problems which came up in the course of his teaching.[174] Plotinus' various *logoi*, situated as they are within a highly specific problematic, are responses to precise questions. They are adapted to the needs of his disciples, and are an attempt to bring about in them a specific psychagogic effect. We must not make the mistake of imagining that they are the successive chapters of a vast, systematic exposition of Plotinus' thought. In each of these *logoi*, we encounter the spiritual method particular to Plotinus, but there is no lack of incoherence and contradictions on points of detail when we compare the doctrinal content of the respective treatises.[175]

When we first approach the Neoplatonic commentaries on Plato and Aristotle, we have the impression that their form and content are dictated exclusively by doctrinal and exegetical considerations. Upon closer examination, however, we realize that, in each commentary, the exegetical method and doctrinal content are functions of the spiritual level of the audience to which the commentary is addressed. The reason for this is that there existed a *cursus* of philosophical instruction, based on spiritual progress. One did not read the same texts to beginners, to those in progress, and to those already having achieved perfection, and the concepts appearing in the commentaries are also functions of the spiritual capacities of their addressees. Consequently, doctrinal content can vary considerably from one commentary to another, even when written by the same author. This does not mean that the commentator changed his doctrines, but that the needs of his disciples were different.[176] In the literary genre of *parenesis*, used for exhorting beginners, one could, in order to bring about a specific effect in the interlocutor's soul, utilize the arguments of a rival school. For example, a Stoic might say, "even if pleasure *is* the good of the soul (as the Epicureans would have it), *nevertheless* we must purify ourselves of passion." [177] Marcus Aurelius exhorted himself in the same manner. If, he writes, the world is a mere aggregate of atoms, as the Epicureans would have it, then death is not to be feared.[178]

Moreover, we ought not to forget that many a philosophical demonstration derives its evidential force not so much from abstract reasoning as from an experience which is at the same time a spiritual exercise. We have seen that this was the case for the Plotinian demonstration of the immortality of the soul. Let the soul practice virtue, he said, and it will understand that it is immortal.[179] We find an analogous example in the Christian writer Augustine. In his *On the Trinity*, Augustine presents a series of psychological images of the Trinity which do not form a coherent system, and which have consequently been the source of a great deal of trouble for his commentators. In fact, however, Augustine is not trying to present a systematic theory of trinitarian analogies. Rather, by making the soul turn inward upon itself, he wants to make it *experience* the fact that it is an image of the Trinity. In his words: "These trinities occur within us and *are* within us, when we recall, look at, and wish for such things." [180] Ultimately, it is in the triple act of remembering God, knowing God, and loving God that the soul discovers itself to be the image of the Trinity.

From the preceding examples, we may get some idea of the change in perspective that may occur in our reading and interpretation of the philosophical works of antiquity when we consider them from the point of view of the practice of spiritual exercises. Philosophy then appears in its original aspect: not as a theoretical construct, but as a method for training people to live and to look at the world in a new way. It is an attempt to transform mankind. Contemporary historians of philosophy are today scarcely inclined to pay attention to this aspect, although it is an essential one. The reason for this is that, in conformity with a tradition inherited from the Middle Ages and from the modern era, they consider philosophy to be a purely abstract-theoretical activity. Let us briefly recall how this conception came into existence.

It seems to be the result of the absorption of *philosophia* by Christianity. Since its inception, Christianity has presented itself as a *philosophia*, insofar as it assimilated into itself the traditional practices of spiritual exercises. We see this occurring in Clement of Alexandria, Origen, Augustine, and monasticism.[181] With the advent of medieval Scholasticism, however, we find a clear distinction being drawn between *theologia* and *philosophia*. Theology became conscious of its autonomy *qua* supreme science, while philosophy was emptied of its spiritual exercises which, from now on, were relegated to Christian mysticism and ethics. Reduced to the rank of a "handmaid of theology," philosophy's role was henceforth to furnish theology with conceptual – and hence purely theoretical – material. When, in the modern age, philosophy regained its autonomy, it still retained many features inherited from this medieval conception. In particular, it maintained its purely theoretical character, which even evolved in the direction of a more and more thorough systematization.[182] Not until Nietzsche, Bergson, and existentialism does philosophy consciously return to being a concrete attitude, a way of life and of seeing the world. For their part, however, contemporary historians of ancient thought have, as a general rule, remained prisoners of the old, purely theoretical conception of philosophy. Contemporary structuralist tendencies do not, moreover, incline them to correct this misconception, since spiritual exercises introduce into consideration a subjective, mutable, and dynamic component, which does not fit comfortably into the structuralists' models of explanation.

We have now returned to the contemporary period and our initial point of departure, the lines by G. Friedmann we quoted at the beginning of this study. We have tried to reply to those who, like Friedmann, ask themselves the question: how is it possible to practice spiritual exercises in the twentieth century? We have tried to do so by recalling the existence of a highly rich and varied Western tradition. There can be no question, of course, of mechanically imitating stereotyped schemas. After all, did not Socrates and Plato urge their disciples to find the solutions they needed by themselves? And yet, we cannot afford to ignore such a valuable quantity of experience, accumulated over millennia. To mention but one example, Stoicism and Epicureanism do seem to correspond to two opposite but inseparable poles of our inner life: tension and relaxation, duty and serenity, moral conscience and the joy of existence.[183]

Vauvenargues said, "A truly new and truly original book would be one which made people love old truths."[184] It is my hope that I have been "truly new and truly original" in this sense, since my goal has indeed been to make people love a few old truths. Old truths: . . . there are some truths whose meaning will never be exhausted by the generations of man. It is not that they are difficult; on the contrary, they are often extremely simple.[185] Often, they even appear to be banal. Yet for their meaning to be understood, these truths must be *lived*, and constantly re-experienced. Each generation must take up, from scratch, the task of learning to read and to re-read these "old truths."

We spend our lives "reading," that is, carrying out exegeses, and sometimes even exegeses of exegeses. Epictetus tells us what he thinks of such activities:

"Come and listen to me read my commentaries . . . I will explain Chrysippus to you like no one else can, and I'll provide a complete analysis of his entire text . . . If necessary, I can even add the views of Antipater and Archedemos" . . . So it's for this, is it, that young men are to leave their fatherlands and their own parents: to come and listen to you explain words? Trifling little words?[186]

And yet we have forgotten *how* to read: how to pause, liberate ourselves from our worries, return into ourselves, and leave aside our search for subtlety and originality, in order to meditate calmly, ruminate, and let the texts speak to us. This, too, is a spiritual exercise, and one of the most difficult. As Goethe said: "Ordinary people don't know how much time and effort it takes to learn how to read. I've spent eighty years at it, and I still can't say that I've reached my goal." [187]

NOTES

1 Georges Friedmann, *La Puissance et la Sagesse*, Paris 1970, p. 359. On June 30, 1977, shortly before his death, Friedmann was kind enough to write me to tell me how much he had been "moved" by my reaction to his book. In the same letter, he referred me to the final remarks he had presented at the close of the Colloquium organdies by the CNRS [National Centre of Scientific Research], 3–5 May, 1977, to commemorate the tricentenary of the death of Spinoza. There, apropos of a passage from Spinoza's *Ethics*, he spoke of the Stoicism of the ancients. Cf. Georges Friedmann, "Le Sage et notre siècle," *Revue de Synthèse* 99 (1978), p. 288.

2 Friedmann, *La Puissance*, pp. 183–284.

3 Epictetus, *Discourses*, 3, 22, 20: "From now on my mind [*dianoia*] is the material with which I have to work, as the carpenter has his timbers, the shoemaker his hides."

4 [Ignatius of Loyola (ca. 1491–1556), founder of the Jesuit Order, wrote his handbook entitled *Spiritual Exercises* beginning in 1522. The goal of the work was to purify its reader from sin and lead him to God, via a four-stage meditation: beginning with meditation on sin, the reader progresses to considering the kingdom of Christ, the passion, and finally the risen and glorified Lord. – Trans.]

5 In Latin literature, cf., for example, Rufinus, *History of the Monks* [written ca. AD 403], ch. 29, PL 21, 410D: "Cum quadraginta annis fuisset in exercitiis spiritualibus conversatus" ["After he had become conversant with spiritual exercises for forty years" – Trans.], and ch. 29 (*ibid.*, col. 453D): "Ad acriora semetipsum spiritalis vitae extendit exercitia" ["He exerted himself to the more zealous exercises of the spiritual life." – Trans.].

In the Greek world, we find this terminology already in Clement of Alexandria, *Stromata*, 4, 6, 27, 1. Cf. J. Leclercq, "Exercices spirituels," in *Dictionnaire de Spiritualité*, vol. 4, cols 1902–8.

6 In his very important work *Seelenführung. Methodik der Exerzitien in der Antike*, Munich 1954, Paul Rabbow situated Ignatius of Loyola's *Exercitia spiritualia* back within the ancient tradition.

7 There have been relatively few studies devoted to this subject. The fundamental work is that of Rabbow, *Seelenführung*; cf. also the review of Rabbow's work by G. Luck, *Gnomon* 28 (1956), pp. 268–71; B.-L. Hijmans Jr ἌΣΚΕΣΙΣ, *Notes on Epictetus' Educational System*, Assen 1959; A.C. Van Geytenbeek, *Musonius Rufus*

and Greek Diatribes, Assen 1963; W. Schmid, "Epikur," in *Reallexikon für Antike und Christentum*, vol. 5, 1962, cols 735–40; I. Hadot "Épicure et l'enseignement philosophique hellénistique et romain," in *Actes du VIIIe Congrès Budé*, Paris 1969; H.-G. Ingenkamp, *Plutarchs Schriften über die Heilung der Seele*, Göttingen 1971; V. Goldschmidt, *Le système stoïcien et l'idée de temps*, 4th edn, Paris 1985.

8 Pseudo-Galen, *Philosophical History*, 5, in H. Diels, ed., *Doxographi Graeci*, p. 602, 18; Pseudo-Plutarch, *Placita*, I, 2, *ibid*, p. 273, 14. The idea originates with the Cynics; cf. Diogenes Laertius, 6, 70–1, and now the important work of M.-O. Goulet-Cazé, *L'Ascèse cynique. Un commentaire de Diogène Laërce, VI, 70, 71*, Paris 1986. Lucian (*Toxaris*, 27; *Vitarum auctio*, 7) uses the word *askesis* to designate philosophical sects themselves. On the need for philosophical exercises, cf. Epictetus, *Discourses*, 2, 9, 13; 2, 18, 26; 3, 8, 1; 3, 12, 1–7; 4, 6, 16; 4, 12, 13; Musonius Rufus, p. 22, 9ff Hense; Seneca, *Letter*, 90, 46.

9 Seneca, *Letter*, 20, 2: "Philosophy teaches us how to act, not how to talk."

10 Epictetus, *Discourses*, I, 4, 14ff: spiritual progress does not consist in learning how to explain Chrysippus better, but in transforming one's own freedom; cf. 2, 16, 34.

11 Epictetus, *Discourses*, I, 15, 2: "The subject-matter of the art of living (i.e. philosophy) is the life of every individual;" cf. I, 26, 7. Plutarch, *Table-talk*, I, 2, 623B: "Since philosophy is the art of living, it should not be kept apart from any pastime."

12 Galen, *Galen On the Passions and Errors of the Soul*, I, 4, p. 11, 4 Marquardt: "make yourself better."

13 On conversion, cf. Arthur Darby Nock, *Conversion*, Oxford 1933, pp. 164–86; Pierre Hadot "Epistrophè et Metanoia dans l'historie de la philosophie," in *Actes du IIe Congrès International de Philosophie* 12, Brussels 1953, pp. 31–6; Pierre Hadot, "Conversio," in *Historiches Wörterbuch der Philosophie*, vol. 1, cols 1033–6, 1971.

14 Seneca, *Letter*, 6, 1: "I feel, my dear Lucilius, that I am being not only reformed, but transformed . . . I therefore wish to impart to you this sudden change in myself."

15 Cicero, *Tusculan Disputations*, 3, 6: "Truly, philosophy is the medicine of the soul"; cf. Epictetus, *Discourses*, 2, 21, 15; 22. Chrysippus wrote a *Therapeutics of the Passions*; cf. *SVF*, vol. 3, §474. Cf. also the aphorism attributed to Epicurus by Usener (*Epicurea*, fr. 221 = Porphyry *Ad Marcellam*, 31, p. 294, 7–8 Nauck): "Vain is the word of that philosopher which does not heal any suffering of man." According to H. Chadwick, *The Sentences of Sextus*, Cambridge 1959, p. 178, n. 336, this sentence is Pythagorean. Cf. Epictetus, *Discourses*, 3, 23, 30: "The philosopher's school is a clinic."

16 The Epicurean method must be distinguished from that of the Stoics. According to Olympiodorus, *Commentary on the First Alcibiades of Plato*, pp. 6, 6ff; 54, 15ff; 145, 12ff Westerink, the Stoics cure contraries by contraries; the Pythagoreans let the patient taste the passions with his fingertips; and Socrates treats his patients by homeopathy, leading them, for example, from the love of terrestrial

beauty to the love of eternal beauty. Cf. also Proclus, *In Alcibordem*, p. 151, 14, vol. 2, p. 217 Segonds.

17 Cf. below. We find the distinction between what depends on us and what does not depend on us in Epictetus, *Discourses*, I, 1, 7; I, 4, 27; I, 22, 9; 2, 5, 4; and Epictetus, *Manual*, ch. 4.

18 Many Stoic treatises entitled *On Exercises* have been lost; cf. the list of titles in Diogenes Laertius, 7, 166–7. A short treatise entitled *On Exercise*, by Musonius Rufus, has been preserved (pp. 22–7 Hense). After a general introduction concerning the need for exercises in philosophy, Rufus recommends physical exercises: becoming used to foul weather, hunger, and thirst. These exercises benefit the soul, giving it strength and temperance. He then recommends exercises designed particularly for the soul, which, says Rufus, consist in steeping oneself in the demonstrations and principles bearing on the distinction between real and apparent goods and evils. With the help of these exercises, we will get into the habit of not fearing what most people consider as evils: poverty, suffering, and death. One chapter of Epictetus' *Discourses* is dedicated to *askesis* (3, 12, 1–7). Cf. below. The treatise *On Exercise* by the PseudoPlutarch, preserved in Arabic (cf. J. Gildmeister and F. Bücheler, "PseudoPlutarchos *Peri askêseôs*," *Rheinisches Museum* NF 27 (1872), pp. 520–38), is of no particular interest in this context.

19 Philo Judaeus, *Who is the Heir of Divine Things*, 253.

20 Philo Judaeus, *Allegorical Interpretations*, 3, 18.

21 The word *therapeiai* can also mean acts of worship, and this meaning would be entirely possible in Philo's mind. Nevertheless, in the present context it seems to me that it designates the therapeutics of the passions. Cf. Philo Judaeus, *On the Special Laws*, I, 191; 197; 230; 2, 17.

22 *Ton kalon mnemai*. Cf. Galen, *Galen On the Passions and Errors of the Soul*, I, 5, 25, pp. 19, 8 Marquardt.

23 On this theme, cf. Rabbow, *Seelenführung*, pp. 249–50; Hijmans, *ΑΣΚΕΣΣΙΣ*, pp. 68–70. Cf. especially Epictetus, *Discourses*, 4, 12, 1–21.

24 The idea of tension (*tonos*) is particularly in evidence in Epictetus, *Discourses*, 4, 12, 15 and 19. The concept of *tonos* is central to Stoicism, as is that of relaxation (*anesis*) in Epicureanism. Cf. F. Ravaisson, *Essai sur la Metaphysique d'Austote*, Paris, 1846, repr. Hildesheim 1963, p. 117.

25 Epictetus, *Discourses*, 4, 12, 7; cf. Marcus Aurelius, *Meditations*, 3, 13; Galen, *Galen On the Passions and Errors of the Soul*, 1, 9, 51, p. 40, 10 Marquardt.

26 Epictetus, *Discourses*, 4, 12, 15–18.

27 Cf. below.

28 Marcus Aurelius, *Meditations*, 7, 54; cf. 3, 12; 8, 36; 9, 6.

29 Only the present depends on us, since our free action cannot be extended either to the past or to the future. Free action is that which either brings about something in the present, or else accepts the present event, which has been willed by fate; cf. Marcus Aurelius, *Meditations*, 2, 14; 4, 26, 5; 12, 26; Seneca, *On Benefits*, 7, 2, 4: "Rejoicing in these present events."

30 Marcus Aurelius, *Meditations*, 3, 10; 2, 14; 8, 36.

31 Cf., for instance, Marcus Aurelius, *Meditations*, 4, 23. Marcus also stresses the cosmic value of the instant in 5, 8, 3: "This event occurred for you, was prescribed for you, and had some kind of relationship to you, having been woven since the beginning, from the most ancient causes."

32 Epictetus, *Discourses*, 2, 16, 2–3; 3, 8, 1–5.

33 Cf. Rabbow, *Seelenführung*, pp. 124–30, 334–6; I. Hadot, *Seneca und die griechisch-römische Tradition der Seelenleitung*, Berlin 1969, pp. 57–8. See also Galen, *Galen On the Passions and Errors of the Soul*, 1, 5, 24, p. 18, 19 Marquardt; Seneca, *On Benefits*, 7, 2, 1; Marcus Aurelius, *Meditations*, 7, 63.

34 Seneca, *On Benefits*, 7, 2, 1–2; Epictetus, *Discourses*, 3, 3, 14–16.

35 On the role of rhetoric in spiritual exercises, see Rabbow, *Seelenführung*, pp. 55–90; Hijmans, *ΑΣΚΕΣΙΣ*, p. 89; I. Hadot, *Seneca*, pp. 17, 184. For examples in Plutarch, see Ingenkamp, *Plutarchs Schriften*, pp. 99ff.

36 Marcus Aurelius, *Meditations*, 7, 58: "In every contingency, *keep before your eyes* those who, when the same thing befell them, were saddened, astonished, resentful. Where are they now? Nowhere." Epictetus, *Manual*, ch. 21: "*Keep before your eyes* every day death and exile, and everything that seems terrible, but most of all death; and then you will never have any abject thought, nor excessive desire." On this exercise, see Rabbow, *Seelenführung*, p. 330.

37 Cf. the passage from Philo cited above. Hijmans, *ΑΣΚΕΣΙΣ*, p. 69, calls attention to the frequency of the expression "Remember!" in Epictetus. It recurs quite often in Marcus Aurelius, for instance, *Meditations*, 2, 4; 8, 15; 29. Cf. Galen, *Galen On the Passions and Errors of the Soul*, 1, 5, 25, p. 19, 8–10 Marquardt: "With the help of memory, keep 'at hand' the ugliness of those who succumb to anger, and the beauty of those who master it."

38 It is only after much hesitation that I have translated *melete* by "meditation." In fact, *melete* and its Latin equivalent *meditatio* designate "preparatory exercises," in particular those of rhetoricians. If I have finally resigned myself to adopting the translation "meditation," it is because the exercise designated by *melete* corresponds, in the last analysis, rather well to what we nowadays term *meditation*: an effort to assimilate an idea, notion, or principle, and make them come alive in the soul. We must not, however, lose sight of the term's ambiguity: meditation is exercise, and exercise is meditation. For instance, the "pre-meditation" of death is a "pre-exercise" of death; the *cottidiana meditatio* cited in the following note could just as well be translated as "daily exercises."

39 See Rabbow, *Seelenführung*, pp. 23–150, 325–8; and Seneca, *On Benefits*, 7, 2, 1: "These are the things that my friend Demetrius says the beginner in philosophy must grasp with both hands, these are the precepts that he must never let go. Rather, he must cling fast to them and make them a part of himself, and by daily meditation reach the point where these salutary maxims occur to him of their own accord." Cf. also Galen, *Galen On the Passions and Errors of the Soul*, 1, 5, 25, p. 19, 13 Marquardt.

40 ["Pre-meditation of misfortunes" – Trans.] On the *praemeditatio malorum*, see Rabbow, *Seelenführung*, pp. 169–70; I. Hadot, *Seneca*, pp. 60–1.

41 See above.

42 See above.

43 Cf. Ingenkamp, *Plutarchs Schuften*, pp. 99–105; Rabbow, *Seelenführung*, pp. 148, 340–2.

44 Cf. Galen, *Galen On the Passions and Errors of the Soul*, I, 5, 24, p. 18, 12 Marquardt: "As soon as we get up in the morning, we must consider in advance, with regard to the various acts we will perform throughout the day, whether it is better to live as a slave of our passions, or to utilize reason against all of them." Marcus Aurelius, *Meditations*, 2, 1, 1: "At the break of dawn, say to yourself: 'I'm going to come across a nosy person, an ingrate, a thug, a cheat, a jealous man, and an anti-social man. All these defects have afflicted them because of their ignorance of what is truly good and evil.' " Cf ibid, 5, 1, 1: "In the morning, when you have trouble getting up, have this thought at hand [*procheiron*]: 'I'm getting up to do a man's work.' "

45 On the examination of the conscience, see Rabbow, *Seelenführung*, pp. 180–8, 344–7; I. Hadot, *Seneca*, pp. 68–70; Hijmans, *ΑΣΚΕΣΙΣ*, p. 88.

46 Cf. Plutarch, *How One may Know One is Making Progress in Virtue*, §12, 82F: "It was Zeno's belief that everyone could, thanks to his dreams, have knowledge of what progress he was making. One has made real progress if he no longer dreams that he is giving in to some shameful passion, or giving his consent to something evil or unjust – or even committing it – and if, instead, the soul's faculties of representation and affectivity, relaxed by reason, shine as if in an ocean of diaphanous serenity, untroubled by waves."

47 See below.

48 This is the domain of spiritual guidance; see I. Hadot, *Seneca*, pp. 5–97. Note especially Galen, *Galen On the Passions and Errors of the Soul*, 1, 7, 36, p. 27, 22 Marquardt: we are to ask an older man to tell us frankly about our defects.

49 Cf. Rabbow, *Seelenführung*, p. 311, n. 64; I. Hadot, *Seneca*, p. 59. Marcus Aurelius' *Meditations* are, of course, the example *par excellence* of this. Note also Horace, *Satires*, I, 4, 138: "When I have some spare time, I amuse myself by writing these thoughts down on paper."

50 The phrase is Descartes', but it gives good expression to the Stoic ideal of inner coherence. [This is the third of René Descartes' well-known "four laws" which he exposes in Part 2 of his *Discourse on the Method*. – Trans.]

51 On this subject, see P. Laín Entralgo, "Die platonische Rationalisienung der Besprechung (ἐπῳδή) und die Erfindung der Psychotherapie durch das Wort," *Hermes* 68 (1958), pp. 298–323; P. Laín Entralgo, *The Therapy of the Word in Classical Antiquity*, New Haven 1970; and the review of this latter work by F. Kudlien, *Gnomon* 45 (1973), pp. 410–12.

52 ["Collections of aphorisms" – Trans.] Cf. Rabbow, *Seelenführung*, pp. 215–22, 352–4; G.A. Gerhard, *Phoinix von Kolophon*, Leipzig 1909, pp. 228–84; I. Hadot, *Seneca*, pp. 16–17. See also Seneca, *Letter*, 94, 27; 43; 98, 5; 108, 9. On collections of poetical and philosophical aphorisms, see W. Spoerri, "Gnome," in *Der kleine Pauly*, vol. 2, 1967, cols 822–9; Chadwick, *Sentences of Sextus*;

T. Klauser, "Apophthegma," *Reallexicon für Antike und Christentun* I (1950), pp. 545–50. See also P. Wendland, *Anaximenes von Lampsakos*, Berlin 1905, pp. 100ff.

53 The term *akroasis* as used by Philo could designate, among other things, attending a course in philosophy; cf. Epictetus, *Discourses*, 3, 23, 27; 38. Normally, the course included the reading, with commentary, of a philosophical text (*anagnosis*), often done by the disciple and criticized by the master (cf. Epictetus, *Discourses*, I, 26, 1; Porphyry, *Life of Plotinus*, ch. 14). See also I. Bruns, *De schola Epictetc*, Kiel 1897. This does not, of course, exclude the individual reading of philosophical texts; cf. Epictetus, *Discourses*, 4, 4, 14–18 (where Epictetus reproaches his disciples for reading texts without putting them into practice). After the reading with commentary, a philosophy class would normally include a discussion (*diatribe*) with the audience, as well as individual discussions (cf. I. Hadot, *Seneca*, p. 65). For the listener, this entire ensemble could be a spiritual exercise. With regard to reading, we should add that exegesis, whether literal or allegorical, was one of the most important spiritual exercises at the end of antiquity, among both pagans and Christians.

54 On the educational program in Hellenistic schools, with its transition from aphorisms to *epitomai* (summaries of basic principles), and finally to full-scale treatises, see I. Hadot 1969a, pp. 53–6; 1969b.

55 On the exercise of definition, see below.

56 On this exercise, see Rabbow, *Seelenführung*, pp. 42–9.

57 Philo's expression "indifference to indifferent things" corresponds exactly to the spiritual exercises mentioned by Marcus Aurelius, *Meditations*, 11, 16: "Our soul finds within itself the power to live a perfectly happy life, if we can remain indifferent towards indifferent things." This formula seems to be a reminiscence of the definition of the goal of human life according to Aristo of Chios (*SVF*, I, §360, = Clement of Alexandria, *Stromata*, 2, 21, 129, 6, p. 183, 14–16 Stählin): "And why should I mention Aristo? He said the goal was indifference, but he leaves 'the indifferent' as simply 'the indifferent.'" On this theme, see below. We must bear in mind that here "indifference" does not mean a lack of interest, but rather equal love for each of life's instants; that is, we are not to make any "difference" between them.

58 See Rabbow, *Seelenführung*, pp. 223–49; Ingenkamp, *Plutarchs Schüften*, pp. 105–18. The technical term for this process is *ethismos*.

59 Epicurus, *Gnomologium Vaticanum*, §64. Cf. also *Letter to Menoecus*, §122: "No one can come too early or too late to secure the health of his soul."

60 Epicurus, *Ratae Sententiae*, §11: "If we were not troubled by our suspicions of the phenomena of the sky and about death, fearing that it concerns us, and also by our failure to grasp the limits of pains and desires, we should have no need of natural science [*physiologia*]." On Epicurean theology, see Schmid, "Epikur"; D. Lemke, *Die Theologie Epikurs*, Munich 1973.

61 Epicurus, *Ratae Sententiae*, §29; Epicurus, *Letter to Menoecus*, §127.

62 Epicurus, *Gnom. Vat.* §33. Cf. A.-J. Festugière, *Epicure et ses dieux*, Paris 1946, p. 44.

63 Epicurus Fr. 469, p. 300, 26ff Usener.

64 On these Epicurean exercises of meditation, see Schmid, "Epikur," p. 744; Rabbow, *Seelenführung*, pp. 129, 336–8; I. Hadot, *Seneca*, pp. 52–3. Cf. Epicurus, *Letter to Menoecus*, §135, 5–8: "Meditate therefore on these things and things like them night and day by yourself, and with someone similar to yourself, and you shall be disturbed, either awake or asleep, but you shall live like a god among men." Ibid, §123, 1–2: "That which I used constantly to recommend to you, put it into practice and *meditate upon it* [*meleta*], considering them to be the elements of the living well." Ibid, §124, 7–8: "*Become accustomed* [*sunethize*] to considering that death is nothing to us."

65 Cf. Philodemus, *Adversus sophistas*, col. 4, 10–14, p. 87 Sbordone, cited by Festugière, *Epicure*, p. 46, n. 1, Schmid, "Epikur," col. 744; translation by A.A. Long and D.N. Sedley, *The Hellenistic Philosophers*, vol. 1: *Translations of the Principal Sources, with Philosophical Commentary*, Cambridge 1987, repr. 1988, p. 156, section J; Greek text, vol. 2, *Greek and Latin Texts with Notes and Bibliography*, p. 161. The technical term used here to indicate that this aphorism must always be "at hand" is *parhepomenon*.

66 For instance, the *Ratae Sententiae* or *Kuriai Doxai* ["Principal Doctrines"], which were known to Cicero (*On Ends*, 2, 20), and the *Gnom. Vat.*

67 On the curriculum in the Epicurean school, see above.

68 Epicurus, *Letter to Pythocles*, §85 = Long and Sedley, *Hellenistic Philosophers*, section 18 C (1), vol. 1, pp. 91–2; Greek text, vol. 2, p. 94. Cf. *Letter to Herodotus*, §37: "I recommend . . . constant occupation in the investigation of the science of nature, since I consider that this activity provides the greatest serenity in life."

69 Lucretius, *On the Nature of Things*, 3, 16f, 28ff. This passage is quite remarkable. On the one hand, it illustrates the fact that Epicurean physics was a true source of pleasure for the sage: it allowed him to have a grandiose imaginative vision of the formation and dissolution of the universe in the infinity of space. On the other, it throws light on one of the most fundamental feelings of the human experience: *horror* in the face of the enigma of nature. One thinks of Goethe's formulation in *Faust*, Part 2, 6272ff: "The shudder is the best part of man. However dearly the world makes him pay for it, he feels the Prodigious deep inside, seized with astonishment." ("Das Schaudern ist der Menschheit bestes Teil. Wie auch die Welt ihm das Gefühl verteure, Ergriffen fühlt er tief das Ungeheure.") On Epicurean spiritual exercises in general, see P.-H. Schrijvers, *Horror ac Divina Voluptas. Études sur la poétique et la poésie de Lucrèce*, Amsterdam 1970.

70 I. Hadot, *Seneca*, pp. 62–3; Rabbow, *Seelenführung*, p. 280. Cf. Cicero, *On Ends*, I, 17, 55; I, 19, 62; *Tusculan Disputations*, 15, 32–3.

71 Epicurus, *Gnom. Vat.*, §75: "The saying, 'Wait till the end of a long life' (to know if you've been happy) is ungrateful towards the good things of the past." Cf. ibid, §69; §19: "He who has forgotten yesterday's good fortune is already an old man."

72 Cf. E. Hoffmann, "Epikur," in M. Dessoir, ed., *Die Geschichte der Philosophie*, vol. I, Wiesbaden 1925, p. 223: "Existence is to be considered, first and foremost, as a pure accident, so that it may then be lived as a completely unique

miracle. We must first realize that existence, inevitably, is a one-shot affair, in order to be able to celebrate that in it which is irreplaceable and unique."

73 Epicurus, *Gnom. Vat.*, §14. Cf. Lucretius, *On the Nature of Things*, 3, 957–60, and G. Rodis-Lewis, *Épicure et son école*, Paris, 1975, pp. 269–83.

74 Horace, *Odes*, I, 11, 7: "Dum loquimur, fugerit invida / aetas: carpe diem, quam minimum credula postero." Cf. ibid, 2, 16, 25: "A soul content with the present."

75 On Epicurean friendship, see Schmid, "Epikur," cols 740–55; Festugière, *Epicure*, pp. 36–70; I. Hadot 1969a, pp. 63ff; Rodis-Lewis, *Epicure*, pp. 362–9.

76 Cf. S. Sudhaus, "Epikur als Beichtirater," *Archiv für Religionswissenschaft* 14 (1911), pp. 647ff. The fundamental text is Philodemus, *Peri parrhêsias* ["On Free Speech"], ed. A. Olivieri, Leipzig 1914; cf. I. Hadot, *Seneca*, p. 63; M. Gigante 1968, pp. 196–217.

77 Schmid, "Epikur," cols. 741–3.

78 Festugière, *Epicure*, p. 69.

79 The prehistory of spiritual exercises is to be sought, first of all, in traditional rules of life and popular exhortation (cf. I. Hadot, *Seneca*, pp. 10–22). Must we go back further still, and look for it first of all in Pythagoreanism, and then, beyond Pythagoras, in magico-religious/shamanistic traditions of respiratory techniques and mnemonic exercises? This theory, defended by E.R. Dodds, *The Greeks and the Irrational* (= Sather Classical Lectures 25), 3rd edn, Berkeley/London 1963; L. Gernet, *Anthropologie de la Grèce antique*, Paris 1968, pp. 423–5; J.-P. Vernant, *Mythe et pensée chez les Grecs*, Paris 1971, pp. 94ff, 108ff; M. Détienne, *De la pensée religieuse à la pensée philosophique. La notion de Daimon dans le pythagoisme ancien*, Paris 1963; M. Détienne, *Les maîtres de vénilé dans la Grèce archaïque*, Paris 1967, pp. 124ff; H. Joly, *Le renversement platonicien*, Paris 1974, pp. 67–70; is entirely plausible. However, I shall not go into the matter here, first of all owing to my lack of competence in the field of the anthropology of prehistory and of archaic Greece, and secondly, because it seems to me that the problems inherent in the history of Pythagoreanism are extremely complex, so that it presupposes a rigorous criticism of our sources (many of which are late, idyllic projections, reflecting Stoic and Platonic concepts). Thirdly, the spiritual exercises under discussion here are mental processes which have nothing in common with cataleptic trances, but, on the contrary, respond to a rigorous demand for rational control, a demand which, as far as we are concerned, emerges with the figure of Socrates.

80 The *historical* Socrates is a probably insoluble enigma. But the *figure* of Socrates, as it is sketched by Plato, Xenophon, and Aristophanes, is a well-attested historical fact. When, in what follows, I speak of "Socrates," I shall be referring to this *figure* of Socrates. See below, ch. 5, "The Figure of Socrates."

81 By using quotation marks, I wish to underline the fact that we are not dealing with authentically Socratic dialogues, but with literary compositions which imitate – more or less faithfully – the dialogues of Socrates, or in which the figure of Socrates plays a role. It is in this sense that Plato's dialogues are Socratic.

82 Plato, *Laches*, 187e–188b.

83 Aristotle, *Sophistical Refutations*, 183b8: "Socrates used to ask questions and not to answer them – for he used to confess that he did not know." Cf. Plato, *Apology*, 21d5: "I do not think that I know what I do not know."

84 Plato, *Apology*, 30e1–5: "If you put me to death, you will not easily find anyone to take my place . . . God has specially appointed me to this city, as though it were a large thoroughbred horse which . . . needs the stimulation of some stinging fly."

85 On taking care of oneself, cf. Plato, *Apology*, 29d; 31b; 36c.

86 Ibid, 29d5–e3. Cf. 30a6–b1: "For I spend my time going about trying to persuade you, young and old, to make your first and chief concern not for your bodies nor for your possessions, but for the highest welfare of your souls."

87 Plato, *Apology*, 36b4–c6.

88 Plato, *Symposium*, 215e6–216a5.

89 In this respect, Stoic exhortation remains Socratic. More than one of Epictetus' *Discourses* seems to imitate the Socratic style; cf., for instance, *Discourses*, I, 11, 1–40. Epictetus praises the Socratic method at 2, 12, 5–16, but he emphasizes that, in his day, it is no longer easy to practice it: "Nowadays, especially in Rome, it is not at all a safe business" (2, 12, 17; 24). Epictetus pictures a philosopher trying to have a Socratic dialogue with a consular personage, and ending up receiving a fist in the face. If we can trust Diogenes Laertius, *Lives of the Philosophers*, 2, 21, a similar incident had happened to Socrates himself.

90 On the history of this theme, see Pierre Courcelle, *Connais-toi toi-même. De Socrate à saint Bernard*, 3 vols, Paris 1974–5.

91 Plato, *Symposium*, 174d.

92 Plato, ibid, 220c–d.

93 Aristophanes, *Clouds*, 700–6, 761–3; cf. 740–5. As a matter of fact, the true meaning of these verses is not entirely clear. They could be interpreted as an allusion to an exercise of mental concentration; this is the view of G. Méautis, *L'âme hellénique*, Paris 1932, p. 183; A.-J. Festugière, *Contemplation et vie contemplative selon Platon*, 2nd edn, Paris 1950, pp. 67–73; W. Schmid, "Das Sokratesbild der Wolken," *Phitologus* 97 (1948), pp. 209–28; A.E. Taylor, *Vaina Socratica*, Oxford 1911, pp. 129–75. The terms *phrontizein* and *ekphrontizein*, used in Aristophanes' description, became – perhaps under Aristophanes' influence – technical terms for designating Socrates' habits. Cf. Plato, *Symposium*, 220c: Socrates stays standing, *phrontizon ti*; Xenophon, *Symposium*, 6, 6: Socrates is nicknamed the *phrontistes*. But it is not certain that, in Aristophanes, this *phrontizein* corresponds to an exercise of meditation directed towards oneself. In the first place, the comparison with the may-beetle gives us to understand that thought takes flight toward "elevated" things. In his *Symposium*, Xenophon tells us it relates to the "*meteora*," in other words to celestial phenomena (cf. Plato, *Apology*, 18b). Secondly, in the *Clouds*, Strepsiades *phrontizei* about the means he will use to settle a business affair, not about himself. It is more a question of the methodology of research (cf. 1. 742: *divide* and *examine*). The most interesting detail seems to me to be the phrase: "If you come up against an insoluble point,

jump to another" (702–4), repeated at 743ff: "If an idea gets you into any difficulty, let go of it, withdraw for a bit, then submit it to your judgement again, shift it around and weigh it carefully." This means that, when one arrives at an *aporia*, one must take up the question again, from a new point of departure. This method is constantly applied in the Platonic dialogues, as has been shown by René Schaerer, *La Question platonicienne. Études sur les rapports de la pensée et de l'expressions dans les Dialogues* (= Mémoires de l'Université de Neuchâtel 10), 2nd edn with postscript, Neuchâtel 1969, pp. 84–7; citing *Meno*, 79e; *Phaedo*, 105b; *Theaetetus*, 187a–b; *Philebus*, 60a. As Schaerer points out (p. 86), we have to do with a process "which forces the mind indefatigably to turn around in circles, in search of the True." It is perhaps this aspect of Socratic methodology which explains Aristophanes' allusions to detours and circuits of thought. Be this as it may, this method is also discernible in Aristotle, as we can see by the examples collected by H. Bonitz, *Index aristotelicus*, Berlin 1870, repr. Graz 1955, col. 111, 35ff: "Taking another point of departure, we shall say." We find Plotinus using the same method, for instance in *Ennead*, 5, 8, 4, 45; 5, 8, 13, 24; 6, 4, 16, 47. On Aristotle, cf. the remarks of I. Düring, "Aristotle and the heritage from Plato," *Eranos* 62 (1964), pp. 84–99.

94 Diogenes Laertius, *Lives of the Philosophers*, 6, 6. Ancient man frequently spoke to himself out loud. Some examples: Pyrrho in Diogenes Laertius 9, 64 (= Long and Sedley, *Hellenistic Philosophers*, 1A, vol. 1, p. 13; vol. 2, p. 3): "When once discovered talking to himself, he was asked the reason, and said that he was training to be virtuous." Philo of Athens, in Diogenes Laertius, *Lives of the Philosophers*, 9, 69: "Philo . . . had a habit of very often talking to himself . . . that is why Timon says of him: 'Philo . . . he who, apart from mankind, used to speak and converse with himself, with no concern for glory or disputes.' " Cleanthes, in Diogenes Laertius, *Lives of the Philosophers*, 7, 171: [Cleanthes] used often to scold himself out loud. Upon hearing him, Ariston once asked him: 'Who are you scolding?' Cleanthes laughed and replied, 'Some old man who has grey hair but no brains.' " Horace, *Satires*, I, 4, 137: "Thus, with lips shut tight, I debate with myself." ("Haec ego mecum compressis agito labris.") Epictetus, *Discourses*, 3, 14, 2: "Man – if you really are a man – then walk by yourself, talk to yourself, and don't hide yourself in the chorus." On meditating while walking, cf. Horace, *Letter*, I, 4, 4–5: "strolling peacefully amid the healthful woods, bearing in mind all the thoughts worthy of a sage and a good man." – On the problems posed by interior and exterior dialogue with oneself, see F. Leo, "Der Monolog im Drama," *Abhandlungen der Götting. Gesellschaft der Wissenschaft*. NF 10, 5 (1908); Wolfgang Schadewelt, *Monolog und Selbstgespäch. Untersuchungen zur Formgeschichte der griechischen Tragödie*, Berlin 1926; F. Dirlmeier, "Vom Monolog der Dichting zum 'inneren' Logos bei Platon und Aristoteles," in *Augewählte Schriften zu Dichtung und Philosophie der Griechen*, Heidelberg 1970, pp. 142–54; G. Misch, *Geschichte der Autobiographie*, vol. I, Berlin 1949, pp. 86, 94, 363, 380, 426, 450, 468. Concerning the prehistory of this spiritual exercise, one may note Homer, *Odyssey*, 20, 17–23:

He struck himself on the chest and spoke to his heart and scolded it:
"Bear up, my heart. You have had worse to endure before this
on that day when the irresistible Cyclops ate up my strong companions . . ."
So he spoke, addressing his own dear heart within him;
and the heart in great obedience endured and stood it
without complaint, but the man himself was twisting and turning.

This passage is quoted by Plato, *Republic*, 441b: "there Homer has clearly represented that in us which has reflected about the better and the worse as rebuking that which feels unreasoning anger as if it were a distinct and different thing." Cf. *Phaedo*, 94d–e.

95 Thus, according to Porphyry, *Life of Plotinus*, 8, 19: "Plotinus was present at the same time to himself and to others." [On this theme, see Pierre Hadot, *Plotin ou la simplicité du regard*, 3rd edn, Paris 1989. An English translation of this work is in preparation. – Trans.]

96 Plato, *Meno*, 75c–d.

97 V. Goldschmidt, *Les dialogues de Platon. Structure et méthode dialectique* (=Bibliothèque de philosophie contemporaine, Histoire de la Philosophie et Philosophie générale), 2nd edn, Paris 1963, pp. 337–8.

98 See above. In *La Question platonicienne*, pp. 84–7, Schaerer has admirably demonstrated the significance of this Platonic method.

99 Plato, *Seventh Letter*, 344b; 341c–d. Cf. Goldschmidt, *Les dialogues*, p. 8; Schaerer, *La Question platonicienne*, p. 86. For the perspective we are adopting, these two works are of fundamental importance.

100 Plato, *Republic*, 450b.

101 "The dialogue's goal is more to form than to inform," writes Goldschmidt, *Les dialogues*, p. 3, citing Plato, *Statesman*, 285–6. Cf. ibid, pp. 162–3; Schaerer, *La Question platonicienne*, p. 216.

102 Plato, *Statesman*, 285c–d.

103 Ibid, 286d. In the words of Schaerer (*La Question platonicienne*, p. 87): "Definitions are worthless in and of themselves. Their entire value consists in the road travelled to achieve them. Along the way, the interlocutor acquires more *mental penetration* (*Sophist*, 227a–b), more *confidence* (*Theaetetus*, 187b), and more *skillfulness in all things* (*Statesman*, 285dff). His soul is thereby *purified*, as he rejects the opinions which formerly barred the way to enlightenment (*Sophist*, 230b–c). But whatever words one uses to designate this dialectical progress, it always takes place in the soul of the interlocutor – and, by the same token, in the soul of the intelligent reader."

104 Cf. Schaerer, *La Question platonicienne*, pp. 38–44; Goldschmidt *Les dialogues*, pp. 79–80, 292, and 341: "The *Republic* solves the problem of Justice and its advantages. At the same time, and by the same token, it urges us on towards Justice." On the exhortatory character of the dialogues, see K. Gaiser, *Protreptik und Paränese bei Platon. Untersuchungen zur Form des platonischen Dialogs*, Stuttgart 1959; K. Gaiser, *Platone come scrittore filosofico*, Naples 1984.

105 Plato, *Meno*, 81e.

106 Plato, *Republic*, 505e.

107 The dialectical exercise, as it rids our thought of the illusions of the senses, brings about the apprenticeship for death which we are about to discuss; cf. Plato, *Phaedo*, 83a.

108 Brice Parain, "Le langage et l'existence" ["Language and existence"], in *L'Existence*, Paris 1945, p. 173. Parain's novels, especially *La mort de Socrate* ["The Death of Socrates"], Paris 1950, try to make comprehensible this relationship between language and death.

109 Sallustius, *Sallustius: Concerning the Gods and the Universe*, 5, 3, p. 11 Nock.

110 Plato, *Apology*, 28b–30b.

111 Plato, *Phaedo*, 67e. Cf. ibid, 64a, 80e.

112 Plato, ibid, 67c. Note the use of the verb "to accustom" (*ethisai*), which presupposes the practice of exercises.

113 Cf. above.

114 Cf. Plato, *Phaedo*, 84a: "The philosophical soul calms the sea of the passions, following the course of reasoning and always being present within it, contemplating and drawing nourishment from the true, the divine, and that which is not subject to opinion." Cf. ibid, 65e, 66c, 79c, 81b, 83b–d.

115 Plato, *Republic*, 571d.

116 Plato, *Republic*, 571d–572a.

117 Plato, *Phaedo*, 64a–b. This is probably an allusion to Aristophanes, *Clouds*, verses 103, 504.

118 La Rochefoucauld, *Maximes*, no. 26.

119 Horace, *Letter*, I, 4, 13–14: "Omnem crede diem tibi diluxisse supremum; gratia superveniet quae non sperabitur hora." Once again, we encounter the Epicurean theme of gratitude.

120 Michel de Montaigne, *Essays*, bk I, ch. 20, vol. 1, p. 87 Villey/Saulnier = vol. 1, p. 111 Ives. Cf. Seneca, *Letter*, 26, 8: "Meanwhile Epicurus will oblige me with these words: 'Think on death,' or rather, if you prefer the phrase, on 'migration to heaven.' The meaning is clear – that it is a wonderful thing to learn thoroughly how to die . . . 'think on death.' In saying this, he bids us think on freedom . . . He who has learned to die has un-learned slavery. [*Qui mori didicit, servire dedidicit.*]" As we can see, the Stoic Seneca borrowed the maxim "*Meditare mortem*" from Epicurus.

121 Epictetus, *Manual*, ch. 21. Cf. Marcus Aurelius, *Meditations*, 2, 11: "Let your every deed and word and thought be those of one who might depart from this life this very moment."

122 See above.

123 Cf. A. de Waelhens, *La philosophie de Martin Heidegger* (= Bibliothèque Philosophique de Louvain 2), 4th edn, Louvain 1955, pp. 135–51; and especially Heidegger, *Sein und Zeit*, §53, pp. 260ff. As R. Brague pointed out in his review of the first edition of this work (*Études philosophiques*, 1982), Heidegger here "is careful to distinguish Being-for-Death from the *meditatio mortis*." It is perfectly true that Heideggerian Being-for-Death only takes on its full meaning within the perspective particular to Heidegger; it is nonetheless true that we have here a system which makes of the anticipation or forestalling of death a precondition of authentic existence. We must not forget that in Platonic philosophy, the point is

not simply to think about death, but to carry out a *training for dying* which is, in reality, a *training for life.*

124 Cf. Plato, *Republic*, 525c, 532b8, and especially 518c: "the true analogy for this indwelling power in the soul and the organ whereby each of us learns is that of an eye that could not be converted to the light from the darkness except by turning the whole body. Even so this organ of knowledge must be turned around from the world of becoming together with the entire soul . . . until it is able to endure the contemplation of that which is. Education is the art of turning this eye of the soul."

125 Plato, *Republic*, 604b–d.

126 Should we call this exercise *already* Stoic, or should we rather say that Stoic exercises are *still* Platonic?

127 Plato, *Republic*, 486a. This passage is quoted by Marcus Aurelius in his *Meditations*, 7, 35.

128 Cf. I. Hadot, *Seneca*, pp. 115–17, 128–30.

129 Aristotle, *Parts of Animals*, 2, 3, 5, 645a 9–10.

130 See above.

131 Epictetus, *Discourses*, I, 6, 19–25: "God has brought man into the world to be a spectator of himself and his works, and not merely a spectator, but also an interpreter . . . Nature . . . did not end [i.e. in the case of mankind] until she reached contemplation and understanding and a manner of life harmonious with nature. Take heed, therefore, lest you die without ever having been spectators of these things. You are willing to travel to Olympia to look at the work of Pheidias, and each of you regards it as a misfortune to die without seeing such sights; yet when there is no need to travel at all, when you have such works near you and under your noses, will you not yearn to look at these works and know them? Will you consequently refuse to learn either who you are, or for what you have been born, or what is the meaning of the spectacle to which you have been admitted?"

132 Philo Judaeus, *On the Special Laws*, 2, chs. 44–6; cf. the other passages from Philo on the contemplation of the world quoted by A.-J. Festugière, *La révélation d'Hermès Trismègiste*, vol. 2, Paris 1949, p. 599.

133 Plutarch, *On Peace of Mind*, §20, 477c.

134 On this theme, see Festugière, *La révélation*, vol. 2, pp. 441–57; P. Courcelle, *La Consolation de Philosophie dans la tradition littéraire*, Paris 1967, pp. 355–72.

135 Marcus Aurelius, *Meditations*, 12, 24. Cf. ibid, 9, 30: "Contemplate from up above."

136 Seneca, *Natural Questions*, I, Preface, 7–9.

137 Marcus Aurelius, *Meditations*, 8, 54; 9, 32.

138 Plotinus, *Ennead*, 6, 5, 12, 19–29.

139 For example, Plotinus, *Ennead*, I, 2; Porphyry, *Sentences*, ch. 32; Macrobius, *Commentary on the Dream of Scipio*, I, 8, 3–11; Olympiodorus, *Commentary on Plato's Phaedo*, pp. 23, 25ff, 45, 14ff. Cf. O. Schissel von Fleschenberg, *Marinos von Neapolis und die neuplatonischen Tugendgrade*, Athens 1928, with the review by W. Theiler in *Gnomon* 5 (1929), pp. 307–17; I. Hadot, *Le problème du néoplatonisme alexandrin, Hiéroclès et Simplicius*, Paris 1978, pp. 152ff. On the important role played by this theme in the systematization of Christian mysticism, see H. van Lieshout, *La théorie plotinienne de la vertu. Essai sur la genèse*

d'un article de la Somme Théologique de saint Thomas, Fribourg 1926, as well as the texts cited in P. Henry, *Plotin et l'Occident. Firmicus Maternus, Marius Victorinus, Saint Augustin et Macrobe* (= Spicileguim sacrum Lovaniense, Études et Documents 15), Louvain 1934, pp. 248–50.

140 Marinus, *Life of Proclus*, chs 14, 18, 21, 22, 24, 28.

141 Cf. P. Hadot, "La métaphysique de Porphyre," in *Porphyre* (= Entretiens Hardt sur l'Antiquité Classique 12), Vandoeuvres/Geneva 1966, pp. 127–9.

142 Porphyry, *On Abstinence*, I, 30.

143 Ibid, I, 29 (*physiosis kai zoe*).

144 Plotinus, *Ennead*, 1, 5, 7, 10, 28–32.

145 Ibid, 1, 6, 9, 8–26.

146 To put this observation into relation with what we have said above, we may say that the spirit of Platonism consists precisely in making knowledge into a spiritual exercise. In order to know, one must transform oneself.

147 As, for example, at *Ennead*, 5, 8, 11, 1–39. As has been shown by P. Merlan, *Monopsychism, Mysticism, Metaconsciousness. Problems of the Soul in the Neo-aristotelian and Neoplatonic Tradition* (= Archives internationaux d'Histoire des idées 2), The Hague 1963, this experiential knowledge of the Intellect has much in common with certain aspects of the Aristotelian tradition.

148 Plotinus, *Ennead*, 6, 7, 36, 6–9.

149 Ibid, 6, 7, 33, 1–2.

150 Ibid, 6, 7, 34, 2–4.

151 Ibid, 5, 3, 17, 38.

152 Ibid, 6, 9, 10, 14–17. At this point, we ought to take into account the entire post-Plotinian tradition. Perhaps it will suffice to recall that Damascius' *Life of Isidore*, one of the last works of the Neoplatonic school, is full of allusions to spiritual exercises.

153 This comparison is quite frequent in Epictetus; cf. *Discourses*, 1, 4, 13; 2, 17, 29; 3, 21, 3. The metaphor of the Olympic games of the soul is also quite common; cf. Epictetus, *Manual*, ch. 51, 2; Plato, *Phaedrus*, 256b; Porphyry, *On Abstinence*, 1, 31.

154 According to J. Delorme, *Gymnasion*, Paris 1960, pp. 316ff, 466: "Athletic exercises were always accompanied by intellectual exercises."

155 Cf. above.

156 Cf. K. Borinski, *Die Antike in Poetik und Kunsttheorie*, vol. 1, Leipzig 1914, pp. 169ff.

157 Plato, *Republic*, 611d–e.

158 Cf. K. Schneider, *Die schweigenden Götter*, Hildesheim 1966, pp. 29–53.

159 Cf. Lucretius, 5, 8 (referring to Epicurus): "He was a god" (*Deus ille fuit*); Epicurus, *Letter to Menoecus*, §§135; 23, J, Long and Sedley, *Hellenistic Philosophers* vol. 2, p. 152; vol. 1, p. 144: "You will live like a god among men."

160 The philosopher is neither a sage, nor a non-sage; cf. H.-J. Krämer, *Plotonismus und hellenistische Philosophie*, Berlin/New York 1971, pp. 174–5, 228–9.

161 Heidegger's analyses of the authentic and inauthentic modes of existence can help to understand this situation; cf. A. de Waelhens, *La philosophie de Martin Heidegger*, pp. 109, 169.

162 [On conversion, cf. above. – Trans.]

163 Diogenes Laertius, *Lives of the Philosophers*, 6, 103.

164 Damascius, *Life of Isidorus*, §147, p. 127, 12–13 Zinzten.

165 Sextus Empiricus, *Against the Logicians*, 2, vol. 2, pp. 426–8 Bury; *Against the Physicists*, 1, vol. 3, pp. 26–8 Bury; *Against the Physicists*, 2, vol. 3, p. 292 Bury; *Outlines of Pyrrhonism*, vol. 1, pp. 324–6 Bury. Cf. Diogenes Laertius, *Lives of the Philosophers*, 9, 61–2: "He lived in conformity with everyday life [*bios*]." Such was Pyrrho's life-style, which, at least on the surface, was not very different from the average man's: "He lived in fraternal piety with his sister, a midwife . . . now and then even taking things for sale to market, poultry or pigs for instance, and with complete indifference he would clean the house. It is said that he was so indifferent that he washed a piglet himself." (Diogenes Laertius, *Lives of the Philosophers*, 9, 66.) All that mattered was one's inner attitude; therefore the sage conformed to "life," i.e. to the opinions of non-philosophers. But he did so with indifference, that is, with an inner freedom which preserved his serenity and peace of mind. This is, incidentally, the same Pyrrho who, when frightened by a dog, replied to his mocking onlookers: "It is difficult to strip oneself completely of being human." (Diogenes Laertius, *Lives of the Philosophers*, 9, 66, fr. 1C Long and Sedley, *Hellenistic Philosophers*, vol. 1, p. 14; vol. 2, p. 3.)

166 Cf., with regard to Plato, V. Goldschmidt, "Sur le problème du 'système de Platon'," *Rivista critica di stonia della filosofia* 5(1959), pp. 169–78. The recent researches of K. Gaiser and H.-J. Krämer on Plato's unwritten teachings have once again raised doubts about the existence of systematic thought in antiquity.

167 Plato, *Phaedrus*, 264c.

168 I. Düring, *Aristoteles. Darstellung und Interpretation seines Denkens*, Heidelberg 1966, pp. 29, 33, 41, 226.

169 Cf. I. Düring, "Von Aristoteles bis Leibniz. Einige Haupttinien in der Geschichte des Aristotelismus," in P. Mordux, ed., *Aristoteles in der neuren Forschung* (= Wege der Forschung 61), Darmstadt 1968, p. 259: "In reality, Aristotle thought in terms of problems: he was a creator of methods, a pedagogue, and an organizer of collaborative scientific work. He did, of course, have strong systematic tendencies, but what he was striving after was a systematic way of approaching problems . . . The idea of creating a self-contained system, however, never even entered his mind."

170 Düring, "Aristotle and the heritage from Plato," pp. 97–8.

171 See above.

172 Düring, *Aristoteles*, p. 41, n. 253.

173 Ibid, pp. 5, 289, 433.

174 Porphyry, *Life of Plotinus*, 4, 11; 5, 60.

175 Cf., for instance, with regard to Plotinus' doctrine of the soul, Henry Blumenthal, "Soul, world-soul, and individual soul in Plotinus," in *Le Néoplatonisme*, 1971.

176 Cf. I. Hadot, "Le système théologique de Simplicius dans son commentaire sur le Manuel d'Epictete," in *Le Neoplatonisme*, 1971, pp. 266, 279; I. Hadot, *Le problème*, pp. 47–65, 147–67.

177 Cf. the quotation from Chrysippus' *Therapeutikos* in *SVF* 3, § 474, pp. 124–5, taken from Origen, *Against Celsus*, I, 64; 8, 51. Note how Origen introduces his

citation: "Chrysippus . . . in his endeavours to restrain the passions of the human soul, not pretending to determine what doctrines are the true ones, says that those who have been brought under the dominion of the passions are to be treated according to the principles of the various schools." On this theme, cf. I. Hadot, *Seneca*, pp. 3, 21, 44, 54, 83; 1969b, p. 351. We ought therefore not to be surprised to find the Stoic Seneca utilizing Epicurean aphorisms to exhort his disciple Lucilius; cf. I. Hadot, *Seneca*, p. 83. A concrete example of this parenetic eclecticism may be found in the manuscript *Vaticanus Graecus* 1950. According to Festugière, *La révélation*, vol. 2, p. 90, n. 2: "It is interesting to note that the second half of *Vat. gr.* 1950 . . . which forms an independent whole, contains the *Memorabilia* of Xenophon (f. 280ff), followed by the *Meditations* of Marcus Aurelius (f. 341ff), then the *Manual* of Epictetus (f. 392ᵛ), and finally, after a page of rhetorical pieces (f. 401), the collection of Epicurean aphorisms entitled *Gnomologium Vaticanum* (f. 401ᵛff.). This whole ensemble, including the selections from Epicurus, is the work of a Stoic, who has gathered together for his personal use a number of fundamental texts on moral doctrine – a kind of 'book of devotion', as it were. Now, the first item on the list is the Socrates of the *Memorabilia*."

178 Marcus Aurelius, *Meditations*, 9, 39; 4, 3, 2.

179 See above.

180 Augustine, *On the Trinity*, 15, 6, 10: "Quia in nobis fiunt vel in nobis sunt, cum ista meminimus, aspicimus, volimus." Memory, knowledge, and will are, for Augustine, the three trinitary images. On the *exercitatio animi* ("exercise of the soul") in Augustine, see H.-I. Marrou, *Saint Augustin et la fin de la culture antique*, Paris 1938, p. 299.

181 On the utilization of the word *philosophia* in Christianity, see A.N. Malingrey, *"Philosophia." Étude d'un groupe de mots dans la littérature grecque, des Présocratiques au IVe siècle ap. J.-C.*, Paris 1961. Clement of Alexandria is one of the best witnesses for the ancient tradition of spiritual exercises. He emphasizes the importance of the master–disciple relationship (*Stromata*, I, 1, 9, 1), the value of psychagogy (ibid, I, 2, 20, 1), and the need for exercises and a hunt after the truth (ibid, I, 2, 21, 1: "the truth reveals itself full of sweetness when one has searched for it and obtained it at the cost of great efforts.")

182 For H. Happ, *Hyle*, Berlin 1971, p. 66, n. 282, the concern for "systems" goes back to Francisco de Suarez (1548–1617).

183 Cf. K. Jaspers, "Epikur," in *Weltbewohner und Weimarianer (Festschift E. Beutter)*, Zurich 1960, p. 132; and Immanuel Kant, *Die Metaphysik der Sitten* (1797), *Ethische Methodenlehre, Zwieter Abschnitt. Die ethische Asketik*, in *Immanuel Kant's Werke*, ed. Ernst Cassirer, Berlin 1916, §53. Here Kant shows how the practice of virtue – which he calls ascetics – should be carried out with Stoic energy combined with Epicurean *joie de vivre*.

184 Vauvenargues, *Réflections et maximes*, §400 [Luc de Clapiers, Marquis de Vauvenargues (1715–1747), friend of Voltaire. – Trans.], together with §398: "Every thought is new when the author expresses it in his own way," and above all §399: "There are many things we do not know well enough, and that it is good to have repeated."

185 "It is contained in the very briefest statements," says Plato, speaking of the essence of his own doctrine (*Seventh Letter*, 334e). "The essence of philosophy is the spirit of simplicity . . . always and everywhere, complication is superficial, construction is an accessory, and synthesis an appearance. Philosophizing is a simple act" (Henri Bergson, *La pensée et le mouvant*, Paris 1946, p. 139).

186 Epictetus, *Discourses*, 3, 21, 7–8.

187 Johann Wolfgang von Goethe, *Conversations with Eckermann*, trans. John Oxenford, 2 vols, 1850, 25 January, 1830.

4

Ancient Spiritual Exercises and "Christian Philosophy"

It was the great merit of Paul Rabbow to have shown, in his *Seelenführung*,[1] in what sense the methods of meditation set forth and practiced in Ignatius of Loyola's *Exercitia spiritualia*[2] were deeply rooted in the spiritual exercises of ancient philosophy. Rabbow begins his book by discussing the various techniques by means of which rhetoricians throughout antiquity sought to persuade their audiences. These included, for example, oratorical amplification and lifelike, stirring descriptions of events.[3] Above all, Rabbow gives a remarkable analysis of the exercises practiced by the Stoics and Epicureans, emphasizing the point that they were *spiritual* exercises of the same kind as we find in Ignatius of Loyola. On both these points, Rabbow's book opened the way to new areas of research. It is possible, however, that even the author himself did not foresee all the consequences of his discovery.

In the first place, Rabbow seems to me to have linked the phenomenon of spiritual exercises too closely to what he terms the "inward orientation" (*Innenwendung*)[4] which, he claims, took place in the Greek mentality in the third century BC, and which manifested itself in the development of the Stoic and Epicurean schools. As a matter of fact, however, this phenomenon was much more widespread. We can already detect its outlines in the Socratic/Platonic dialogues, and it continues right up until the end of antiquity. The reason for this is that it is linked to the very essence of ancient philosophy. It is *philosophy itself* that the ancients thought of as a spiritual exercise.

If Rabbow tends to limit the extent of spiritual exercises to the Hellenistic/Roman period, the reason is perhaps that he restricts himself to considering their ethical aspect alone. Moreover, he considers ethics only in philosophies like Stoicism and Epicureanism, which appear to accord predominance to ethical questions in their instruction. In fact, Rabbow goes so far as to define spiritual exercises as moral exercises:

> By "moral exercise," we mean a procedure or determinate act, intended to influence oneself, carried out with the express goal of achieving a determinate moral effect. It always looks beyond itself, in as much as it repeats itself, or at least is linked together with other acts to form a methodical ensemble.[5]

With the advent of Christianity, Rabbow continues, these moral exercises were transformed into spiritual exercises:

> Spiritual exercises, then, which resemble moral exercises like a twin, both in essence and structure, were raised to their classical rigor and perfection in the *Exercitia spiritualia* of Ignatius of Loyola. Spiritual exercises thus belong properly to the religious sphere, since their goal is to fortify, maintain, and renew life "in the Spirit," the *vita spiritualis*.[6]

Christian spiritual exercises did indeed take on a new meaning by virtue of the specific character of Christian spirituality, inspired as it is by the death of Christ and the Trinitarian life of the divine Persons. But to speak, apropos of the philosophical exercises of antiquity, of simple "moral exercises" is to misunderstand their importance and significance. As we showed above, these exercises have as their goal the transformation of our vision of the world, and the metamorphosis of our being. They therefore have not merely a moral, but also an existential value. We are not just dealing here with a code of good moral conduct, but with a *way of being*, in the strongest sense of the term. In the last analysis, then, the term "spiritual exercises" is the best one, because it leaves no doubt that we are dealing with exercises which engage the totality of the spirit.[7]

Secondly, one gets the impression from reading Rabbow that Ignatius of Loyola rediscovered spiritual exercises thanks to the sixteenth-century renaissance of rhetorical studies.[8] In fact, however, rhetoric for the ancients was only one of many ingredients of exercises which were first and foremost *philosophical* in the strict sense of the term. Moreover, ever since the first centuries of the church's existence, Christian spirituality has been the heir of ancient philosophy and its spiritual practices. There was thus nothing to prevent Ignatius from finding the methodology for his *Exercitia* within the Christian tradition itself. In the following pages, we hope to show, with the help of a few quotations, in what way ancient spiritual exercises were preserved and transmitted by an entire current of ancient Christian thought: that current, namely, which defined Christianity itself as a philosophy.

Before we begin our study, we must be more specific about the notion of spiritual exercises. "Exercise" corresponds to the Greek terms *askesis* or *melete*. Let us be clear at the outset about the limits of the present inquiry: we shall not be discussing "asceticism" in the modern sense of the word, as it is defined, for instance, by Heussi: "Complete abstinence or restriction in the use of food, drink, sleep, dress, and property, and especially continence in sexual matters."[9] Here, we must carefully distinguish between two different phenomena. On the one hand, there is the Christian – and subsequently modern – use of the word "asceticism", as we have just seen it defined. On the other, there is use of the word *askesis* in ancient philosophy. For ancient philosophers, the word *askesis* designated exclusively the spiritual exercises we have discussed above:[10] inner activities of the thought and the will. Whether or not sexual or alimentary practices analogous to those of Christian asceticism existed among certain ancient philosophers – the Cynics, for example, or the Neoplatonists – is a wholly different question. Such practices have nothing to do with philosophical thought-exercises. This question has been competently dealt with by many authors,[11] who have shown both the analogies and the differences between asceticism (in the modern sense of the word) in ancient philosophy and in Christianity. What we propose to examine here is rather the way in which *askesis*, in the *philosophical* sense of the term, was received into Christianity.

In order to understand the phenomenon under consideration, it is essential to recall that there was a widespread Christian tradition which portrayed Christianity as a *philosophy*. This assimilation began with those Christian writers of the second century who are usually referred to as the Apologists, and in particular with Justin. The Apologists considered Christianity a philosophy, and to mark its opposition to Greek philosophy, they spoke of Christianity as "our philosophy" or as "Barbarian philosophy."[12] They did not, however, consider Christianity to be just one philosophy among others; they thought of it as *the* philosophy. They believed that that which had been scattered and dispersed throughout Greek philosophy had been synthesized and systematized in Christian philosophy. Each Greek philosopher, they wrote, had possessed only a portion of the *Logos*,[13] whereas the Christians were in possession of the *Logos* itself, incarnated in Jesus Christ. If to do philosophy was to live in accordance with the law of reason, then the Christians were philosophers, since they lived in conformity with the law of the divine *Logos*.[14]

Clement of Alexandria dwells at length on this theme. He establishes a close link between philosophy and *paideia*, by which he means the education of mankind. Already within Greek philosophy, the *Logos*, or divine pedagogue, had been at work educating humanity, but Christianity itself, as the complete revelation of the *Logos*, was the true philosophy[15] which "teaches us to conduct ourselves so that we may resemble God, and to accept the divine plan [*oikonomia*] as the guiding principle of all our education."[16]

The identification of Christianity with true philosophy inspired many aspects of the teaching of Origen, and it remained influential throughout the Origenist tradition, especially among the Cappadocian Fathers: Basil of Caesarea, Gregory Nazianzen, and Gregory of Nyssa. It is also in evidence in John Chrysostom.[17] All these authors speak of "our philosophy"; of the "complete philosophy"; or of "the philosophy according to Christ."

We may well ask ourselves if such an identification was legitimate, and wonder whether it did not contribute to a large extent to the notorious "Hellenization" of Christianity, about which so much has been written. I will not go into this complex problem here, but shall limit myself to pointing out that in portraying Christianity as a philosophy, this tradition was the heir – almost certainly consciously so – of a tendency already at work in the Jewish tradition, particularly in Philo of Alexandria.[18] Philo portrayed Judaism as a *patrios philosophia*: the traditional philosophy of the Jewish people. The same terminology was used by Flavius Josephus.[19]

When, a few centuries later, monasticism came to represent the culmination of Christian perfection, it, too, could be portrayed as a *philosophia*. From the fourth century on, this is exactly how it was in fact described, by church Fathers such as Gregory Nazianzen,[20] Gregory of Nyssa, and John Chrysostom,[21] and especially by Evagrius Ponticus.[22] This viewpoint was still current in the fifth century, for instance in Theodoret of Cyrrhus.[23]

Here again, it was Philo of Alexandria who had shown the way. He had given the name "philosophers" to the Therapeutae, who, according to his description,[24] lived in solitude, meditating on the law and devoting themselves to contemplation. Jean Leclercq[25] has shown that, under the influence of Greek tradition, the monastic life continued to be designated by the term *philosophia* throughout the Middle Ages. Thus, a Cistercian monastic text tells us that Bernard of Clairvaux used to initiate his disciples "into the disciplines of celestial philosophy."[26] Finally, John of Salisbury maintained that it was the monks who "philosophized" in the most correct and authentic way.[27]

The importance of this assimilation between Christianity and philosophy cannot be over-emphasized. Let us be clear on one point, however: there can be no question of denying the incomparable originality of Christianity. We shall return to this point later; in particular, we shall emphasize the specifically Christian character of this "philosophy," as well as the care Christians have taken to connect it with the biblical/evangelical tradition. Moreover, the tendency to assimilation was confined within strict historical limits, and always linked more or less closely to the tradition of the Apologists and of Origen. This tendency did, however, exist; its importance was considerable, and its result was the introduction of philosophical spiritual exercises into Christianity.

Along with its absorption of spiritual exercises, Christianity acquired a specific style of life, spiritual attitude, and tonality, which had been absent from primitive Christianity. This fact is highly significant: it shows that if Christianity was able to be assimilated to a philosophy, the reason was that philosophy itself was already, above all else, a way of being and a style of life. As Jean Leclercq points out: "In the monastic Middle Ages, just as much as in Antiquity, *philosophia* did not designate a theory or a means of knowledge, but a lived, experienced wisdom, and a way of living according to reason." [28]

We remarked above[29] that the fundamental attitude of the Stoic philosopher was *prosoche*: attention to oneself and vigilance at every instant. For the Stoics, the person who is "awake" is always perfectly conscious not only of what he *does*, but of what he *is*. In other words, he is aware of his place in the universe and of his relationship to God. His self-consciousness is, first and foremost, a moral consciousness.

A person endowed with such consciousness seeks to purify and rectify his intentions at every instant. He is constantly on the lookout for signs within himself of any motive for action other than the will to do good. Such self-consciousness is not, however, merely a moral conscience; it is also cosmic consciousness. The "attentive" person lives constantly in the presence of God and is constantly remembering God, joyfully consenting to the will of universal reason, and he sees all things with the eyes of God himself.

Such is the philosophical attitude *par excellence*. It is also the attitude of the Christian philosopher. We encounter this attitude already in Clement of Alexandria, in a passage which foreshadows the spirit which was later to reign in philosophically-inspired monasticism: "It is necessary that divine law inspire fear, so that the philosopher may acquire and conserve peace of mind [*amerimnia*], by dint of prudence [*eulabeia*] and attention to himself [*prosoche*], and that he may remain exempt from sins and falls in all things." [30] For Clement, the divine law is simultaneously the universal reason of the philosophers, and the divine word of the Christians. It inspires fear, not in the sense of a passion – which, as such, would be condemned by the Stoics – but rather in the sense of a certain circumspection in thought and action. Such attention to oneself brings about *amerimnia* or peace of mind, one of the most sought-after goals in monasticism.

Attention to oneself is the subject of a very important sermon by Basil of Caesarea.[31] Basil bases his sermon on the Greek version of a passage from *Deuteronomy*: "Give heed to yourself, lest there be a hidden word in your heart." [32] On this basis, Basil develops an entire theory of *prosoche*, strongly influenced by the Stoic and Platonic traditions. We shall return to this point later. For the moment, let us simply note that Basil's reason for commenting on this particular passage of *Deuteronomy* is that, for him, it evokes a technical term of ancient philosophy. For Basil, attention to oneself consists in awakening the rational principles of thought and action which God has placed in our souls.[33] We are to watch over *ourselves* – that is, over our spirit and our soul – and not over that which is *ours* (our body) or that which is *round about* us (our possessions).[34] Thus, *prosoche* consists in paying attention to the beauty of our souls, by constantly renewing the examination of our conscience and our knowledge of ourselves.[35] By so doing, we can correct the judgments we bring upon ourselves. If we think we are rich and noble, we are to recall that we are made of earth, and ask ourselves where are the famous men who have preceded us now. If, on the contrary, we are poor and in disgrace, we are to take cognizance of the riches and splendors which the cosmos offers us: our body, the earth, the sky, and the stars, and we shall then be reminded of our divine vocation.[36] It is not hard to recognize the philosophical character of these themes.

Prosoche or attention[37] to oneself, the philosopher's fundamental attitude, became the fundamental attitude of the monk. We can observe this phenomenon in Athanasius' *Life of Antony*, written in AD 357. When describing the saint's conversion to the monastic life, Athanasius simply says: "He began to *pay attention to himself*."[38] Antony himself, we read later, is supposed to have said to his disciples on his deathbed: "Live as though you were dying every day, *paying heed to yourselves* [*prosechontes heautois*] and remembering what you heard from my preaching."[39]

In the sixth century, Dorotheus of Gaza remarked: "We are so negligent that we do not know why we have gone out of the world . . . That is why we are not making progress . . . The reason for it is that there is no *prosoche* in our hearts."[40] As we have seen,[41] attention and vigilance presuppose continuous concentration on the present moment, which must be lived as if it were, simultaneously, the first and last moment of life. Athanasius tells us that Antony used to make no attempt to remember the time he had already spent at his exercises, but rather made a brand new effort every day, as if starting afresh from zero.[42] In other words, he lived the present moment as if it were his first, but also his last. We also saw that Antony told his disciples to "Live as though you were dying every day."[43] Athanasius reports another of Antony's sayings: "If we live as if we were going to die each day, we will not commit sin."[44] We are to wake up thinking it possible that we may not make it until the evening, and go to sleep thinking that we shall not wake up.[45] Epictetus had spoken along similar lines: "Let death be before your eyes every day, and you will never have any abject thought nor excessive desire."[46]

In the same vein, Marcus Aurelius wrote: "Let your every deed and word and thought be those of one who might depart from this life this very moment."[47] Dorotheus of Gaza also established a close link between *prosoche* and the imminence of death: "Let us pay heed to ourselves, brothers, and be vigilant while we still have time . . . Look! Since the time we sat down at this conference we have used up two or three hours of our time and got that much nearer to death. Yet though we see that we are losing time, we are not afraid!"[48] And again: "Let us pay heed to ourselves and be vigilant, brothers. Who will give us back the present time if we waste it?"[49]

Attention to the present is simultaneously control of one's thoughts, acceptance of the divine will, and the purification of one's intentions with regard to others. We have an excellent summary of this constant attention to the present in a well-known *Meditation* of Marcus Aurelius:

> Everywhere and at all times, it is up to you to rejoice piously at what is occurring *at the present moment*, to conduct yourself with justice towards the people who are *present here and now*, and to apply rules of discernment [*emphilotekhnein*] to your *present* representations [*phantasiai*], so that nothing slips in that is not objective.[50]

We encounter the same continuous vigilance over both thought and intentions in monastic spirituality, where it is transformed into the "watch of the heart,"[51] also known as *nepsis*[52] or vigilance. We are not dealing here with a mere exercise of the moral conscience. Rather, *prosoche* relocates man within his genuine being: that is, his relationship to God. It is thus equivalent to the continuous exercise of the presence of God. In the words of Plotinus' disciple Porphyry: "Let God be present as overseer and guardian of every action, deed and word!"[53] Here we have one of the fundamental themes of philosophical *prosoche*: presence both to God and to oneself.

"Have your joy and your rest in one thing only: in progressing from one action done for the sake of others to another such act, always accompanied by the remembrance of God."[54] This *Meditation* of Marcus Aurelius has to do, once again, with the theme of exercises involving the presence of God. At the same time, it introduces to us an expression which was later to play an important role in monastic spirituality. The "remembrance of God" is a perpetual reference to God at each instant of life. Basil of Caesarea links it explicitly with the "watch of the heart": "We must keep watch over our heart with all vigilance . . . to avoid ever losing the thought of God."[55] Diadochus of Photice often evokes this theme. For him, the remembrance of God is entirely equivalent to *prosoche*: "Only they know their failures who never let their intellects be distracted from the remembrance of God."[56] "Since then [i.e. since its fall], it is only with difficulty that the human intellect can remember God and His commandments."[57] We are to

> close off all the intellect's avenues of escape, by means of the remembrance of God.[58]

> What distinguishes a man who is virtue's friend is that he constantly consumes everything that is earthly in his heart by means of the remembrance of God, so that, bit by bit, the evil in it is dispersed by the fire of the remembrance of the Good, and his soul

returns in perfection to its natural brilliance; nay, even with increased splendor.[59]

Clearly, remembrance of God is, in some sense, the very essence of *prosoche*. It is the most radical method for ensuring one's presence to God and to oneself.[60] Vague intentions, however, are not sufficient for true attention to one's self. We noted that Diadochus of Photice speaks of the "remembrance of God *and* of His commandments." In ancient philosophy as well, *prosoche* required meditating on and memorizing rules of life (*kanones*), those principles which were to be applied in each particular circumstance, at each moment in life. It was essential to have the principles of life, the fundamental "dogmas," constantly "at hand."

We encounter this same theme once again in the monastic tradition. Here, however, philosophical dogmas are replaced by the Commandments as an evangelical rule of life, and the words of Christ, enunciating the principles of Christian life. Yet the rule of life could be inspired not only by the evangelical commandments, but also by the words of the "ancients;" in other words, of the first monks. We have only to recall Antony, on his deathbed, recommending that his disciples remember his exhortations.[61] Evagrius Ponticus declares: "It is a very necessary thing . . . to examine carefully the ways of the monks who have traveled, in an earlier age, straight along the road and to direct oneself along the same paths." [62]

Both the evangelical commandments and the words of the ancients were presented in the form of short sentences, which – just as in the philosophical tradition – could be easily memorized and meditated upon. The numerous collections of *Apophthegmata* and of *Kephalaia* we find in monastic literature are a response to this need for memorization and meditation. *Apophthegmata*[63] were the famous sayings which the ancients – that is to say, the Desert Fathers – pronounced in specific circumstances. This literary genre was already in existence in the philosophical tradition, and we find numerous examples of it in the works of Diogenes Laertius. As for *Kephalaia*,[64] these are collections of relatively short sentences, usually grouped into "centuries." This, too, was a literary genre much in vogue in traditional philosophical literature; some examples are Marcus Aurelius' *Meditations* and Porphyry's *Sentences*. Both these literary genres are responses to the requirements of meditation.

Like philosophical meditation, Christian meditation flourished by using all available means of rhetoric and oratorical amplification, and by mobilizing all possible resources of the imagination. Thus, for example, Evagrius Ponticus used to invite his disciples to imagine their own death, the decomposition of their bodies, the terrors and sufferings of their souls in Hell, and eternal fire; then, by way of contrast, they were to picture the happiness of the just.[65]

Meditation must, in any case, be constant. Dorotheus of Gaza insists strongly on this point:

> Meditate constantly on this advice in your hearts, Brothers. Study the words of the holy Elders.[66]

> If we remember the sayings of the holy Elders, brothers, and meditate on them constantly, it will be difficult for us to sin.[67]

> If you wish to possess these sayings at the opportune moment, meditate on them constantly.[68]

In the spiritual life, there is a kind of conspiracy between, on the one hand, normative sayings, which are memorized and meditated upon, and, on the other, the events which provide the occasion for putting them into practice. Dorotheus of Gaza promised his monks that, if they constantly meditated on the "works of the holy Elders," they would "be able to profit from everything that happens to you, and to make progress by the help of God."[69] Dorotheus no doubt meant that after such meditation, his monks would be able to recognize the will of God in all events, thanks to the words of the Fathers, which were likewise inspired by the will of God.

Vigilance and self-attention clearly presuppose the practice of examining one's conscience. We have already seen, in the case of Basil of Caesarea,[70] the close link between *prosoche* and the examination of conscience. It seems that the practice of the examination of the conscience occurs for the first time, within the Christian tradition, in Origen's *Commentary on the Song of Songs*.[71] In the course of his interpretation of verse 1: 8, "Unless thou know thyself, O fair one among women,"[72] Origen explains that the soul must examine its feelings and actions. Does it have the good as a goal? Does it seek after the various virtues? Is it making progress? For instance, has it completely suppressed the passions of anger, sadness, fear, and love of glory? What is its manner of giving and receiving, or of judging the truth?

This series of questions, devoid as it is of any exclusively Christian feature, takes its place in the philosophical tradition of the examination of conscience, as it had been recommended by the Pythagoreans, the Epicureans, the Stoics – especially Seneca and Epictetus – and many other philosophers, such as Plutarch and Galen.[73] We find the practice recommended again by John Chrysostom,[74] and especially by Dorotheus of Gaza:

> We ought not only to examine ourselves every day but also every season, every month, and every week, and ask ourselves: "What stage am I at now with regards to the passion by which I was overcome last week?"

Similarly every year: "Last year I was overcome by such and such a passion; how about now?"

The Fathers have told us how useful it is for each of us to purify himself in turn, by examining, every evening, how we have spent the day, and every morning, how we have spent the night. . . . Truly, however, we who sin so much and are so forgetful, really need to examine ourselves every six hours also, so that we may know how we have spent these hours and in what way we have sinned.[75]

In this regard there is an interesting detail in Athanasius' *Life of Antony*. According to his biographer, Antony used to recommend to his disciples that they take written notes of the actions and movements of their souls. It is possible that written examinations of conscience were already part of the philosophical tradition;[76] they would have been useful, if not necessary, in order to ensure that the investigation was as precise as possible. For Antony, however, the important aspect was the therapeutic value of writing: "Let each one of us note and record our actions and the stirrings of our souls as though we were going to give an account of them to each other."[77] Surely, he continues, we would not dare to commit sins in public, in full view of others: "Let this record replace the eyes of our fellow ascetics." According to Antony, the act of writing gives us the impression of being in public, in front of an audience. We can also discern the therapeutic value of writing in a passage in which Dorotheus of Gaza reports that he felt "help and relief"[78] by the mere fact of having written to his spiritual director.

Another interesting psychological point: Plato and Zeno had remarked that the quality of our dreams allows us to judge the spiritual state of our soul.[79] We find this observation repeated by Evagrius Ponticus[80] and Diadochus of Photice.[81]

Finally, *prosoche* implies self-mastery. That is, it implies the triumph of reason over the passions, since it is the passions that cause the distraction, dispersion, and dissipation of the soul. Monastic literature insists tirelessly on the misdeeds of the passions, which were often personified in demoniacal form.

Many recollections of ancient philosophy were preserved in monastic exercises of self-mastery. For instance, we find Dorotheus of Gaza, like Epictetus, advising his disciples to begin by training themselves in little things, so as to create a habit,[82] before moving on to greater things. Similarly, he advises them to diminish the number of their sins bit by bit, in order to defeat a passion.[83] We find Evagrius Ponticus proposing that one passion ought to be combated by means of another – fornication, for instance, by the concern for one's good reputation – as long as it remains impossible to combat the passion directly by the virtue which is opposed to it. This was the method already suggested by Cicero in his *Tusculan Disputations*.[84]

We said above that Christianity's acceptance of spiritual exercises had introduced into it a certain spiritual attitude and style of life which it had previously lacked. As an example, let us consider the concept of exercises as a whole. In the very process of performing repetitious actions and undergoing a training in order to modify and transform ourselves, there is a certain reflectivity and distance which is very different from evangelical spontaneity. Attention to oneself – the essence of *prosoche* – gives rises to a whole series of techniques of introspection. It engenders an extraordinary finesse in the examination of conscience and spiritual discernment. Most significantly, the ideal sought after in these exercises, and the goals proposed for the spiritual life, became tinged with a strong Stoico-Platonic coloration; that is to say, since by the end of antiquity Neoplatonism had integrated Stoic ethics within itself, that they were deeply infused with Neoplatonism. This is the case, for instance, in Dorotheus of Gaza, who describes spiritual perfection in completely Stoic terms: it is the transformation of the will so that it becomes identified with the Divine Will:

> He who has no will of his own always does what he wishes. For since he has no will of his own, everything that happens satisfies him. He finds himself doing as he wills all the time, for he does not want things to be as he wills them, but he wills that they be just as they are.[85]

The most recent editors of Dorotheus compare this text with a passage from the *Manual* of Epictetus: "Do not seek to have everything that happens happen as you wish, but wish for everything to happen as it actually does happen, and your life will be serene."[86]

Spiritual perfection is also depicted as *apatheia* – the complete absence of passions – a Stoic concept taken up by Neoplatonism. For Dorotheus of Gaza, *apatheia* is the end-result of the annihilation of one's own will: "From this cutting off of self-will a man procures for himself detachment [*aprospatheia*], and from detachment he comes, with the help of God, to perfect *apatheia*."[87] We may note in passing that the means Dorotheus recommends for cutting off self-will are wholly identical to the exercises of self-mastery of the philosophical tradition. In order to cure curiosity, for instance, Plutarch advised people not to read funeral epitaphs, not to snoop on their neighbors, and to turn their backs on street scenes.[88] Similarly, Dorotheus advises us *not* to look in the direction where we *want* to look; not to ask the cook what he's preparing for dinner; and not to join in a conversation we find already underway.[89] This is what Dorotheus means by "cutting off self-will."

It is with Evagrius, however, that we can see most clearly just how closely Christian *apatheia* can be linked to philosophical concepts. In Evagrius' *Praktikos*, we find the following definition: "The Kingdom of Heaven is *apatheia* of the soul along with true knowledge of existing things."[90] When we turn to comment on a formula such as this, we find how great is the distance separating such speculations from the evangelical spirit. As we know, the evangelical message consisted in the announcement of an eschatological event called "the Kingdom of Heaven" or "the Kingdom of God." Evagrius begins by differentiating between the two expressions, and interpreting them in a highly personal way. Enlarging upon the Origenist tradition,[91] he considers that the two expressions designate two inner states of the soul. More precisely, they designate two stages of spiritual progress:

> The Kingdom of Heaven is *apatheia* of the soul along with true knowledge of existing things.
>
> The Kingdom of God is knowledge of the Holy Trinity co-extensive with the capacity of the intelligence and giving it a surpassing incorruptibility.[92]

Two levels of knowledge are distinguished here: the knowledge of beings and the knowledge of God. We then realize that this distinction corresponds exactly to a division of the parts of philosophy which was well known to Origen, and is attested in Platonism at least since the time of Plutarch.[93] In this division, three separate stages or levels of spiritual progress are distinguished, which correspond to the three parts of philosophy: ethics – or "practics," as Evagrius calls it – physics, and theology. Ethics corresponds to initial purification, physics to definitive detachment from the sensible world and contemplation of the order of nature; finally, theology corresponds to contemplation of the principle of all things. According to the Evagrian schema, however, ethics corresponds to *praktike*, physics to "the Kingdom of Heaven," which includes the true knowledge of beings, and theology corresponds to "the Kingdom of God," which is the knowledge of the Trinity. In Neoplatonic systematization, these degrees also correspond to degrees of virtue. According to Porphyry,[94] the soul begins by utilizing the *political* virtues to dominate the passions *via* the state of *metriopatheia*. It then rises to the level of the *kathartic* virtues. These virtues begin to detach the soul from the body, but do not yet do so completely; this is only the beginning of *apatheia*. Not until the level of the *theoretical* virtues does the soul attain to full *apatheia* and perfect separation from the body. It is at this level that the soul is able to contemplate the forms within the divine intellect, which are the models for the phenomenal world.[95] This level, characterized by *apatheia* and the contemplation of existents, corresponds to Evagrius' "Kingdom of Heaven." According to Evagrius, the soul now contemplates the multiplicity of *physeis* ("natures"; hence the denomination "physical"): on the one hand, the intelligible forms, and on the other the logoi of sensible beings.[96] The final stage, noetic in nature, is the contemplation of God Himself. Thus, Evagrius sums up his thought in these terms: "Christianity is the doctrine of Christ our Savior. It is composed of *praktike*, of physics, and of theology." [97]

Apatheia plays an essential role, not only in theoretical constructions such as Evagrian metaphysics, but also in monastic spirituality. There, its value is closely linked to that of peace of mind and absence of worry: *amerimnia*[98] or *tranquillitas*.[99] Dorotheus of Gaza[100] does not hesitate to declare that peace of mind is so important that one must, if necessary, drop what one has undertaken if one's peace of mind is endangered. Peace of mind – *tranquillitas animi* – had, moreover, always been a central value within the philosophical tradition.[101]

For Porphyry, as we have seen, *apatheia* was a result of the soul's detachment from the body. Here we touch once again upon the philosophical exercise *par excellence*. As we saw above, Plato had declared: "those who go about philosophizing correctly are in training for death." [102] As late as the seventh century, we still find the echo of this saying in Maximus Confessor: "In conformity with the philosophy of Christ, let us make of our life a training for death." [103]

Yet Maximus himself is only the inheritor of a rich tradition, which repeatedly identified Christian philosophy with training for death. We encounter this theme already in Clement of Alexandria,[104] who understood such training in a thoroughly Platonic sense, as the attempt spiritually to separate the soul from the body. For Clement, perfect knowledge, or *gnosis*, is a kind of death. It separates the soul from the body, and promotes the soul to a life entirely devoted to the good, allowing it to devote itself to the contemplation of genuine realities with a purified mind. Again, the same motif recurs in Gregory Nazianzen: "Make of this life, as Plato said, a training for death, while – to speak in his terms – separating the soul from the body as far as possible." [105] "This," he tells us, "is the practice of philosophy." Evagrius, for his part, expresses himself in terms strikingly similar to Porphyry's:

> To separate the body from the soul is the privilege only of Him who has joined them together. But to separate the soul from the body lies as well in the power of the person who pursues virtue. For our Fathers gave to the training for death and to the flight from the body a special name: *anachoresis* [i.e. the monastic life].[106]

It is easy to see that the Platonic concept of the flight from the body, which exercised such an attraction upon the young Augustine, was an element *added on* to Christianity, and not essential to it. Nevertheless, this concept determined the orientation of the whole of Christian spirituality in a quite specific direction.

So far, we have noted the permanent survival of certain philosophical spiritual exercises in Christianity and monasticism, and we have tried to make comprehensible the particular tonality that their reception introduced into Christianity. We must not, however, exaggerate the importance of this phenomenon. In the first place, as we have said, it manifested itself only in a rather restricted circle: among Christian writers who had received a philosophical education. Even in their case, however, the final synthesis is essentially Christian.

To be sure, our authors strove to Christianize their borrowings as much as possible; but this is perhaps the least important aspect of the matter. They believed they recognized spiritual exercises, which they had learned through philosophy, in specific scriptural passages. Thus, we saw Basil of Caesarea making a connection between *prosoche* and a text from Deuteronomy.[107] Then, in Athanasius' *Life of Antony*, and throughout monastic literature, *prosoche* was transformed into the "watch of the heart," under the influence of *Proverbs*, 4:23: "Above all else, guard your heart."[108] Examination of one's conscience was often justified by the *Second Letter to the Corinthians*, 13:5: "Examine yourselves . . . and test yourselves."[109] Finally, the meditation on death was recommended on the basis of *First Corinthians*, 15: 31: "I die every day."[110]

Nevertheless, it would be a mistake to believe that these references were enough, all by themselves, to Christianize spiritual exercises. The reason why Christian authors paid attention to these particular biblical passages was that they were *already* familiar, from other sources, with the spiritual exercises of *prosoche*, meditation on death, and examination of the conscience. By themselves, the texts from scripture could never have supplied a method for practicing these exercises. Often, in fact, a given scriptural passage has only a distant connection with a particular spiritual exercise.

More important is the overall spirit in which Christian and monastic spiritual exercises were practiced. They always presupposed the assistance of God's grace, and they made of humility the most important of virtues. In the words of Dorotheus of Gaza: "The closer one comes to God, the more one sees oneself as a sinner."[111] Such humility makes us consider ourselves inferior to others. It leads us to maintain the greatest reserve in both conduct and speech, and to adopt certain significant bodily positions, for instance prostration before other monks.

Two other fundamental virtues were penitence and obedience. Penitence, inspired by the fear and love of God, could take the form of extremely severe self-mortification. The remembrance of death was intended not only to make people realize the urgency of conversion, but also to develop the fear of God. In turn, it is linked to meditation on the Last Judgment, and thereby to the virtue of penitence. The same holds true of the examination of conscience.

Obedience – the renunciation of one's own will, in complete submission to the orders of a superior – completely transformed the philosophical practice of spiritual direction. We can see to just what extremes such obedience could be taken in Dorotheus' *Life of Dositheus.*[112] The director of conscience had an absolute power of decision over his disciple's possessions, eating habits, and entire way of life.

In the final analysis, all these virtues were transfigured by the transcendent dimension of the love of God and of Christ. Thus, to train for death, or to separate the soul from the body, was at the same time to participate in the death of Christ. To renounce one's will was to adhere to divine love.

Generally speaking, we can say that monasticism in Egypt and Syria[113] was born and developed in a Christian milieu, spontaneously and without the intervention of a philosophical model. The first monks were not cultivated men, but Christians who wanted to attain to Christian perfection by the heroic practice of the evangelical prescriptions, and the imitation of the Life of Christ. It was, therefore, natural that they should seek their techniques of perfection in the Old and the New Testament. Under Alexandrian influence, however – the distant influence of Philo, and the more immediate influence of Origen and Clement of Alexandria, magnificently orchestrated by the Cappadocians – certain philosophical spiritual techniques were introduced into Christian spirituality. The result of this was that the Christian ideal was described, and, in part, practiced, by borrowing models and vocabulary from the Greek philosophical tradition. Thanks to its literary and philosophical qualities, this tendency became dominant, and it was through its agency that the heritage of ancient spiritual exercises was transmitted to Christian spirituality: first to that of the Middle Ages, and subsequently to that of modern times.

NOTES

1 See above.
2 See above.
3 Paul Rabbow, *Seelenführung. Methodik der Exerzitien in der Antike*, Munich 1954, p. 23.
4 Ibid, p. 17.
5 Ibid, p. 18.
6 Ibid.
7 See above.
8 Rabbow, *Seelenführung* p. 301, n. 5; p. 306, nn. 14, 17.
9 K. Heussi, *Der Ursprung des Mönchtums*, Tübingen 1936, p. 13.
10 See above.
11 For example, G. Kretschmar, "Der Ursprung der früchristlichen Askese," *Zeitschrift für Theologie und Kirche* 61 (1964), pp. 27–67; P. Nagel, *Die Motivierung der Askese in der alten Kirche und der Ursprung des Mönchums* (= Texte und Untersuchungen zur Geschichte der altchristlichen Literatur 95), Berlin 1966; B. Lohse, *Askese und Mönchtum in der Antike und in der alten Kirche*,

Munich/Vienna 1969; K.S. Frank, ed., *Askese und Mönchtum in der alten Kirche* (= Wege der Forschung 409), Darmstadt 1975; R. Hauser and G. Lanczkowski, "Askese," in *Historisches Wörterbuch der Philosophie*, vol. I, cols 538–41, 1971 (with good bibliography); J. de Guibert, "Ascèse," in *Dictionnaire de Spiritualité*, vol. 1, cols 936–1010.

12 Justin, *Dialogue with Trypho*, 8, 1; Tatian, *Address to the Greeks*, 31, 35, 55; Melito in Eusebius, *Ecclesiastical History*, 4, 26, 7.

13 Justin, *Second Apology*, 2, 13, 3; Lactantius, *Divine Institutes*, 7, 7, 7: "if someone had arisen who could collect the truth scattered and dispersed among the individual philosophers and sects and reduce it to one body, that one . . . would not disagree with us"; 7, 8, 3: "We . . . are able to pick out the truth by surer signs; we who gather it, not from fluctuating suspicion, but who know it from divine tradition."

14 Justin, *Apology*, I, 46, 1–4.

15 Clement of Alexandria, *Stromata*, I, 13, 57, 1–58, 5; I, 5, 28, 1–32, 4.

16 Ibid, I, 11, 52, 3.

17 Most of the relevant texts have been assembled in A.N. Malingrey, *"Philosophia." Étude d'un groupe de mots dans la littérature grecque, des Présocratiques au IVe siècle ap. J.-C.*, Paris 1961.

18 Philo Judaeus, *The Legation to Gaius*, 156; 345; *Life of Moses*, 2, 216; *On the Contemplative Life*, 26.

19 Flavius Josephus, *Antiquities of the Jews*, 18, 11; 23.

20 Gregory Nazianzen, *Apologetica*, 103, *PG* 35, 504A.

21 John Chrysostom, *Against the Opponents of the Monastic Life*, 3, 13, *PG* 47, col. 372.

22 See below.

23 Theodoret of Cyrrhus, *History of the Monks of Syria*, 2, 3, 1; 4, 1, 9; 4, 2, 19; 4, 10, 15; 6, 13, 1; 8, 2, 3 Canivet.

24 Philo Judaeus, *On the Contemplative Life*, 2; 30.

25 J. Leclercq, "Pour l'histoire de l'expression 'philosophic chrétienne'," *Mélanges de Science Religeuise* 9 (1952), pp. 221–6.

26 *Exordium magnum Cisterciense, PL* 185, 437.

27 John of Salisbury, *Polycraticus*, 7, 21, *PL* 199, 696.

28 Leclercq "Pour l'histoire," p. 221.

29 See above.

30 Clement of Alexandria, *Stromata*, 2, 20, 120, 1.

31 Basil of Caesarea, *In Illud Attende tibi ipsi, PG* 31, cols 197–217. P. Adnès, "Garde du cœur," *Dictionnaire de Spiritualité*, vol. 6, col. 108, points to the existence of a multitude of sermons relating to this theme. He cites C. Baur, *Initia Patrum Graecorum* (= Studi e Testi 181, 2), Vatican City 1955, p. 374.

32 *Deuteronomy*, 15: 9. [The Septuagint Greek version of the Bible renders this phrase as *prosche seautoi me genetai rhema krypton en tei kardiai sou*: "Pay attention to yourself, lest a hidden word come to be in your heart," which the King James Version renders as "Beware that there be not a thought in thy wicked heart." The Greek title of Basil's sermon is consequently *eis to Prosche seautoi*: "On the words, 'Give heed to yourself' " – Trans.]

33 Basil, *In Illud Attende*, 2, 201B, pp. 433–4 Wagner.

34 Ibid, 3, 204A, p. 435 Wagner. This distinction was current in Platonic circles; cf. Plato, *First Alcibiades*, 130–1d; *Apology*, 36b4–c6.

35 Ibid, 3, 204B; 5, 209B, pp. 435, 440 Wagner.

36 Ibid, 5–6, 209C–213A, pp. 440–2 Wagner.

37 On the following exercises, the reader may consult the following articles in the *Dictionnaire de Spiritualité*: "Attention," "Apatheia," "Contemplation," "Examen de Conscience," "Direction spirituelle," "Exercices spirituels," "Garde du coeur."

38 *Prosechon heautoi*. Athanasius, *Life of Antony*, 3, PG 26, 844B, p. 32 Gregg.

39 Ibid, 91, 969B, p. 97 Gregg.

40 Dorotheus of Gaza, *Didaskaliai*, 10, §104, line 9 Regnault/de Préville = p. 163 Wheeler. The concept of *prosoche* plays a very important role throughout the monastic tradition; cf. for instance Diadochus of Photice, *Kephalaia Gnostica*, §27, p. 98, 19 Des Places.

41 See above.

42 Athanasius, *Life of Antony*, 853A; 868A; 969B; pp. 37, 43, 97 Gregg/Clebsch.

43 Cf. above.

44 Ibid, 19, 872A, p. 45 Gregg/Clebsch.

45 Ibid.

46 Epictetus, *Manual*, 21. See above.

47 Marcus Aurelius, *Meditations*, 2, 11.

48 Dorotheus of Gaza, *Didaskaliai*, §114, 1–15 Regnault/de Préville = p. 173 Wheeler.

49 Ibid, §104, 1–3 Regnault/de Préville = p. 163 Wheeler.

50 Marcus Aurelius, *Meditations*, 7, 54.

51 Athanasius, *Life of Antony*, 873C; Basil of Caesarea, *Regulae fusius tractatae*, PG 31, 921 B = p. 243 Wagner. Cf. John Cassian, *Collationes*, vol. 1, p. 84 Pichery = p. 84 Luibheid: "we must practice the reading of the Scripture, together with all the other virtuous activities, and we do so to *trap and to hold our hearts* free of the harm of every dangerous passion." [Basil and Athanasius use the term *phulake*, among whose many meanings are "protection," "control," "guarding," and "observance." It can also mean a prison or a prisoner. Originally, however, *phulake* meant a night-watch or the person charged with this duty (the Latin *custodia*); and this is the meaning I have tried to convey by translating *he tes kardias phulake* by "watch of the heart." All the other meanings, however, are relevant and should be borne in mind. – Trans.]

52 Dorotheus of Gaza, *Didoskaliai*, §104 Regnault/de Préville = p. 163 Wheeler.

53 Porphyry, *Porphyry the Philosopher, To Marcella*, 12.

54 Marcus Aurelius, *Meditations*, 6, 7.

55 Basil, *In Illud attende*, p. 243 Wagner.

56 Diadochus of Photice, *Kephalaia Gnostica*, 27, p. 98, 11 Des Places.

57 Ibid, 56, p. 117, 15.

58 Ibid, 59, p. 119, 1–2.

59 Ibid, 97, p. 160, 3.

60 On the theme of presence, see above.

61 See above.
62 Evagrius of Pontis, *Praktikos*, §91, p. 91 Bamberger.
63 Cf. T. Klauser, "Apophthegmata," *Reallexicon für Antike und Christentum* I (1950), pp. 545–50.
64 Cf. E. von Ivánka, "Kephalaia," *Byzantinische Zeitschrift* 47 (1954), pp. 258–91.
65 *Apophthegmata Patrum, PG* 65, 173A–B.
66 Dorotheus of Gaza, *Didaskaliai*, §60, 27, p. 120 Wheeler.
67 Ibid, §69, 2, p. 131 Wheeler.
68 Ibid, §189, 4–5.
69 Ibid, §60, 30, pp. 120–1 Wheeler.
70 See above.
71 Origen, *Commentary on the Song of Songs*, pp. 143, 27ff. Baehrens = pp. 128ff Lawson.
72 [Again, while the King James Bible reads "If thou know not, O thou fairest among women", the Greek Septuagint version gives "Unless you know yourself" (*Ean me gnois seauten*) – Trans.]
73 See the references in I. Hadot, *Seneca und die griechisch-römische Tradition der Seelenleitung*, Berlin 1969, pp. 66–71.
74 John Chrysostom, *Non esse ad gratiam concionandum, PG* 50, 659–60.
75 Dorotheus of Gaza, *Didaskaliai*, §§111, 13; 117, 7, pp. 170; 175 Wheeler.
76 Cf. I. Hadot, *Seneca*, p. 70.
77 Athanasius, *Life of Antony, PG* 26, 924B, p. 73 Gregg/Clebsch.
78 Dorotheus of Gaza, *Didaskaliai*, §25, 11, p. 91 Wheeler.
79 See above.
80 Evagrius of Pontis, *Praktikos*, §§54–6, p. 31 Bamberger. Cf. F. Refoulé, "Rêves et vie spirituelle d'après Evagre le Pontique," *Supplément de la Vie Spirituelle* 59 (1961), pp. 470–516.
81 Diadochus of Photice, *Kephalaia Gnostica*, 37, p. 106 Des Places.
82 Dorotheus of Gaza, *Didskaliai*, §20, p. 89 Wheeler. L. Regnault and J. de Préville, editors of the *Sources Chrétiennes* edition, cite as a parallel Epictetus, *Discourses*, I, 18, 18.
83 Ibid, §120, p. 178 Wheeler. Regnault and de Préville compare Epictetus, *Discourses*, 2, 18.
84 Evagrius of Pontis, *Praktikos*, §58, p. 32 Bamberger. In their *Sources Chrétiennes* edition, A. and C. Guillaumont cite as a parallel Cicero, *Tusculan Disputations*, 4, 75.
85 Dorotheus of Gaza, *Didaskaliai*, §202, 12.
86 Epictetus, *Manual*, 8.
87 Dorotheus of Gaza, *Didaskaliai*, §20, 11–13, p. 88 Wheeler.
88 Plutarch, *On Curiosity*, 520Dff.
89 Dorotheus of Gaza, *Didaskaliai*, 20, pp. 88–9 Wheeler.
90 Evagrius of Pontis, *Praktikos*, 2, p. 15 Bamberger.
91 See the texts cited by A. and C. Guillaumont in the notes to their commentary on the *Praktikos* (SC 171), p. 499, n. 2; p. 501, n. 3.
92 Evagrius of Pontis, *Praktikos*, §§2–3, pp. 15–16 Bamberger.
93 Cf. P. Hadot, "La division des parties de la philosophie dans l'Antiquité," *Museum Helveticum* 36 (1979), pp. 201–23.

94 Cf. I. Hadot, *Le problème du néoplatonisme alexandrin, Hiéroclès et Simplicus*, Paris 1978, pp. 152–8.

95 Porphyry, *Sentences*, p. 27, 9, Lamberz.

96 Cf. the note in A. and C. Guillaumont, 1971, p. 500.

97 Evagrius of Pontis, *Praktikos*, §I, p. 15 Bamberger.

98 On *amerimnia*, see Diadochus of Photice, *Kephalaia Gnostica*, 25, p. 97, 7; 30, p. 100, 19; 65, p. 125, 12; 67, p. 127, 22 Des Places. For Dorotheus of Gaza, see, *inter alia*, *Didaskaliai*, §68, 2.

99 For occurrences of *tranquillitas*, cf. John Cassian, *Conferences*, I, 7, vol. I, p. 85 Pichery = p. 42 Luibheid; 19, 11, vol. 3, p. 48 Pichery.

100 Dorotheus of Gaza, *Didaskaliai*, §§58–60, pp. 118–20 Wheeler.

101 In the treatises of Plutarch and Seneca, for instance.

102 See above.

103 Maximus Confessor, *Commentary on the Our Father*, *PG* 90, 900A = p. 114 Berthold.

104 Clement of Alexandria, *Stromata*, 5, 11, 67, 1, pp. 370–1 Stählin.

105 Gregory Nazianzen, *Epistula* 31, vol. 1, p. 39 Gallay.

106 Evagrius of Pontis, *Praktikos*, §52, p. 30 Bamberger. Compare Porphyry, *Sentences*, 8, p. 3, 6 Lamberz: "What nature has bound together, she also unbinds, but that which the soul binds, the soul likewise unbinds. It was nature that bound the body within the soul, but it was the soul which bound itself within the body. Therefore, while it is nature that unbinds the body from the soul, it is the soul which unbinds itself from the body."

107 Cf. above.

108 Athanasius, *Life of Antony*, 873C, p. 47 Gregg/Clebsch.

109 Ibid, 924A, p. 72 Gregg/Clebsch.

110 Ibid, 872A, p. 45 Gregg/Clebsch.

111 Dorotheus of Gaza, *Didaskaliai*, §151, 47.

112 Dorotheus of Gaza, *Life of Dositheus*, §§5–9, edited among Dorotheus' *Spiritual Works* in Regnault/de Préville 1963, pp. 129ff.

113 Cf. A. Vööbus, *A History of Asceticism in the Syrian Orient* (= CSCO vol. 184, Subsidia 14, vol. 197, Subsidia 17), Louvain 1958–60.

Part III

Figures

5

The Figure of Socrates

Since the dawn of Greek thought, the sage has functioned as a living, concrete model. Aristotle testifies to this in a passage from his *Protrepticus*: "What more accurate standard or measure of good things do we have than the Sage?"[1] There were several reasons for the fact that my research on the sage as a model gradually became fixed upon Socrates. In the first place, I found in him a figure who had exercised a widespread influence of the greatest importance on the entire Western tradition. Secondly, and most importantly, the figure of Socrates – as sketched by Plato, at any rate – had, it seemed to me, one unique advantage. It is the portrait of a mediator between the transcendent ideal of wisdom and concrete human reality. It is a paradox of highly Socratic irony that Socrates was not a sage, but a "philo-sopher": that is, a lover of wisdom.

To speak about Socrates is, of course, to expose oneself to all sorts of historical difficulties. The accounts we have of him by Plato and by Xenophon have transformed, idealized, and deformed the historical Socrates.[2] I shall not attempt here to uncover or reconstruct the historical Socrates. Instead, what I shall try to set forth is the *figure* of Socrates, as it has influenced our Western tradition. Since this is a phenomenon of immense proportions, however, I shall restrict myself to two of its aspects: the figure of Socrates as depicted in Plato's *Symposium*, and as it was perceived by those two great Socratics, Kierkegaard[3] and Nietzsche.[4]

1 Silenus

Socrates thus functions as a mediator between ideal norms and human reality. The concepts of "mediation" and "intermediate" call to mind the ideas of equilibrium and the Golden Mean. We should therefore expect to see in Socrates a harmonious figure, combining divine and human characteristics in delicate nuances.

Nothing could be further from the truth. The figure of Socrates is ambiguous, troubling, and strangely disconcerting. The first surprise in store for us is his physical ugliness, which is well attested by the testimony of Plato, Xenophon, and Aristophanes.[5] "It is significant," wrote Nietzsche, "that Socrates was the first great Hellene to be ugly."[6] "Everything in him is exaggerated, *buffo*, a caricature."[7] Nietzsche goes on to evoke his "crab-like eyes, puffed-up lips, and hanging belly,"[8] and he takes pleasure in telling the story of how the physiognomist Zopyrus once told Socrates he was a monster, keeping hidden within himself the worst vices and appetites. Socrates, says Nietzsche, simply replied: "How well you know me!"[9] If Socrates really did resemble a Silenus, as he is depicted in Plato's *Symposium*,[10] such suspicions were quite understandable. In popular imagination, Sileni and satyrs were hybrid demons, half-animal, half-men, who made up the escort of Dionysos. These impudent, ribald buffoons also constituted the chorus of satyr-plays, a literary genre of which Euripides' *Cyclops* is one of the few remaining examples.

The Sileni were purely natural beings. They stood for the negation of culture and civilization, for grotesque buffoonery, and for the license of the instincts.[11]

To use Kierkegaard's expression, Socrates was a cobold.[12] To be sure, Plato gives us to understand that Socrates' resemblance to Silenus was only an appearance, beneath which something else was hidden. Alcibiades, in his famous speech in praise of Socrates at the end of the *Symposium*,[13] compares Socrates to the little statues of Sileni that could be found in sculptors' shops, which concealed little figurines of the gods inside themselves. Similarly, Socrates' exterior appearance – ugly, buffoon-like, impudent, almost monstrous – was only a mask and a facade.

Here we are led to another paradox: Socrates was not only ugly, but a dissimulator as well. Nietzsche writes: "Everything in him is concealed, ulterior, subterranean."[14] Socrates masks himself, and at the same time is used as a mask by others.

Socrates masks himself: here we encounter that famous Socratic irony, the meaning of which we shall have to clarify later on. Socrates pretends to be ignorant and impudent. "He spends his whole life," says Alcibiades, "playing the part of a simpleton and a child."[15] "The nouns and verbs which form the outer envelope of his words are like the hide of an impudent satyr."[16] His ignorant appearance and amorous attentions "are what he has wrapped around himself, like a carved Silenus."[17]

Socrates pulled off his enterprise of dissimulation so well that he succeeded in definitively masking himself from history. He wrote nothing, engaging only in dialogue. All the testimonies we possess about him hide him from us more than they reveal him, precisely because Socrates has always been used as a mask by those who have spoken about him.

Because he was himself masked, Socrates became the *prosopon*, or mask, of personalities who felt the need to take shelter behind him. It was from him that they got the idea both to mask themselves, and to use Socratic irony as a mask. We have here a phenomenon extremely rich in its literary, pedagogical, and psychological implications.

The original nucleus of this phenomenon was the irony of Socrates himself. Socrates, the eternal interrogator, used skillful questions to bring his interlocutors to admit their ignorance. By so doing, he disturbed them so much that they were eventually led to question their entire lives. After Socrates' death, the memory of his Socratic conversations inspired a new literary genre, the *logoi sokratikoi*, which imitated the conversations Socrates had had with a wide variety of interlocutors. In these *logoi sokratikoi*, Socrates became a *prosopon* – an interlocutor or character – and hence, if we recall the meaning of *prosopon* in the ancient theater, a mask. Especially in the subtle, refined form given it by Plato, the Socratic dialogue was intended to provoke in its readers an effect analogous to that produced by the living discourse of Socrates himself. Thus, the reader of these dialogues finds himself in the same situation as Socrates' interlocutors: he does not know where Socrates' questions are going to lead him. Socrates' elusive, unsettling *prosopon*/mask sows disquiet in the soul of the reader, leading it to a heightening of consciousness which may go as far as far as a philosophical conversion. As Konrad Gaiser has convincingly shown,[18] the reader himself is invited to take refuge behind the mask of Socrates. In almost all Plato's Socratic dialogues, there comes a moment of crisis, when the interlocutors are overcome by discouragement. They no longer have confidence in the possibility of continuing the discussion, and it seems as though the dialogue is about to be broken off. This is where Socrates intervenes: he takes the others' doubt, uneasiness, and discouragement upon himself. He assumes all the risks of the dialectical adventure, and carries out a complete switching of roles. If the enterprise fails, it will henceforth be his responsibility. In this way, he shows his interlocutors a projection of their own selves. They can now transfer their personal uneasiness onto Socrates, and regain confidence in dialectical research and in the logos itself.

In his dialogues, Plato too uses Socrates as a mask, or, in Nietzsche's terminology, as a "semiotics."[19] As Paul Friedländer[20] has pointed out, whereas the "ego" had long since made its appearance in Greek literature – Hesiod, Xenophanes, Parmenides, Empedocles, the Sophists, and even Xenophon do not hesitate to speak in the first person – Plato completely effaces himself behind Socrates in his dialogues, and systematically avoids the use of the first person singular. We are dealing here with an extremely subtle relationship, whose significance is extremely hard to grasp. Are we to suppose, with Gaiser and H.-J. Krämer,[21] that Plato carefully distinguished between two kinds of teaching: his own, which was oral, secret, and reserved for members of the Academy, and his written dialogues, in which he utilized the mask of Socrates to exhort his readers to philosophy? Alternatively, should we conclude that Plato uses the figure of Socrates to set forth his doctrines with a certain degree of distance and irony? In any case, this initial situation has indelibly influenced Western consciousness. Whenever thinkers have been aware of – and frightened by – the radical renewal of which they were the bearers, they too have used a mask to confront their contemporaries. They have usually chosen to use the ironic mask of Socrates.

When, in the nineteenth century, J.G. Hamann praised Socrates in his *Socratic Memorabilia*, he did so, to use his own term, to *mimike*.[22] In other words, Hamann himself took up the mask of Socrates – the rationalist par excellence in the eyes of the eighteenth century[23] – in order to make people see, behind the mask, a figure prophetic of Christ.

What, for Hamann, was only a temporary expedient became a fundamental, existential attitude for Kierkegaard. Kierkegaard's penchant for masks is most evident in his use of pseudonyms. As is well known, most of Kierkegaard's works were first published under a variety of pseudonyms: Victor Eremita, Johannes Climacus, etc. We are not dealing here with an editorial caprice. Rather, for Kierkegaard, all these pseudonyms correspond to different levels – the "aesthetic," "ethical," and "religious" – at which the author was supposed to be situated. Kierkegaard speaks successively of Christianity as an aesthete, then as a moralist, in order to force his contemporaries into the awareness that they are not true Christians. "He hid himself beneath the mask of an artist and half-believing moralist to speak about what he believed most deeply."[24]

Kierkegaard was perfectly aware of the Socratic character of his method:

> From the point of view of my whole activity as an author, integrally conceived, the aesthetic work is a deception, and herein is to be found the deeper significance of the use of pseudonyms. A deception, however, is a rather ugly thing. To this I would make answer: One must not let oneself be deceived by the word "deception." One can deceive a person for the truth's sake, and (to recall old Socrates) one can deceive a person into the truth. Indeed, it is only by this means, i.e. by deceiving him, that it is possible to bring into the truth one who is in an illusion.[25]

Kierkegaard's goal was to make the reader aware of his mistakes, not by directly refuting them, but by setting them forth in such a way that their absurdity would become clearly apparent. This is as Socratic as can be. At the same time, Kierkegaard used pseudonymy to give voice to all the different characters within him. In the process, he objectified his various selves, without recognizing himself in any of them, just as Socrates, by means of his skillful questions, objectified the self of his interlocutors without recognizing himself in any of them. Thus we find Kierkegaard writing: "Because of my melancholy, it was years before I was able to say 'thou' to myself. Between my melancholy and my 'thou,' there was a whole world of fantasy. I exhausted it, in part, in my pseudonyms."[26] Yet Kierkegaard was not content to mask himself behind pseudonyms. His real mask was Socratic irony itself; it was Socrates himself: "O Socrates! Yours and mine are the same adventure! I am alone. My only analogy is Socrates. My task is a Socratic task."[27]

Kierkegaard termed this Socratic method his "method of indirect communication."[28] We encounter it once again in Nietzsche, for whom it is the method of the great educator: "An educator never says what he himself thinks, but always only what he thinks of a thing in relation to the requirements of those he educates. He must not be detected in this dissimulation."[29] This method is justified by the educator's transcendent mission: "Every profound spirit needs a mask; better yet, around every profound spirit a mask is continually growing, thanks to the constantly false – that is to say, superficial – interpretation of his every word, step, and manifestation of life."[30] The mask of the Socratic Silenus served as the model for Nietzsche's theory of the mask. As he wrote in the unpublished writings of the last period of his life:

> I believe that this was the magic of Socrates: he had one soul, and another one in behind it, and behind it still another one. It was in the first one that Xenophon lay down to sleep; in the second, Plato; and in the third one Plato again, but this time Plato with his own second soul. Plato himself is a man with many a hidden cave behind and facades out front.[31]

As for Kierkegaard, so for Nietzsche: masks were a pedagogical necessity, but also a psychological need. Nietzsche himself could be included in his category of "men who want only to be seen shining through others. And there's a lot of wisdom in this."[32] In his *Ecce Homo*,[33] Nietzsche himself admits that he used his masters Schopenhauer and Wagner as masks in writing his *Untimely Meditations*, just as Plato had used Socrates as a "semiotics." There is indeed a relationship comparable to that between Plato and Socrates here: Nietzsche was speaking of an *ideal* Wagner and an *ideal* Schopenhauer, who were really nothing other than Nietzsche himself. As Bertram[34] has convincingly shown, one of Nietzsche's masks was certainly Socrates himself; Socrates, whom he pursued with the same amorous hatred that Nietzsche feels for Nietzsche; that same Socrates who, he tells us, "is so close to me, that I am almost always fighting with him."[35] The side of Socrates Nietzsche hates is identical with the Nietzsche who dissolves myths, replacing the gods by the knowledge of good and evil; the Nietzsche who brings men's minds back to things human, all too human. The side of

Socrates which Nietzsche loves, and of which he is jealous, is what he himself would like to be: the seducer, the educator, and the guide of souls. We shall have occasion to return to this amorous hatred.

The Socratic mask is the mask of irony. If we examine the texts – by Plato,[36] Aristotle,[37] or Theophrastus[38] – in which the word *eironeia* appears, we can conclude that irony is a psychological attitude in which the individual uses self-deprecation in an attempt to appear inferior to what he really is. In the art and usage of discourse, it takes the form of pretending to concede that one's interlocutor is right, and to adopt the point of view of one's adversary. The rhetorical figure of *eironeia*, then, consists in using words or speeches which the audience would rather have expected to hear coming from the mouth of one's adversary.[39] This is certainly the form assumed by Socratic irony. In the words of Cicero: "By disparaging himself, Socrates used to concede more than was necessary to the adversaries he wanted to refute. Thus, thinking one thing and saying another, he enjoyed using the kind of dissimulation which the Greeks call 'irony'."[40] Socratic irony is thus a feigned self-deprecation, which consists primarily in passing oneself off as someone completely ordinary and superficial. As Alcibiades puts it in his praise of Socrates:

> His speech is for all the world like those Sileni that open up down the middle. When you listen to it for the first time, you just can't help finding it absolutely ridiculous. He talks about pack asses and black-smiths and shoemakers and tanners, and he always seems to be repeating the same thing, so that anyone who wasn't used to his style and wasn't very quick on the uptake would naturally take it for the most utter nonsense.[41]

Not only was Socrates guilty of banality in the subjects he discussed, but his interlocutors were banal, as well. He sought out and found his audience in the marketplace, the gymnasia, artists' workshops, and shops. He was a street person. In the words of Nietzsche: "Mediocrity is the most appropriate mask the superior spirit can wear."[42] Socrates talked and debated, but he refused to be considered a master. "When people came to see him," remarks Epictetus, "and asked him to introduce them to other philosophers, he complied readily, and willingly accepted to pass unnoticed himself."[43]

Here we touch the heart of Socratic irony: if Socrates refused to teach or be considered a master, it was because he had nothing to say or to communicate, for the excellent reason that, as he frequently proclaimed, he did not know anything. Since he had nothing to say, and no thesis to defend, all Socrates could do was to ask questions, even though he himself refused to answer them. In the first book of the *Republic*, Thrasymachus cries out: "Ye gods! Here we have the well-known *eironeia* of Socrates, and I knew it and predicted that when it came to replying you would refuse and dissemble and do anything rather than answer any question that anyone asked you."[44] Aristotle described the situation even more clearly: "Socrates used to ask questions and not answer them – for he used to confess that he did not know."[45]

Obviously, we cannot know exactly how Socrates' discussions with the Athenians took place. Plato's dialogues – even the most "Socratic" – are only a doubly weak imitation of them. In the first place, they are not spoken, but written, and, as Hegel remarked, "in printed dialogue, answers are altogether under the author's control; but to say that in actual life people are found to answer as they are here made to do, is quite another thing."[46] Moreover, beneath the surface charm of literary fiction, we can recognize in Plato's dialogues the trace of the scholastic exercises of the Platonic Academy. Aristotle codified the rules of these dialectical jousts in his *Topics*.[47] There were well-defined roles for both questioner and respondent in these argumentation exercises, and the rules of this intellectual fencing were rigorously defined.

It is not our task here to try to disentangle what may be properly "Socratic" in the conversations reported by Plato; rather, we are concerned to uncover the significance of Socratic irony as it was known to tradition, and the movements of consciousness to which it corresponds.

Otto Apelt[48] has given a good description of the mechanism of Socratic irony: *Spaltung und Verdoppelung*.[49] Socrates splits himself into two, so that there are two Socrates: the Socrates who knows in advance how the discussion is going to end, and the Socrates who travels the entire dialectical path along with his interlocutor. Socrates' interlocutors do not know where he is leading them, and therein lies the irony. As he travels the path along with his interlocutors, Socrates constantly demands total agreement from them. He takes his partner's position as his starting point, and gradually makes him admit all the consequences of his position. This a priori agreement is founded on the rational demands of the Logos,[50] or reasonable discourse. By constantly demanding assent, Socrates leads his interlocutor to recognize that his initial position was contradictory, and he thereby objectifies their common undertaking. As a rule, Socrates chooses an activity familiar to his interlocutor as the subject of discussion, and tries to define, together with him, the practical knowledge required to carry out this activity. For example, a general must know how to fight bravely, and a soothsayer must behave piously towards the gods. At the end of the road, however, the general turns out to have no idea of what courage really is, and the soothsayer doesn't know what piety is. It is then that the interlocutor realizes that he doesn't really know the reasons for his actions. Suddenly, his whole value-system seems to him without foundation. Up until then, he had, to a certain extent, identified with the value-system which had dictated to him his way of thinking and speaking. Henceforth, he is opposed to it.

Thus, the interlocutor, too, is cut in two: there is the interlocutor as he was *before* his conversation with Socrates, and there is the interlocutor who, in the course of their constant mutual accord, has identified himself with Socrates, and who henceforth will never be the same again.

The absolutely essential point in this ironical method is the path which Socrates and his interlocutor travel together. Socrates pretends he wants to learn something from his interlocutor, and this constitutes his ironic self-deprecation. In fact, however, even while Socrates *appears* to identify himself with the interlocutor, and enter completely into his discourse, in the last analysis it is the interlocutor who unconsciously enters into Socrates' discourse and identifies himself with *him*. Let us not forget: to identify oneself with Socrates is to identify oneself with *aporia* and doubt, for Socrates doesn't know anything; all he knows is that he knows nothing. Therefore, at the end of the discussion, the interlocutor has not learned anything; in fact, he no longer even knows anything. And yet, throughout the duration of the discussion, he has experienced what true activity of the mind is. Better yet, he has *been* Socrates himself. And Socrates is interrogation, questioning, and stepping back to take a look at oneself; in a word, he is consciousness.

Such is the profound meaning of Socratic maieutics. In a famous passage of the *Theaetetus*,[51] Socrates tells how he practices the same trade as did his mother, who was a midwife, attending corporeal births. Socrates himself, he claims, is a midwife of the mind, and it is to the birth of minds that he attends. Socrates himself does not engender anything, since he knows nothing; he merely helps others to engender themselves. As Kierkegaard was well aware, Socratic maieutics stands the master–disciple relationship on its head:

> to be a teacher does not mean simply to affirm that such a thing is so, or to deliver a lecture, & etc. No, to be a teacher in the right sense is to be a learner. Instruction begins when you, the teacher, learn from the learner, put yourself in his place so that you may understand what he understands and in the way he understands it.[52]

> The disciple is the opportunity for the master to understand himself, as the master is the opportunity for the disciple to understand himself. When he dies, the master has no claim on the disciple's soul, no more than the disciple has on that of the master . . . The best way to understand Socrates is precisely to understand that we do not owe him anything. That is what Socrates preferred, and it is good that he was able to prefer this.[53]

Here we touch upon one of the possible meanings of Socrates' enigmatic declaration: "I only know one thing: that is, that I don't know anything."[54]

This statement could be interpreted as meaning that Socrates did not possess any transmissible knowledge, and was unable to cause ideas to pass from his mind into that of others. As Socrates is made to say in Plato's *Symposium,* "My dear Agathon . . . I only wish that wisdom were the kind of thing that flowed . . . from the vessel that was full to the one that was empty." [55]

In Xenophon's *Memoirs of Socrates,* Hippias tells Socrates that, instead of always asking questions about justice, he would do better simply to say, once and for all, what justice is. Socrates replies: "If I don't reveal my views on justice in words, I do so by my conduct." [56] To be sure, Socrates was a passionate lover of words and dialogue. With just as much passion, however, he sought to demonstrate to us the limits of language. What he wanted to show us is that we can never understand justice if we do not *live* it. Justice, like every authentic reality, is indefinable, and this is what Socrates sought to make his interlocutor understand, in order to urge him to "live" justice. The questioning of discourse leads to the questioning of the individual, who must decide whether or not he will resolve to live according to his conscience and to reason. In the words of one of Socrates' interlocutors: "Anyone who enters into conversation with Socrates is liable to be drawn into an argument, and whatever subject he may start, he will be continually carried round and round by him, until at last he finds that he has to give an account both of his present and past life." [57] The individual thus finds himself called into question in the most fundamental bases of his action, and he becomes aware of the living problem he himself represents for himself. All values are consequently turned upside down, as is the importance previously accorded them. As Socrates says in Plato's *Apology*:

> I care nothing for what most people care about: money-making, administration of property, generalships, success in public debates, magistracies, coalitions, and political factions . . . I did not choose that path, but rather the one by which I could do the greatest good to each of you in particular: by trying to persuade each of you to concern himself less about what he *has* that about what he *is*, so that he may make himself as good and as reasonable as possible. [58]

The Socratic enterprise is existential in that it appeals to the individual. This is why Nietzsche and Kierkegaard, each in his own way, tried to repeat it. In the following text by Nietzsche, where he describes the "Schopenhauerian man," isolated in the midst of his contemporaries, it is hard not to think of Socrates' constant appeal to "take care of yourself," [59] and his continual calling into question of the individual:

> his fellow men . . . strut about in a hundred masquerades, as youths, old men, fathers, citizens, priests, officials, merchants, mindful solely of

their comedy and not at all of themselves. To the question: "To what end do you live?" they would all quickly reply with pride: "To become a good citizen, or scholar, or statesman!" [60]

the objective of all human arrangements is through distracting one's thoughts to cease to be aware of life. [61]

Haste is universal because everyone is in flight from himself. [62]

Already in Plato's *Symposium*, Alcibiades had said: "Socrates makes me admit to myself that, even though I myself am deficient in so many regards, I continue to take no care for myself, but occupy myself with the business of the Athenians." [63] This passage allows us to glimpse the political consequences of such a reversal of values and upending of the guiding norms of life. Concern for one's individual destiny cannot help but lead to conflict with the state. [64] This is the deepest meaning of the trial and death of Socrates. Socratic irony becomes especially dramatic when, thanks to the evidence of Plato's *Apology of Socrates*, we see it being used at the expense of the philosopher's accusers, and, in a sense, bringing about his condemnation to death. [65]

Here we have an instance of the "seriousness of existence" of which Kierkegaard speaks. [66] For Kierkegaard, Socrates' merit was that he was an *existing* thinker, not a speculative philosopher who has forgotten what it means to exist. Kierkegaard's fundamental category of existence is the individual, or the unique, isolated in the solitude of his existential responsibility. For Kierkegaard, Socrates was its discoverer. [67]

Here we come upon one of the most profound reasons for Socratic irony: direct language is not adequate for communicating the experience of existing, the authentic consciousness of being, the seriousness of life as we live it, or the solitude of decision making. To speak is to be doubly condemned to banality. In the first place, there can be no direct communication of existential experience, and in this sense, every speech-act is "banal." Secondly, however, it is this same banality which, in the form of irony, can make indirect communication possible. [68] In the words of Nietzsche: "I believe I sense that Socrates was profound; his irony was above all the necessity to pass himself off as superficial, in order to be able to associate with people at all." [69] For the existential thinker, banality and superficiality are a vital necessity. The existentialist must remain in contact with mankind, even if the latter is at a level of less-than-adequate consciousness. At the same time, however, we have here to do with a pedagogical artifice. The circuitous detours of irony, and the shock of *aporia*, can cause the reader to attain to the seriousness of existential consciousness, especially if, as we shall see later, the power of Eros is thrown in for good measure.

Socrates had no system to teach. Throughout, his philosophy was a spiritual exercise, an invitation to a new way of life, active reflection, and living consciousness.

Perhaps the Socratic formula: "I know that I know nothing" ought to be given a deeper meaning. We are thus brought back to our starting point: Socrates knows that he is not a sage.[70] As an individual, his conscience was aroused and spurred on by this feeling of imperfection and incompleteness.

In this regard, Kierkegaard can help us to understand the significance of the figure of Socrates. Kierkegaard asserts that he knows only one thing: that he is not a Christian. He was intimately convinced of this fact, because to be a Christian is to have a genuine personal and existential relationship with Christ; it is to interiorize Christ in a decision emanating from the depths of the self. Since such interiorization is so very difficult, it is virtually impossible for anyone truly to be a Christian. The only true Christian was Christ. At any rate, the least we can say is that the best Christian is he who is aware of not being a Christian, insofar as he recognizes that he is not a Christian.[71]

Like every existential consciousness, Kierkegaard's was divided. It existed only in its consciousness of not truly existing. Kierkegaardian consciousness is identical to Socratic consciousness:

> O Socrates, you had the accursed advantage of making it painfully obvious, by means of your ignorance, that others were even less wise than you. They didn't even know that they were ignorant. Your adventure was the same as mine. People become exasperated with me when they see that I can show that others are even less Christian than I; I who respect Christianity so much that I see and admit that I am not a Christian![72]

Socratic consciousness is also torn and divided: not by the figure of Christ, but by the transcendent norm of the figure of the sage.

Justice, as we have seen, cannot be defined. It must be lived. All the human discourse in the world could never suffice to express the depth of one person's resolution to be just. All human decisions are, however, fragile and precarious. When a person chooses to be just in the context of a particular act, he has the inkling of an existence which could be just in the full sense of the term. Such a fully just existence is that of the sage, who is not *sophos*, but *philo-sophos:* not a wise man, but one who desires wisdom, precisely because he lacks it. Paul Friedländer puts it well: "Socratic irony, at its center, expresses the tension between ignorance – that is, the impossibility ultimately to put into words 'what justice is' – and the direct experience of the unknown, the existence of the just man, whom justice raises to the level of the divine."[73]

Just as Kierkegaard was only Christian insofar as he was conscious of not being a Christian, Socrates was a sage only insofar as he was conscious of not being wise. An immense desire arises from such an awareness of privation, and this is why, for Western consciousness, Socrates the philosopher takes on the features of Eros, the eternal vagabond in search of true beauty.

2 Eros

It could be said that Socrates was the first individual in the history of Western thought. Werner Jaeger[74] was right to point out that Plato and Xenophon, in their Socratic writings, strive to make the reader sense Socrates' originality and uniqueness as they sketch his literary portrait. This need of theirs was certainly the result of the extraordinary experience of having known an incomparable personality, and, as Kierkegaard pointed out,[75] it is the true explanation of the terms *atopos*, *atopia*, and *atopotatos*, which recur so often in the Platonic corpus[76] to describe Socrates' character. In the *Theaetetus*, for instance, Socrates declares: "They say I am *atopotatos*, and all I create is *aporia*."[77] Etymologically, *atopos* means "out of place," hence strange, extravagant, absurd, unclassifiable, and disconcerting. In the *Symposium*, Alcibiades insists on this point in his speech in praise of Socrates. Normally, he says, there are classes of men, ideal types to which individuals correspond. For example, there is the type of the "great general, noble and courageous," represented in Homeric antiquity by Achilles, and among contemporary figures by the Spartan leader Brasidas. Then there is the type of the "clever and eloquent statesman," represented in antiquity by Nestor the Greek and Antenor the Trojan, and by Pericles among contemporaries. Socrates, however, does not fit into any category. He cannot be compared to any man, concludes Alcibiades; only to Sileni or satyrs.[78]

Socrates was indeed an individual: that individual so dear to Kierkegaard that he would have liked to have as an epitaph: "He was That Individual."[79]

And yet, although Socrates was unlike anyone else, we shall now see him take on the mythic characteristics of Eros;[80] an Eros, that is, conceived as a projection of the figure of Socrates.

In Socrates, erotic irony is intimately connected to dialectical irony, and it leads to reversals of situation quite analogous to those caused by the latter. Let us be quite clear: the love in question here is homosexual love, precisely because it is educative love. In the Greece of Socrates' day, masculine love was a vestige and remainder of archaic warrior education, in which the young nobleman was trained in the aristocratic virtues, within the framework of virile friendship, and under the direction of an older man. The master–disciple relationship was conceived during the period of the Sophists, on the model of this archaic relationship, and it was frequently spoken of in erotic terms. We must not, of course, forget the role played by rhetoric and literary fiction in this way of speaking.[81]

Socrates' erotic irony consisted in pretending to be in love until, thanks to the reversal brought about by irony, the object of his amorous attentions fell in love himself. Such is the story Alcibiades tells in his speech in praise of Socrates. Alcibiades, believing in the sincerity of the numerous declarations of love Socrates had made to him, invited Socrates home one night in order to seduce him. He slipped into bed with him, and wrapped his arms around him. Much to Alcibiades' surprise, however, Socrates remained in complete control of himself, and did not let himself be seduced at all. "Since that time," declares Alcibiades,

> I am the one who has been reduced to slavery, and I'm in the state of a man bitten by a viper.[82]

> I've been bitten in the heart, or the mind, or whatever you like to call it, by Socrates' philosophy ... the moment I hear him speak I am smitten with a kind of sacred rage, worse than any Corybant, and my heart jumps into my mouth and the tears start into my eyes ... I'm not the only one, either; there's Charmides, and Euthydemus, and ever so many more. He's made fools of them all, just as if he were the beloved, not the lover.[83]

It is hard to imagine a better commentary on this passage than the following one, by Kierkegaard:

> one might possibly call him a seducer, for he deceived the youth and awakened longings which he never satisfied ... He deceived them all in the same way as he deceived Alcibiades who ... observes that instead of the lover, Socrates became the beloved ... he attracted the youth to him, but when they looked up to him, when they sought repose in him, when forgetting all else they sought a safe abode in his love, when they themselves ceased to exist and lived only in being loved by him – then he was gone, then the enchantment was over, then they felt the deep pangs of unrequited love, felt that they had been deceived and that it was not Socrates who loved them but they who loved Socrates.[84]

Socrates' erotic irony consisted in pretending to be in love. In dialectic irony, Socrates pretended, as he asked his questions, that his real desire was that his interlocutor communicate to him his knowledge or wisdom. In fact, however, this game of questions and answers resulted in the interlocutor realizing that he was incapable of curing Socrates' ignorance, for he in fact had neither wisdom nor knowledge to give to Socrates. What the interlocutor really desired, then, was to enrol in Socrates' school: the school of the consciousness of not-knowing.

In erotic irony, Socrates used amorous declarations to pretend that he wanted his ostensible lover to hand over to him not his knowledge, but his physical beauty. This situation is understandable: Socrates was not attractive, whereas the young man was. In this case, however, the beloved – or supposedly beloved – discovered through Socrates' attitude that he was incapable of satisfying Socrates' love, because there was no true beauty within him. Upon discovering his shortcomings, the beloved would then fall in love with Socrates. It was not beauty with which the beloved fell in love – Socrates did not have any – rather, he fell in love with the love which, according to Socrates' definition in the *Symposium*,[85] is desire for the beauty which all of us lack. To be in love with Socrates, then, was to be in love with love.

This is precisely the meaning of the *Symposium*.[86] The whole dialogue is constructed so as to make the reader guess the identity between the figures of Socrates and Eros. Plato depicts the guests taking turns, going from left to right, giving speeches in praise of Eros. In succession, we hear Phaedrus and Pausanias, then Eryximachus the doctor, Aristophanes the comic poet, and finally the tragic poet Ariston. When Socrates' turn comes, he does not give a straightforward speech in praise of love, for that would be contrary to his method. Instead, he reports the conversation he had once had with Diotima, a priestess from Mantinea, who told him the myth of the birth of Eros. Theoretically, the dialogue would have ended here, were it not for Alcibiades' sudden intrusion into the banquet room. Crowned with violets and ivy leaves and rather drunk, Alcibiades submits to the rules of the banquet, but instead of praising Eros, he gives a speech in praise of Socrates.

The identity between Socrates and Eros is underlined in several ways: not only does the speech in praise of Socrates take its place in the series of speeches already given in praise of Eros, but, in addition, there are many significant features in common between the portrait of Eros, as sketched by Diotima, and the portrait of Socrates given by Alcibiades.

On the day of Aphrodite's birth, recounts Diotima, the gods had a banquet. Penia – that is, "Poverty" or "Privation" – came begging at the end of the meal. There she espied Poros – "Means," "Expedient," or "Wealth" – drunk on nectar and asleep in Zeus' garden. As a way out of her destitution, Penia decided to have a child by Poros, so she lay with him while he slept, and conceived Eros.

This account of the genealogy of Eros allows Diotima to give a description of him so subtle that it can be interpreted on a variety of levels. In the first place, following the exact words of the myth, we can recognize in Eros the features of both his mother and his father. From his father's side, he gets his clever, inventive mind (in Greek *euporia*). From his mother, he inherits the condition of a poverty-stricken beggar: *aporia*. Behind this description, we can distinguish a quite particular conception of love. Whereas the other guests had described Eros in an idealized way, Socrates recounts his conversation with

Diotima in order to introduce some realism into the vision of love. Contrary to what the other guests assume, says Socrates, it is not the case that love is beautiful. If it were, it would no longer be love, for Eros is essentially desire, and the only thing that can be desired is that which one does not have. Eros, then, cannot be beautiful: as the son of Penia, he lacks beauty, but as the son of Poros, he knows how to remedy his lack. Agathon has confused love with its object, the beloved.

For Socrates, love is a *lover*. It is therefore not, as most people think, a god, but only a *daimon*; a being intermediate between the human and the divine.

This is why there is something comic about Diotima's description of Eros. In it, we can perceive the beggarly existence to which love can condemn us. This is the familiar theme of "Militat omnis amans": [87] in which the lover stands guard on his beloved's doorstep, or spends the night sleeping on the ground. Eros is both beggar and soldier, but also inventor, sorcerer, magician, and clever talker, for love makes him ingenious. For him, life is an uninterrupted suite of discouragement and hope, need and satisfaction, which succeed one another in accordance with the successes and defeats of his love.

This is Eros in his monstrous aspect – good-for-nothing, shameless, obstinate, loud-mouthed and savage – whose misdeeds are depicted with such relish in Greek poetry, right down to the Byzantine period.[88]

And yet, with astonishing skill, Plato makes the features of Socrates "the philosopher" appear beneath the figure of Eros the hunter. Agathon may think Eros is delicate and lovely, but Diotima asserts he is, in reality, always poor, rough, dirty, and barefoot. In his speech in praise of Socrates, Alcibiades likewise portrays Socrates as barefoot, covered only by a coarse coat which barely protects him from the winter cold.[89] From the context of the dialogue, we learn that Socrates has, exceptionally, taken a bath before coming to the symposium.[90] The comic poets, too, had a good laugh at the expense of Socrates' bare feet and old cloak.[91]

The figure of Socrates as Eros the beggar was subsequently taken up by the Cynic philosophers, in particular Diogenes. Diogenes, who seems to have designated himself as a "furious Socrates," used to go wandering with only his cloak and knapsack, bereft of hearth and home.[92] As Friedländer points out,[93] barefooted Eros also calls to mind primitive man, as he is depicted by Plato in the *Protagoras* (321c5) and the *Statesman* (272a5).

We are thus brought back to the figure of that purely natural being, Silenus, with his primitive strength, more primal than culture and civilization. The fact that this element enters into the complex portrait of Socrates/Eros is not a matter of indifference. Rather, it corresponds perfectly to the reversal of values brought about by Socratic consciousness. For the person concerned about his soul, what is essential is not to be found in appearance, dress, or comfort, but in freedom.

And yet, Diotima stresses that Eros has inherited some features from his father: "he sets traps for noble souls, for he is bold, headstrong, and full of endurance. He's a dangerous hunter, always plotting some trick; he lusts after cleverness,[94] is full of resources, and is always thinking up some scheme; he's a terrible sorcerer, magician, and sophist."[95] We could very well be listening to Strepsiades in Aristophanes' *Clouds*, describing what he wants to become after his Socratic education: "audacious, glib, daring and head-strong . . . never at a loss for words, a real fox."[96] In his speech prais-ing Socrates, Alcibiades had called him an impudent Silenus,[97] and Agathon had bestowed upon Socrates the epithet of *hybristes*.[98] For Alcibiades, Socrates is a magician[99] and a smooth talker, skilled in attracting pretty boys.[100]

Eros' toughness appears once again in the portrait which Alcibiades sketches of Socrates on campaign with the army. He could, Alcibiades says, put up with cold, hunger, and fear, and hold his wine as easily as he endured long bouts of meditation.[101] During the retreat from Delion, Alcibiades tells us, Socrates walked as calmly as if he were in the streets of Athens, where Aristophanes describes him as "holding his head high . . . rolling his eyes, barefoot, looking solemn."[102] As we can see, this portrait of Socrates/Eros is not very flattering; we are clearly smack in the midst of Platonic – if not Socratic – irony. Nevertheless, this image is not without its profound psychological truth.

Eros, Diotima tells us, is a *daimon*: that is, a being intermediate between gods and men. Once more, we are forced to consider the problem of intermediary states, and we realize once more just how uncomfortable such a situation is. Eros the *daimon*, as Diotima describes him to us, is undefinable and unclassifiable: he too, like Socrates, is *atopos*. He is neither god nor man, fair nor ugly, wise nor foolish, good nor evil.[103] Yet he still embodies desire, for, like Socrates, he is *aware* that he is neither handsome nor wise. This is why he is a *philo-sopher* – a lover of wisdom. In other words, he desires to attain to the level of being of divine perfection. Thus, according to Diotima's description, Eros is the desire for his own perfection, which is to say, for his true self. He suffers from being deprived of the plenitude of being, and he strives to attain it. When other men fall in love with Socrates/Eros – that is, when they fall in love with love, such as Socrates reveals it to them – what they love in Socrates is his love for, and aspiration toward, beauty and the perfection of being. In Socrates, they find the path toward their own perfection.

Eros, like Socrates, is merely a call and a possibility; he is neither wisdom nor beauty itself. To be sure, if one opens up the little Sileni mentioned by Alcibiades, they turn out to be full of statues of gods.[104] The Sileni, however, are not themselves the statues. They only open up so that one can get at them. The etymological meaning of Poros, Eros' father, is "means of access" or "way out." Socrates is only a Silenus, opening up onto something beyond himself.

The philosopher, too, is nothing other than this: a summons to existence. As Socrates puts it ironically to the handsome Alcibiades: "If you love me, it must be because you have seen in me a beauty which bears no resemblance to your own physical beauty . . . But consider the matter more carefully, lest you make a mistake both about me and about me and about my real nothingness." [105] Here Socrates gives Alcibiades a warning. In loving Socrates, he is really only loving Eros: not Aphrodite's son, but the son of Poros and Penia. The cause of his love is that he senses that Socrates can open up to him a path toward an extraordinary beauty, transcending all earthly beauties. Socrates' virtues – those statues of the gods hidden within the ironical Silenus – which Alcibiades admires so much,[106] are only a reflection and a foretaste of that perfect wisdom which Socrates desires, and which Alcibiades desires through Socrates.

In Socratic Eros, we find the same basic structure as in Socratic irony: a divided consciousness, passionately aware that it is not what it ought to be. It is from this feeling of separation and lack that love is born.

One of Plato's greatest merits will always be that he was able, via the myth of Socrates/Eros, to introduce into the philosophical life the dimension of love – that is, of desire and the irrational. He accomplished this in several ways: in the first place, in the experience of dialogue itself, in which two interlocutors experience a passionate will to clarify a problem together. Quite apart from the dialectical movement of the logos, the path traveled together by Socrates and his partner, and their common will to come to an agreement, are already a kind of love. There is a great deal more philosophy in spiritual exercises like Socrates' dialogues than in the construction of a philosophical system. The task of dialogue consists essentially in pointing out the limits of language, and its inability to communicate moral and existential experience. Yet the dialogue itself, qua event and spiritual activity, already constitutes a moral and existential experience, for Socratic philosophy is not the solitary elaboration of a system, but the awakening of consciousness, and accession to a level of being which can only be reached in a person-to-person relationship.

Just like ironical Socrates, Eros teaches nothing, for he is ignorant. He does not make people more wise; he makes them *other*. He, too, is maieutic: he helps souls to engender themselves.

It is touching to trace the influence of Socratic Eros throughout history.[107] In third-century Alexandria, for instance, the Christian writer Gregory Thaumaturgus praised his master Origen in the following terms:

And thus, like some spark lighting upon our inmost soul, love was kindled and burst into flame within us – a love at once for the *Logos* . . . and for this man, its friend and advocate . . . sometimes he would approach us in the genuine Socratic fashion, and trip us up by his argumentation whenever he saw us getting restive under him, like so many unbroken horses.[108]

As Bertram has shown in some splendid pages,[109] we encounter the tradition of Socratic Eros and the educative *daimon* in Nietzsche. According to Bertram, three sayings sum up perfectly this erotic dimension of pedagogy. One is by Nietzsche himself: "The deepest insights spring from love alone."[110] Another is by Goethe: "We learn only from those we love."[111] Finally, there is Hölderlin's dictum: "Mortal man gives his best when he loves."[112] These three maxims go to show that it is only through reciprocal love that we can accede to genuine consciousness.

Using Goethe's terminology, we could characterize this dimension of love, desire, and the irrational as the "demonic." Plato had encountered this dimension in the person of Socrates himself. As is well known, Socrates' *daimon* was a kind of inspiration which sometimes came over him in a completely irrational way, as a negative sign telling him not to do such and such a thing. It was, in a sense, his real "character," or true self. Moreover, this irrational element in Socratic consciousness is probably not without relation to Socratic irony. It is possible that Socrates' reason for asserting that he did not know anything was that, when it came time for action, he trusted in his own *daimon*, as he also trusted in the *daimon* of his interlocutors. In any case, as James Hillman pointed out in 1966, if Plato was able to bestow upon Socrates the figure of the great *daimon* Eros, it was probably because, in Socrates, he had encountered a demonic man.[113]

How can we describe this dimension of the demonic? No one could be a better guide for us in this matter than Goethe, who was fascinated and troubled by the mystery of the "demonic" all throughout his life. His first encounter with the demonic had probably been Socrates' *daimon*, as depicted in Hamann's *Socratic Memorabilia*.[114] Socrates fascinated Goethe to such an extent that we find the following extraordinary exclamation in his letter to Herder of 1772: "If only I could be Alcibiades for one day and one night, and then die!"[115] For Goethe, the demonic had all the ambiguous and ambivalent features of Socratic Eros. It is, as he writes in Book 20 of *Poetry and Truth*,[116] a force which is neither divine nor human, neither diabolical nor angelic, which simultaneously unites and separates all beings. Just as in the case of Eros in the *Symposium*, it can only be defined by simultaneous and contradictory negations. Yet it is a force which gives its holders an incredible power over beings and things. The demonic represents a kind of natural magic within the dimension of the irrational and inexplicable. This irrational element is the motor force indispensable for all creation; it is the blind, inexorable dynamic which we cannot escape, but must rather learn how to use. In his *Urworte*, Goethe writes as follows about the *daimon* of individuals:

So must you be; you cannot escape yourself.
. . . no time nor power may destroy
Form marked with a seal, which develops as it lives.[117]

In Goethe, the creatures who most faithfully represent this demonic element take on the features of Eros in the *Symposium*. As Raabe has demonstrated, this is particularly true in the case of Mignon.[118] Mignon, like Eros, is indigent, but she aspires to purity and beauty. Although her clothing is poor and coarse, her musical gifts reveal her inner riches. Like Eros, she sleeps on the bare ground, or on Wilhelm Meister's doorstep. Finally, like Eros, she is the projection and incarnation of Wilhelm Meister's nostalgia for a higher form of life.

Another demonic figure in Goethe is Ottilia, heroine of the *Elective Affinities*. She is depicted as a natural force, powerful, strange, and fascinating. Her profound relationship to Eros is more discreetly indicated than in the case of Mignon, but it is no less real. Mention should also be made of the hermaphroditic figure of Homunculus, whose relationship to Eros is emphasized so clearly in Act II of the *Second Faust*.[119]

As an ambiguous, ambivalent, indecisive element, the demonic is neither good nor evil. Only mankind's moral decision can give it its definitive value. And yet, this irrational, inexplicable element is inseparable from existence. The encounter with the demonic, and the dangerous game with Eros, cannot be avoided.

3 Dionysos

We shall now return to Nietzsche's odd, amorous hatred for Socrates. To be sure, Bertram has already stated the essential on this point,[120] but perhaps Nietzsche's complex attitude can be better understood by considering some of the less frequently noticed elements which go to make up the Socrates of the *Symposium*.

Nietzsche was quite familiar with the strange seductive powers of Socrates, whom he termed "This mocking and enamored monster and pied piper of Athens, who made the most overweening youths tremble and sob."[121] Nietzsche tries to define the mechanism of this seduction: "I have made understandable how it was that Socrates could repel: it is therefore all the more necessary to explain his fascination."[122] Nietzsche then goes on to propose several explanations: Socrates flattered the Greeks' taste for combat with his dialectics; he was a great erotic; he understood his historical role of counteracting instinctive decadence by means of rationality. The truth is that none of these explanations is particularly fascinating. Nietzsche does, however, suggest a more profound cause: the seduction Socrates exercised on all posterity came from his attitude in the face of death. More specifically, it came from the semi-voluntary nature of his death. As early as his first work, *The Birth of Tragedy*, Nietzsche summed up the last pages of the *Phaedo* and the *Symposium* in a grandiose image:

> that he was sentenced to death, not exile, Socrates himself seems to have brought about with perfect awareness and without any natural awe of death. He went to his death with the calm with which, according to Plato's description, he leaves the Symposium at dawn, the last of the revelers, to begin a new day, while on the benches and on the ground his drowsy table companions remain behind to dream of Socrates, the true Eroticist. *The dying Socrates* becomes the new ideal, never seen before, of noble Greek youths.[123]

Nietzsche sensed and foresaw, in the concluding scene of Plato's *Symposium*, a symbol of Socrates' death. Taken by itself, Plato's description of the scene was as simple as could be:

> Only Agathon, Aristophanes and Socrates were still awake, and they were passing a huge bowl from left to right, and drinking from it. Socrates was holding a discussion with them . . . he was gradually forcing them to admit that one and the same author ought to be able to compose both comic and tragic poetry . . . Aristophanes was the first to fall asleep, and then, when the sun had already risen, Agathon. Socrates . . . then got up and left. He headed for the Lyceum, and, after splashing himself with water, he spent the rest of the day just like he would have any other.[124]

The ambiguous symbolism latent in this sober passage has not been lost on modern poets. C.F. Meyer, for instance, gave the following picture of the figure of the dying Socrates, in that dawn when only the philosopher is still awake:

> While Socrates' friends drank with him
> And their heads sank down on their pillows
> A young man came in – I remember it well
> Along with two lithe flute-players.
> We drained our cups to the dregs,
> And our lips, tired from so much talk, fell silent
> A song hovered above the withered garlands . . .
> Silence! The sleepy flutes of death are sounding![125]

By contrast, what Hölderlin saw in this episode was Socrates the lover of life:

> Yet each of us has his measure.
> For hard to bear
> Is misfortune, but harder still good fortune.
> Yet one wise man was able
> From noon to midnight, and on
> Till morning lit up the sky
> To keep wide awake at the banquet.[126]

Herein lies the enigma Socrates posed for Nietzsche. How could someone who loved life as much as Socrates loved it seem, by his will to die, to hate existence? For Nietzsche was quite familiar with the Socrates who loved life; indeed, he loved him:

> If all goes well, the time will come when one will take up the *Memorabilia*[127] of Socrates rather than the Bible as a guide to morals and reason, and when Montaigne and Horace will be employed as forerunners and signposts to an understanding of Socrates, that simplest and most imperishable of intercessors. The pathways of the most various philosophical modes of life lead back to him ... Socrates excels the founder of Christianity in possessing a joyful kind of seriousness and that *wisdom full of roguishness* that constitutes the finest state of the human soul.[128]

We can see Socrates' *"wisdom full of roguishness"* in Xenophon's depiction of Socrates dancing;[129] in the jesting, ironical Socrates of the Platonic dialogues; and in the figure of the life-loving philosopher in Hölderlin's poem "Socrates and Alkibiades":

> "Holy Socrates, why do you always
> Pay court to this young man?
> Do you know nothing greater?
> Why do your eyes gaze lovingly on him
> As on a god?"
> "He who has thought most deeply
> Loves that which is the most alive.
> He who has seen the world
> Can understand lofty Youth.
> And often, in the end,
> The wise bow down before the fair."[130]

In Nietzsche's essay *Schopenhauer as Educator*, the figure of Schopenhauer is merged with this figure of Socrates-as-lover-of-life. In the following

extraordinary passage, Nietzsche has recourse to Hölderlin's verses in order
to describe the sage's gaiety:

> Nothing better or happier can befall a man than to be in the proximity
> of one of those victorious ones, who, precisely because *they have thought
> most deeply, must love what is most living and*, as *sages, incline in the end to
> the beautiful* . . . They are active and truly alive . . . which is why, in their
> proximity, we feel human and natural for once, and feel like exclaiming
> with Goethe: "How glorious and precious is a living thing! how well
> adapted to the conditions it lives in, how true, how existent!" [131]

In *The Birth of Tragedy*,[132] Nietzsche thought he could foresee the coming
of a musical Socrates. Socrates the musician, he thought, would answer the
call which, in Socrates' dreams, had invited the philosopher to devote himself
to music; he would thereby reconcile the ironic lucidity of rational consciousness with demonic enthusiasm. Such a figure, says Nietzsche in his unpublished writings, would be a true example of "tragic man." Nietzsche projected
his own dream of a reconciliation between Apollo and Dionysos into this
image of Socrates as musician.

In the dying Socrates, Nietzsche saw yet another reflection of his own
drama. Socrates *wanted* to die – this is what was so shocking to Nietzsche –
and at the moment of his death his spoke these enigmatic words: "O Crito,
we owe a rooster to Asclepius." [133] It was as if he had been cured from some
illness, and owed a debt to the god of healing.

> This ridiculous and terrible "last word" means, for those who have ears:
> "O Crito, *life is a disease*." Is it possible that a man like him . . . should
> have been a pessimist? He had merely kept a cheerful mien while
> concealing all his life long his ultimate judgment, his inmost feeling.
> Socrates, Socrates *suffered life!* And then he still revenged himself – with
> this veiled, gruesome, pious, and blasphemous saying . . . I wish he had
> remained taciturn also at the last moment of his life; in that case he
> might have belonged to a still higher order of spirits.[134]

As Bertram has shown so well, Nietzsche here gives us the clue to his own secret,
intimate doubt, and to the drama of his entire existence. Nietzsche would have
liked to be the bard of the joy of life and existence; yet, in the final analysis,
wasn't he, too, afraid that life might be nothing but a disease? By letting what he
thought of terrestrial existence be known, Socrates gave his secret away. Yet
Nietzsche *wanted* to belong to that "higher order of spirits": those, that is, who
can keep quiet about this terrifying secret. In Bertram's words: "Was his extreme,
Dionysiac paean to life, and to life alone, only the kind of silence, beneath which
a great educator for life did not believe in life?" [135]

In the *Twilight of the Idols*, we find one final reversal in Nietzsche's reinterpretation of Socrates' last words. Here, the sickness from which Socrates is to be cured is not life itself, but the kind of life Socrates led: " 'Socrates is no physician,' he said softly to himself; 'here death alone is the physician. Socrates himself has merely been sick for a long time.' "[136] On this interpretation, Socratic lucidity and Socratic morality correspond to a sickness gnawing away at life. Yet, here again, might not Socrates' illness be the same as that of Nietzsche himself? This myth-dissolving lucidity, this pitiless consciousness; are they not those of Nietzsche himself? Nietzsche's amorous hatred for Socrates was, in the last analysis, identical with the amorous hatred Nietzsche felt for himself. Perhaps the ambiguity of the figure of Socrates in Nietzsche was rooted in the ambiguity of the central figure of Nietzschean mythology: Dionysos, god of death and of life.

For reasons which, in the last analysis, remain rather mysterious for us, Plato in his *Symposium* surrounded Socrates with a whole cluster of Dionysiac symbols.[137] In fact, the entire dialogue could have been entitled *The Judgment of Dionysos*, since Agathon tells Socrates that, when it comes to finding out who is wiser, he or Socrates, they will leave the question up to Dionysos. In other words, whoever drinks the most will win this contest of *sophia* – wisdom and knowledge – placed as it is under the sign of the god of wine.[138] When Alcibiades later bursts into the banquet room, he is crowned with violets and ivy leaves, just like Dionysos.[139] As soon as he comes in, Alcibiades places a crown of headbands around Socrates' head, as it was the custom to do for the victor in poetry contests.[140] We recall that Dionysos was the god both of tragedy and of comedy. In the course of his speech in praise of Socrates, Alcibiades composes what Socrates later terms "a drama of satyrs and Sileni,"[141] since these are the beings to which he compares Socrates. Again, we recall that satyrs and Sileni formed the accompanying entourage of Dionysos, and that the centre of satyric drama was, originally, the passion of Dionysos. In the final scene of the *Symposium*, we find Socrates alone with the tragic poet Agathon and the comic poet Aristophanes, gradually convincing them that one and the same man should be able to be both a tragic and a comic poet.[142] Agathon, in his praise of Eros, had said that love was the greatest of poets.[143] Thus, Socrates, who excels in the field of Eros, also excels in that of Dionysos. After all, he has no rival when it comes to holding his wine,[144] and if, as a result of the "Judgment of Dionysos," he wins the wisdom contest, it is because he is the only one still awake at the end of the banquet.[145] Can we discern yet another Dionysiac characteristic in his prolonged ecstasies and transports, which are mentioned twice in the dialogue?[146]

Thus, we find in Plato's *Symposium* what seems to be a conscious and deliberate ensemble of allusions to the Dionysiac nature of the figure of Socrates. This ensemble culminates in the final scene of the dialogue, in which Socrates emerges victorious from the judgment of Dionysos, as the best drinker and the best poet.

We should not be surprised if, paradoxically, secretly, and perhaps unconsciously, the figure of Socrates comes, for Nietzsche, to coincide with the figure of Dionysos.

At the end of *Beyond Good and Evil*, Nietzsche dedicates to Dionysos an extraordinary panegyric of the "genius of the heart," which he repeats, as evidence of his skill in psychological mastery, in the *Ecce Homo*,[147] although this time he makes a point of refusing to say whom he is addressing. In this hymn, it is as though we hear an echo of the *Veni Sancte Spiritus*,[148] that old medieval encomium of the Holy Ghost (of which Hamann[149] considered Socrates' *daimon* to be a prefiguration): "Flecte quod est rigidum, fove quod est frigidum, rege quod est devium." [150] For Nietzsche, the genius of the heart has the same marvelously delicate power of softening, warming, and straightening. In his portrait of the spiritual guide with demonic powers, Nietzsche intended to describe the action of Socrates. But as Bertram has suggested,[151] wasn't he also thinking – consciously or unconsciously – of Socrates?

We will conclude with Nietzsche's encomium, since it sums up admirably all the themes of our discussion:

The genius of the heart, as that great concealed one possesses it, the tempter god and born pied piper of consciences, whose voice knows how to descend into the netherworld of every soul; who does not say a word or cast a glance in which there lies no secret goal of seduction . . . the genius of the heart who silences all that is loud and self-satisfied, teaching it to listen; who smooths rough souls and lets them taste a new desire – to lie still as a mirror, that the deep sky may mirror itself in them . . . the genius of the heart from whose touch everyone walks away richer, not having received grace and surprised, not as blessed and oppressed by alien goods, but richer in himself, newer to himself than before, broken open and sounded out by a thawing wind; more uncertain, perhaps; tenderer, more fragile, more broken, but full of hopes that as yet have no name.[152]

NOTES

1 Aristotle, *Protrepticus*, frg. 5, p. 33 Ross. Cf. the German translation in I. Düring *Aristoleles. Darstellung und Interpretationen seines Denkens*, Heidelberg 1966, p. 414 and n. 87 = frg. B 39 in Düring's 1969 German translation of the *Protepticus*, p. 47.

2 On the problem of the historical Socrates, see the collection of articles in Andreas Patzer, ed., *Der historische Sociates* (= Wege der Forschung 585), Darmstadt 1987.

3 On Kierkegaard and Socrates, cf. J. Himmelstrup, *S. Kierkegaards Sokrates-*

Auffassung, Neumünster 1927; J. Wild, "Kierkegaard and classical philology," *Philosophical Review* 49 (1940), pp. 536–7; J. Wahl, *Études kierkegaardiennes*, 3rd edn, Paris 1967; E. Pivcevic, *Ironie als Daseinsform bei Sören Kierkegaard*, Gütersloh 1960; T. Bohlin 1941.

4 On Nietzsche and Socrates, see E. Bertram, *Nietzsche. Versuch einer Mythologie*, Berlin 1918, repr. Bonn, 8th edn, 1965; H. Hasse, *Das Problem des Sokrates bei F. Nietzsche*, Leipzig 1918; K. Hildebrandt, *Nietzsches Wettkampf mit Sokrates und Platon*, Dresden 1922; E. Sandvoss, *Sokrates und Nietzsche*, Leiden 1966; H.J. Schmidt, *Nietzsche and Sokrates*, Meisenheim 1969; Walter Kaufmann, *Nietzsche. Philosopher, Psychologist, Antichrist*, 4th edn, Princeton NJ 1974. On the vast phenomenon of Socrates' influence in the West, the reader will find a handy collection of texts in H. Spiegelberg, *The Socratic Enigma*, New York 1964. For the eighteenth and nineteenth centuries, see B. Böhm, *Sokrates im achtzehnten Jahrhundert Studien zum Werdegang des modernen Persönlichkeitsbewusstseins*, Leipzig 1929; H.-G. Seebeck, *Das Sokratesbild vom 19. Jahrhundert*, Göttingen 1947.

5 Plato, *Symposium*, 215b-c; Xenophon, *Symposium*, 4, 19; 5, 7; Aristophanes, *Clouds*, 362 (Socrates as cross-eyed). Cf. Plato, *Phaedo*, 117b.

6 Friedrich Nietzsche, "Socrates and Tragedy," *Posthumous Writings 1870–1873*, *Second Lecture*, in *Friedrich Nietzsche, Sämtliche Werke*, eds G. Colli and M. Montinari, 15 vols, Berlin 1980 (hereafter Colli/Montinari), vol. 1, p. 545.

7 Friedrich Nietzsche, *Twilight of the Idols. The Problem of Socrates*, 3–4, vol. 6, pp. 68–9, Colli/Montinari = *The Portable Nietzsche*, trans., intro., preface and notes Walter Kaufmann (= Viking Portable Library 62), New York 1954, repr. 1968 (hereafter *PN*), pp. 474–5.

8 Nietzsche, "Socrates and Tragedy," vol. 1, p. 544, Colli/Montinari.

9 Nietzsche, *Twilight of the Idols. The Problem of Socrates*, 3. On this anecdote, cf. Cicero, *On Fate*, 5, 10; *Tusculan Disputations*, 4, 37, 80; Alexander of Aphrodisias, *On Fate*, p. 171, 11 Bruns. According to Zopyrus, Socrates was stupid and slow because he lacked a hollow space between his collar-bones. We can perhaps detect an echo of this notion in Carus' description of the "Boeotian type"; cf. C.G. Carus, *Symbolik der menschlichen Gestalt*, 1858, repr. Hildesheim/Damstadt 1962, p. 267.

10 See above.

11 In *The Birth of Tragedy*, 8, Nietzsche insists on the alliance between wisdom and primitive instinct in the figure of the Sileni and Satyrs. Compare Jung's remarks on the alliance between wisdom and buffoonery in the nature of the elf (C.G. Jung, *Von den Wurzeln des Bewussteins*, Zurich 1954, p. 42). See also the following note.

12 Søren Kierkegaard, *The Concept of Irony with Constant Reference to Socrates*, GW 31, p. 10 = trans., intro., and notes Lee M. Capel, New York 1965 (hereafter Capel), p. 50.

13 Plato, *Symposium*, 215b.

14 Nietzsche, *Twilight of the Idols. The Problem of Socrates*, 4, vol. 6, p. 69 Colli/Montinari = *PN*, p. 475.

15 Plato, *Symposium*, 216e.

16 Ibid, 221e.

17 Ibid, 216d.

18 K. Gaiser, *Protreptik und Paränese bei Platon. Untersuchungen zur Form des platonischen Dialogs*, Stuttgart 1959, pp. 26, 149ff, 197.

19 Friedrich Nietzsche, *Ecce Homo*, 3, vol. 6, p. 320 Colli/Montinari = in *Friedrich Nietzsche, On the Genealogy of Morals*, trans. Walter Kaufmann and R.J. Hollingdale, New York 1969 (hereafter Kaufmann and Hollingdale), p. 280.

20 P. Friedländer, *Plato = An Introduction* (= Bollingen Series 59.1), trans. H. Meyerhoff, vol. 1, 2nd edn, Princeton NJ 1969, p. 126.

21 Cf. K. Gaiser, *Platons ungeschriebene Lehre. Studien zur systematischen und geschichtlichen Begründung der Wissenschaften in der platonischen Schule*, Stuttgart 1963, 2nd edn 1968; H.-J. Krämer, *Arete bei Platon und Aristoteles. Zum Wesen und zur Geschichte der platonischen Ontologie*, Heidelberg 1959; 2nd edn, Amsterdam 1967. On the history and current state of the question, see J. Wippern, ed., *Das Problem der ungeschriebenen Lehre Platons* (= Wege der Forschung 186), Darmstadt 1972; M.-D. Richard, *L'Enseignement oral de Platon, une nouvelle interprétation du platonisme*, preface Pierre Hadot, Paris 1986.

22 J.G. Hamann, *Sokratische Denkwürdigkeiten*, with notes by F. Blanke, Gütersboh 1959, p. 74. ["In an imitative way." – Trans.]

23 Cf. Böhm, *Sokrates*, cited above, n. 4.

24 J. Wahl, *Études kierkegaardiennes*, 3rd edn, Paris 1967, p. 282.

25 Søren Kierkegaard, *The Point of View for my Work as an Author*, GW 33, II, 1, A&5, p. 48 = trans., intro. and notes Walter Lowrie, New York 1962, 1st edn 1939 (hereafter Lowrie), pp. 39–40.

26 Søren Kierkegaard, *Tägebücher* (*Diaries*), Düsseldorf/Cologne 1982, vol. 2, p. 84 [= 8, A 27 (1847)].

27 Søren Kierkegaard, *The Instant*, GW 34, p. 329.

28 Cf. Søren Kierkegaard, *Concluding Unscientific Postscript* (*GW* 16, p. 240: "Socrates was very careful that there should be no direct relationship between the teacher and the student." On indirect communication, see Wahl, *Études Kierkagaardiennes*, pp. 281–8, 584 (on Nietzsche's theory of the mask).

29 Friedrich Nietzsche, *Posthumous Fragments*, June–July 1885, 37 (7), vol. 11, p. 580 Colli/Montinari = WP 980 (1885), p. 512.

30 Friedrich Nietzsche, *Beyond Good and Evil*, §40, vol. 5, p. 58 Colli/Montinari = trans. with commentary Walter Kaufmann, New York 1966 (hereafter Kaufmann), p. 51.

31 Nietzsche, *Posthumous Fragments*, April–June 1885, 34 (66), vol. 11, p. 440 Colli/Montinari.

32 Nietzsche, *The Dawn*, 4, §421, vol. 3, p. 257 Colli/Montinari.

33 Nietzsche, *Ecce Homo*, §3, vol. 6, pp. 319–21 Colli/Montinari = pp. 280–2 Kaufmann and Hollingdale.

34 E. Bertram, *Nietzsche. Versuch einer Mythologie*, Berlin 1918, repr. Bonn, 8th edn 1965, p. 182. Bertram's entire chapter on Nietzsche and the Mask is essential reading.

35 Nietzsche, *Posthumous Fragments*, 6 (3), Summer 1875, vol. 8, p. 97 Colli/Montinari.

36 Plato, *Republic*, 337a; *Symposium*, 216e 5; *Apology*, 38a 1.

37 Aristotle, *Nicomachean Ethics*, 1108a 22; 1127a 22.
38 Theophrastus, *Characters*, §1.
39 Cf. H. Lausberg, *Handbuch der literarischen Rhetorik*, Munich 1960, §§582; 902, with abundant references. One of the finest examples of the rhetorical use of irony is the praise of slavery in Montesquieu's *L'Esprit des Lois*, 15, 5.
40 Cicero, *Lucullus*, 15; *Brutus*, 292–300.
41 Plato, *Symposium*, 221e.
42 Nietzsche, *Human, All Too Human*, §175, vol. 2, p. 627 Colli/Montinari = (Texts in German Philosophy), trans. R.J. Hollingdale, Cambridge 1986 (hereafter Hollingdale), p. 352.
43 Epictetus, *Manual*, §46. Cf. F. Schweingruber, "Sokrates und Epiktet," *Hermes* 78 (1943), pp. 52–79.
44 Plato, *Republic*, 337a. Cf. *Gorgias*, 489e; *Theaetetus*, 150c.
45 Aristotle, *On Sophistical Refutations*, 183b8.
46 G.W.F. Hegel, *Vorlesungen über die Geschichte der Philosophie*, vol. 2, p. 65 = *Hegel's Lectures* 3 vols, London 1892, repr. London 1955 (hereafter Haldane), vol. 1, p. 203. The pages Hegel devoted to Socrates in this work are of great profundity, permeated as they are by the great problem of romantic irony.
47 Cf. P. Moraux, "La joute dialectique d'après le huitième livre des Topiques," in G.E.L. Owends, ed., *Aristotle on Dialectic* (= Proceedings of the Third Symposium Aristotelicum), Oxford 1968. On the philosophical significance of such dialectical jousts, cf. E. Weil, "La place de la logique dans la pensée aristotélicienne," *Revue de la Métaphysique et de Morale* 56 (1951), pp. 283–315.
48 O. Apelt, *Platonische Aufsätze*, Berlin 1912, pp. 96–108. On Socratic irony, the reader may consult the important work of M. Landmann, *Elenktik und Maieutuk*, Bonn 1950, and the excellent article by René Schaerer, "Le mécanisme de l'ironie dans ses rapports avec la dialectique," *Revue de Métaphysique et de Morale* 49 (1941), pp. 181ff. On irony in general, see Vladimir Jankélévitch, *L'Ironie*, Paris 1964.
49 ["Splitting" and "doubling" – Trans.]
50 The logos common to Socrates and to his interlocutors is personified in Plato, *Protagoras*, 361a.
51 Plato, *Theaetetus*, 149aff.
52 Kierkegaard, *Point of View*, §2, *GW* 33, II, 1, A, p. 40 = pp. 29–30 Lowrie.
53 Søren Kierkegaard, *Philosophical Fragments*, *GW* 10, pp. 58, 21.
54 Plato, *Apology*, 21d5.
55 Plato, *Symposium*, 175d.
56 Xenophon, *Memorabilia*, 4, 4, 10.
57 Plato, *Laches*, 187e.
58 Plato, *Apology*, 36b.
59 Plato, *Alcibiades*, 120d4; *Apology*, 36c.
60 Nietzsche, *Untimely Meditations*, 3, 4, vol. 1, p. 374 Colli/Montinari = trans. R.J. Hollingdale, intro. J.P. Stern, Cambridge 1983, repr. 1990 (hereafter Hollingdale and Stern), pp. 154–5.
61 Ibid, p. 373 Colli/Montinari = p. 154 Hollingdale and Stern.
62 Ibid, 3, 5, p. 379 Colli/Montinari = p. 158 Hollingdale and Stern.

63 Plato, *Symposium*, 216a.

64 Hegel insists strongly on this point; cf. *History of Philosophy*, 1, 2B, 36, = vol. 1, p. 442 Haldane: "no people, and least of all a free people like the Athenians, has by this freedom to recognize a tribunal of conscience."

65 Socrates' will to die posed a grave problem for Nietzsche; we shall return to this point later.

66 Kierkegaard, *Concluding Unscientific Postscript*, pp. 82ff Lowrie.

67 Kierkegaard, *Point of View*, Part II, ch. 2, B p. 61 Lowrie.

68 Cf. Wahl, *Études Kierkegaardiennes*, pp. 281ff; and especially the author's remarks on the relationship between the divine *incognito* and the *incognito* of the writer, p. 285, n. 1.

69 Nietsche, *Posthumous Fragments*, April–June 1885, 34 (148), vol. 11, p. 470 Colli/Montinari.

70 Cf. Plato, *Apology*, 23b: "The wisest [*sophotatos*] of you men is he who has realized, like Socrates, that in respect of wisdom [*sophia*] he is really worthless."

71 Cf. Wahl, *Études kierkegaardiennes*, pp. 387, 409 n. 1 (on Kierkegaard's negative theology).

72 Søren Kierkegaard, *Der Augenblick* (*The Instant*), 10, *GW* 34, pp. 330–1.

73 Friedländer, *Plato*, p. 153.

74 Werner Jaeger, *Paideia*, vol. 2, Berlin 1954, p. 64.

75 Kierkegaard, *Point of View*, *GW* 33, p. 64 = p. 61 Lowrie.

76 Plato, *Symposium*, 215a; *Phaedrus*, 229–30; *Alcibiades*, 106a.

77 Plato, *Theaetetus*, 149a.

78 Plato, *Symposium*, 221c–d.

79 Kierkegaard, *Point of View*, *GW* 33, p. 113 = p. 102 Lowrie.

80 On Socrates and Eros, see J. Hillman, "On psychological creativity," *Eranos-Jahrbuch* 35 (1966), pp. 370–98. The author emphasizes the demonic aspect of Socratic Eros, and I believe our investigations are mutually complementary.

81 Cf. H.-I. Marrou, *Histoire de l'éducation dans l'Antiquité*, 6th edn, Paris 1971, ch. 3: "De la pédérastie comme éducation" ["On pederasty as education" – Trans.].

82 Plato, *Symposium*, 217–18.

83 Ibid, 218a, 215e, 222b.

84 Kierkegaard, *Concept of Irony*, ch. 2, *GW* 31, p. 194 = p. 213 Capel.

85 Plato, *Symposium*, 200–1.

86 See, above all, Léon Robin, "Introduction," in *Platon, Le Banquet* (Budé), Paris 1951, pp. CI–CIX; Robin, *La théorie platonicienne de l'amour*, Paris 1933, p. 195; Friedländer, *Plato*, ch. 2: "Demon and Eros."

87 ["Every lover is a soldier." – Trans.]

88 On the genealogy of Eros, see M. Détienne and J.-P. Vernant, *Les ruses de l'intelligence. La mètis des Grecs*, Paris 1974, p. 140; A. Spies, *Militat omnis amans. Ein Beitrag zur Bildersprache der antiken Erotik*, Tübingen 1930. On Eros as a good-for-nothing, see the *Anthologia Palatina*, Book 5, Epigrams 176–80.

89 Plato, *Symposium*, 203c–d, 220b. On Socrates and Eros, see Jankélévitch, *L'Ironie*, pp. 122–5; T. Gould, *Platonic Love*, London 1963, p. 57.

90 Plato, *Symposium*, 174a.

91 See the passages quoted by Diogenes Laertius, *Lives*, 2, 27–8.

92 On the life-style of Diogenes the Cynic, see Diogenes Laertius, *Lives*, 6, 20 ff. The passage containing the definition of Diogenes as a "furious Socrates" (6, 54) is poorly attested textually, but is nevertheless not lacking in psychological verisimilitude.

93 Friedländer, *Plato*, p. 368, n. 6.

94 The Greek words chosen by Plato are intentionally ambiguous: Eros lusts after *phronesis*, that is, wisdom; he is "resourceful" (*porimos*); and he "philosophizes" (*philosophon*) all through his life.

95 Plato, *Symposium*, 203d.

96 Aristophanes, *Clouds*, 445ff.

97 Plato, *Symposium*, 221e.

98 ["Insolent, outrageous" – Trans.] Ibid, 175e.

99 Ibid, 215c; cf. *Meno*, 80a3; *Charmides*, 155e; *Phaedo*, 77e.

100 Ibid, 218a–b.

101 Ibid, 220a–d.

102 Aristophanes, *Clouds*, 362–3. Cf. Plato, *Symposium*, 221b.

103 Cf. Plato, *Symposium*, 203–4. On the philosophical significance of these simultaneous negations, cf. H.-J. Krämer, *Platonismus und hellenistische Philosophie*, Berlin/New York 1971, pp. 174–5, 229–30.

104 Plato, *Symposium*, 215b.

105 Ibid, 218e.

106 At *Symposium*, 217–21, Alcibiades insists on Socrates' temperance and strength.

107 Cf. Soren Kierkegaard, *Christliche Reden* (*Christian Speeches*), 1848, *GW* 20, p. 260: "When, in the course of my readings, I ran across Socrates, my heart began to pound like that of the young men who held discussions with him. The thought of Socrates inspired my entire youth, and filled my soul to overflowing." See also Goethe's comment, below.

108 Gregory Thaumaturgus, *Speech in Praise of Origen*, 6, 83; 7, 97.

109 E. Bertram, *Nietzsche. Versuch einer Mythologie*, Berlin 1918, repr. Bonn, 8th edn, 1965, pp. 318ff. Friedländer, *Plato*, p. 50, also alludes to this section of Bertram's work.

110 Nietzsche, "Introduction to the Study of Classical Philology," in *Nietzsches Werke*, vol. 17: *Philologica*, Leipzig 1910, p. 333.

111 Johann Wolfgang von Goethe, *Conversations with Eckermann*, trans. John Oxenford, 2 vols, 1850, May 12, 1825.

112 Friedrich Hölderlin, *The Death of Empedocles*, First Version, Act 2, Scene 4.

113 Hillman, "Psychological creativity," p. 380.

114 Hamann, *Sokratische Denkwurdigkeiten*, pp. 149ff *Hamann's Socratic Memorabilia, A Translation and Commentary*, trans. James C. O'Flaherty, Baltimore 1967 (hereafter O'Flaherty), pp. 169ff.

115 Johann Wolfgang von Goethe, letter to Herder, July 1772: "Wär' ich einen Tag und eine Nacht Alzibiades und dann wollt'ich sterben."

116 Johann Wolfgang von Goethe, *Poetry and Truth*, Hamburger Ausgabe (hereafter *HA*), vol. 10, p. 175.

117 Johann Wolfgang von Goethe, "Urworte, Orphisch. The Demon," *HA*, vol. 1,
   p. 359, lines 5–8: "So musst du sein, dir kannst du nicht entfliehen . . ./und
   keine Zeit und keine Macht zerstückelt/Geprägte Form die lebend sich
   entwickelt."
118 On Mignon's aspirations, cf. Johann Wolfgang von Goethe, *Wilhelm Meister's
   Apprenticeship and Travels, From the German of Goethe*, trans. Thomas Carlyle, 2
   vols, 2nd edn, 1839, vol. 2, p. 89:

> Such let me seem, till such I be;
> Take not my snow-white dress away! Soon from this dusk
>   of earth I flee
> Up to the glittering lands of day.
> There first a little space I rest,
> Then wake so glad, to scenes so kind
> In earthly robes no longer drest,
> This band, this girdle left behind.
> And those calm shining sons of morn,
> They ask not who is maid or boy;
> No robes, no garments there are worn,
> Our body pure from sin's alloy.
> [So lasst mich scheinen, bis ich werde,
> Zieht mir das weisse Kleid nicht aus!
> Ich eile von der schönen Erde
> Hinab in jenes feste Haus.
> Dort ruh' ich, eine kleine Stille,
> Dann öffnet sich der frische Blick;
> Ich lasse dann die reine Hülle,
> Den Gürtel und den Kranz zurück.
> Und jene himmlische Gestalten
> Sie fragen nicht nach Mann und Weib
> Und keine Kleider, keine Falten
> Umgeben den verklärten Leib.

Cf. M. Delcourt, "Ultrumque-neutrum," in *Mélanges H.-Ch. Puech*, Paris 1974,
p. 122: "A stolen child, unhappy, dressed as a boy and hiding her sex, Mignon is
depicted as a *zwitterhaftes Wesen* ["hybrid being" – Trans.]. Finally reconciled with
herself, she plays the role of an angel in a children's celebration and sings a Lied in
which she foretells her imminent death: *Ich eile von der schönen Erde . . .* "I am leaving
the lovely earth in haste / for that solid home . . . and the heavenly Forms who live
there / do not ask if one is man or woman / and no clothing, no veils / surround
one's transfigured body." On the figure of Mignon, cf. also W. Emrich, *Die Symbolik
von Faust II*, Frankfurt 1957, pp. 172, 459, with further bibliography.
119 On Ottilia and the Demonic, in relation to the concept of the *Ungeheures*
   ["monstrous" – Trans.], cf.–Emrich, *Die Symbolik*, p. 217. On hermaphroditism
   in general, see ibid, pp. 171–6.

120 Bertram, *Nietzsche*, ch. 20 ("Sokrates"). This is not the place to enter into a lengthy discussion of this point, but it seems to me that Bertram's position on the relationship between Nietzsche and Socrates has not been surpassed by the more recent work on the subject.

121 Friedrich Nietzsche, *The Gay Science*, §340, vol. 3, p. 569 Colli/Montinari = trans. Walter Kaufmann, New York 1974 (hereafter Kaufmann 1974), p. 272.

122 Nietzsche, *Twilight of the Idols, The Problem of Socrates*, §8, vol. 6, p. 71 Colli/Montinari = *PN*, p. 477.

123 Nietzsche, *The Birth of Tragedy*, §13, vol. 1, p. 91 Colli/Montinari = p. 89 Kaufmann.

124 Plato, *Symposium*, 223c.

125 C.F. Meyer, *Das Ende des Festes*, in *Gedichte*, vol. 4:

> Da mit Sokrates die Freunde tranken
> Und die Häupter auf die Polster sanken
> Kam ein Jüngling, kann ich mich entsinnen,
> Mit zwei schlanken Flöterbläserinnen.
> Aus dem Kelchen schütten wir die Neigen,
> Die gesprächsmüden Lippen schweigen,
> Um die welken Kränze zieht ein Singen . . .
> Still! Des Todes Sclummerflöten klingen!

[Conrad Ferdinand Meyer (1825–98) was one of Switzerland's greatest poets and novelists. – Trans.]

126 Friedrich Hölderlin, *Der Rhein*:

> Nur hat ein jeder sein Mass.
> Denn schwer ist zu tragen /Das Unglük, aber schwerer das Glük
> Ein Weiser aber vermocht es/Vom Mittag bis in die Mitternacht,
> Und bis der Morgen erglänzte,
> Beim Gastmahl helle zu bleiben.

=*Friedrich Hölderlin, Poems and Fragments*, trans. M. Hamburger, London 1966, p. 421.

127 "The most attractive book in Greek literature," said Nietzsche in his *Posthumous Fragments*, July 1879, 41, 2, vol. 8, p. 584 Colli/Montinari.

128 Nietzsche, *Friedrich Nietzsche: Human, All Too Human, A Book for Free Spirits*, §86, vol. 2, pp. 591–2 Colli/Montinari = p. 332 Hollingdale.

129 Xenophon, *Symposium*, 2, 16.

130
> "Warum huldigest du, heiliger Sokrates,
> Diesem Jünglinge stets? kennest du Grössers nicht?
> Warum siehet mit Liebe,
> Wie auf Götter, dein Aug' auf ihn?"
> "Wer das Tiefste gedacht, liebt das Lebendigste
> Hohe Jugend versteht, wer in die Welt geblikt
> Und es neigen die Weisen
> Oft am Ende zu Schönem sich."

131   während dem Menschen nichts Fröhlicheres und Besseres zu Theil
       werden kann, als einem jener Siegreichen nahe zu sein, die, weil sie das
       Tiefste gedacht, gerade *das Lebendigste lieben* müssen *und* als *Weise am Ende
       zum Schönen neigen* . . . Sie bewegen sich und leben wirklich . . . weshalb
       es uns in ihrer Nähe wirklich einmal menschlich und natürlich zu Muthe
       ist and wir wie Goethe ausrufen möchten: "Was ist doch ein Lebendiges
       für ein herrliches köstliches Ding! wie abgemessen zu seinem Zustande,
       wie wahr, wie seiend!"

       Nietzsche, *Untimely Meditations*, 3, *Schopenhauer as Educator*, 2, vol. 1, p. 349
       Colli/Montinari = p. 136 Hollingdale and Stern. [The quotation is taken from
       Goethe's *Italienische Reise*, October 9, 1786. – Trans.].
132   Nietzsche, *The Birth of Tragedy*, §14–15, vol. 1, pp. 96; 102 Colli/Montinari =
       pp. 93–8 Kaufmann. Socrates' dream, in which the gods order him to devote
       himself to music, is recounted in Plato's *Phaedo*, 60–1.
133   Plato, *Phaedo*, 118a.
134   Nietzsche, *The Gay Science*, §340, vol. 3, pp. 569–70 Colli/Montinari = p. 272
       Kaufmann 1974.
135   Bertram, *Nietzsche*, p. 341.
136   Nietzsche, *Twilight of the Idols. The Problem of Socrates*, §12, vol. 6, p. 73,
       Colli/Montinari = *PN*, p. 479.
137   Cf. Helen H. Bacon, "Socrates Crowned," *The Virginia Quarterly Review* 35
       (1959), pp. 415–30.
138   Plato, *Symposium*, 175e.
139   Ibid, 212e. Cf. Gould, *Platonic Love*, p. 40.
140   Ibid, 213e.
141   Ibid, 222d.
142   Ibid, 223d.
143   Ibid, 196e.
144   Ibid, 176c, 220a, 223d.
145   Ibid, 223d.
146   Ibid, 174d, 220c.
147   Nietzsche, *Ecce Homo*, §6, vol. 6, pp. 307–8 Colli/Montinari = pp. 268–9
       Kaufmann and Hollingdale.
148   ["Come, Holy Spirit." Otherwise known as the "Golden Sequence,"
       this Whitsun sequence is now commonly considered the work of Stephen
       Langton (ca. 1150–1228), Archbishop of Canterbury and opponent of King John.
       – Trans.]
149   Hamann, *Sokratische Denkwürdigkeiten*, pp. 149ff = pp. 141ff O'Flaherty.
150   ["Bend what is stubborn, warm what is cold, straighten what is crooked." –
       Trans.]
151   Bertram, *Nietzsche*, pp. 345–6.
152   Nietzsche, *Beyond Good and Evil*, §295, vol. 5, p. 237 Colli/ Montinari =
       pp. 218–19 Kaufmann.

6

Marcus Aurelius

1 The *Meditations* as a Spiritual Exercise

The *Meditations* of Marcus Aurelius – a better translation of the Greek title would be *Exhortations to Himself* – were first published in the West by the Zurich humanist Andreas Gesner, in 1558–9. Since their first appearance, the *Meditations* have continued to fascinate readers. Not all of these readers, however – and this includes many historians as well – have always understood what Marcus Aurelius intended to accomplish by writing this book. The seventeenth-century English editors and translators Meric Casaubon and Thomas Gataker still had an intimate sense for ancient realities, and were well aware of the nature of the work with which they were dealing. The *Meditations*, they realized, were a collection of *hypomnemata* (*commentaria* in Latin): notes written on a daily basis for the author's personal use.

Many authors allude to the existence of this literary genre in antiquity. Since they were not intended for publication, however, such writings were destined to disappear. We owe the preservation of Marcus' *Meditations* to some happy set of circumstances, quite possibly to the piety of one of the members of the emperor's immediate entourage.

Most historians, however, have anachronistically projected the literary prejudices of their own epoch back upon the *Meditations*. In the seventeenth and eighteenth centuries, when systematic treatises were considered the perfect form of philosophical production, it was generally thought that the *Meditations* should be brought into relation with the composition of some such treatise. Scholars consequently imagined that the *Meditations* were the extracts or *disjecta membra* of such a hypothetical opus, or perhaps a series of notes written with a view to its publication.

In the nineteenth century, characterized as it was by romanticism, it was widely recognized that the *Meditations* were a collection of *hypomnemata* or personal notes. Frequently, however, as in Renan's great study *Marcus*

Aurelius or the End of the Ancient World,[1] it was maintained that Marcus had written "a personal diary of his inner states."

In the twentieth century, the age of psychology, psychoanalysis, and suspicion, the very fact of having written this personal diary has been interpreted as the symptom of a psychological malaise. It has become a cliché to speak of the "pessimism" of Marcus Aurelius. E.R. Dodds,[2] for example, insisted on the perpetual self-criticism which Marcus carried out upon himself, and related this tendency to a dream of Marcus', which is preserved for us by Dio Cassius.[3] On the night of his adoption, says Dio, the emperor dreamed that his shoulders were made of ivory. According to Dodds,[4] this suggests that Marcus suffered from an acute identity crisis.

In a collaborative study, H. van Effenterre and the psychosomatist R. Dailly undertook to diagnose the pathological aspects – both psychic and physiological – of what they termed "the case of Marcus Aurelius."[5] Basing themselves on the testimony of Dio Cassius,[6] they supposed that Marcus suffered from a gastric ulcer, and that the emperor's personality corresponded to the psychological correlates of this illness:

> The ulcer-sufferer is someone closed in on himself, worried, and uneasy . . . a kind of hypertrophy of the self renders him unable to see his fellow men . . . in the last analysis, it is himself that he is looking for in others . . . He is conscientious to the point of punctiliousness, and is more interested in the technical perfection of administration than in human relationships, although the former should be only the sum total of the latter. If he is a thinking man, the ulcer-sufferer will be inclined to search for justifications, to fabricate superior personalities, and to adopt Stoic or Pharisaic attitudes.[7]

For these authors, Marcus' *Meditations* are a response to his need for "self-persuasion" and "justification in his own eyes."[8]

The acme of this kind of interpretation is no doubt the article by Thomas W. Africa, entitled "The opium addiction of Marcus Aurelius."[9] Basing himself on passages in Galen and Dio Cassius, the author tries to detect a genuine addiction to opium on the part of Marcus Aurelius, and he believes he can discover its symptoms in the *Meditations*. In fact, however, the texts he cites do not constitute conclusive proof of Marcus' drug addiction. As for the texts from the *Meditations* themselves cited as symptoms of intoxication, Africa's interpretation of them is pure nonsense.

Dio Cassius does not mention opium at all; he only mentions that, during the Danubian campaign, Marcus did not eat at night, and during the day consumed only a bit of theriac to ease his chest and stomach.[10] Galen does indeed mention opium,[11] but in such a way that it is impossible to deduce from his words a genuine addiction to opium. He merely says that, during the Danubian campaign, Marcus took a little bit of theriac every day – "in the quantity of an Egyptian bean" – for reasons of security. This was a frequent custom among Roman emperors, since theriac was considered an excellent antidote against poisons. Because theriac contained poppy-juice – that is, opium – Marcus experienced chronic fatigue during the day when he took it. He therefore had the poppy-juice removed from the mixture, but then began to suffer from insomnia. He again returned to taking theriac with poppy-juice, but this time the theriac was aged and much less strong. After the death of Marcus' official doctor Demetrius, Galen himself was charged with the composition of the emperor's theriac, and Marcus was entirely satisfied with his services. Galen explained to him that his theriac was the best, precisely because it was composed according to traditional proportions.

Marcus' problems with fatigue and insomnia were, as we can see, merely temporary. Marcus never sought out opium for its own sake, but for its medicinal effects, and thanks to Galen he seems to have found the proper balance in his dosage.

In the last note to his article, Africa himself admits that, even if one consumed as much theriac as Marcus did, the quantity of opium it contained was, in all probability, insufficient to produce an opium addiction. But, he adds, we must *suppose* that the prescribed doses were not always respected, because we must find some way of explaining the strangeness of the emperor's *Meditations* and the bizarre nature of the visions he describes.

Here the weakness of Africa's reasoning leaps to the eyes. We are not at all certain, he argues, that Marcus Aurelius was an opium addict, but we have to *presume* that he was, since we have somehow to explain the strangeness of the *Meditations*. This is a double sophism: first, even if Marcus' visions in the *Meditations* are bizarre, nothing obliges us to explain them by means of opium; after all, Dailly and van Effenterre were content to explain them by a gastric ulcer!

Africa thinks he can detect analogies between the *Meditations* and Thomas De Quincey's *Confessions of an English Opium-eater*. But is such a comparison really possible?

We shall let Africa speak for himself:[12]

Marcus' vision of time as a raging river carrying all before it into the abyss of the future was no school doctrine of life viewed from the Porch but an attempt to express the extended perspectives of time and space which opium had opened up to him. Temporal and spatial dimensions were accelerated until Europe was but a speck and the present a point and men insects crawling on a clod. History was no longer a reference but an actual pageant of the past and Marcus shared the exacerbated sensations of his fellow-addict, De Quincey: "The sense of space, and in the end the sense of time, were both powerfully affected. Buildings, landscapes, etc., were exhibited in proportions so vast as the bodily eye is not fitted to receive. Space swelled and was amplified to the extent of unutterable and self-repeating infinity. This disturbed me very much less than the vast expansion of time. Sometimes I seemed to have lived for seventy or a hundred years in one night; nay, sometimes had feelings representative of a duration far beyond the limits of human experience."[13]

The passages from Marcus Aurelius to which Africa refers are the following:

Eternity is a kind of river of events, and a violent torrent; no sooner has each thing been seen, than it has been carried away; another is being carried along, and it too will be swept away.[14]

Think often of the speed with which all that is and comes to be passes away and vanishes; for Being is like a river in perpetual flux, its activities are in constant transformation, and its causes in myriad varieties. Scarcely anything is stable, even that which is close at hand. Dwell, too, on the infinite gulf of the past and the future, in which all things vanish away.[15]

Pace Mr Africa, this theme is abundantly attested in Stoicism. Take, for example, the following passages from Seneca:

Place before your mind's eye the vast spread of time's abyss and embrace the universe; and then compare what we call human life with infinity . . .[16]

Everything falls into the same abyss . . . time passes infinitely quickly . . . Our existence is a point; nay, even less; but nature, by dividing this puny thing, has given it the appearance of a longer duration.[17]

This image is a venerable one; we find it in the following fine verses of Leonidas of Tarentum: "O man, infinite was the time before you came to the dawn, and infinite will be the time awaiting you in Hades. What portion of life remains for you, but that of a point, or if there is anything tinier than a point?"[18] To be sure, Marcus' river is none other than the Stoic river of being, which "flows without ceasing,"[19] but in the last analysis, it is also the river of Heraclitus, who, Plato tells us, compared all beings to a river's flow.[20] It is also, moreover, the river of the Platonists as mentioned by Plutarch: "All things simultaneously come to be and perish: actions, words, and feelings – for Time like a river carries everything away."[21] The same river is mentioned by Ovid: "Time itself flows on in constant motion, just like a river . . . wave is pushed on by wave."[22]

When, in the passage quoted above, Seneca uses the expression *propone* – "place before your mind's eye", that is, "represent to yourself the abyss of time" – he makes it clear that he is talking about an exercise of the imagination which the Stoic must practice. It is an instance of the same kind of exercise when, in his *Meditations*, Marcus Aurelius tries to embrace the dimensions of the universe in his imagination, and to look at things from on high,[23] in order to reduce them to their true value.

Think of the whole of being, in which you participate to only a tiny degree; think of the whole of eternity, of which a brief, tiny portion has been assigned to you; think about fate, of which you are such an insignificant part.[24]

If you were to find yourself suddenly raised up into the air, and observed from on high the busy hodgepodge of human affairs, you would despise them, as you saw at the same time how vast is the domain of the beings inhabiting the air and the ether.[25]

You have the power to strip off many superfluous things that are obstacles to you, and that depend entirely upon your value-judgements; you will open up for yourself a vast space by embracing the whole universe in your thoughts, by considering unending eternity, and by reflecting on the rapid changes of each particular thing; think of how short is the span between birth and dissolution, and how vast the chasm of time before your birth, and how the span after your dissolution will likewise be infinite.[26]

The rational soul . . . travels through the whole universe and the void that surrounds it . . . it reaches out into the boundless extent of infinity, and it examines and contemplates the periodic rebirth of all things.[27]

Asia and Europe are little corners of the world; every sea is a droplet in the world; each present instant of time is a point in eternity; everything is puny, unstable, and vanishing.[28]

How puny a portion of infinite, gaping eternity has been assigned to each man; it vanishes with all speed into the Unending. How puny a portion of the substance of the All; how puny a portion of the soul of the All. Of the whole of the earth, how puny is the lump you are crawling on![29]

The difference between these texts and the passage quoted above from De Quincey leaps to the eye. For the latter, the distortion of time and space is, as it were, imposed upon him from outside; the addict is the passive victim of his impressions. For Marcus, by contrast, the consideration of the infinity of time and space is an *active* process; this is made quite clear by his repeated admonitions to "represent to himself" and "think of" the totality of things. We have to do here with a traditional spiritual exercise which utilizes the faculties of the imagination. De Quincey speaks of a distortion of the instant, which takes on monstrous proportions. Marcus, by contrast, speaks of an *effort* to imagine the infinite and the all, in order that all instants and places may be seen reduced to infinitesimal proportions. In Marcus' case, this voluntary exercise of the imagination presupposes a belief in the classical Stoic cosmological scheme: the universe is situated within an infinite void, and its duration is comprised within an infinite time, in which periodic rebirths of the cosmos are infinitely repeated. Marcus' exercise is intended to provide him with a vision of human affairs capable of replacing them within the perspective of universal nature.

Such a procedure is the very essence of philosophy. We find it repeated – in identical form, beneath superficial differences of vocabulary – in all the philosophical schools of antiquity.[30] Plato, for instance, defines the philosophical nature by its ability to contemplate the totality of time and being, and consequently to hold human affairs in contempt.[31] We encounter this same theme[32] among Platonists like Philo of Alexandria[33] and Maximus of Tyre;[34] in Neopythagoreanism[35] among the Stoics,[36] and even among the Epicureans, as we have seen in the passage from Metrodorus quoted above.[37]

In Cicero's *Dream of Scipio*, the grandson of Scipio Africanus contemplates the earth from on top of the Milky Way. The earth appears so small to him that the Roman empire seems imperceptible, the inhabited world resembles a tiny island in the midst of the ocean, and life itself seems less substantial than a point.[38] This theme was kept alive throughout Western tradition. One thinks of Pascal's "two infinities": "Let the earth seem like a point . . . compared to the vast orbit described by this star . . ."[39]

Marcus Aurelius' notes to himself give us very little information about his personal experiences. To be sure, in some chapters of the *Meditations* we can discern some minimal autobiographical data, but these are few and far between (only 35–40 chapters, out of 473, contain such information). Often, these details consist in no more than a name, such as Pantheia, mistress of Lucius Verus, who sat next to her lover's tomb, or the mimes Philistion, Phoibos, and Origanion. Marcus tells us practically nothing about himself.

But what about those numerous statements by Marcus which seem steeped in pessimism? Don't they tell us anything about his psychological states? If one gathers them together, they certainly give the impression of a complete disdain for human affairs. We seem to find in them the expression of bitterness, disgust, and even "nausea"[40] in the face of human existence: "Just like your bath-water appears to you – oil, sweat, filth, dirty water, all kinds of loathsome stuff – such is each portion of life, and every substance."[41] In the first instance, this kind of contemptuous expression is reserved for the flesh and the body, which Marcus calls "mud," "dirt," and "impure blood." [42] Yet the same treatment is reserved for things mankind usually considers as important values:

> These foods and dishes . . . are only dead fish, birds and pigs; this Falernian wine is a bit of grape-juice; this purple-edged toga is some sheep's hairs dipped in the blood of shellfish; as for sex, it is the rubbing together of pieces of gut, followed by the spasmodic secretion of a little bit of slime. [43]

Marcus takes a similarly illusion-free view of human activities: "Everything highly prized in life is empty, petty, and putrid; a pack of little dogs biting each other; little children who fight, then laugh, then burst out crying." [44] The war in which Marcus defended the borders of the empire was, for him, like a hunt for Sarmatian slaves, not unlike a spider's hunt for flies. [45] Marcus cast a pitiless glance on the chaotic agitation of human marionettes: "Think about what they're like when they're eating, sleeping, copulating, defecating. Then think of what they're like when they're acting proud and important, when they get angry and upbraid their inferiors." [46] Human agitation is all the more ridiculous because it lasts only an instant, and ends up as very little indeed: "Yesterday, a little bit of slime, tomorrow ashes or a mummy." [47]

Two words suffice to sum up the human comedy: all is banal, and all is ephemeral. Banal, because nothing is new under the sun:

> Always bear in mind that everything is exactly the way it comes to pass right now; it has happened that way before, and it will happen that way again. Make them come alive before your mind's eye, these monotonous dramas and scenes, which you know through your own experience or through ancient history; picture the whole court of Hadrian, of Antoninus, of Philip, Alexander, and Croesus. All these spectacles were identical; the only thing that changed were the actors. [48]

Banality and boredom reach the point of being sickening:

> Just as you get sick of the games in the arena and such places, because they are always the same, and their monotony makes the spectacle tedious, so feel the same way about life as a whole. From top to bottom, everything is the same, and comes from the same causes. How long will this go on? [49]

Not only are human affairs tedious: they are also transitory. Marcus tries to make the human swarms of past ages come alive in his imagination, [50] picturing the days of Trajan or Vespasian, with their weddings, illnesses, wars, feasts, trading, agriculture, ambition, and intrigues. All these human masses have disappeared without a trace, observes Marcus, along with their activities. Marcus also tries to imagine this incessant process of destruction at work upon those around him.[51]

Marcus has no patience for those who would try to console themselves for the brevity of existence by the hope that they will survive in the name they leave to posterity. "What's in a name?" he asks: "A mere noise, or a faint echo."[52] At best, this miserable, fleeting thing will be transmitted to a few generations, each of which will last as long as a lightning-flash in the infinity of time.[53] We ought not to be fooled by such an illusion: "How many do not even know your name, and how many will very soon forget it."[54] "Soon you will have forgotten everything; soon, too, everything will have forgotten you."[55]

Such an accumulation of pessimistic utterances is indeed impressive. We should be careful, however, of deducing from them over-hasty conclusions about Marcus' own psychology. It is too facile for us to imagine that, like many modern authors, ancient writers wrote in order directly to communicate information, or the emotions they happened to be feeling. We assume, for instance, that Marcus' *Meditations* were intended to transmit his everyday feelings to us; that Lucretius was himself an anxious person, and used his poem *On the Nature of Things* to try to combat his anxiousness; that Augustine was really confessing himself in his *Confessions*. In fact, however, it is not enough to consider the obvious, surface meaning of the phrases in an ancient text in order fully to understand it. Rather, we must try to understand *why* these phrases were written or spoken; we must discover their *finality*.

Generally speaking, we can say that Marcus' seemingly pessimistic declarations are not expressions of his disgust or disillusion at the spectacle of life; rather, they are a *means* he employs in order to change his way of evaluating the events and objects which go to make up human existence. He does this by defining these events and objects as they really are – "physically," one might say – separating them from the conventional representations people habitually form of them. Marcus' definitions of food, wine, purple togas, or sexual union are intended to be "natural." They are technical, almost medical definitions of objects which, when considered in a purely "human" way, provoke the most violent passions, and we are to use them to free ourselves from the fascination they exercise upon us. Such definitions do not express Marcus' impressions; on the contrary, they correspond to a point of view intended to be *objective*, and which is by no means Marcus' invention. Already in antiquity, for instance, Hippocrates and Democritus were said to have defined sexual union as "a little epilepsy."

When Marcus pitilessly imagines the intimate life of the arrogant "eating, sleeping, copulating, defecating," he is trying to give a *physical* vision of human reality. We find a similar reflection in Epictetus, concerning people who are content just to discourse about philosophy: "I'd like to stand over one of these philosophers when he's having sex, so as to see how he sweats and strains, what kind of grunts and groans he utters; whether he can even remember his own name, much less the philosophical discourses he has heard, declaimed, or read!" [56] Marcus applies the same method to our idea of death: "consider what it is to die; and that, if one looks at death in and of itself, dissolving the images associated with death by taking apart our common conception of it, he will not suspect it to be anything other than a product of Nature." [57]

As we have seen, Marcus' effort to confront existence in all its naked reality leads him to glimpse processes of decay and dissolution already at work in the people and things around him, or to make the court of Augustus come alive before his eyes for an instant, so as to realize that all these people, so alive in his imagination, are in fact long dead. Yet we have no more right to interpret this as obsession with death or morbid complacency than when, in the film *Dead Poets' Society*, Robin Williams makes his students study a picture of the school's old boys. Williams' character is trying to make his charges understand the meaning of *carpe diem* ("seize the day"), the irreplaceable value of each instant of life, and it is with this goal in mind that he emphasizes that all the faces in the class photograph, so young and alive, are now long dead.

Moreover, when Marcus speaks of the monotony of human existence, it is not in order to express his own boredom, but in order to persuade himself that death will not deprive us of anything essential. In Lucretius, the same argument is used by nature herself, to console man for the misfortune of death: "There is no new invention I can think up to please you; everything is always the same . . . what lies in store for you is always the same . . . even if you were never to die." [58]

In the case of Marcus Aurelius, all these declarations are the conscious, voluntary application of a method which he formulates in the following terms:

> always make a definition or description of the object that occurs in your representation, so as to be able to see it as it is in its essence, both as a whole and as divided into its constituent parts, and say to yourself its proper name and the names of those things out of which it is composed, and into which it will be dissolved. [59]

This method is quintessentially Stoic: it consists in refusing to add subjective value-judgments – such as "this object is unpleasant," "that one is good," "this one is bad," "that one is beautiful," "this is ugly" – to the "objective" representation of things which do not depend on us, and therefore have no moral value. The Stoics' notorious *phantasia kataleptike* – which we have translated as "objective representation" – takes place precisely when we

refrain from adding any judgment value to naked reality.[60] In the words of
Epictetus: "we shall never give our assent to anything but that of which we
have an objective representation,"[61] and he adds the following illustration:

> So-and-so's son is dead.
> What happened?
> His son is dead.
> Nothing else?
> Not a thing.
>
> So-and so's ship sank.
> What happened?
> His ship sank.
>
> So-and-so was carted off to prison.
> What happened?
> He was carted off to prison.
> – But if we now add to this "He has had bad luck," then each of us is
>   adding this observation on his own account.[62]

In these objective/realistic definitions, some historians[63] believe they can
discover the traces of an attitude of repugnance in the face of matter and the
objects of the physical world. Thus, according to this view, Marcus Aurelius
renounced the Stoic doctrine of the immanence of divine reason in the world
and in matter, and there is no longer any trace in him of the admiration felt
by Chrysippus for the phenomenal world. We can therefore, it is alleged, find
traces in Marcus of a tendency to affirm the transcendence of a divinity
existing apart from the phenomenal world.

Some passages in Marcus do indeed seem provocative in this regard, but
they require the most painstaking interpretation. When, for instance, Marcus
evokes "the putridity of the matter underlying all things . . . liquid, dust,
bones, stench,"[64] he does not mean to say that matter itself is putrefaction;
rather, he wants to emphasize that the transformations of matter, qua natural
processes, are necessarily accompanied by phenomena which *seem to us* to be
repugnant, although in reality they too are natural.

The passage we have cited above[65] may seem even more provocative: "Just
like your bath-water appears to you – oil, sweat, filth, dirty water, all kinds
of loathsome stuff – such is each portion of life, and every substance." This
concise text can be interpreted in several different ways. In the first place, we
could say that Marcus is here applying his method of objective definitions.
What he means to say would be this: "when I observe physical and
physiological phenomena as they truly are, I have to admit that there are
many aspects of them which seem to me to be disgusting or trivial: they

consist of dust, the filth which covers abandoned objects, bad smells, and stenches. Our objective representation must recognize all these aspects of reality, without seeking to conceal any of them." Yet this realist vision has a threefold function. In the first place, it is intended to prepare us to confront life such as it is. As Seneca remarks,

> To be offended by these things is just as ridiculous as to complain that you got splashed in the bath, or that you got pushed around in a crowd, or that you got dirty in a mud-puddle. The same things happen in life as in the baths, in a crowd, or on the road . . . Life is not a delicate thing.[66]

Secondly, the realistic outlook is not intended to deny the immanence of reason in the world, but to persuade us to search for reason where it can be found in its purest state: in the *daimon* or inner genius, that guiding principle within man, source of freedom and principle of the moral life.

Finally, by reinforcing the sombre tones of disgust and repulsion, such definitions are intended to provide a contrast with the splendid illumination which transfigures all things when we consider them from the perspective of universal reason. Elsewhere, Marcus does not hesitate to declare:

> Everything comes from above, whether it has originated directly in that common directing principle, or whether it is a necessary consequence thereof. Thus, the gaping jaws of a lion, poison, and all kinds of unpleasant things, like thorns and mud, are by-products of those venerable, beautiful things on high. Don't imagine, therefore, that these unpleasant things are alien to that principle you venerate, but rather consider that *source* of all things.[67]

Here it is quite clear that filth, dust, and other such apparently repulsive aspects of reality are the necessary consequence of a natural process which, in the last analysis, goes back to universal reason. It is thus not matter itself which seems repulsive to us, but the accessory phenomena which accompany its transformations. Here Marcus[68] is in complete accord with Stoic orthodoxy, according to which matter is docile and subservient to reason, which molds and governs it. The function of Marcus' physico/objective definitions is precisely to make us realize that the feelings of repulsion we feel in the presence of some phenomena which accompany natural processes are nothing but an anthropocentric prejudice. In the following charming passage, Marcus expresses his belief that nature is beautiful in *all* its aspects:

> There is something pleasant and attractive about even the incidental by-products of natural phenomena. For instance, when bread is being

baked, some parts of it split open, and it is precisely those parts which split apart in this way, and which, in a sense, have nothing to do with bread-making itself, which are somehow quite appropriate, and excite our appetite in a most particular way. The same is true of figs: it is when they are at their ripest that they burst open. In the case of very ripe olives, it is precisely their proximity to decay which adds to them a certain beauty. The same is true with ripe ears of corn which bend towards the ground; with the lion's wrinkled forehead; with the foam spuming forth from the mouths of wild pigs, and many other such things: if we look at them in isolation, they are far from being beautiful. Nevertheless, because they are incidental by-products of natural processes, they add to the beauty of these processes and have an attractive effect on us. Thus, as long as one has a feeling for, and a deep understanding of Nature's processes, there is scarcely any of the things that occur as incidental by-products which will not present itself to one as pleasant, at least in some of its aspects. Such a person . . . will look upon the actual gaping jaws of wild beasts with no less pleasure than upon all the imitations of them that sculptors and painters offer us. With his wise vision, he will be able to discern the rich maturity of old men and women, as well as the lovely charm in young children; and there are many such things, which do not appeal to everyone; only to that person who has truly familiarized himself with nature and its workings.[69]

It is instructive to compare this text with the passage from Aristotle quoted above.[70]

Already in Aristotle, but especially in Marcus Aurelius, we can see a revolution taking place. In the place of an idealistic aesthetics, which considers as beautiful only that which is rational and functional, manifesting beautiful proportions and an ideal form, there appears a realistic aesthetics which finds beauty in things just the way they are, in everything that lives and exists. We know from Aulus Gellius,[71] moreover, that Marcus' distinction between nature's original plan and the unforeseen consequences resulting from this plan goes back to Chrysippus. Thus, in this case as well, Marcus stands firmly within orthodox Stoic tradition.

To return to the "provocative" passage with which we began:[72] it appears that Marcus' meaning is as follows. When dealing with what the Stoics termed *indifferentia*[73] – that is, things which depend not upon us, but upon universal nature– we must not make any distinction between what is repulsive and what is pleasant; any more than does nature itself.[74] Dirt, mud, and thorns, after all, come from the same source as the rose and the springtime. Thus, from the point of view of nature, and therefore also of whoever is familiar with nature, there is no distinction to be made between bath-water and the rest of creation: everything is equally "natural."

We can hardly hope to deduce Marcus' psychological states from any of the preceding. Was he an optimist or a pessimist? Did he suffer from a stomach ulcer? The *Meditations* do not allow us to respond to these questions. All we can learn from them is about spiritual exercises, as they were traditionally practiced by the Stoics.

2 Epictetus

In Marcus Aurelius' day, the greatest authority in questions of Stoicism was Epictetus. As the slave of Epaphroditus, one of Nero's freedmen, Epictetus had attended the classes of the Stoic Musonius Rufus. When Epictetus in turn was subsequently freed by Epaphroditus, he opened a philosophy school at Rome. In AD 93–4, Epictetus fell victim to the edict by which the emperor Domitian banished philosophers from Rome and Italy, and he set himself up in Nicopolis in Epirus. There he opened another school, where one of his regular students was the future civil servant and historian Arrian of Nicomedia. It was Arrian who was responsible for transmitting what we know about Epictetus' teaching; for Epictetus, like many philosophers in antiquity, never wrote anything down.

What Arrian thus preserved for us was not the technical part of Epictetus' philosophical instruction – his commentaries on Stoic authors such as Chrysippus, for example, or his more general explanations of doctrine. Rather, what Arrian copied down was the discussions which, as was usual in ancient philosophical schools, took place *after* the technical part of the class. In these discussions, the master would reply to questions from his audience, or enlarge upon particular points which were of importance for leading a philosophical life.[75] It is important to emphasize this point, for it means that we must not expect to find technical, systematic expositions of every aspect of Stoic doctrines in Epictetus' *Discourses*. Instead, they deal with a rather limited number of problems, for the most part restricted to ethical matters. This does not prove, of course, that Epictetus did not take up the whole of the Stoic system in the course of his theoretical teaching. Besides, only the first four books of Arrian's work have survived. We know from a passage in Aulus Gellius,[76] who cites an extract from the fifth book of Epictetus' *Discourses*, that a part of the work has been lost. For these two reasons, then, we must be wary of concluding, on the basis of these collections of Arrian's notes, that theoretical philosophical teaching gradually became impoverished in the course of later Stoicism.

What we *can* say is that Epictetus did insist very strongly upon a concept that was traditional in Stoicism:[77] the difference between *discourse about* philosophy and the *practice of* philosophy itself.

It is sometimes claimed that the Stoics recognized two parts of philosophy: on the one hand, they distinguished a theoretical-discursive part, comprising physics and logic; that is, the study of nature and of the rules of discourse. On the other, there was the practical part of philosophy, corresponding to ethics. This is incorrect. Rather, both theoretical philosophical discourse *and* philosophy itself as it was lived and experienced were made up of three constituent parts.

In theoretical philosophical discourse, the three parts of philosophy were necessarily distinguished. They were made the object of separate explanations, developed according to a logical principle of succession, and they laid the foundations for and developed the basic principles of Stoic doctrine. On the level of theoretical discourse, then, the parts of philosophy were in a sense external to one another, in accordance with the requirements of didactic exposition. Philosophy itself, however, is the *exercise* of wisdom; it is a unique act, renewed at each instant, and it may be just as well described as the exercise of logic, physics, or ethics, according to the subject-matter on which it is exercised, without its unity being in any way diminished. On this level, we are no longer concerned with theoretical logical – that is, the theory of correct reasoning – rather, we are concerned not to let ourselves be deceived in our everyday lives by false representations. We are no longer concerned with theoretical physics – the theory of the origin and evolution of the cosmos – we are concerned with being aware at every instant that we are *parts* of the cosmos, and that we must make our desires conform to this situation. We no longer do ethical theory – the definition and classification of virtues and duties – we simply *act* in an ethical way.

Concrete philosophical praxis requires that we always bear in mind the Stoics' fundamental dogmas. These dogmas were intended to constitute the basis for our rectitude of judgment, our attitude toward the cosmos, and the conduct we should adopt towards our fellow citizens within the city. Philosophy as it was lived and experienced thus implied continuous exercises of meditation and constant vigilance, in order to keep alive in one's mind the principles taught by theoretical discourse.

If we want to understand why Epictetus attaches so much importance to what he terms "the three areas of exercises," we shall have to bear in mind this distinction between theoretical philosophical discourse and concrete philosophy as it is lived and experienced. In the *Discourses* as reported by Arrian, these three areas are presented with such systematic rigor that we are justified in suspecting that this doctrine had an important role to play in Epictetus' theoretical teaching.

Epictetus bases his doctrine on the traditional Stoic distinction between things which depend on us and things which do not: "What depends on us is value-judgments, inclinations to act, desires, aversions, and, in a word, everything that is our doing. What does not depend on us is the body, wealth, glory, high political positions, and, in a word, everything that is not our own doing." [78] What depends upon us is the acts of our own soul, because we are able freely to choose them. What does *not* depend on us is those things that depend on the general course of nature and of fate. Among the acts of the soul which do depend on us, some correspond to the area of judgment and assent, others to the area of desire, and, finally, still others correspond to the area of inclinations to action.

For Epictetus, then, it is these three areas, acts of the soul, or aspects of "that which depends on us" which define the three forms of philosophical exercises. By comparing the relevant passages in Epictetus' *Discourses*,[79] we can present the theory of the three forms or areas of philosophical exercises as follows.

The first area is that of desire and aversion. People are unhappy because they desire things they may either lose or fail to obtain, and because they try to avoid misfortunes which are often inevitable. This happens because such desiderata as wealth and health, for example, do not depend on us. The discipline of desire consequently consists in accustoming ourselves to the gradual renunciation of such desires and aversions, so that, in the end, we shall desire only that which *does* depend on us – moral virtue – and shall also avoid only that which depends on us – moral evil. We are to regard everything which does *not* depend on us as indifferent; that is to say, we must not make any *difference* between such things. Rather, we must accept them all, willed as they are by universal nature. The discipline of desire concerns the passions or emotions (*pathe*) which we feel as a result of what happens to us.

The second area of exercises is that of motivating inclinations, or action. For Epictetus, this area is related first and foremost to human relationships within the city. It corresponds to what the Stoics traditionally called "the duties" (*ta kathekonta*): those actions which are appropriate to the inclinations of our nature. Duties are actions – they thus fall under the category of things which depend on us – bearing upon objects which do *not* depend on us – such as other people, politics, health, art, etc. As we have seen, such objects ought to be matters of indifference; yet, by dint of a reasonable justification, they can be considered as corresponding to that deeply-embedded instinct which impels rational human nature to act for its own conservation. Duties are thus actions "appropriate" to our rational nature, and they consist in placing ourselves in the service of the human community, in the form of the city/state and of the family.

The third area of exercises is that of assent (*sunkatathesis*). Epictetus urges us to criticize each representation (*phantasia*) as it presents itself to us, and give our assent only to that which is "objective." In other words, we are to set aside all subjective value-judgments. Epictetus formulates the principle guiding this exercise as follows: "People are not troubled by things, but by their judgements *about* things."[80]

For Epictetus, these three areas (*topoi*) of exercise correspond to the three aspects of philosophy as it is lived and experienced, as opposed to the three parts of philosophical *discourse*. This becomes clear from a passage in the *Discourses* in which he criticizes pseudo-philosophers, who are content just to read theoretical discourses about philosophy. Here we can clearly see that the second and third areas correspond respectively to ethics and to dialectics. The connection between logic and the third of our *topoi* is particularly evident:

> It is as if, in the area of the exercise of assent, we were surrounded by representations, some of them "objective" and others not, and we did not want to distinguish between them, but preferred to read treatises with titles like *On Comprehension*! How does this come about? The reason is that we have never carried out our reading or our writing in such a way that, when it comes to action, we could use the representations we receive in a way consonant with nature; instead, we are content when we have learned what is said to us, and can explain it to others; when we can analyze syllogisms and examine hypothetical arguments.[81]

In this passage, Epictetus underlines the opposition between, on the one hand, theoretical logic, as it was set forth in treatises with titles like *On Comprehension*; and, on the other, what we might term "lived logic," or logic as applied to life, which consists in the discipline of assent, and the critique of those representations which *actually do* present themselves to us. In the rest of this passage, we find the same opposition between theoretical discourse and practical, "lived" exercises, this time with regard to the second area. Epictetus shows that the only justification for reading theoretical treatises like *On Inclination* or *On Duties* is so that, in concrete situations, we can act in conformity with mankind's rational nature.

    In the tripartite division of philosophy,[82] the areas of logic and ethics are followed by that of physics. Can physics, then, be made to correspond to the discipline of desire? It would seem as though the passage we have just quoted prohibits such an identification. When, in the context of the discipline of desire, Epictetus speaks of treatises entitled *On Desire and Aversion*, we have every reason to believe these were treatises relating to ethics. However, even though the abstract theory of "desire" as such, insofar as it is an act of the soul, pertains to the areas of ethics and psychology, the lived attitude which corresponds to the discipline of desire does indeed seem to be a kind of applied physics, which one lives and experiences in the manner of a spiritual exercise. On several occasions, Epictetus insists that the discipline of desire consists in "learning to desire that everything happen just the way it *does* happen."[83] We are to "keep our will in harmony with what happens,"[84] and to "be well-pleased with the divine government of things."[85] "If a good man could foresee the future, he would cooperate with sickness, death, and mutilation; for he would be aware that this had been ordained by the universal order of things, and that the whole is more important than its parts."[86] We have here a true case of physics lived and experienced as a spiritual exercise. Since, in order to discipline their desires, people need to be intensely conscious of the fact that they are a part of the cosmos, they must replace each event within the perspective of universal nature.

Such, for Epictetus, is the practice and exercise of philosophy, and we find this fundamental scheme repeated throughout the *Discourses*. Epictetus' disciple Arrian, who was responsible for the redaction of both the *Discourses* and the *Manual*, made no mistake in this regard, when he chose to group the sayings which make up the *Manual* according to the three disciplines or areas we have just distinguished.[87]

3 Marcus Aurelius and Epictetus

It is fair to say that the essential substance of Marcus Aurelius' *Meditations* comes from Epictetus. In the first place, it is probably from Epictetus that Marcus got the very idea of the literary genre of meditation by means of writing: "These are the kinds of things on which lovers of wisdom ought to meditate; they ought to write them down every day, and use them to train themselves."[88] "Let these thoughts be 'at hand' for you, day and night. Write them down and re-read them; talk about them, both to yourself and with others."[89]

The idea of dialogue with oneself had existed for a long time; one thinks of Homer's depiction of Odysseus admonishing himself: "Bear up, my heart."[90] The custom of writing down, for one's personal use, either one's own thoughts or the sayings one has read is also no doubt extremely old. Nevertheless, we have every reason to believe that it was from Epictetus that Marcus derived the idea of this particular form of self-exhortation and conversation with oneself, bearing as it does upon the same rules of life and principles of action upon which Epictetus had advised his readers to meditate.

The object of Marcus' meditations and exercises was none other than Epictetus' three fundamental themes: the discipline of desire, the discipline of inclinations, and the discipline of judgment. This conceptual structure is peculiar to Epictetus, and is found nowhere else in the philosophical literature of antiquity.[91] Moreover, in the course of a series of quotations from Epictetus, Marcus cites a fragment which clearly sets forth the three themes we have been examining:

What must be found is a method with regard to *assent* [*to sugkatatithes-thai*]. In the area [*topos*] of the *inclinations* [*hormai*], we must keep vigilant our attentive faculty, so that these inclinations may operate with reserve, in the service of the community, and in a way corresponding to the value of their objects. Finally, when it comes to things that do not

depend on us, we must abstain totally from *desire* [*orekseos apekhesthai*]
and feel no aversion towards any of them.[92]

Additionally, Marcus repeatedly formulates the triple rule of life himself. We
can easily recognize it in the following passages:

What is enough for you?
– Your present value-judgement, so long as it is objective;
– The action you are accomplishing at the present moment, so long as it
is done for the benefit of the human community;
– Your present inner disposition, as long as it rejoices in every event
brought about by causes outside yourself.[93]

A rational nature is proceeding as it should if it fulfills the following
conditions:
– If, in its representations [*phantasiai*], it does not give its assent
[*sugkatatithemene*] either to what is false, or to what is unclear;
– If it guides its inclinations [*hormas*] only towards those actions which
serve the human community;
– If it has desire [*orekseis*] or aversion only for things that depend on us,
while joyfully greeting everything allotted to it by universal nature.[94]

Wipe out your representations [*phantasian*].
Check your inclinations [*hormai*].
Extinguish your desire [*oreksin*].
Keep your directing principle [*hegemonikon*] under your control.[95]

On what, then, should we exert our efforts? Only this:
– correct intentions;
– actions [*prakseis*] carried out in the service of the community;
– speech [*logos*] which could never be used to deceive;
– an inner disposition [*diathesis*] which joyfully greets each event like
something necessary and familiar, since it flows from so grand a
principle, and so great a source.[96]

The reader will perhaps have noticed that, although it is quite obvious that
Marcus Aurelius took over his tripartite structure from Epictetus, there is
nevertheless a difference in tone and emphasis in Marcus' presentation of it.
When, for instance, Marcus speaks of the discipline of desire, he does not, as
Epictetus had done, insist on the necessity of desiring only those things which
depend on us – that is, moral good – so that our desires may not be frustrated.
Rather, Marcus, in a much more explicit way than Epictetus, conceives of this
exercise as putting our desires in harmony with the will of fate and of

universal reason. Its goal is to bring about within us an attitude of indifference to indifferent things; that is, whatever does not depend on us. For Marcus, much more than for Epictetus, the discipline of desire takes on the form of applied "physics," or physics transformed into a spiritual exercise.

The discipline of desire culminates in a joyful, loving satisfaction[97] in the events willed by nature. But in order to achieve this state, we must totally change our way of looking at things. We must consider them from the point of view of universal nature, and this implies learning to recognize the chain of causes which produce each event. We are to consider each event as woven by destiny, and as flowing forth by natural necessity from the first causes. The discipline of desire thus obliges us to relocate the totality of human life within a cosmic perspective, and become aware of the fact that we are a *part* of the world: "He who doesn't know what the world is doesn't know where he himself is, either. He who doesn't know for what purpose the world exists, doesn't know who he is himself. Whoever doesn't know the answer to one of these questions is unable to say for what purpose he himself exists."[98]

In order to practice this kind of "physics," Marcus, as we have seen, tries to follow a rigorous method of definition,[99] which consists in relocating all objects within the totality of the universe, and all events within the nexus of causes and effects. They are to be defined in and for themselves, and separated from the conventional, anthropomorphic representations mankind habitually makes of them.

Here we can perhaps glimpse in what way the three disciplines, like the three parts of philosophy, imply one another within the single act of philosophizing. The method of "physical" definition discussed by Marcus corresponds to the discipline of assent, which prescribes that we must give our assent only to those representations which are objective and freed from all subjective value-judgments.

Once prolonged experience has allowed us to come to know nature's ways and laws, "physics," when practiced as a spiritual exercise, leads us to "familiarity" with nature.[100] Thanks to this familiarity, we can perceive the links between all phenomena which seem strange or repugnant to us, and between these phenomena and universal reason, the source from which they flow. From such a perspective, every event will seem to us beautiful and worthy of our affectionate assent. To be *indifferent* to indifferent things means to make no *difference* between them; in other words, to love them equally, just as nature does: " 'The earth loves the rain; she also loves the venerable Ether.'[101] And the Universe, too, loves to produce all that must be produced. Thus, I say to the Universe: 'I love along with you!' Isn't this, after all, the meaning of of the phrase, 'Such-and-such an event "loves" to happen?' "[102] When, in ancient Greek, one wished to say that something "usually occurs," or "is accustomed to occur," a common idiom made it possible to say the event "loves" to occur (*philei ginesthai*). Here, Marcus gives us to understand that events *literally* "love" to happen. We are to "love" to see them happen, because universal nature "loves" to produce them.

In the last analysis, such an attitude of joyful consent to the world corresponds to an attitude of obedience to the divine will. This is why Marcus sometimes describes the discipline of desire as an invitation to "follow the gods" or "God," as in the following presentation of the three disciplines: "Keep the *daimon* within you in a state of serenity; so that it may *follow God* in an appropriate way, neither saying anything contrary to the *truth*, nor doing anything contrary to *justice*."[103] In the formulation of the second theme, Epictetus placed more emphasis on the fact that our inclinations and actions must be related to our duties (*kathekonta*) toward our fellow-men. Marcus, by contrast, speaks more often about *just* actions, done in the service of the human community. As was the case with the first theme, the second theme takes on a strongly emotional tonality for Marcus: we must love other people with all our hearts, he writes,[104] for rational beings are not only parts of the same whole, but the limbs of the same body. Moreover, we are to extend our love even toward those who commit injustices against us, bearing in mind that they belong to the same human race as we do, and that, if they sin, they do so involuntarily, and out of ignorance.[105]

Marcus differs the least from Epictetus in his presentation of the third theme, the discipline of assent. The discipline Marcus imposes on himself relates, however, not only to the inner logos – that is, to the assent we give to our representations (*phantasiai*) – but also to the outer logos; that is, our manner of expressing ourselves.[106] Here, the fundamental virtue is that of truth, understood as rectitude of thought and speech. Lies, even when involuntary, are the result of the deformation of our faculty of judgment.[107]

When formulating the triple rule of life, Marcus also likes to insist on the fact that we must concentrate on the *present* moment: the *present* representation, the *present* action, and the *present* inner disposition (whether of desire or of aversion). We find nothing of the sort in Epictetus, yet Marcus' attitude here is in complete accord with the fundamental Stoic attitude of attention (*prosoche*) as directed toward the present moment.[108] Nothing must escape the vigilance of consciousness: neither our relationship to destiny and the way of the world – this is the discipline of desire – nor our relationship with our fellow men (discipline of the active will), nor, finally, our relationship to ourselves (discipline of assent).

Elsewhere, Marcus links the three philosophical exercises to their corresponding virtues. We thus have the following schema:

Discipline	*Corresponding virtue*
Of desire	Temperance (*sophrosyne*); absence of worries (*ataraxia*)
Of inclinations	Justice (*dikaiosyne*)
Of assent	Truth (*aletheia*); absence of hurry (*aproptosia*).

Marcus enumerates the three virtues corresponding to the three disciplines in the following terms: "Absence of hurry, love of our fellow-men, obedience to the gods." [109]

This vocabulary is totally absent from Epictetus' *Discourses*. How are we to explain these differences in the way Marcus and Epictetus present the three fundamental exercises of philosophy?

In the first place, it seems certain that Marcus possessed more information about Epictetus' teachings than we do today. In the first book of his *Meditations*,[110] Marcus tells us that he came to know the writings of Epictetus thanks to Quintus Iunius Rusticus, a statesman who had taught Marcus the fundamentals of Stoic doctrine before going on to become one of his counsellors. Marcus states that Rusticus loaned him his personal copy of Epictetus' *hypomnemata*; that is, a book of notes taken down at his classes. This statement can be interpreted in two ways:

1 The book in question could be a copy of the work by Arrian. In the prefatory letter he placed at the beginning of his edition of Epictetus' *Discourses*, Arrian himself describes his work as a collection of *hypomnemata*:

> Whatever I heard him say, I tried to write down, using his very words as far as possible, so that I should have in the future some "notes intended to help me remember" [*hypomnemata*] of his thought and his frankness. As was to be expected, these notes often have the appearance of an improvised, spontaneous conversation between two men, not such as one would write if he was expecting them to be read one day.[111]

Now, Arrian had come to attend the classes of Epictetus sometime between AD 107 and 109. His prefatory letter to Lucius Gellius was probably written after Epictetus' death, some time between 125 and 130, and the *Discourses* themselves were published ca. AD 130. Aulus Gellius recounts[112] that, in the year he spent studying at Athens – around AD 140 – he had been present at a discussion in the course of which the famous millionaire Herod Atticus had brought to him from a library a copy of what Gellius refers to as the *dissertationes* of Epictetus, arranged (*digestae*) by Arrian. He also tells how, on the way from Cassiopeia to Brindisium, he came across a philosopher who had a copy of the same work in his baggage. This shows that is was at least possible that Marcus read a copy of this book, which had been loaned to him by Rusticus.

2 We might also consider another suggestion, which has already been proposed by Farquharson. What Rusticus loaned to Marcus, on this hypothesis, would have been Rusticus' own notes, which he himself had taken during Epictetus' lectures. From the chronological point of view, if we grant that Epictetus died between AD 125 and 130, and if Rusticus was

born at the beginning of the second century, as we are entitled to deduce from his official *cursus*, it would then be entirely possible for Rusticus to have been Epictetus' student. Moreover, it is hard to imagine that there was no copy of Epictetus' *Discourses* available in Rome around AD 145–6, even though the work had been widely diffused in Greece by 140. Besides, Marcus represents Rusticus' gift as something exceptional; we are thus entitled to wonder if the gift may not, after all, have been Rusticus' own notes. It is, moreover, more or less certain that Marcus had read Arrian's work, since the *Meditations* are full of literal citations taken from it.

Whether Marcus had read only the *Discourses* as arranged by Arrian, or whether he had read Rusticus' notes as well, one thing is beyond doubt: Marcus was familiar with more texts concerning Epictetus' teaching than we are today. We possess only a part of Arrian's work; and if Rusticus' notes did in fact exist, they may well have revealed to Marcus some aspects of Epictetus' teachings which had not been noted down by Arrian.

It is thanks to Marcus that we know some otherwise unknown fragments of Epictetus, such as the following: "You are a little soul, bearing the weight of a dead body." [113] This fragment also goes to show that "pessimistic" features are not exclusively characteristic of Marcus Aurelius, as has often been claimed. Thus, we may suppose that the differences in presentation of the three exercises which we find in Marcus and in the extant works of Epictetus can be explained by the influence of passages of Epictetus which were known to Marcus, but subsequently were lost.

Finally, we must not forget that there is a profound difference between the literary genre of Epictetus' *Discourses* and Marcus Aurelius' *Meditations*. Arrian's work, even if it was more extensively rearranged than its author is willing to admit in his preface, is quite literally a series of *Discourses* given before an audience. Their subject-matter was inspired by specific circumstances: questions directed to the master, or visits of people from outside the school. The argumentation was adapted to the capacities of the audience, and its goal was to persuade them.

By contrast, Marcus was alone with himself. For my part, I cannot discern in the *Meditations* the hesitations, contradictions, and strugglings of a man abandoned to his solitude, which some scholars have thought to detect in them.[114] On the contrary, one is rather astounded by the firmness of thought and technical nature of the philosophical vocabulary one encounters from beginning to end of the *Meditations*. Everything points to the conclusion that either Marcus had perfectly assimilated the teachings of Rusticus and Epictetus, or else that he always had Epictetus' own texts at hand, for the practice of his meditation exercises. One is also astonished, moreover, by the extraordinary literary quality of the majority of the *Meditations*. Marcus' former teacher of rhetoric, Fronto, had taught him how to finely chisel his sentences, and Marcus always sought to give to his thoughts the clarity, rigor, and striking formulations necessary to give them the sought-after therapeutical and psychagogic effect. After all, it is not enough merely to repeat some rational principle to oneself, in order to be persuaded of it;[115] everything depends on how you formulate it. The *Meditations* have the appearance of variations, sometimes executed with supreme virtuosity, on a small number of fundamental themes; indeed, they are variations almost exclusively on the three themes first taken up by Epictetus. In some passages, such as those we have seen cited above, the triple schema, enunciating the three philosophical exercises we must practice at each instant, is presented in its entirety, with only some slight variations. Elsewhere, only two of the themes, or even a single one, are presented. As for the variations: sometimes they develop one or another of the three themes, at other times they set forth motifs associated with these principal themes. For instance, under the heading of the discipline of desire, we are presented with the theme of destiny weaving for us in advance all that is going to happen to us;[116] or a discussion of the "physical" definition of objects;[117] the natural character of the accessory phenomena which accompany natural phenomena;[118] or the theme of death.[119] Under the heading of the second discipline, that of inclinations, we find the associated themes of love for others,[120] or of rational action.[121]

Thus Marcus, in the course of his solitary meditations, was led to orchestrate and make explicit everything that was implied by the doctrine of the three disciplines as proposed by Epictetus. Often, Marcus does little more than expand upon brief notes which were already sketched in the *Discourses* arranged by Arrian: this is the case for the theme of joyous satisfaction with the events willed by universal reason, for example, or with the theme of obedience to the gods.[122]

To conclude: each time Marcus wrote down one of his *Meditations*, he knew exactly what he was doing: he was exhorting himself to practice one of the disciplines: either that of desire, of action, or of assent. At the same time, he was exhorting himself to practice philosophy itself, in its divisions of physics, ethics, and logic.[123]

Perhaps now we are in a better position to understand what it is that gives Marcus Aurelius' *Meditations* the fascinating power they have exerted over generations of readers. It is precisely the fact that we have the feeling of witnessing the practice of spiritual exercises – captured live, so to speak. There have been a great many preachers, theoreticians, spiritual directors, and censors in the history of world literature. Yet it is extremely rare to have the chance to see someone in the process of training himself to be a human being: "When you have trouble getting up in the morning, let this thought be in your mind: I'm waking up in order to do a man's work." [124]

We have already stressed that Marcus seldom seems to hesitate, stumble, or feel his way as he practices exercises which follow the directions Epictetus had sketched in advance so precisely. Nonetheless, we feel a quite particular emotion as we catch a person in the process of doing what we are all trying to do: to give a meaning to our life, to strive to live in a state of perfect awareness and to give each of life's instants its full value. To be sure, Marcus is talking to himself, but we still get the impression that he is talking to each one of us as well.

NOTES

1 [Ernest Renan (1823–92) dominated French religious studies in the nineteenth century, not without provoking occasional scandalous controversies. His *Marc Aurèle* was published in 1882. – Trans.]
2 E.R. Dodds, *Pagan and Christian in an Age of Anxiety*, Cambridge 1965, p. 29, n. 1, with reference to Marcus Aurelius, *Meditations*, 8, 1, 1; 10, 8, 1–2; 11, 18, 5; 5, 10, 1.
3 Dio Cassius, 71, 36, 1.
4 Dodds, *Pagan and Christian*, p. 29, n. 1.
5 R. Dailly and H. van Effenterre, "Le cas Marc Aurèle. Essai de psychosomatique historique," *Revue des Études Anciennes* 56 (1954), pp. 347–65.
6 Dio Cassius, 71, 6, 4.
7 Dailly and Effenterre, "Le cas Marc Aurèle," p. 354.
8 Ibid, p. 355.
9 T.W. Africa, "The opium addiction of Marcus Aurelius," *Journal of the History of Ideas* (Jan.–Mar. 1961), pp. 97–102.
10 Dio Cassius, *Roman Histories*, 71, 6, 4.
11 Galen, *Works*, vol. 14, p. 3 Kühn.
12 Africa, "Opium addiction," p. 101.
13 Thomas De Quincey, *Confessions of an English Opium-eater*, 1st edn in *London Magazine*, Sept./Oct. 1821–Dec. 1822, repr. New York 1950, p. 60.
14 Marcus Aurelius, *Meditations*, 4, 43.
15 Ibid, 5, 23.
16 Seneca, *Letter*, 99.
17 Seneca, *Letter*, 49, 3.
18 Leonidas of Tarentum, in *The Greek Anthology*, 7, 472, vol. 2 Paton.
19 *SVF* vol. 2, §762 (= Plutarch, *On Common Conceptions*, 1083 D): "substance . . . always in flux and in motion."
20 Plato, *Cratylus*, 402a; cf. A.A. Long, "Heracleitus and Stoicism," in *Philosophia* (Academy of *Athens*) 5–6 (1975–6).
21 Plutarch, *On the Obsolescence of Oracles*, 432a.
22 Ovid, *Metamorphoses*, 15, 179.
23 On the view from on high, see below.
24 Marcus Aurelius, *Meditations*, 5, 24.
25 Ibid, 12, 24.
26 Ibid, 9, 32.
27 Ibid, 11, 1, 3.
28 Ibid, 6, 36, 1.

29 Ibid, 12, 32.
30 See above.
31 Plato, *Republic*, 486a.
32 See below.
33 Philo Judaeus, *On the Special Laws*, 3, 1–2.
34 Maximus of Tyre, 22, 6, p. 91 Dübner.
35 Ovid, *Metamorphoses*, 15, 147.
36 For instance, Seneca, *Natural Questions*, "Preface," 7–13, quoted above.
37 See above.
38 Cicero, *Scipio's Dream*, 3, 16ff. Cf. the remarks on this passage by A.-J. Festugière, *La révélation d'Hermès Trismégiste*, vol. 2, Paris 1949, pp. 441ff.
39 Blaise Pascal, *Pensées*, Section 2, §72, p. 347 Brunschvicg. Cf. the quotation from Ernest Renan, below.
40 [The word "nausea" is here used in the Sartrean sense of sudden, almost physical disgust before the absurd meaninglessness of life; cf. Jean-Paul Sartre, *La Nausée*, Paris 1938. – Trans.]
41 Marcus Aurelius, *Meditations*, 8, 24.
42 Ibid, 2, 2.
43 Ibid, 6, 13.
44 Ibid, 5, 33, 2.
45 Ibid, 10, 10.
46 Ibid, 10, 19.
47 Ibid, 4, 48, 3.
48 Ibid, 10, 27.
49 Ibid, 6, 46.
50 Ibid, 4, 32.
51 Ibid, 10, 18; 31.
52 Ibid, 5, 33.
53 Ibid, 3, 10.
54 Ibid, 9, 30.
55' Ibid, 7, 21.
56 Epictetus, *Discourses*, 4, 1, 143.
57 Marcus Aurelius, *Meditations*, 12, 2, 3.
58 Lucretius, *On the Nature of Things*, 3, 944–9.
59 Marcus Aurelius, *Meditations*, 4, 11, 1–2.
60 [In Stoic epistemology, a *phantasia kataleptike* was a sense-presentation so clear and irrefutable that it entailed immediate assent. Since the correspondence between representations and objects could not otherwise be verified, it was thus the Stoics' only criterion of judgment between truth and falsehood. – Trans.]
61 Epictetus, *Discourses*, 3, 8, 4.
62 Ibid.
63 E.g. R.B. Rutherford, *The Meditations of Marcus Aurelius: A Study*, Oxford 1989, p. 243.
64 Marcus Aurelius, *Meditations*, 9, 36.
65 Ibid, 8, 24, cited above., n. 41.
66 Seneca, *Letters to Lucilius*, 107, 2.

67 Marcus Aurelius, *Meditations*, 6, 36, 2.
68 Ibid, 6, 1; 6, 5.
69 Ibid, 3, 2.
70 Cf. above.
71 Aulus Gellius, *Attic Nights*, 12, 1.
72 Marcus Aurelius, *Meditations*, 8, 24.
73 Cf. above.
74 Ibid, 9, 1, 9.
75 Cf. I. Hadot, *Seneca und die griectisch-römische Tradition der Seelenleitung*, Berlin 1969, pp. 56–7.
76 Aulus Gellius, *Attic Nights*, 19, 1, 14.
77 Cf. below.
78 Epictetus, *Manual*, I, 1.
79 Cf. esp. Epictetus, *Discourses*, I, 4, 11; 3, 2, 1; 3, 12, 1.
80 Epictetus, *Manual*, 5.
81 Epictetus, *Discourses*, 4, 3, 13ff.
82 [On the tripartite division of philosophy in antiquity, cf. P. Hadot, "La métaphysique du Porphyre," in *Porphyre* (= Entretiens Hardt sur l'Antiquité Classique 12), Vandoeuvres/Geneva 1966; Hadot, "La division des parties de la philosophie dans l'Antiquité," *Museum Heleveticum* 36 (1979), pp. 201–23. – Trans.]
83 Epictetus, *Discourses*, I, 12, 15.
84 Ibid, I, 12, 17.
85 Ibid, I, 12, 8.
86 Ibid, 2, 10, 5.
87 This was already noticed by M. Pohlenz, *Die Stoa. Geschichte einer geistigen Bewegung*, 1948–9; 5th edn, 2 vols, Göttingen 1978–80, vol. 2, p. 162.
88 Epictetus, *Discourses*, I, 1, 25.
89 Ibid, 3, 24, 103. On the importance of having memorable sayings "at hand" (*procheiron*), see above.
90 Homer, *Odyssey*, 20, 18–23.
91 The resemblances which have been proposed between Epictetus and Panaitios, Eudorus, and Seneca (cf. Pohlenz, *Die Stoa*, vol. 2, p. 162) are not very convincing.
92 Marcus Aurelius, *Meditations*, 11, 37.
93 Ibid, 9, 36; cf. above. Cf. also ibid, 7, 54, quoted above.
94 Ibid, 8, 7.
95 Ibid, 9, 7.
96 Ibid, 4, 33.
97 *Euarestein*. The same term is used by Epictetus; cf. *Discourses*, I, 12, 8.
98 Marcus Aurelius, *Meditations*, 8, 52.
99 Ibid, 3, 11.
100 Cf. ibid, 4, 33; 3, 2, 6; 4, 44.
101 [An adaptation of Euripides, fr. 898 Nauck, 2nd edn. The same quotation had already been used by Aristotle in his discussion of friendship at *Nicomachean Ethics*, 8, 2, 1155a32ff. – Trans.]
102 Ibid, 10, 21.

103 Ibid, 3, 16, 2.
104 Ibid, 7, 13.
105 Ibid, 7, 22.
106 [For the Stoics, there was a fundamental identity between the "inner [*endiathetos*] logos," or thought, and the "outer [*prophorikos*] logos," or speech. – Trans.]
107 Ibid, 9, 1, 2–4.
108 On the concept of *prosoche*, cf. above.
109 *Meditations*, 3, 9.
110 Ibid., I, 7, 3.
111 Arrian, *Letter to Lucius Gellius*, in Epictetus, *Discourses*, vol. I, p. 4, 2–4 Oldfather.
112 Aulus Gellius, *Attic Nights*, I, 2.
113 Marcus Aurelius, *Meditations*, 4, 41 = Epictetus fr. 26, vol. 2, p. 471 Oldfather.
114 Cf., for example, Rutherford, *Meditations*, p. 229.
115 Cf. M. Alexandre, "Le travail de la sentence chez Marc Aurèle: philosophie et rhétorique," in *Formes brèves* (= Publications de la Faculté des Lettres et des Langues de l'Université de Poitiers 3), Poitiers 1979.
116 Marcus Aurelius, *Meditations*, 3, 4, 5; 3, 11, 4; 3, 16, 3; 4, 26, 4. In this and in the following notes, I have given only the minimum number of examples, so as not to strain the reader's patience with an excess of tedious references.
117 Ibid, 3, 11; 8, 6; 11, 2.
118 Ibid, 3, 2; 4, 36, 2.
119 Ibid, 2, 12, 3; 2, 14; 2, 17, 4–5; 3, 3.
120 Ibid, 7, 13, 3; 7, 22.
121 Ibid, 2, 16, 6; 12, 20.
122 Cf. ibid, 1, 12, 8.
123 Cf. ibid, 8, 13.
124 Ibid, 5, 1.

7

Reflections on the Idea of the "Cultivation of the Self"

In his preface to *The Use of Pleasure*, as well as in a chapter of *The Care of the Self*,[1] Michel Foucault made mention of my article 'Exercices spirituels', the first version of which dates back to 1976.[2] Foucault seems to have been particularly interested by the following points, which I developed in this article: the description of ancient philosophy as an art, style, or way of life; the attempt I made to explain how modern philosophy had forgotten this tradition, and had become an almost entirely theoretical discourse; and the idea I sketched out in the article, and have developed more fully above, that Christianity had taken over as its own certain techniques of spiritual exercises, as they had already been practiced in antiquity.

Here, I should like to offer a few remarks with a view to delineating the differences of interpretation, and in the last analysis of philosophical choice, which separate us, above and beyond our points of agreement. These differences could have provided the substance for a dialogue between us, which, unfortunately, was interrupted all too soon by Foucault's premature death.

In *The Care of the Self*, Foucault meticulously describes what he terms the "practices of the self" (*pratiques de soi*), recommended in antiquity by Stoic philosophers. These include the care of one's self, which can only be carried out under the direction of a spiritual guide; the attention paid to the body and the soul which the "care of the self" implies; exercises of abstinence; examination of the conscience; the filtering of representations; and, finally, the conversion toward and possession of the self. M. Foucault conceives of these practices as "arts of existence" and "techniques of the self."

It is quite true that, in this connection, the ancients did speak of an "art of living." It seems to me, however, that the description M. Foucault gives of what I had termed "spiritual exercises," and which he prefers to call "techniques of the self," is precisely focused far too much on the "self," or at least on a specific conception of the self.

In particular, Foucault presents Greco-Roman ethics as an ethics of the pleasure one takes in oneself: "Access to the self is liable to replace this kind of violent, uncertain, and temporary pleasures with a form of pleasure one takes in oneself, serenely and forever." [3] To illustrate his point, Foucault cites Seneca's twenty-third *Letter*, where he speaks of the joy one can find within oneself, and specifically within the best portion of oneself. In fact, however, I must say that there is a great deal of inexactitude in this way of presenting the matter. In Letter 23, Seneca explicitly opposes *voluptas* and *gaudium* – pleasure and joy – and one cannot, therefore, speak of "another form of pleasure," as does Foucault (*Care of the Self*, p. 83) when talking about joy. This is not just a quibble over words, although the Stoics did attach a great deal of importance to words, and carefully distinguished between *hedone* – "pleasure" – and *eupatheia* – "joy".[4] No, this is no mere question of vocabulary. If the Stoics insist on the word *gaudium*/"joy," it is precisely because they refuse to introduce the principle of pleasure into moral life. For them, happiness does not consist in pleasure, but in virtue itself, which is its own reward. Long before Kant, the Stoics strove jealously to preserve the purity of intention of the moral consciousness.

Secondly and most importantly, it is not the case that the Stoic finds his joy in his "self;" rather, as Seneca says, he finds it "in the best portion of the self," in "the true good." [5] Joy is to be found "in the conscience turned towards the good; in intentions which have no other object than virtue; in just actions." [6] Joy can be found in what Seneca calls "perfect reason" [7] (that is to say, in divine reason)[8] since for him, human reason is nothing other than reason capable of being made perfect. The "best portion of oneself," then, is, in the last analysis, a transcendent self. Seneca does not find his joy in "Seneca," but by transcending "Seneca"; by discovering that there is within him – within all human beings, that is, and within the cosmos itself – a reason which is a part of universal reason.

In fact, the goal of Stoic exercises is to go beyond the self, and think and act in unison with universal reason. The three exercises described by Marcus Aurelius,[9] following Epictetus, are highly significant in this regard. As we saw above, they are as follows:

1 to judge objectively, in accordance with inner reason;
2 to act in accordance with the reason which all human beings have in common; and
3 to accept the destiny imposed upon us by cosmic reason. For the Stoics, there is only one single reason at work here, and this reason is man's true self.

I can well understand Foucault's motives for giving short shrift to these aspects, of which he was perfectly aware. His description of the practices of the self – like, moreover, my description of spiritual exercises – is not merely an historical study, but rather a tacit attempt to offer contemporary mankind a model of life, which Foucault calls "an aesthetics of existence." Now, according to a more or less universal tendency of modern thought, which is perhaps more instinctive than reflective, the ideas of "universal reason" and "universal nature" do not have much meaning any more. It was therefore convenient to "bracket" them.

For the moment, then, let us say that, from an historical point of view, it seems difficult to accept that the philosophical practice of the Stoics and Platonists was nothing but a relationship to one's self, a culture of the self, or a pleasure taken in oneself. The psychic content of these exercises seems to me to be something else entirely. In my view, the feeling of belonging to a whole is an essential element: belonging, that is, both to the whole constituted by the human community, and to that constituted by the cosmic whole. Seneca sums it up in four words: *Toti se inserens mundo*,[10] "Plunging oneself into the totality of the world." In his admirable *Anthropologie philosophique*,[11] Groethuysen pointed out the importance of this fundamental point. Such a cosmic perspective radically transforms the feeling one has of oneself.

Oddly, Foucault does not have much to say about the Epicureans. This is all the more surprising in that Epicurean ethics is, in a sense, an ethics without norms. It is an autonomous ethics, for it cannot found itself upon nature, which according to its views is the product of chance. It would seem, therefore, to be an ethics perfectly suited to the modern mentality. Perhaps the reason for this silence is to be found in the fact that it is rather difficult to integrate Epicurean hedonism into the overall schema of the use of pleasures proposed by M. Foucault. Be this as it may, the Epicureans did make use of spiritual exercises, for instance the examination of conscience. As we have said, however, these practices are not based on the norms of nature or universal reason, because for the Epicureans the formation of the world is the result of mere chance. Nevertheless, here again, this spiritual exercise cannot be defined simply as culture of the self, a relationship of the self to the self, or pleasure that can be found in one's own self. The Epicurean was not afraid to admit that he needed other things besides himself in order to satisfy his desires and to experience pleasure. He needed bodily nourishment and the pleasures of love, but he also required a physical theory of the universe, in order to eliminate the fear of the gods and of death. He needed the company of the other members of the Epicurean school, so that he could find happiness in mutual affection. Finally, he needed the imaginative contemplation of an infinite number of universes in the infinite void, in order to experience what Lucretius calls *divina voluptas et horror*. Metrodorus, a disciple of Epicurus, gives a good account of the Epicurean sage's immersion in the cosmos: "Remember that, although born mortal with a limited life-span, you have risen in thought as far as the eternity and infinity of things, and that you have seen everything that has been, and everything that shall be." [12] In Epicureanism, there is an extraordinary reversal of perspective. Precisely because existence seems to the Epicurean to be pure chance, inexorably unique, he greets life like a kind of miracle, a gratuitous, unexpected gift of nature, and existence for him is a wonderful celebration.

Let us consider another example to illustrate the differences between our interpretations of the "care of the self." In an interesting article entitled "Écriture de soi," [13] M. Foucault took as his point of departure a remarkable text concerning the therapeutic value of writing, which I had studied in *Exercices spirituels*.[14] According to this text, St Antony used to advise his disciples to write down their actions and the emotions of their souls, as if they were going to make them known to others. "Let writing take the place of the eyes of other people," Antony used to say. This anecdote leads M. Foucault to reflect on the various forms adopted in antiquity by what he calls the "writing of the self." In particular, he examines the literary genre of *hypomnemata*, which one could translate as "spiritual notebooks," in which one writes down other people's thoughts, which may serve for the edification of the person writing them down. Foucault[15] describes the goal of this exercise in the following terms: the point is to "capture what-has-already-been-said [*capter le déjà-dit*]," and to "collect what one may have heard or read, with a view to nothing less than the constitution of the self." He then asks himself, "How can we be placed in the presence of our selves with the help of ageless discourses, picked up from any old place?" And he replies as follows: "this exercise was supposed to allow one to turn back towards the past. The contribution of the *hypomnemata* is one of the means by which one detaches the soul from worries about the future, in order to inflect it toward meditation on the past." Both in Epicurean and in Stoic ethics, Foucault thinks he perceives the refusal of a mental attitude directed toward the future, and the tendency to accord a positive value to the possession of a past which one can enjoy autonomously and without worries.

It seems to me that this is a mistaken interpretation. It is true that the Epicureans – and *only* the Epicureans – did consider the memory of pleasant moments in the past as one of the principal sources of pleasure, but this has nothing to do with the meditation on "what-has-already-been-said" practiced in *hypomnemata*. Rather, as we saw above,[16] Stoics and Epicureans had in common an attitude which consisted in liberating oneself not only from worries about the future, but also from the burden of the past, in order to concentrate on the present moment; in order either to enjoy it, or to act within it. From this point of view, neither the Stoics nor even the Epicureans accorded a positive value to the past. The fundamental philosophic attitude consisted in *living in the present*, and in possessing not the past, but the present. That the Epicureans also attached a great deal of importance to the thoughts formulated by their predecessors is a wholly different matter. But although *hypomnemata* deal with what has already been said, they do not deal with just anything "already said," the only merit of which would be that it is a part of the past. Rather, it is because one recognizes in this "thing already said" – which usually consisted in the dogmas of the school's founding members – that which reason itself has to say *to the present*. It is because one recognizes, in the dogmas of Epicurus or Chrysippus, an *ever-present* value, precisely because they are the very expression of reason. In other words, when one writes or notes something down, it is not an alien thought one is making one's own. Rather, one is utilizing formulae considered as apt to actualize what is already present within the reason of the person writing, and bring it to life.

According to M. Foucault, this method made a deliberate attempt to be eclectic, and therefore implied a personal choice; this then explains the "constitution of the self."

> Writing as a personal exercise, done by oneself and for oneself, is an art of disparate truth; more precisely, it is a way of combining the traditional authority of what has already been said, with the singularity of the truth which asserts itself in it, and the particularity of the circumstances which determine its utilization.

In fact, however, personal choice is not to be found in eclecticism, at least for the Stoics and Epicureans. Eclecticism is only used for converting beginners. At that stage, anything goes. For instance, Foucault finds an example of eclecticism in the *Letters to Lucilius*, in which the Stoic Seneca quotes sayings of Epicurus. The goal of these letters, however, is to *convert* Lucilius, and to cause him to begin to lead a moral life. The utilization of Epicurus appears only in the first *Letters*, and soon disappears.[17] On the contrary, personal choice in fact intervenes only when one adheres exclusively to a precise form of life, be it Stoicism or Epicureanism, considered as in conformity with reason. It is only in the New Academy – in the person of Cicero, for instance – that a personal choice is made according to what reason considers as most likely at a given moment.

It is thus not the case, as Foucault maintains,[18] that the individual forges a spiritual identity for himself by writing down and re-reading disparate thoughts. In the first place, as we have seen, these thoughts are not disparate, but chosen because of their coherence. Secondly, and most importantly, the point is not to forge oneself a spiritual identity by writing, but rather to liberate oneself from one's individuality, in order to raise oneself up to universality. It is thus incorrect to speak of "writing of the self": not only is it not the case that one "writes oneself," but what is more, it is not the case that writing constitutes the self. Writing, like the other spiritual exercises, *changes the level of the self*, and universalizes it. The miracle of this exercise, carried out in solitude, is that it allows its practitioner to accede to the universality of reason within the confines of space and time.

For the monk Antony, the therapeutic value of writing consisted precisely in its universalizing power. Writing, says Antony, takes the place of other people's eyes. A person writing feels he is being watched; he is no longer alone, but is a part of the silently present human community. When one formulates one's personal acts in writing, one is taken up by the machinery of reason, logic, and universality. What was confused and subjective becomes thereby objective.

To summarize: what Foucault calls "practices of the self" do indeed correspond, for the Platonists as well as for the Stoics, to a movement of conversion toward the self. One frees oneself from exteriority, from personal attachment to exterior objects, and from the pleasures they may provide. One observes oneself, to determine whether one has made progress in this exercise. One seeks to be one's own master, to possess oneself, and find one's happiness in freedom and inner independence. I concur on all these points. I do think, however, that this movement of interiorization is inseparably linked to another movement, whereby one rises to a higher psychic level, at which one encounters another kind of exteriorization, another relationship with "the exterior." This is a new way of being-in-the-world, which consists in becoming aware of oneself as a part of nature, and a portion of universal reason. At this point, one no longer lives in the usual, conventional human world, but in the world of nature. As we have seen above,[19] one is then practicing "physics" as a spiritual exercise.

In this way, one identifies oneself with an "Other": nature, or universal reason, as it is present within each individual. This implies a radical transformation of perspective, and contains a universalist, cosmic dimension, upon which, it seems to me, M. Foucault did not sufficiently insist. Interiorization is a going beyond oneself; it is universalization.

The preceding remarks are not intended to be relevant only to an historical analysis of ancient philosophy. They are also an attempt at defining an ethical model which modern man can discover in antiquity. What I am afraid of is that, by focusing his interpretation too exclusively on the culture of the self, the care of the self, and conversion toward the self – more generally, by defining his ethical model as an aesthetics of existence – M. Foucault is propounding a culture of the self which is *too* aesthetic. In other words, this may be a new form of Dandyism, late twentieth-century style. This, however, deserves a more attentive study than I am able to devote to it here. Personally, I believe firmly – albeit perhaps naively – that it is possible for modern man to live, not as a sage (*sophos*) – most of the ancients did not hold this to be possible – but as a practitioner of the ever-fragile *exercise* of wisdom. This can be attempted, starting out from the lived experience of the concrete, living, and perceiving subject, under the triple form defined, as we saw above, by Marcus Aurelius:

1 as an effort to practice objectivity of judgment;
2 as an effort to live according to justice, in the service of the human community; and
3 as an effort to become aware of our situation as a part of the universe. Such an exercise of wisdom will thus be an attempt to render oneself open to the universal.

More specifically, I think modern man can practice the spiritual exercises of antiquity, at the same time separating them from the philosophical or mythic discourse which came along with them. The same spiritual exercise can, in fact, be justified by extremely diverse philosophical discourses. These latter are nothing but clumsy attempts, coming after the fact, to describe and justify inner experiences whose existential density is not, in the last analysis, susceptible of any attempt at theorization or systematization. Stoics and Epicureans, for example – for completely different reasons – urged their disciples to concentrate their attention on the present moment, and free themselves from worries about the future as well as the burden of the past. Whoever concretely practices this exercise, however, sees the universe with new eyes, as if he were seeing it for the first time. In the enjoyment of the pure present, he discovers the mystery and splendor of existence. At such moments, as Nietzsche said,[20] we say yes "not only to ourselves, but to all existence." It is therefore not necessary, in order to practice these exercises, to believe in the Stoics' nature or universal reason. Rather, as one practices them, one lives concretely according to reason. In the words of Marcus Aurelius:[21] "Although everything happens at random, don't you, too, act at random." In this way, we can accede concretely to the universality of the cosmic perspective, and the wonderful mystery of the presence of the universe.

NOTES

1 M. Foucault, *The Care of the Self* (= *History of Sexuality*, vol. 3), trans. Robert Hurley, New York 1986. [References are to the French edition, *Le Souci de soi*, Paris 1984 – Trans.]
2 *Annuaire de la 5ᵉ Section de l'École pratique des Hautes Études*, 1975–6.
3 Foucault, *Souci*, pp. 83–4.
4 We find this distinction again in Plotinus and in Bergson, the latter linking together joy and creation; cf. Henri Bergson, *L'Energie spirituelle*, 14th edn, Paris 1930, p. 24.
5 Seneca, *Letter*, 23, 6.

6 Ibid, 23, 7.
7 Seneca, *Letter*, 124, 23.
8 Seneca, *Letter*, 92, 27.
9 Marcus Aurelius, *Meditations*, 7, 54; 9, 6; 8, 7.
10 Seneca, *Letter*, 46, 6.
11 B. Groethuysen, *Anthropologie philosophique*, Paris 1952, repr. 1980, p. 80.
12 Cf. above.
13 ["Writing of the self"; M. Foucault, "L'écriture de soi," *Corps écrit* 5 (1983), pp. 3–23 – Trans.]
14 Cf. above.
15 *Art. cit.*, p. 8.
16 Above.
17 Cf. I. Hadot, "Épicure et l'enseignement philosophique héllenique et romain," in *Actes du VIIIe Congrès Budé*, Paris 1969, p. 351.
18 *Loc. cit.*, pp. 11–13.
19 Cf. above.
20 Reference [?]
21 Marcus Aurelius, *Meditations*, 10, 28, 3.

Part IV

Themes

8

"Only the Present is our Happiness": The Value of the Present Instant in Goethe and in Ancient Philosophy

"Then the spirit looks neither ahead nor behind. Only the present is our happiness." [1] In this verse from Goethe's *Second Faust*, we find an expression of the art of concentrating on and recognizing the value of the present instant. It corresponds to an experience of time which was lived with particular intensity in such ancient philosophies as Epicureanism and Stoicism, and in what follows we shall be especially concerned with this type of experience. We ought not, however, to forget the literary context in which these lines are spoken, the meaning they take on within the context of the *Second Faust*, and, more generally, within the work of Goethe. In the process, we will find that Goethe himself is a remarkable witness for the type of experience we have mentioned.

The verses quoted mark one of the climaxes of the *Second Faust*; a moment when Faust seems to reach the culminating point of his "quest for the highest existence." [2] Beside him, on the throne which he has had built for her, sits Helen, whom he had evoked in the first act, after a terrifying journey to the realm of the Mothers, in order to amuse the emperor; but had since fallen hopelessly in love with her:

> Has the Source of Beauty, overflowing its banks,
> Flowed into the deepest recesses of my being? . . .
> To you I dedicate the stirring of all strength,
> The essence too of passion;
> To you, affection, love, worship, and madness. [3]

It is Helen for whom he has searched throughout the second act, throughout all the mythical forms of classical Greece. He has spoken of her with the centaur Chiron, and with Manto the Sibyl, and finally, it is she who, in the third act, has come to take refuge in the medieval fortress – perhaps Mistra in the Peloponnese – of which he appears as the lord and master.

It is then that the extraordinary encounter takes place between Faust and Helen; Faust, who, although he appears in the guise of a medieval knight, is really the personification of modern man, and Helen, who, although she is evoked in the form of the heroine of the Trojan War, is, in fact, the figure of beauty itself, and in the last analysis of the beauty of nature. With consummate mastery, Goethe has succeeded in bringing these figures and symbols to life, in such a way that the encounter between Faust and Helen is as highly-charged with emotion as the meeting between two lovers, as laden with historical significance as the meeting between two epochs, and as full of meaning as the encounter of a human being with his destiny.

The choice of poetic form is used very skillfully to represent both the dialogue of the two lovers and the encounter between two historical epochs. Since the beginning of the third act, Helen had been speaking in the manner of ancient tragedy, and her words were set to the rhythm of iambic trimeters, while the chorus of captive Trojan women responded to her in strophe and antistrophe. Now, however, at the moment when Helen meets Faust and hears the watchman Lynceus speak in rhymed distichs, she is astonished and charmed by this unknown poetic form:

> No sooner has one word struck the ear
> Than another comes to caress its predecessor.[4]

The birth of Helen's love for Faust will, moreover, express itself in the same rhymed distichs, which Faust begins and Helen finishes, inventing the rhyme each time. As she learns this new poetic form, Helen learns, as Phorkyas says, to spell out the alphabet of love.[5] Helen begins:

> Tell me, then, how can I, too, speak so prettily?

"That's easy enough," replies Faust;

> It must come from the heart,
> And when one's breast with longing overflows,
> One looks around, and asks –

> *Helen:*   who shall enjoy it with us.

Faust begins again:

> Now the spirit looks not forward, nor behind
> Only the present –

Helen: is our happiness.

Faust: It is our treasure, our highest prize, our possession
and our pledge.
But who confirms it?

Helen: My hand.[6]

The love duet ends, for the moment, with this sign of Helen's yielding, and the rhyme-play thus ends in a "confirmatio" which is now no longer the echo of a rhyme, but the gift of a hand. Faust and Helen then fall silent, and embrace each other without a word, while the chorus, adopting the tone of an epithalamion, describes their embrace. Then the dialogue of love – and also of rhyming verses – starts up again between Faust and Helen, and causes us to live a moment of such intensity and pregnancy that both time and the drama seem to stop. Helen says:

> I feel myself so far away and yet so close;
> And I say only too gladly: Here Am I! Here!

Faust: I can scarcely breathe; my words tremble and falter;
This is a dream, and time and place have disappeared.

Helen: It seems to me that I am broken down with age,
and yet I am so new;
Mingled with you, I am faithful to the Unknown.

Faust: Don't rack your brains about your destiny, so unique!
Existence is a duty, be it only for an instant.[7]

Here the drama seems to stop. We think that Helen and Faust have nothing left to desire, fulfilled as they are by each other's presence. But Mephistopheles, who, in order to adapt himself to the Greek world, has taken on the monstrous mask of Phorkyas, breaks off this perfect moment by announcing the menacing approach of the troops of Menelaus, and Faust reproaches him for his ill-timed interruption. The marvelous instant has now disappeared, but the dispositions of Faust and of Helen will still be reflected in the description of the ideal Arcadia in which Faust and Helen are to engender Euphorion, the genius of poetry.

The dialogue we have quoted may be understood at several levels. First and foremost, it is the dialogue between two lovers, who, as such, resemble all lovers everywhere. Faust and Helen are two lovers absorbed by the living presence of the beloved: they forget everything – both past and future – which is other than this presence. Their excess of happiness gives them an impression of dreamlike unreality: time and space disappear. We are entering the unknown, and it is the moment of love fulfilled.

On a second level of interpretation, however, the dialogue takes place between Faust and Helen as symbolic figures, representing, on the one hand, modern man in his ceaseless striving, and on the other, ancient beauty in its soothing presence; both are miraculously reunited by the magic of poetry, which abolishes the centuries. In this dialogue, Faust as modern man tries to make Helen forget her past, so that she may be wholly in the present instant, which she is incapable of understanding. She feels herself to be so distant and yet so close, abandoned by life and yet in the process of rebirth, living in Faust, mingled with him, and trusting in the unknown. Faust asks her not to reflect upon her strange destiny, but to accept the new existence which is being offered to her. In this dialogue between two symbolic figures, Helen becomes "modernized," if one may say so; as she adopts rhyme, the symbol of modern interiority, she has doubts, and reflects upon her destiny. At the same time, Faust becomes "antiquated": he speaks as a man of antiquity, when he urges Helen to concentrate on the present moment, and not to lose it in hesitant reflection on the past and the future. As Goethe said in a letter to Zelter, this was the characteristic feature of ancient life and art: to know how to live in the present, and to know what he called "the healthiness of the moment." In antiquity, says Goethe, the instant was "pregnant;" in other words, filled with meaning, but it was also lived in all its reality and the fullness of its richness, sufficient unto itself. We no longer know how to live in the present, continues Goethe. For us, the ideal is in the future, and can only be the object of a sort of nostalgic desire, while the present is considered trivial and banal. We no longer know how to profit from the present; we no longer know – as the Greeks did – how to act in the present, and upon the present.[8] Indeed, if Faust speaks to Helen as a man of the ancient world, it is precisely because the presence of Helen – that is, the presence of ancient beauty – reveals to him what presence itself is: the presence of the world, "That splendid feeling of the present" (*Herrliches Gefühl der Gegenwart*) as Goethe wrote in the *East-West Divan*.[9]

This, finally, is the reason why the dialogue can be understood at a third level. Here, it is no longer the dialogue of two lovers, nor of two historical figures, but rather the dialogue of man with himself. The encounter with Helen is not only the encounter with ancient beauty emanating from nature; it is also the encounter with a living wisdom and art of living: that "healthiness of the moment" which we mentioned above. The nihilist Faust had wagered with Mephistopheles that he would never say to an instant: "Stay, you are so beautiful!" But now, following after humble Gretchen, it is ancient, noble Helen who reveals to him the splendor of being – that is, of the present instant – and teaches him to say yes to the world and to himself.

We must now define the ancient experience of time which we saw expressed in the above-quoted verses from *Faust*. Basing ourselves on the letter from Goethe to Zeller we cited above, we might think that we have to do with a generalized, common experience of ancient man, and that it was natural for ancient man to be familiar with what Goethe calls the "healthiness of the moment." Moreover, following Goethe, many historians and philosophers, from Oswald Spengler[10] to the logician Hintikka,[11] have alluded to the fact that the Greeks "lived in the present moment" more than did the representatives of other cultures. In his book *Die Zauberflöte*,[12] Siegfried Morenz gives a good summary of this conception: "No one has better characterized the particular nature of Greece than Goethe . . . in the dialogue between Faust and Helen: '. . . then the spirit looks neither backwards nor ahead. Only the present is our happiness.' "

We must certainly agree that the Greeks in general gave particular attention to the present moment, and this attention could take on several different ethical and artistic meanings. Popular wisdom advised people both to be content with the present, and to know how to utilize it. Being content with the present meant, on the one hand, being content with earthly existence. This is what Goethe admired in ancient art, particularly in funerary art, where the deceased was represented not with his eyes raised toward the heavens, but in the act of living his daily life. On the other hand, knowing how to utilize the present meant knowing how to recognize and seize the favorable and decisive instant (*kairos*). *Kairos* designated all the possibilities contained within a given moment: a good general, for example, knows how to strike at the opportune *kairos*, and sculptors fix in marble the most significant *kairos* of the scene which they wish to bring to life.

It does seem, then, that the Greeks paid particular attention to the present moment. This, however, does not justify us in imagining – as did Winckelmann, Goethe, and Hölderlin – the existence of an idealized Greece, the citizens of which, because they lived in the present moment, were perpetually bathed in beauty and serenity. As a matter of fact, people in antiquity were just as filled with anguish as we are today, and ancient poetry often preserves the echo of this anguish, which sometimes goes as far as despair. Like us, the ancients bore the burden of the past, the uncertainty of the future, and the fear of death. Indeed, it was for this human anguish that ancient philosophies – particularly Epicureanism and Stoicism – sought to provide a remedy. These philosophies were therapies, intended to provide a cure for anguish, and to bring freedom and self-mastery, and their goal was to allow people to free themselves from the past and the future, so that they could live within the present. Here we have to do with an experience of time wholly different from the common, general experience we have been describing. As we shall see, this experience corresponds precisely to that expressed in the verses from *Faust*: "Only the present is our happiness . . . don't think about your destiny. Existence is a duty." We are dealing with a philosophical conversion, implying a voluntary, radical transformation of one's way of living and looking at the world. This is the true "healthiness of the moment," which leads to serenity.

Despite the profound differences between Epicurean and Stoic doctrine, we find an extraordinary structural analogy between the experiences of time as it was lived in both schools. This analogy will perhaps allow us to glimpse a certain common experience of the present underlying their doctrinal divergences. We can define this analogy as follows: both Epicureanism and Stoicism privilege the present, to the detriment of the past and above all of the future. They posit as an axiom that happiness can only be found in the present, that one instant of happiness is equivalent to an eternity of happiness, and that happiness can and must be found immediately, here and now. Both Epicureanism and Stoicism invite us to resituate the present instant within the perspective of the cosmos, and to accord infinite value to the slightest moment of existence.

To begin with Epicureanism: it is a therapy of anguish, and a philosophy which seeks, above all, to procure peace of mind. Its goal is consequently to liberate mankind from everything that is a cause of anguish for the soul: the belief that the gods are concerned with mankind; the fear of post-mortem punishment; the worries and pain brought about by unsatisfied desires; and the moral uneasiness caused by the concern to act out of perfect purity of intention.

Epicureanism does away with all this. With regard to the gods, it affirms that they themselves live in perfect tranquillity. They are not troubled by the worry of producing or governing the universe, since the latter is the result of a fortuitous coming together of eternally existent atoms. With regard to death, Epicureanism asserts that the soul does not survive the body, and that death is not an event within life. With regard to desires, it affirms that they trouble us to the extent that they are artificial and useless. We must reject all those desires which are neither natural nor necessary, and satisfy – with prudence – those of our desires which are natural but not necessary. Above all, we are to satisfy those desires which are indispensable for the continuation of our existence. As for moral worries, they will be completely appeased once we realize that man, like all other living beings, is always motivated by pleasure. If we seek for wisdom, this is simply because it brings peace of mind: in other words, a pleasurable state.

What Epicureanism proposes is a form of wisdom, which teaches us how to relax and to suppress our worries. This only appears to be easy, moreover;

for we must renounce a great deal, in order that we may desire only that
which we are certain of obtaining, and submit our desires to the judgment of
reason. What is required, in fact, is a total transformation of our lives, and
one of the principal aspects of this transformation is the change of our attitude
toward time. According to Epicureanism, senseless people – that is, the
majority of mankind – are tormented by vast, hollow desires which have to
do with wealth, glory, power, and the unbridled pleasures of the flesh.[13] What
is characteristic of all these desires is that they cannot be satisfied in the
present. This is why, for the Epicureans,

> senseless people live in hope for the future, and since this cannot be
> certain, they are consumed by fear and anxiety. Their torment is the
> most intense when they realize too late that they have striven in vain
> after money or power or glory, for they do not derive any pleasure from
> the things which, inflamed with hope, they had undertaken such great
> labors to procure.[14]

According to an Epicurean saying, "The life of a foolish man is fearful and
unpleasant; it is swept totally away into the future." [15] Thus, Epicurean
wisdom proposes a radical transformation, which must be active at each
instant of life, of mankind's attitude toward time. We must, it teaches, learn
how to enjoy the pleasure of the present, without letting ourselves be
distracted from it. If the past is unpleasant to us, we are to avoid thinking
about it, and we must not think about the future, insofar as the idea of it
provokes in us fears or unbridled expectations. Only thoughts about what is
pleasant – of pleasure, whether past or future – are to be allowed into the
present moment, especially when we are trying to compensate for current
suffering. This transformation presupposes a specific conception of pleasure,
peculiar to Epicureanism, according to which the quality of pleasure depends
neither on the quantity of desires it satisfies, nor on the length of time it lasts.

The quality of pleasure does not depend on the quantity of desires it
satisfies. The best and most intense pleasure is that which is mixed to the
least extent with worry, and which is the most certain to ensure peace of
mind. It can therefore be procured by the satisfaction of natural and necessary
desires; that is, those desires which are essential and necessary for the
preservation of existence. Now, such desires can easily be satisfied, without
our having to rely on the future for them, and without our being exposed to
the worry and uncertainty of lengthy pursuit. "Thanks be to blessed nature,
who made necessary things easy to obtain, and things which are hard to obtain
unnecessary." [16]

What causes us to think about the past or the future are such illnesses of
the soul as the human passions, desires for wealth, power, or depravity; but
the purest, most intense pleasure can easily be obtained within the present.

Not only does pleasure not depend upon the quantity of satisfied desires, but –
above all – it does not depend upon duration. It has no need to be long-lasting
in order to be perfect: "An infinite period of time could not cause us more
pleasure than can be derived from this one, which we can see is finite." [17]
"Finite time and infinite time bring us the same pleasure, if we measure its
limits by reason." [18] This may seem paradoxical, but it is founded on a
theoretical conception. As the Stoics were to repeat, a tiny circle is no more
of a circle than a large one. [19] The Epicureans thought of pleasure as a reality
in and for itself, not situated within the category of time. Aristotle had said
that pleasure is total and complete at each moment of its duration, and that
its prolongation does not change its essence. [20] For the Epicureans, a practical
attitude is joined to this theoretical representation: if pleasure limits itself to
that which procures perfect peace of mind, it attains a summit which cannot
be surpassed, and it is impossible for it to by increased by duration. In the
words of Guyau: "In enjoyment, there is a kind of inner plenitude and
over-abundance which makes it independent of time, as well as of everything
else. True pleasure bears its infinity within itself." [21]

Thus, pleasure is wholly within the present moment, and we need not wait
for anything from the future to increase it. Everything we have been saying
so far could be summed up in the following verses from Horace: "Let the soul
which is happy with the present learn to hate to worry about what lies
ahead." [22] The happy mind does not look towards the future. If we limit our
desires in a reasonable way, we can be happy right now. Not only *can* we be
happy, but we *must*: happiness must be found immediately, here and now,
and in the present. Instead of reflecting about our lives as a whole, calculating
our hopes and worries, we must seize happiness within the present moment.
The matter is urgent; in the words of an Epicurean saying:

> We are only born once – twice is not allowed – and it is necessary
> that we shall be no more, for all eternity; and yet you, who are not
> master of tomorrow, you keep on putting off your joy? Yet life is vainly
> consumed in these delays, and each of us dies without ever having
> known peace. [23]

Once again, we find the echo of this idea in Horace: "While we are talking,
jealous time has fled. So seize the day [*carpe diem*], and put no trust
in tomorrow." [24] Horace's *carpe diem* is by no means, as is often believed,
the advice of a sensualist playboy; on the contrary, it is an invitation
to conversion. We are invited to become aware of the vanity of our immensely vain desires, at the same time as of the imminence of death, the
uniqueness of life, and the uniqueness of the present instant. From this
perspective, each instant appears as a marvelous gift which fills its recipient
with gratitude:

Believe that each new day that dawns will be the last for you:
Then each unexpected hour shall come to you as a delightful gift.[25]

There is perhaps an echo here of the Epicurean Philodemus: "Receive each additional moment of time in a manner appropriate to its value; as if one were having an incredible stroke of luck."[26]

We have already encountered the Epicureans' feelings of gratitude and astonishment, in the context of the miraculous coincidence between the needs of living beings and the facilities provided for them by nature. The secret of Epicurean joy and serenity is to live each instant as if it were the last, but also as if it were the first. We experience the same grateful astonishment when we accept the instant as though it were unexpected, or by greeting it as entirely new: "If the whole world were appear to mortals now, for the first time; if it was suddenly and unexpectedly exposed to their view; what could one think of more marvelous than these things, and which mankind would less have dared to believe?"[27] In the last analysis, the secret of Epicurean joy and serenity is the experience of infinite pleasure provided by the consciousness of existence, even if it be only for a moment. In the words of an Epicurean saying: "The cry of the flesh is: Not to be hungry, not to be thirsty, not to be cold. Whoever has these things, and hopes to keep on having them, can rival in happiness with Zeus himself."[28] The lack of hunger and thirst is thus the condition for being able to continue to exist, being conscious of existing, and enjoying this consciousness of existing. God has nothing more than this. It could be objected that God's pleasure consists in his knowledge that he has the happiness of existing forever. Not so, replies Epicurus; for the pleasure of one instant of existence is just as total and complete as a pleasure of infinite duration, and man is just as immortal as God, because death is not a part of life.[29]

In order to show that one single instant of happiness is enough to give such infinite pleasure, the Epicureans practiced telling themselves each day: "I have had all the pleasure I could have expected." In the words of Horace: "He will be master of himself and live joyfully who can say, every day: 'I have lived.' "[30] Seneca also takes up this Epicurean theme:

When we are about to go to sleep, let us say in joyous cheerfulness: "I have lived; I have travelled the route that fortune had assigned to me." If God should grant us tomorrow as well, let us accept it joyfully. That person is most happy and in tranquil possession of himself who awaits tomorrow without worries.[31] Whoever says: "I have lived", gets up every day to receive unexpected riches.[32]

We can also see here the role played in Epicureanism by the thought of death. To say, every evening: "I have lived," is to say "my life is over." It is to practice the same exercise as that which consists in saying: "Today will be the last day of my life." Yet it is precisely this exercise of becoming aware of life's finitude which reveals the infinite value of the pleasure of existing within the present instant. From the point of view of death, the mere fact of existing – even if only for a moment – seems to be of infinite value, and gives us pleasure of infinite intensity. Only once we have become aware of the fact that we have already – in one instant of existence – had everything there was to be had, can we say with equanimity: "my life is over."

It is here, moreover, that the cosmic perspective comes into play. The Epicureans had their own particular vision of the universe. As Lucretius put it: thanks to the doctrine of Epicurus, which explained the origin of the universe by the fall of atoms in a void, the walls of the world burst open for the Epicurean: he saw all things come into being within the immense void,[33] and traversed the immensity of the all. Alternatively, he exclaims, in the words of Metrodorus: "Remember that, born a mortal, with a limited life-span, you have risen up in soul to eternity and the infinity of things, and that you have seen all that has been and all that shall be."[34] Here again, we encounter the contrast between finite and infinite time. Within finite time, the sage grasps all that takes place within infinite time, or as Léon Robin puts it in his commentary on Lucretius: "The sage places himself within the immutability of eternal Nature, which is independent of time."[35]

Thus, the sage perceives the totality of the cosmos within his consciousness of the fact of existing. Nature gives him everything within an instant, and since she has already given him everything, she has nothing left to give him, as she says in Lucretius' poem: "You must always expect the same things, even though the span of your life should triumph over all the ages; nay, even were you never to die."[36]

The fundamental attitude that the Stoic must maintain at each instant of his life is one of attention, vigilance, and continuous tension, concentrated upon each and every moment, in order not to miss anything which is contrary to reason. We find an excellent description of this attitude in Marcus Aurelius:

Here is what is enough for you:
1. the judgment you are bringing to bear at this moment upon reality, as long as it is objective;
2. the action you are carrying out at this moment, as long as it is accomplished in the service of the human community; and
3. the inner disposition in which you find yourself at this moment, as long as it is a disposition of joy in the face of the conjunction of events caused by extraneous causality.[37]

Thus, Marcus used to train himself to concentrate upon the present moment; that is, upon what he was thinking, doing, and feeling within the present instant. "This is enough for you," he tells himself, and the expression has a double meaning:

1 It is enough to keep you busy; you have no need to think about anything else; and
2 It is enough to make you happy; there is no need to seek for anything else.

This is the spiritual exercise Marcus himself calls "delimiting the present." [38] Delimiting the present means turning one's attention away from the past and the future, in order to concentrate it upon what one is in the process of doing.

The present of which Marcus speaks is a present delimited by human consciousness. The Stoics distinguished two ways of defining the present.[39] The first consisted in understanding the present as the limit between the past and the future: from this point of view, no present time ever actually exists, since time is infinitely divisible. This, however, is an abstract, quasi-mathematical division, with the present being reduced to an infinitesimal instant.

The second way consisted in defining the present with reference to human consciousness. In this case, the present represented a certain "thickness" of time, corresponding to the attention-span of lived consciousness. When Marcus advises us to "delimit the present," he is talking about this lived present, relative to consciousness. This is an important point: the present is defined by its reference to man's thoughts and actions.

The present suffices for our happiness, because it is the only thing which belongs to us, and depends upon us. For the Stoics, it was essential to distinguish between what does and does not depend upon us. The past does not belong to us, since it is definitively fixated, and the future does not depend on us, because it does not yet exist. Only the present depends on us, and it is therefore the only thing which can be either good or bad, since it is the only thing which depends upon our will. Since the past and the future do not depend on us, they do not come under the category of moral good or evil, and must therefore be indifferent to us.[40] It is a waste of time to worry about what is long gone, or what will perhaps never occur; we must therefore "delimit the present." "All the happiness you are trying to achieve by long, roundabout ways: you can have it all right now. . . . that is, if you leave everything past behind you, entrust the future to providence, and if you arrange the present in accordance with piety and justice."[41]

Elsewhere, Marcus describes the exercise of delimiting the present in the following terms:

if you separate from yourself, that is, from your thought . . . everything you have said or done in the past, everything that disturbs you about the future; all that . . . attaches itself to you against your will . . . if you separate from yourself the future and the past, and apply yourself exclusively to living the life that you are living – that is to say, the present – you can live all the time that remains to you until your death, in calm, benevolence, and serenity.[42]

Seneca describes the same exercise as follows:

Two things must be cut short:[43] the fear of the future and the memory of past discomfort; the one does not concern me any more, and the other does not concern me yet.[44]

The sage enjoys the present without depending on the future. . . . Liberated from the burden of worries which torture the mind, he does not hope for or desire anything. He does not plunge forward into the unknown, for he is happy with what he has [i.e. the present, which is all that belongs to us]. And don't believe that he is content with not very much, for what he has is everything.[45]

Here we witness the same transformation of the present that we encountered in Epicureanism. In the present, say the Stoics, we have everything, and only the present is our happiness. There are two reasons why the present is sufficient for our happiness: in the first place, Stoic happiness – like Epicurean pleasure – is complete at every instant and does not increase over time. The second reason is that we already possess the whole of reality within the present instant, and even infinite duration could not give us more than what we have right now.

Happiness, then – that is, for the Stoics, moral action or virtue – is always total and complete, at each moment of its duration. Like pleasure for the Epicurean sage, the happiness of the Stoic sage is perfect. It lacks nothing, just as a circle, whether it is large or small, still remains a circle. The same is true of a propitious or opportune moment or favorable opportunity: it is an instant, the perfection of which depends not on its duration, but rather on its quality, and the harmony which exists between one's exterior situation and the possibilities that one has.[46] Happiness is nothing more nor less than that instant in which man is wholly in accord with nature.

Just as was the case for the Epicureans, one instant of happiness is, according to the Stoics, equivalent to an eternity. In the words of Chrysippus: "If a person has wisdom for one instant, he is no less happy than he who possesses it for an eternity."[47] Similarly, as for the Epicureans, so for the Stoics: we will never be happy if we are not so right now. It's now or never. The matter is urgent: we must hurry, for death is imminent, and all we require in order to be happy is to *want* to be so. The past and the future are of no use. What is needed is the immediate transformation of our way of thinking, of acting, and of accepting events. We must think in accordance with truth, act in accordance with justice, and lovingly accept what comes to pass. In the words of Marcus Aurelius: "How easy it is to find oneself, right away, in a state of perfect peace of mind." [48] In other words, it is enough just to want it.

For the Stoics, as for the Epicureans, it is the imminence of death which gives the present instant its value. "We must carry out each action of our lives as if it were the last." [49] This is the secret of concentration on the present moment: we are to give it all its seriousness, value, and splendor, in order to show up the vanity of all that we pursue with so much worry: all of which, in the end, will be taken away from us by death. We must live each day with a consciousness so acute, and an attention so intense, that we can say to ourselves each evening: "I have lived; I have actualized my life, and have had all that I could expect from life." In the words of Seneca: "He has peace of mind who has lived his entire life every day." [50]

We have just seen the first reason why the present alone is sufficient for our happiness: namely, that one instant of happiness is equivalent to a whole eternity of happiness. The second reason is that, within one instant, we possess the totality of the universe. The present instant is fleeting – Marcus insists strongly on this point[51] – but even within this flash, as Seneca says, "we can proclaim, along with God: 'all this belongs to me.' " [52] The instant is our only point of contact with reality, yet it offers us the whole of reality; precisely because it is a passage and a metamorphosis, it allows us to participate in the overall movement of the event of the world, and the reality of the world's coming-to-be.

In order to understand the preceding, we must bear in mind what moral action, virtue, and wisdom meant for the Stoics. Moral good – for the Stoics, the only kind of good there is – has a cosmic dimension: it is the harmonization of the reason within us with the reason which guides the cosmos, and produces the chain of causes and effect which makes up fate. At each moment, we must harmonize our judgment, action, and desires with universal reason. In particular, we must joyfully accept the conjunction of events which results from the course of nature. At each instant, we must therefore resituate ourselves within the perspective of universal reason, so that, at each instant, our consciousness may become a cosmic consciousness. Thus, if one lives in accord with universal reason, at each instant his consciousness expands into the infinity of the cosmos, and the entire universe is present to him. For the Stoics, this is possible because there is a total mixture and mutual implication of everything with everything else: Chrysippus, for example, spoke of a drop of wine being mixed with the whole of the sea, and spreading to the entire world.[53] "He who sees the present moment sees all that has happened from all eternity, and all that will happen throughout infinite time." [54] This explains the attention given to each current

event, and to what is happening to us at each instant. Each event implies the
entire world: "Whatever happens to you has been prepared for you from all
eternity, and the mutual linkage of cause and effect has, from all eternity,
woven together your existence and the occurrence of this event." [55]

One could speak here of a mystical dimension of Stoicism. At each moment
and every instant, we must say "yes" to the universe; that is, to the will of
universal reason. We must want that which universal reason wants: that is,
the present instant, exactly as it is. Some Christian mystics have also
described their state as a continuous consent to the will of God. Marcus, for
his part, cries out: "I say to the universe: 'I love along with you.' " [56] We have
here a profound feeling of participation and identification; of belonging to a
whole which transcends our individual limits, and gives us a feeling of
intimacy with the universe. For Seneca, the sage plunges himself into the
whole of the universe (*toti se inserens mundo*).[57]

Because the sage lives within his consciousness of the world, the world is
constantly present to him. In Stoicism, even more than in Epicureanism, the
present moment takes on an infinite value: it contains within it the entire
cosmos, and all the value and wealth of being.

It is quite remarkable that the two schools of Stoicism and Epicureanism,
in other respects so opposed, should both place the concentration of
consciousness upon the present moment at the very center of their way of life.
The difference between the two attitudes consists only in the fact that the
Epicurean enjoys the present moment, whereas the Stoic wills it intensely; for
the one, it is a pleasure; for the other, a duty.

Our scene from *Faust* echoes this double motif in two key phrases: "Only the
present is our happiness," and "Existence is a duty." [58]

In his conversations with Falk,[59] Goethe had spoken of certain beings who, by
virtue of their innate tendencies, are half Stoic and half Epicurean. He found
nothing surprising, he said, in the fact that they accepted the fundamental
principles of the two systems at the same time, and even that they tried to unite
them as far as was possible. One might say that Goethe himself, in his way of
living the present moment, was also "half Stoic and half Epicurean." He enjoyed
the present moment like an Epicurean, and willed it intensely like a Stoic.

In Goethe, we re-encounter most of the themes we have enumerated above;
in particular, the delimitation of the present followed by expansion into the
totality of the cosmos, which we observed in Epicureanism and in Stoicism.
In this regard, Goethe could have mentioned an opposition that was dear to
him: that between "systole" and "diastole."

First of all, let us consider concentration on and delimitation of the present.
In moments of happiness, these processes take place spontaneously: "Then
the spirit looks neither forward nor behind." This verse from *Faust* is echoed
by a poem dedicated to Count Paar:[60]

> Happiness looks neither forward nor backwards;
> And thus the instant becomes eternal.

The present instant is perceived as a grace which is accorded us, or an opportunity we are offered.

The mind may also, however, turn voluntarily away from the past and the future, in order to more fully enjoy the present state of reality. Such is the attitude of Goethe's Egmont:[61]

> Do I live only in order to think about life? Must I prevent myself from enjoying the present moment, that I may be sure of the one that follows, and then waste that one, too, in cares and useless worries? . . . Does the sun illuminate me today, that I may ponder what happened yesterday? That I may guess at and arrange that which cannot be guessed nor arranged: the fate of the oncoming day?

This is the same secret of happiness which Goethe formulated in the "Rule of Life":[62]

> Would you model for yourself a pleasant life?
> Worry not about the past
> Let not anger get the upper hand
> Rejoice in the present without ceasing
> Hate no man. . . .
> And the future? Abandon it to God.

This is the height of wisdom; the wisdom of the child in the *Marienbad Elegy*:[63]

> Hour by hour, life is kindly offered us
> We have learned but little from yesterday
> Of tomorrow, all knowledge is forbidden,
> And if I ever feared the coming evening,
> The setting sun still saw what brought me joy.
> Do like me, then: with joyful wisdom
> Look the instant in the eye! Do not delay!
> Hurry! Run to greet it, lively and benevolent,
> Be it for action, for joy or for love!
> Wherever you may be, be like a child, wholly and always;
> Then you will be the All; and invincible.

The "rule of life" – that "high wisdom" – consists in looking neither forward nor behind, but in becoming aware of the uniqueness and incomparable value of the present. In Goethe, then, we find the same exercise of delimitation of the present that we had encountered in ancient philosophy. This exercise is, however, inseparable from another exercise, which consists in becoming aware of the inner richness of the present, and of the totality contained within the instant. By delimiting the present, consciousness, far from shrinking, swells to fill the dimensions of the world; for that vision which "looks the instant in the eye" is the disinterested vision of the artist, the poet, and the sage, which is interested in reality for its own sake.

Enjoying the present, without thinking about the past or the future, does not mean living in total instantaneousness. Thoughts about the past and the future are to be avoided only insofar as rehashing past defeats, and cowering in fear of future difficulties, can cause distractions, worries, hopes, or despair, which turn our attention away from the present, where it ought to be concentrated. When we do concentrate our attention on the future, however, we discover that the present itself contains both the past and the future, insofar as it is the genuine passage within which the action and movement of reality are carried out. It is this past and this future which are seized by the artist's vision, in the instant which he chooses to describe or to reproduce. The artists of antiquity, says Goethe, knew how to choose the "pregnant" instant, heavy with meaning, "which marks a decisive turning-point between time and eternity." [64] To use one of Goethe's favorite terms, such instants "symbolize" an entire past, and an entire future.

Likewise, when an artist seizes an instant of the movement of a dancer, it allows us to glimpse both the "before" and the "after": "The marvelous suppleness with which a dancer moves from one figure to another, and provokes our admiration in the face of such artistry: it is fixated for a moment, so that we can see, simultaneously, the past, the present and the future, and we are thus transported into a supraterrestrial state." [65]

Whoever practices the art of living must also recognize that each instant is pregnant: heavy with meaning, it contains both the past and the future; not only of the individual, but also of the cosmos in which he is plunged. This is what Goethe gives us to understand in his poem "The Testament:" [66]

> Let reason be present everywhere
> Where life rejoices in life.

This point at which life rejoices in life is nothing other than the present instant. "Then," continues Goethe,

> the past has gained steadfastness
> The present is alive beforehand,
> The Instant is eternity.

Goethe is even more explicit on this point in one of his conversations with Eckermann:[67] "Hold fast to the present. Every circumstance, every instant is of infinite value, for it is the representative of an entire eternity."

Some commentators have believed they could explain Goethe's conception of the instant as eternity by Neoplatonic or Pietistic influence.[68] It is true that we do find within these traditions the representation of God as eternal present; but such a conception is not to be found in Goethe's writings. When Goethe speaks of the eternal in his poem entitled "Testament," for example, he is talking about the eternity of the cosmic process of becoming:

> Throughout all things, the Eternal pursues its course. . . .
> Being is eternal, for laws
> Protect the living treasures
> With which the All adorns itself.

In order to explain the Goethean notion of the instant as representative of eternity, we must rather think of the Epicurean and Stoic tradition of which I have spoken above. This tradition affirmed, in the first place, that one instant of happiness is equivalent to an eternity; and, secondly, that one instant of existence contains the whole eternity of the cosmos. In Goethean terms, this second idea could be expressed by saying that the instant is the symbol of eternity. Goethe defined the symbol as "the living, instantaneous revelation of the unexplorable,"[69] but we could just as well define the instant as "the living symbol of the unexplorable." The idea of the "unexplorable" corresponds to what, for Goethe, is the inexpressible mystery at the basis of nature and of all reality. It is its very fleetingness and perishable nature that make the instant the symbol of eternity, because its ephemeral nature reveals the eternal movement and metamorphosis which is, simultaneously, the eternal presence of being: "All that is perishable is only a symbol."[70]

It is here that the thought of death comes into play, for life itself is perpetual metamorphosis, and, inseparably, the death of every instant. Sometimes, for Goethe, this theme takes on a mystical tone:

> In order to find himself in the Infinite
> The individual willingly accepts to disappear.
> It is a pleasure to abandon oneself.[71]

I would praise the living creature who aspires to death in the flame.[72]

In the last analysis, then, it is eternity – that is, the totality of being – which gives the present moment its value, meaning, and pregnancy. "If the eternal remains present to us at each instant, we do not suffer from the fleetingness of time."[73] The ultimate meaning of Goethe's attitude toward the present is thus, as it was for ancient philosophy, the happiness and the duty of existing in the cosmos. It is a profound feeling of participation in and identification with a reality which transcends the limits of the individual. "Great is the joy of existence, and greater yet the joy we feel in the presence of the world."[74] "Throughout all things, the Eternal pursues its course. Hold on to Being with delight!"[75]

We ought here to cite the entire song of the watchman Lynceus near the end of the *Second Faust*:

> In all things, I see
> The eternal adornment,
> And since it pleases me,
> I please myself as well.
> You, my happy eyes:
> Whatever you have seen,
> Be it what it may,
> It certainly was beautiful.[76]

In his work on Winckelmann, Goethe presents this wonderstruck consent to being – to the being of the entire cosmos – as characteristic of the ancient soul.

> If man feels at home in the world as within an All, an All which is great, beautiful, noble and precious; if the pleasure of living in harmony with this All gives him a pure, free delight, then the universe – if it could be conscious of itself – would exult with joy; it would have attained its goal, and would be amazed at this summit of its becoming and its being. After all, what good is all this profligate abundance of suns, planets, moons, stars, Milky Ways, comets, nebula, worlds in the process of becoming and which have come to be, if, when all is said and done, one happy man does not rejoice, unconsciously, in his own existence?[77]

When Goethe says "unconsciously," he means that the reasons why people may be happy, and may be in harmony with the universe, are unknown and completely incomprehensible to them. Here we come across another case of the "unexplorable,"[78] to use one of Goethe's favorite expressions. Yet the innocent joy of existing, and the spontaneous, unreflecting pleasure which living beings take in existence, are an original phenomenon which reveals the presence of an unexplorable mystery: "The child is pleased by the cake, without knowing anything about the pastry-cook; and starlings like cherries, without them stopping to think about where they came from." [79]

We again find this "yes" to the world and consent to being in the following passage from Nietzsche, whatever reservations about it he himself may have had:

> Let us assume we say "Yes!" to one single, unique moment: we have thus said yes, not only to ourselves, but to the whole of existence. For nothing is isolated, neither in ourselves nor in things. And if, even once, our soul has vibrated and resounded like a string with happiness, all eternity was necessary to create the conditions for this one event; and all eternity has been approved, redeemed, justified, and affirmed. [80]

Not long ago, Georges Friedmann courageously denounced the tragic lack of balance which has come about in the modern world between "power" and "wisdom." [81] If we have chosen here to present some aspects of one of the fundamental themes of the European spiritual tradition, it was not in order to satisfy some historical or literary curiosity, but to describe a spiritual attitude: an attitude which, for ourselves and for modern man in general, hypnotized as we are by language, images, information, and the myth of the future, seemed to us to provide one of the best means of access to this wisdom, so misunderstood and yet so necessary. The call of Socrates speaks to us more now than ever before: "Take care for yourself." [82] This call is echoed by Nietzsche's remark: "Is it not the case that all human institutions" – to which we might add: "as well as the whole of modern life" – are intended to prevent mankind from feeling their life, by means of the constant dispersion of their thoughts?" [83]

NOTES

1 Johann Wolfgang von Goethe, *Faust*, 9381.
2 Ibid, 4685.
3 Ibid, 6487–500.
4 Ibid, 9370.
5 Ibid, 9419.
6 Ibid, 9377–84.
7 Ibid, 9411–18.
8 Johann Wolfgang von Goethe, Letter to Zelter of October 19, 1829, in *Goethes Briefe*, ed. K.R. Mandelkow, Munich 1967, vol. 4, p. 346.
9 "Book of the Cup-Bearer" ("Das Schenkenbuch"), in *Goethes Werke*, Hamburger Ausgabe (hereafter *HA*), vol. 2, p. 94.
10 O. Spengler, *Der Untergang des Abendlandes*, Munich 1923, vol. I, p. 11.
11 J. Hintikka, *Time and Necessity*, Oxford, 1973, p. 86.
12 S. Morenz, *Die Zauberflöte*, Münster, 1952, p. 89.

13 Cicero, *De finibus*, I, 18, 59.

14 Ibid, I, 18, 60.

15 Seneca, *Letters to Lucilius*, 15, 9.

16 Epicurus, fr. 240, p. 567 Arrighetti = Stobaeus vol. III, 17, 22 Hense.

17 Cicero, *De finibus*, I, 19, 63.

18 Epicurus, *Ratae Sententiae*, 19, p. 127 Arrighetti.

19 Seneca, *Letters to Lucilius*, 74, 27.

20 Aristotle, *Nichomachean Ethics*, 10, 3, 1174a17ff; cf. H.-J. Krämer, *Platonismus und hellenistische Philosophie*, Berlin/New York 1971, pp. 188ff.

21 J.M. Guyau, *La morale d'Épicure*, Paris 1927, pp. 112ff.

22 Horace, *Odes*, 2, 16, 25f.

23 Epicurus, *Gnomologicum Vaticanum* §14, p. 143 Arrighetti.

24 Horace, *Odes*, I, 11, 7.

25 Horace, *Letter*, I, 4, 13.

26 Cf. M. Gigante, *Richerche Filodemee*, Naples 1983, pp. 181, 215–16.

27 Lucretius, *On the Nature of Things*, 1033–6.

28 Epicurus, *Gnomologicum Vaticanum*, §33, p. 146 Arrighetti.

29 Epicurus, *Letter to Menoeceus*, §§124–5, p. 108 Arrighetti.

30 Horace, *Odes*, 3, 29, 42.

31 Without worries (*sine sollicitudine*), because he knows that on that day he has received all that it was possible to have, and that there is nothing left to be desired.

32 Seneca, *Letters to Lucilius*, 12, 9.

33 Lucretius, *On the Nature of Things*, 3, 16–17.

34 The most accessible text of this saying has been preserved by Clement of Alexandria, *Stromata*, V, 14, 138, 2. Cf. the commentary of A. Le Boulluec in *Clément d'Alexandrie, Stromates, V*, Paris 1981, p. 369.

35 L. Robin, *Lucrèce, De la Nature, Commentaire des livres III–IV*, Paris 1926, repr. 1962, p. 151.

36 Lucretius, *On the Nature of Things*, III, 947–9.

37 Marcus Aurelius, *Meditations*, 9, 6.

38 Ibid, 7, 29, 3; 3, 12, 1.

39 The principal text may be found in *SVF* 2, 509 [= Arius Didymus fr. 26 Diels, in Stobaeus vol. I, p. 105, 5ff. Wachsmuth]; for a commentary cf. P. Hadot, "Zur Vorgeschichte des Begriffs Existenz," *Archiv für Begriffsgeschichte* 13 (1969), pp. 118–19.

40 Marcus Aurelius, *Meditations*, 6, 32, 3.

41 Ibid, 12, 1, 1–2.

42 Ibid, 12, 3, 3–4.

43 [*Circumcidenda*. Literally, to cut a circle off the bark of a tree, thereby pruning or even killing it. – Trans.]

44 Seneca, *Letters to Lucilius*, 78, 14.

45 Seneca, *On Benefits*, 7, 2, 4–5.

46 Cicero, *De finibus*, 3, 14, 45.

47 Plutarch, *On Common Conceptions*, 8, 1062a.

48 Marcus Aurelius, *Meditations*, 5, 2.

49 Ibid, 2, 5, 2; 7, 69.

50 Seneca, *Letters to Lucilius*, 101, 10.
51 Marcus Aurelius, *Meditations*, 2, 14, 3.
52 Seneca, *On Benefits*, 7, 3, 3.
53 Plutarch, *On Common Conceptions*, 37, 1078e.
54 Marcus Aurelius, *Meditations*, 6, 37.
55 Ibid, 10, 5.
56 Ibid, 10, 21.
57 Seneca, *Letters to Lucilius*, 66, 6.
58 Goethe, *Faust*, 9382, 9418.
59 Conversation with J.D. Falk, in F. von Biedermann, ed., *Goethes Gespräche*, Leipzig 1910, vol. 4, p. 469.
60 "An Grafen Paar," in *Goethes Sämtliche Werke* (Cottasche Jubiläumsausgabe), Stuttgart 1902, vol. 3, p. 13.
61 Johann Wolfgang von Goethe, *Egmont*, Act 2.
62 Johann Wolfgang von Goethe, "Lebensregel," in *Sprüche*, 97ff, in *Goethes Werke*, *HA*, vol. I, p. 319.
63 Johann Wolfgang von Goethe, *Elegie*, v. 91ff, in *Goethes Werke*, *HA*, vol. I, p. 384.
64 Goethe, Letter to Zelter of October 19, 1829, in *Goethes Briefe*, vol. 4, p. 347.
65 Goethe, Letter to Sickler of April 28, 1812, in ibid, vol. 3, p. 184.
66 Johann Wolfgang von Goethe, *Vermächtnis*, in *Goethes Werke*, HA, vol. I, p. 370.
67 J.P. Eckermann, *Gespräche mit Goethe*, Wiesbaden 1955 (conversation of November 3, 1823), p. 61.
68 Neoplatonism: H. Schmitz, *Goethes Altesdenken*, Bonn 1959, pp. 152ff. Pietism: W. Schadewelt, *Goethestudien*, Zurich 1963, p. 445.
69 *Maximen und Reflexionen*, 314 Hecker = *Goethes Werke*, *HA*, 752.
70 Goethe, *Faust*, 12104.
71 "Eins und Alles," in *Goethes Werke*, *HA*, vol. I, p. 368.
72 "Selige Sehnsucht," in *Diwan*, in *Goethes Werke*, *HA*, vol. 2, p. 18.
73 Letter to August von Bernstorff of April 17, 1823, in *Goethes Briefe*, vol. 4, p. 63.
74 *Book of Suleika*, in the *East–West Divan*, in *Goethes Werke*, *HA*, vol. 2, p. 70.
75 "Testament," *loc. cit.*
76 *Faust*, 11296–303.
77 "Winckelmann," in *Goethes Werke*, *HA*, vol. 12, p. 98.
78 Cf. *Maximen und Reflexionen* 1207 Hecker = *Goethes Werke*, *HA* vol. 12, 718.
79 Eckermann, *Gespräche* (conversation of February 28, 1831), p. 438.
80 Friedrich Nietzsche, *Posthumous Fragments*, Ende 1886-Früjahr 1887, 7[38], in *Friedrich Nietzsche, Sämtliche Werke*, eds G. Colli and M. Montinari, 15 vols, Berlin 1980 (hereafter Colli/Montinari), vol. 12, pp. 307–8.
81 G. Friedmann, *La Puissance et la Sagesse*, Paris 1970.
82 Plato, *Alcibiades*, 120d4; *Apology*, 36c.
83 Friedrich Nietzsche, *Untimely Meditations*, 3, 4: *Schopenhauer as Educator*, 3, 4, vol. I, p. 373 Colli/Montinari.

9

The View from Above

No one has better expressed our longing for a view from above and flight of the soul than Goethe's Faust, as he went for his Easter promenade with Wagner and glimpsed the evening sunset:[1]

> O why does no wing lift me from the ground
> To strive after the sun for ever?
> In an endless evening dusk, I'd see
> The silent earth beneath my feet.
> Each hill would be ablaze, each vale bestilled,
> And silver brooks would flow in golden streams . . .
>
> Before me day, behind the night
> Heaven above and underneath the waves:
> A lovely dream, until it disappears! . . .
> Alas! To the Spirit's wings
> No mortal wing can join so easily.
> And yet, when high above us, lost in vast blue spaces
> The skylark sings her warbling tune,
> It is inborn in every man,
> That his mind surges onwards and upwards.

To the casual reader, this text seems to be nothing more than a dream about flying: the banal desire, innate in every human being, to be able to fly. A mere topos, in other words, as historians are often only too quick to categorize it. In fact, however, the theme of the flight of the soul plays a role of extraordinary importance in Goethe, as we can already glimpse from the following lines of his letter to Schiller of May 12, 1798: "Your letter found me . . . in the *Iliad*, to which I always return with delight. It is always as if one were in a balloon, far above everything earthly; as if one were truly in that intermediate zone where the gods float hither and thither."[2] In fact, man had succeeded in freeing himself from the weight of the earth only a few years previously. The Montgolfier brothers had carried out their first flight on November 21, 1783. Goethe had been deeply impressed by this event, and in an entirely unexpected way, this experience helped him to understand Homeric poetry.

Besides the events they narrate, the Homeric epics show us the whole world from the point of view of the gods, who look down upon mankind's battles and passions from the heights of the heavens or the mountaintops, without, however, being able to resist the temptation of intervening from time to time on behalf of one or the other contending parties. For example, in the fifth book of the *Iliad*, we speed through the space between heaven and earth together with the steeds of Hera:

> The horses winged their way unreluctant
> through the space between the earth and the starry heaven.
> As far as into the hazing distance a man can see with
> his eyes, who sits in his eyrie gazing on the wine-blue water,
> as far as this is the stride of the gods' proud neighing horses.[3]

At the beginning of book 13, we adopt the point of view of Zeus, and observe along with him the lands of the Thracians, the Mysians, and other such peoples, while elsewhere, sitting with Poseidon high on the loftiest peak of the green-wooded island of Samothrace, we gaze at the battle and the clamor of arms before the walls of Troy.

For Goethe, the reason Homeric poetry can raise us above all earthly things, and allow us to observe them from the point of view of the gods, is because it represents the paradigm of true poetry. As Goethe puts it in *Poetry and Truth*:

> True poetry can be recognized by the fact that, like a secular Gospel, through the inner cheerfulness and outward pleasure it procures us, it can free us from the mundane burdens which weigh upon us. Like a hot-air balloon, it lifts us up into higher regions, along with the ballast that clings to us, and lets us see, from a bird's-eye view, the mad labyrinths of the world spread out before us.[4]

In the last sentence, Goethe has in mind not only the view from above of the Homeric gods, but also the wings which Daedalus fashioned, in order to free himself from the Labyrinth in which Minos had imprisoned him. We shall later see in more detail why it is that, in Goethe's view, poetry has such an astonishing power.

The intimately connected themes of the bird's-eye view and flight of the soul have a long, complex history. Before we go on to examine the moral and existential meaning attributed to them, first by ancient philosophy, and then by Goethe, it may be useful to attempt to classify the various forms in which they appear. Since our discussion will be concerned only with philosophical and literary texts, we can leave aside the question of the real or ostensible Shamanic origin of these themes.[5]

First of all, we should emphasize that ancient philosophy and literature do not seem to have linked the theme of the flight of the soul with the ability to fly; that is, with the mere sensory experience of flight. Rather, it went hand in hand with a specific conception of the power of thought and the divine nature of the soul, which is able to raise itself above the categories of space and time. We cannot consider this power as a natural capacity of the human soul qua inhabitant of the terrestrial regions, nor it is a supernatural phenomenon. With regard to the first point, it is only natural that thought or the thinking soul can transport itself rapidly, even instantaneously, to wherever the object of thought happens to be. Already in the seventh book of the *Odyssey*,[6] the swiftness of ships is compared with that of wings and of thought, while Xenophon, in his *Memorabilia*, remarks that the thought of the soul, just like the divine thought, can instantaneously transport itself to Egypt or to Sicily.[7] This idea was frequently taken up by Philo of Alexandria, who used it to illustrate the themes of the immortality of the soul, the greatness of man, and his likeness to God.[8]

According to another conception, however, the flight of the soul did not consist in the mere experience of thinking, which is in a sense a banal, everyday phenomenon. Rather, it was something that could only be experienced under extraordinary circumstances: in particular, it came about as a consequence of the separation of the soul from the body.

Here we recognize the doctrine of Plato: according to the myth of the *Phaedrus*,[9] the soul is provided with wings by nature. Prior to its incarnation in a terrestrial body, the soul is thus able to rise up to the outermost limits of the heavens, and follow the procession of the winged chariots of the gods. If, however, the soul proves itself to be too weak for celestial existence, it loses its wings and falls into a body. The soul can only win back its wings when it separates itself from the body; in other words, after death. When Cicero in the *Tusculan Disputations*,[10] or Seneca in his *Consolation to Marcia*,[11] speak of the soul's post-mortem existence, they describe how souls discover the secrets of nature and look down on the earth from above. Plato, however, would above all have underlined the fact that, during its celestial journeys, the soul can contemplate the supracelestial world of eternal forms, as it did in its previous life, before its fall into the corporeal world.

Shortly before death, the soul already begins to feel the effects of its imminent separation from the body; hence it is able to journey into the beyond. In the tenth book of the *Republic*, Plato tells the story of Er the Pamphylian, who was left for dead on the battlefield, and whose soul was temporarily separated from his body. When Proclus discusses this passage in his *Commentary on Plato's Republic*,[12] he reports a number of similar stories, about Aristeas of Proconnesus, Hermodorus of Clazomenae, and Epimenides of Crete. Democritus also seems to have made a collection of such stories,[13] and Clearchus of Soloi, a pupil of Aristotle, told the tale of the psychic flight of a certain Cleonymus of Athens, whose soul had risen high up above the earth, and from there had had glimpses of completely unknown regions of the earth.[14] Plutarch, in his essay *On the Delays of Divine Vengeance*, recounts the experiences of a certain Thespesius of Soloi, who had also been left for dead:

> He saw nothing like what he had seen before: the stars were enormously large, and immeasurably far from one another, and they shone forth with a light of great force and marvelous colours, so that the soul, gently and lightly transported by this light like a ship on a calm sea, could quickly move to wherever it wished.[15]

In the view of the ancients, even the most insignificant dream was a separation of soul from body, in the course of which the soul could rise up to celestial heights. We need only think of the example of Cicero's *Dream of Scipio*.[16]

The separation of soul from body can also occur by purely spiritual means. This spiritual "death to the body" was carried out by means of philosophy, for according to Plato, philosophy is nothing but training for death:

> Shall we not say that purification occurs . . . when man separates the soul as much as possible from the body, and accustoms it to gather itself together from every part of the body and concentrate itself until it is completely independent, and to have its dwelling, so far as it can, both now and in the future, alone and by itself, freed from the shackles of the body?[17]

We shall have occasion later on to return to the precise meaning of this philosophical exercise. For the moment, suffice it to say that when Plato wants to describe the philosophical life, he does so by means of the image of the soul's gathering itself together, and its subsequent flight into the infinity of the heavens. This flight allows the soul to look down from above at human affairs, in the truest sense of the phrase.

As for the philosopher himself, Plato describes him as follows in the *Theaetetus*:

> In fact, it is only his body that lives and has its residence in the state; his soul, however, holds all this to be puny and meaningless, and contemptuously wanders all over the place, "under the earth," as Pindar says, and measuring whatever is on its surface, and "above the heavens,"

observing the stars, and in general thoroughly investigating the nature of everything that is, but without lowering itself to the level of any of the objects in its vicinity.[18]

In the *Republic*, Plato expresses the view that greatness of soul consists in precisely such an attitude: "For smallness is particularly contrary to the soul which always strives after the complete and perfect, both divine and human."[19] Such a soul, capable of observing the totality of space and time, has no fear even of death.

Here it might not be inappropriate to try to formulate more precisely two concepts with which we have been dealing: on the one hand, the concept of philosophy as a means of achieving spiritual death, and, on the other, the idea of philosophy as the ascent of the soul into the celestial heights. Plato developed these ideas and concepts in a specifically Platonic direction, but in and of themselves they are not specifically Platonic. Rather, they are to be found in all the ancient philosophical schools, be they Epicurean, Stoic, or Cynic.

In other words, in all schools – with the exception of Skepticism – philosophy was held to be an exercise consisting in learning to regard both society and the individuals who comprise it from the point of view of universality. This was accomplished partly with the help of a philosophical theory of nature, but above all through moral and existential exercises. The goal of such exercises was to help people free themselves from the desires and passions which troubled and harassed them. These needs and desires, it was thought, were imposed on the individual by social conventions and the needs of the body. The goal of philosophy was to eliminate them, so that the individual might come to see things as nature herself sees them, and consequently desire nothing other than that which is natural. If we leave aside for the moment terminological and conceptual differences, we can say that, within each school, philosophy signified the attempt to raise up mankind from individuality and particularity to universality and objectivity. For example, philosophical death for the Platonists consisted in getting rid of one's passions, in order to attain to the autonomy of thought. For the Stoics, philosophical death consisted in putting oneself in accord with universal reason, the all-embracing Logos, both interior and exterior.

Thus, in each philosophical school we encounter one and the same conception of philosophy. Similarly, in each philosophical school we find the same conception of the the cosmic flight and the view from above as the philosophical way par excellence of looking at things. In particular, Platonists, Stoics, and Epicureans all discovered, in addition to their theoretical physics, a practical physics, which was conceived of as an exercise in which the imagination speeds through the infinite vastnesses of the universe. Especially for the Platonists and the Stoics, the goal of this lived physics of the universe was to attain to greatness of soul, and in all schools its function was to teach people to despise human affairs and to achieve inner peace.

The exercise of practical physics is already hinted at in Plato's *Timaeus*,[20] where the soul is urged to bring its inner movements into accord with the movements and harmony of the all. Again, we find the same theme in the area of *meteorologia*: that is, speech which – according to the Hippocratic method, as Plato says in the *Phaedrus*[21] – places the soul and human affairs within the perspective of the all. Such a method, Plato adds, leads to nobility of thought.

Epicurean physics also opens up a wide field for mental flight, in the infinity of space and the infinite number of worlds. Thus Lucretius: "Since space stretches far beyond the boundaries of our world, into the infinite, our mind seeks to sound out what lies within this infinity, in which the mind can plunge its gaze at will, and to which the mind's thoughts can soar in free flight."[22] Elsewhere, Lucretius says that Epicurus has "boldly broken down the tightly shut gates of nature," and "Advanced far beyond the the flaming walls of our world."[23] In mind and thought, claims Lucretius, Epicurus has sped through the whole of infinity, thence to return victoriously and teach us what can and cannot come into being.[24]

This spiritual conquest of space kindled the enthusiasm of the eighteenth century, which dreamed of producing a new Lucretius. André Chénier[25] sought to give new life to this ideal in his unfinished poem "Hermes":

> Equipped with the wings of Buffon
> And lit by the torch of Newton, my flight
> Often soars, with Lucretius, beyond the azure girdle
> That stretches around the globe.
> I see Being, Life, and their unknown Source;
> And all the worlds tumbling through the Ether.
> I follow the comet with its fiery tail
> And the stars, with their weight, form and distance;
> I voyage with them in their immense orbits . . .
> Before my avid gaze, the diverse Elements unfold,
> With their Strife and their Love, the Causes and the Infinite.[26]

To return to Epicurean cosmic flights: the Epicurean sage's gaze upon infinity probably corresponds to that of the Epicurean gods. Unconcerned by mundane affairs in their bright, eternal tranquillity, they spend their time contemplating the infinity of space, time, and the multiple worlds.

We encounter this same tranquillity in the Stoic tradition, especially in the text from Philo of Alexandria cited more fully below, which describes philosophers in the following terms:

> As their goal is a life of peace and serenity, they contemplate nature and everything found within her: they attentively explore the earth, the sea,

the air, the sky, and every nature found therein. In thought, they accompany the moon, the sun, and the rotations of the other stars, whether fixed or wandering. Their bodies remain on earth, but they give wings to their souls, so that, rising into the ether, they may observe the powers which dwell there, as is fitting for those who have truly become citizens of the world.[27]

For Marcus Aurelius, only the "physical" viewpoint on things is capable of giving us greatness of soul; thus we have often found him practicing those spiritual exercises which have to do with the "physical" viewpoint on things. As he says in book 9 of the *Meditations*: "You have the power to strip off many superfluous things that are obstacles to you, and that depend entirely upon your value-judgments; you will open up for yourself a vast space by embracing the whole universe in your thoughts, by considering unending eternity."[28] In book 7, he admonishes himself as follows:

Watch and see the courses of the stars as if you were running alongside them, and continually dwell in your mind upon the changes of the elements into one another; for these imaginations wash away the foulness of life on the earth. When you are reasoning about mankind, look upon earthly things below as if from some vantage point above them.[29]

We shall return later to the final phrase. Elsewhere, Marcus describes the way in which the soul plunges itself into the totality of space and the infinity of time: "it traverses the whole Universe and the surrounding void, and surveys its shape, reaches out into the boundless extent of time, embracing and pondering the periodic rebirth of the all."[30] The goal of physics as a spiritual exercise was to relocate human existence within the infinity of time and space, and the perspective of the great laws of nature. This is what Marcus means by the all-embracing metamorphosis he mentions,[31] but he also has in mind the correspondence of all things, and the mutual implication of each thing in everything else.

Here, I believe, we have the reason why Goethe, in the passage quoted above, considered true poetry as an exercise consisting in spiritually elevating oneself high above the earth. For Goethe, poetry in the truest sense is a kind of physics, in the sense we have defined above: it is a spiritual exercise, which consists in looking down at things from above, from the point of view of the nature or the all, and the great laws of nature. By "laws of nature" we are to understand not only the all-embracing metamorphosis and unity of all things, but also the two universal principles Goethe refers to as "polarity" and "increase," and which he loved to observe both in nature and in individual human life.[32] We can detect the inspiration of these ideas not only in Goethe's youthful poetic cycle "God and the World," but also in the more modest and unassuming poems of the older Goethe. Like the physics of antiquity, poetry thus conceived is intended to bring about in its readers or listeners greatness of soul and inner peace.

We now move on to another aspect of this spiritual exercise. The view from above can also be directed pitilessly upon mankind's weaknesses and shortcomings. All the philosophical schools dealt with this theme at length, but, as we shall see, it was treated with particular relish by the Cynic tradition. In Ovid's *Metamorphoses*, we find a Neo-Pythagorean version of the theme: "It is a delight to travel along the starry firmament and, leaving the earth and its dull regions behind, to ride on the clouds, to stand upon stout Atlas' shoulders and see, far below, men wandering aimlessly, devoid of reason, anxious and in fear of the hereafter, thus to exhort them and unroll the book of fate!" [33] We encounter an Epicurean version of it at the beginning of book 2 of Lucretius' *On the Nature of Things*: "nothing is more delightful than to possess well-fortified sanctuaries serene, built up by the teachings of the wise, whence you may look down from on high upon others and behold them all astray, wandering abroad and seeking the paths of life." [34]

The theme takes on a Stoic coloration in Seneca's *Natural Questions*.[35] Here the soul of the philosopher, looking down from the heights of the heavens, becomes aware of the puniness of the earth, and the ridiculousness of the wars fought by human armies – which resemble swarms of ants – over minuscule stretches of territory. In Marcus Aurelius, the theme appears in a particularly realistic form: "look upon earthly things below as if from some place above them – herds, armies, farms, weddings, divorces, births, deaths, the noise of law courts, lonely places, various foreign nations, festivals, mournings, market places: a mixture of everything and an order composed of contraries." [36] Elsewhere, Marcus enjoins us to: " 'Look from above' at the spectacle of myriad herds, myriad rites, and manifold journeyings in storm and calm; diversities of creatures who are being born, coming together, passing away." [37] The view from above thus leads us to consider the whole of human reality, in all its social, geographical, and emotional aspects, as an anonymous, swarming mass, and it teaches us to relocate human existence within the immeasurable dimensions of the cosmos. Everything that does not depend on us, which the Stoics called indifferent (*indifferentia*) – such as health, fame, wealth, and even death – is reduced to its true dimensions when considered from the point of view of the nature of the all.

When the view from above takes on this specific form of observing human beings on earth, it seems more than ever to belong to the Cynic tradition. We find it being used with particular effectiveness by Lucian, a contemporary of Marcus Aurelius who was strongly influenced by Cynic doctrines. In Lucian's dialogue entitled *Icaromenippus, or the Sky-man*, the Cynic Menippus confides to a friend that he was so disillusioned by the contradictory teachings of the philosophers concerning the ultimate principles and the universe that he resolved to fly up heaven to see for himself how things were.[38] He fitted himself out with a pair of wings – on the left side a vulture's wing and on the right side that of an eagle – and soared upwards towards the moon. Once there, he reported, "I rested myself, looking down on the earth from on high and like Homer's Zeus, now observing the land of the horse-loving Thracians, now the land of the Mysians, and presently, if I liked, Greece, Persia and India; and from all this I got my fill of kaleidoscopic pleasure."[39] Once his eyes had become accustomed to the tiny dimensions of human beings, however, Menippus began to observe mankind. He could see "not only the *nations* and cities but the people themselves as clear as could be, the traders, the soldiers, the farmers, the litigants, the women, the animals, and, in a word, all the life that the good green earth supports."[40] Not only could Menippus see what people were doing in the open air, but also what they were about inside their own homes, when they thought no one was observing them.[41]

After Menippus has recited a long list of the crimes and adulteries he had seen committed inside people's homes, he sums up his overall impression: what he saw was a cacophonous, ridiculous hodge-podge of a play. What he found most ridiculous of all were those people who fought over the borders of their cities and private land-holdings, since the earth itself appeared to him so absurdly tiny and insignificant. Rich people, says Menippus, are proud of completely unimportant things. Their domains are no bigger than one of Epicurus' atoms, and the sight of man's cities reminded him of an anthill, with all its inhabitants scurrying about aimlessly.

Once he leaves the moon, Menippus travels among the stars until he arrives at the dwelling-place of Zeus. There, he has a good laugh over the ridiculously contradictory nature of the prayers mankind address to Zeus.

In another of Lucian's dialogues, entitled *Charon, or the Inspectors*,[42] Charon, ferryman of the dead, asks for a day off, so that he can go up to the surface of the earth and see just what this earthly existence is which people miss so much once they arrive in the underworld. With the help of Hermes, he piles up several mountains on top of one another, so as to be able to observe mankind better from on high. There follows the same kind of description we have already seen in Marcus Aurelius and in the *Icaromenippus*: Charon sees sea-travellers, trials, farmers – in a word, every kind of human activity, but all with one thing in common: an existence full of pain. Charon remarks: "If only humans could get it straight from the beginning: that they're going to die; that, after a brief stay in life, they have to depart from this life like a dream and leave everything on earth behind, then they'd live more wisely and die with fewer regrets." But man is thoughtless; he resembles the bubbles thrown up by a waterfall, which burst as soon as they come into existence.

As we have said, this kind of view from above, directed toward mankind's earthly existence, is a typical manifestation of Cynicism. We can see this by the fact that the dialogue *Charon* bears the Greek subtitle *Episkopountes*, "The Observers," or rather "The Overseers." The Cynic philosopher saw it as his duty to supervise the actions of his fellow men, like a kind of spy, lying in wait for their mistakes, so as to denounce them.[43] The Cynic had the task of watching over his fellow men like their censor, surveying their behavior from the heights of a watchtower. The words *episkopos* or *kataskopos* – "overseer" or "spy" – were used in antiquity as nicknames for the Cynics.[44] For them, the view from above was intended to denounce the absurdity of human life. It is no accident if, in one of Lucian's dialogues, it is precisely Charon, ferryman of the dead, who plays the role of observing human affairs from above; he is, after all, peculiarly well placed to observe them from the perspective of death.

To observe human affairs from above means, at the same time, to see them from the point of view of death. It is only this perspective which brings about the necessary elevation and loosening of the spirit, which can provide the distance we need in order to see things as they really are. The Cynic never ceases denouncing mankind's delusions: forgetful of death, people passionately attach their hearts to some object – luxury or power, for example – which, in the course of time, they will inevitably be forced to give up. This is why the Cynics called upon mankind to rid themselves of superfluous desires, and to reject social conventions, and the whole of artificial civilization, as being nothing but a source of worries, care, and suffering. The Cynics would have us return to a simple, purely natural way of life.

To return to Lucian: we learn from his short essay *How One Should Write History* that the view from above is appropriate not only to the philosopher but also to the historian. More precisely, the historian's gaze must be the same as the philosopher's: courageous, free of party affiliations, not bound to any nation, but equally well disposed towards all, making no concessions either to friendship or to hate. This attitude must be expressed in the historian's presentation of his materials. The historian, says Lucian, must be like Homer's Zeus: gazing now at the land of the Thracians, now at the land of the Mysians.[45]

For the third time now, we encounter the Homeric topos of a god casting his gaze down at the earth. This time, however, the Homeric source is quoted so as to serve as a model of that impartiality which must characterize historical reporting, thanks to the elevated viewpoint the historian has elected as his own. This is what a modern writer might refer to as "the viewpoint of Sirius." Thus we find Ernest Renan writing in 1880: "Viewed from the solar system, our revolutions have scarcely the extent of the movements of atoms. Considered from Sirius, they are even smaller still."[46] To adopt the viewpoint of Sirius means, here again, to undertake the spiritual exercise of letting go and using reserve, so as to achieve impartiality, objectivity, and critical judgment.

I have only been able to bring up here a few aspects of an extraordinarily rich tradition. If – as I hope to do one day – one were to write the complete history of the theme of the view from above, many other texts would have to be taken into consideration. Here, by way of conclusion, I shall restrict myself to citing Baudelaire's poem "Élévation," in which the great Symbolist describes the experience of the poet. For him, the poet was a being not meant for this world (as he put it in "The Albatross," "His huge wings prevent him from walking"). Yet, thanks to his poetic gifts, which allow him to observe things from above, the poet is also a being capable of seizing the hidden correspondences in things. We thus return to the theme of Goethe's "true poetry," which is really a kind of physics in the sense in which we have defined this term above: an intensive attempt to plunge into the secrets of nature.

[Elevation]

Above the ponds, above the valleys,
The mountains, woods, the clouds, and seas,
Beyond the sun, beyond the ether,
Beyond the limits of the starry spheres,

My spirit, you move with swift agility.
Like a good swimmer at home in the sea,
You slice gay furrows through the measureless depths,
With ineffable, masculine joy.

Fly far away from these pestilent fumes,
Go cleanse yourself in the upper air.
Go drink, like a pure, celestial liquor,
The bright fire that fills transparent space.

Left behind, all cares and endless sorrow
That weigh upon our foggy life like stones!
Oh happy man, who soars on sturdy wings
To calm and luminous fields!

In the morning, his thoughts, in their freedom,
soar up to the heavens like larks.
– He sails over life, understanding with ease
The language of flowers and voiceless things.[47]

NOTES

1 Johann Wolfgang von Goethe, *Faust*, I, 1074–9, 1088–95.
2 Johann Wolfgang von Goethe, Letter to Schiller, in *Goethes Briefen*, in *Goethes Werke*, Hamburger Ausgabe (hereafter *HA*), vol. 2, p. 344.
3 Homer, *Iliad*, bk 5, 767–73.
4 Johann Wolfgang von Goethe, *Dichtung und Wahrheit*, bk 13, *HA*, vol. 9, p. 580.
5 See above.
6 Homer, *Odyssey*, 7, 36.
7 Xenophon, *Memorabilia*, I, 4, 17.
8 Philo Judaeus, *Legum Allegoriae*, I, 62; *Quod deterius*, 86; *De mutatione nominum*, 178–80; *De opificio mundi*, 69–71.
9 Plato, *Phaedrus*, 246c–8c.
10 Cicero, *Tusculan Disputations*, I, 19, 43–5.
11 Seneca, *Consolatio ad Marciam*, 25, 2.
12 Proclus, *In Rempublicam*, vol. 2, p. 113, 20ff Kroll; French trans. A.-J. Festugière 1970, vol. 3, p. 58.
13 Cf. Proclus, *In Rempublicam*, p. 113, 6 Kroll.
14 Ibid, p. 114, 1 Kroll. Cf. F. Wehrli, *Die Schule des Aristoteles*, vol. 3, Basel 1948, fragment 8, pp. 11, 47–9.
15 Plutarch, *De sera numinis vindicta*, 22, 563b–8a.
16 Cf. above, *Meditations*.
17 Plato, *Phaedo*, 67c.
18 Plato, *Theaetetus*, 173c.
19 Plato, *Republic*, 486a.
20 Plato, *Timaeus*, 90c. It is instructive to compare this text with the description of Makarie in Goethe's *Wilhelm Meisters Apprenticeship and Travels* (3, 15, in *Goethes Werke*, *HA*, vol. 8, p. 449): "Makarie's relationship to our solar system can scarcely be described. Not only does she preserve and observe it in her mind, her spirit and imagination, but she makes herself as it were a part of it. She pictures herself swept away into the celestial spheres, but in a highly peculiar way: since her childhood, she has been wandering around the sun . . . in a spiral, getting farther and farther away from the middle point and circling ever closer to the outermost regions."
21 Plato, *Phaedrus*, 270a–c.
22 Lucretius, *On the Nature of Things*, 2, 1044.
23 Ibid, 2, 72–7.
24 Ibid, 2, 74–5.
25 [The French Romantic poet André Chénier, born 1762 in Constantinople, was guillotined during the French Revolution on July 25, 1794. – Trans.]
26 André Chénier, "Hermès," in A. Chénier, *Œuvres complètes*, Paris 1966, p. 392.
27 Philo Judaeus, *On the Special Laws*, 2, 44. Cf ibid, 3,1.
28 Marcus Aurelius, *Meditations*, 9, 32.
29 Ibid, 7, 47–8.
30 Ibid, 11, 1–2.
31 *Loc. cit.*, 2, 17.

32 Cf. C.F. von Weizsäcker, "Einige Begriffe aus Goethes Naturwissenschaft," in *Goethes Werke, HA*, vol. 13, p. 548.

33 Ovid, *Metamorphoses*, 15, 147 ff.

34 Lucretius, *On the Nature of Things*, 2, 7 ff.

35 Seneca, *Natural Questions, Preface*, 7–11.

36 Marcus Aurelius, *Meditations*, 7, 48.

37 Ibid, 9, 30.

38 Lucian, *Icaromenippus*, vol. 2, pp. 268 ff. Harmon.

39 Ibid, 11, p. 287.

40 Ibid, 12, p. 289.

41 This is also the theme of Lesage's eighteenth-century novel, *Le diable boiteux* [*"The Limping Devil"* – Trans.]. The idea of a trip to the moon or to the stars was the inspiration for many a seventeenth- and eighteenth-century novel; an example would be Voltaire's *Micromegas*.

42 Lucian, *Charon sive contemplantes*, vol. 2, pp. 397ff. Harmon.

43 Lucian himself describes the Cynic in this way. Cf. *Dialogues of the Dead*, 10, 2.

44 Cf. E. Norden, "Beiträge zur Geschichte der griechischen Philosophie," *Jahrbücher für classische Philologie*, supplementary vol. 19, Leipzig 1893; Epictetus, *Discourses*, 3, 22, 24.

45 Lucian, *Quomodo historia conscribenda sit*, ch. 49.

46 Ernest Renan, *Œuvres complètes*, vol. 2, Paris, 1948, p. 1037.

47 Charles Baudelaire, "Élévation."

10

The Sage and the World

1 Definition of the Problem

No one has described the relationship between the ancient sage and the world around him better than Bernard Groethuysen:

> The sage's consciousness of the world is something peculiar to him alone. Only the sage never ceases to have the whole constantly present to his mind. He never forgets the world, but thinks and acts with a view to the cosmos. . . . The sage is a part of the world; he is cosmic. He does not let himself be distracted from the world, or detached from the cosmic totality. . . . The figure of the sage forms, as it were, an indissoluble unity with man's representation of the world.[1]

This is particularly true of the Stoic sage, whose fundamental attitude consisted in a joyful "Yes!" accorded at each instant to the movement of the world, directed as it is by universal reason. We recall Marcus Aurelius' well-known prayer to the universe: "All that is in tune with you, O universe, is in tune with me."[2] Perhaps less well known is the aesthetic theory Marcus developed from the same point of view:

> If a person has experience and a deeper insight into the processes of the universe, there will be hardly any phenomenon accompanying these processes that does not appear to him, at least in some of its aspects, as pleasant. And he will look upon the actual gaping jaws of wild beasts with no less pleasure than upon all the imitations of them that sculptors and painters offer us. . . . and there are many such things, which do not appeal to everyone; only to that person who has truly familiarized himself with nature and her workings.[3]

We recall, moreover, that the Stoic sage, like Seneca, was conscious of being a part of the world, and plunged himself into the totality of the cosmos: *toti se inserens mundo*.[4]

The same could be said of the Epicurean sage, even though the physics he professed considered the world to be the result of chance, excluding all divine intervention. Nevertheless, this conception of the world suited the Epicurean perfectly: it brought with it pure pleasure and peace of mind, freed him from unreasonable fear of the gods, and made him consider each instant as a kind of unexpected miracle. As Hoffmann pointed out,[5] it is precisely because the Epicurean considered existence to be the result of pure chance that he greeted each moment with immense gratitude, like a kind of divine miracle. The sage's pleasure came from contemplating the world in peace and serenity; and in this he resembled the gods, who took no part in the management of the world, lest their eternal repose be disturbed. Describing the sage's contemplation, analogous to that of the gods, Lucretius exclaimed:

the terrors of the mind fly away, the walls of the world part asunder, I see things moving on through all the void . . . At these things, as it were, some godlike pleasure and a thrill of awe seizes on me, to think that thus . . . nature is made so clear and manifest, laid bare to sight on every side.[6]

This cosmic dimension is thus essential to the figure of the antique sage.

Here the reader may object: it could well be that ancient wisdom – whether Platonic, Aristotelian, Stoic, or Epicurean – was intimately linked with a relationship to the world; but isn't this ancient vision of the world out of date? The quantitative universe of modern science is totally unrepresentable, and within it the individual feels isolated and lost. Today, nature is nothing more for us than man's "environment"; she has become a purely human problem, a problem of industrial hygiene. The idea of universal reason no longer makes much sense.

All this is quite true. But can the experience of modern man be reduced to the purely technico-scientific? Does not modern man, too, have his own experience of the world qua world? Finally, might not this experience be able to open up for him a path toward wisdom?

2   The World of Science and the World of Everyday Perception

It would be stating the obvious to affirm that the world which we perceive in our everyday experience is radically different from the unrepresentable world constructed by the scientist. The world of science does indeed, by means of its multiple technical applications, radically transform some aspects of our daily life. Yet it is essential to realize that our way of perceiving the world in everyday life is not radically ·affected by scientific conceptions. For all of us – even for the astronomer, when he goes home at night – the sun rises and sets, and the earth is immobile.

Following Husserl, Merleau-Ponty developed some noteworthy reflections on this opposition between the world of science and the world of perception:

> The entire world of science is constructed on the basis of the world as we experience it [*sur le monde vécu*], and if we want rigorously to think through science itself, in order precisely to appreciate its range and its meaning, we must first of all reawaken this experience of the world, of which science is the secondary expression.[7]

For lived, existential experience, the earth is nothing other than the immobile ground[8] in relation to which I move, the fundamental referent of my existence. It is this earth, immobile in relation to our experienced movements, that even the astronaut uses as a reference point, including when, from the depths of space, the earth appears to him like a little blue ball. The analyses of Husserl and Merleau-Ponty thus let us see that the Copernican revolution, of which so much is made in philosophy handbooks, upset only the theoretical discourse of the learned *about* the world, but did not at all change the habitual, day-to-day perception we have *of* the world.

We must, however, be more specific about the opposition between the world of science and the world of everyday perception. The reason why Husserl and Merleau-Ponty want us to return to the world of lived perception, or rather to this perception-as-a-world, is so that we may become *aware* of it. This awareness, in turn, will radically transform our very perception of the world, since it will no longer be a perception of distinct objects, but perception of the world *as* a world, and, especially for Merleau-Ponty, perception of the *unity* of the world and of perception. In their view, philosophy is nothing other than this process by means of which we try "to relearn to see the world."[9]

In a sense, one might say that the world of science and the world of philosophy are both, in their own way, opposed to the world of habitual perception. In the case of science, this opposition takes the form of the elimination of perception. Science discloses to us a universe reduced, by both mathematical and technological means, to its quantitative aspects. Philosophy, for its part, deepens and transforms habitual perception, forcing us to become aware of the very fact the we *are perceiving the world*, and that the world *is* that which we perceive.

We find a similar distinction between habitual and philosophical perception in the writings of Bergson. He describes this difference as follows:[10]

Life requires that we put on blinkers; we must not look to the right, to the left, or behind, but straight ahead, in the direction in which we are supposed to walk. In order to live, we must be selective in our knowledge and our memories, and retain only that which may contribute to our action upon things.

Bergson continues: "We could say the same thing about perception. As an auxiliary of action, it isolates, out of the totality of the real, that which interests us." Some people, however, are born detached: artists.

When they look at a thing, they see it *for itself*, and no longer *for them*. They no longer perceive merely for the sake of action: they perceive for the sake of perceiving; that is, for no reason, for the pure pleasure of it . . .

That which nature does once in a long while, out of distraction, for a few privileged people; might not philosophy . . . attempt the same thing, in another sense and in another way, for everybody? Might not the role of philosophy be to bring us to a more complete perception of reality, by means of a kind of displacement of our attention?

The "displacement of attention" of which Bergson speaks, as in the case of Merleau-Ponty's "phenomenological reduction," is in fact a conversion:[11] a radical rupture with regard to the state of unconsciousness in which man normally lives. The utilitarian perception we have of the world, in everyday life, in fact hides from us the world qua world. Aesthetic and philosophical perceptions of the world are only possible by means of a complete transformation of our relationship to the world: we have to perceive it *for itself*, and no longer *for ourselves*.

3 Aesthetic Perception

Bergson and, as we shall see later, Merleau-Ponty consider the aesthetic perception of the world as a kind of model for philosophical perception. In fact, as J. Ritter has pointed out,[12] it is only with the flourishing of modern science, from the eighteenth century on, and the transformation of the philosopher's relationship to nature which came about as a result, that we find an awareness of the necessity of an "aesthetic" mode of perception, in order to allow existence – man's *Dasein* – to maintain the cosmic dimension essential to human existence. As early as 1750, Baumgarten,[13] in his *Aesthetica*, had opposed *veritas logica* to *veritas aesthetica*[14]: *veritas logica* was, for example, the knowledge of an eclipse appropriate to an astronomer, while aesthetic truth might be, for example, a shepherd's emotional perception of the same phenomenon, as he describes it to his beloved. In his *Critique of Judgement* of

1790, Kant also opposed aesthetic perception to scientific knowledge. In order to perceive the ocean as sublime, writes Kant, it is not necessary to associate with it all sorts of geographical or meteorological knowledge while we look at it. Rather: "one must come to see the ocean, all by itself – just as the poets do, exclusively *according to what it displays to the eye*, when it is contemplated either at rest, in the form of a limpid mirror of water, or when it is violently stirred, like an abyss threatening to swallow up everything." [15] When, between 1815 and 1830, C.G. Carus wrote his *Lettres sur la peinture de paysage*,[16] he characterized landscape-painting as the "art of the representation of the life of the earth [*Erdlebenbildkunst*]." For Carus, it is thanks to aesthetic perception that we may continue to live in that perceptive, lived relationship with the earth, which constitutes an essential dimension of human existence.

Thus, a disinterested, aesthetic perception of the world can allow us to imagine what cosmic consciousness might signify for modern man. Modern artists, reflecting on their art, regard it as inseparable from a completely characteristic experience of the world.

In the first place, the modern artist consciously participates in cosmic life *as* he creates. "The dialogue with nature," writes Paul Klee,[17] "remains for the artist the condition *sine qua non*. The artist is a man. He is himself nature, a part of nature within the domain of nature." This dialogue with nature presupposes an intense communication with the world, carried out not merely through visual channels: "Today, the artist is better and more subtle than a camera . . . he is a creature upon earth and a creature within the universe; a creature on one star among the other stars." This is why there are, according to Klee, means other than visual for establishing the relationship between the self and its object. There is the fact that we plunge our roots into the same soil, and that we share a common participation in the cosmos. This means that the artist must paint in a state in which he *feels* his unity with the earth and with the universe.

For Klee, then, abstract art appears as a kind of prolongation of the work of nature:

> [The artist's] progress in the observation and vision of nature gradually lets him accede to a philosophical vision of the universe which allows him freely to create abstract forms . . . Thus, the artist creates works of art, or participates in the creation of works, which are an image of the creative work of God . . . Just as children imitate us while playing, so we, in the game of art, imitate the forces which created, and continue to create, the world . . . *Natura naturans* is more important to the painter than *natura naturata*.[18]

We re-encounter this cosmic consciousness in Cézanne.[19] "Have you seen that gigantic Tintoretto in Venice," he writes, in which the earth and the sea, the terraqueous globe, are hanging above people's heads? The horizon is moving off into the distance; the depth, the ocean distances, and bodies are taking flight, an immense rotundity, a mappamundi; the planet is hurled, falling and rolling in mid-ether! . . . He was prophesying for us. He already had the same *cosmic obsession* which is consuming us now. . . . As for me, I want to lose myself in nature, to grow again with her, like her. . . . In a patch of green, my whole brain will flow along with the flowing sap of the trees. . . . The immensity, the torrent of the world, in a tiny thumb's worth of matter.

As we saw, the painter, according to Klee, feels himself to be a "piece of nature, within the domain of nature." We find the same theme in Roger Caillois' *Generalized Aesthetics*,[20] apropos of the experience of beauty:

Natural structures constitute both the initial and the final reference point of all imaginable beauty, although beauty is *human* appreciation. Since man himself belongs to nature, the circle can easily be closed, and the feeling man has of beauty merely reflects his condition as a living being and integral part of the universe. It does not follow from this that nature is the model of art, but rather that art constitutes a particular instance of nature: that which occurs when the aesthetic act undergoes the additional process of design and execution.

The artistic process shares with the creative process of nature the characteristic of rendering things visible, causing them to appear. Merleau-Ponty laid great stress on this idea:[21] "Art no longer imitates visible things; it makes things visible.[22] It is the blueprint of the genesis of things. Paintings show how things become things and how the world becomes a world. . . . how mountains become, in our view, mountains." Painting makes us feel the presence of things: the fact that "things are *here*." "When Cézanne strives after depth," continues Merleau-Ponty, "what he's really seeking is the combustion of being."

The experience of modern art thus allows us to glimpse – in a way that is, in the last analysis, philosophical – the miracle of perception itself, which opens up the world to us. Yet we can only perceive this miracle by reflecting on perception, and converting our attention. In this way, we can change our relationship to the world, and when we do so, we are astonished by it. We break off "our familiarity with the world, and this break can teach us nothing other than the unmotivated surging-forth of the world."[23] At such moments, it is as if we were seeing the world appear before our eyes for the first time.

4 *Spectator Novus*

There is nothing new in what we have said so far. Our reason for recalling it was in order to define the area of our experience in which there might be possible a relationship to the world bearing some resemblance to that which existed between the ancient sage and the cosmos: the world, that is, of perception. We are now in a position to show that, since ancient times, there have existed exercises by means of which philosophers have tried to transform their perception of the world, in a way analogous to Merleau-Ponty's phenomenological reduction, or to the conversion of attention spoken of by Bergson. Obviously, the philosophical discourses by which Bergson, Merleau-Ponty, and the philosophers of antiquity express or justify the procedure which leads to the transformation of perception are very different from one another, just as the discussions of Klee or Cézanne about painting are not to be confused with the phenomenology of Merleau-Ponty. Be that as it may, Merleau-Ponty was deeply conscious of the sense in which, above and beyond differences of discourse, the experiences of Klee or Cézanne coincided with his own. One could say the same about the similar experience which can be glimpsed behind certain quite striking texts from antiquity.

For example, let us consider this passage from one of Seneca's *Letters to Lucilius*: "As for me, I usually spend a great deal of time in the contemplation of wisdom. I look at it with the same stupefaction with which, on other occasions, I look at the world; this world that I quite often feel as though I were seeing for the first time [*tamquam spectator novus*]."[24] If Seneca speaks of stupefaction, it is because he sometimes finds that he discovers the world all of a sudden, "as though [he] were seeing it for the first time." At such moments, he becomes conscious of the transformation taking place in his perception of the world. Normally, he had not been in the habit of seeing the world, and consequently was not astonished by it. Now, all of a sudden, he is stupefied, because he sees the world with new eyes.

The Epicurean Lucretius was familiar with the same experience as the Stoic Seneca. In book 2 of his *On the Nature of Things*, he announces that he is going to proclaim a new teaching: "A truth wondrously new is struggling to fall upon your ears, and a new face of things to reveal itself." Indeed, it is not surprising if this new teaching strikes the imagination: Lucretius is about to assert the existence of infinite space, and, within this infinite space, of a plurality of worlds. In order to prepare his reader for this novelty, Lucretius introduces some considerations about mankind's psychological reactions to novelties. On the one hand, he says, we find that which is new difficult to believe; whatever disturbs our mental habits seems to us a priori false and inadmissible. Once we have admitted it, however, the same force of habit which made the novelty surprising and paradoxical subsequently makes it seem banal, and our admiration gradually diminishes. Lucretius then describes how the world would look to us if we saw it for the first time:

> First of all, the bright, clear colour of the sky, and all it holds within it, the stars that wander here and there, and the moon and the radiance of the sun with its brilliant light; all these, if now they had been seen for the first time by mortals, if, unexpectedly, they were in a moment placed before their eyes, what story could be told more marvelous than these things, or what that the nations would less dare to believe beforehand? Nothing, I believe; so worthy of wonder would this sight have been. Yet think how no one now, wearied with satiety of seeing, deigns to gaze up at the shining quarters of the sky![25]

These texts are extremely important for our purpose. They show that, already in antiquity, people were not conscious of living in the world. They had no time to look at the world, and philosophers strongly sensed the paradox and scandal of the human condition: man *lives in* the world without *perceiving* the world. Bergson correctly grasped the reason for this situation, when he distinguished between habitual, utilitarian perception, necessary for life, and the detached, disinterested perception of the artist or philosopher. What separates us from the world is thus not the irrepresentable character of the scientific universe – the world we live in is, after all, that of lived perception – and neither is it contemporary doubts about the rational character of the world: Lucretius had already denied this rationality. People in antiquity were unfamiliar with modern science, and did not live in an industrial, technological society; yet the ancients didn't *look* at the world any more than we usually do. Such is the human condition. In order to live, mankind must "humanize" the world; in other words transform it, by action as well as by his perception, into an ensemble of "things" useful for life. Thus, we fabricate the objects of our worry, quarrels, social rituals, and conventional values. That is what *our* world is like; we no longer see the world qua world. In the words of Rilke, we no longer see "the Open"; we see only the "future." Ideally, we would

> see everything
> and ourselves *in* everything
> healed and whole
> forever.[26]

The obstacle to perceiving the world is not to be found in modernity, but within man himself. We must separate ourselves from the world qua world in order to live our daily life, but we must separate ourselves from the "everyday" world in order to rediscover the world qua world.

5 The Instant

There is a well-known text, in which we can see both the echo of ancient traditions and the anticipation of certain modern attitudes: Rousseau's *Rêveries du promeneur solitaire*.[27] What is remarkable in this passage is that we cannot help but recognize the intimate connection which exists, for Rousseau, between cosmic ecstasy and the transformation of his inner attitude with regard to time. On the one hand, "every individual object escapes him; he sees and feels nothing which is not in the whole."[28] Yet, at the same time, "Time no longer means anything [to him]... the present lasts forever, without letting its duration be sensed, and without any trace of succession. There is no sensation – either of privation or of enjoyment, pleasure or pain, desire or fear – other than the one single sensation of our existence."[29] Here Rousseau analyzes, in a most remarkable way, the elements which constitute and make possible a disinterested perception of the world. What is required is concentration on the present moment, a concentration in which the spirit is, in a sense, without past nor present, as it experiences the simple "sensation of existence." Such concentration is not, however, a mere turning in upon oneself. On the contrary: the sensation of existence is, inseparably, the sensation of being *in* the whole and the sensation of the existence *of* the whole.

In Rousseau, all this is a passive, almost mystical state. For the ancients, however, it is quite apparent that the transformation of one's view of the world was intimately linked to exercises which involved concentrating one's mind on the present instant.[30] In Stoicism as well as in Epicureanism, such exercises consisted in "separating oneself from the future and past," in order to "delimit the present instant."[31] Such a technique gives the mind, freed from the burden and prejudices of the past, as well as from worry about the future, that inner detachment, freedom, and peace which are indispensable prerequisites for perceiving the world qua world. We have here, moreover, a kind of reciprocal causality: the mind acquires peace and serenity by becoming aware of its relationship with the world, to the extent that it re-places our existence within the cosmic perspective.

This concentration on the present moment lets us discover the infinite value and unheard-of miracle of our presence in the world. Concentration on the present instant implies the suspension of our projects for the future. In other words, it implies that we must think of the present moment as the *last* moment, and that we live each day and each hour as if it were our last. For the Epicureans, this exercise reveals the incredible stroke of luck thanks to which each moment we live in the world is made possible.

Believe that every day that dawns will be the final one for you. If you do, you will receive each unexpected hour with gratitude.[32]

Receive each moment of accumulating time as though it came about by an incredible stroke of luck.[33]

Let the soul find its joy in the present, and learn to hate worries about the future.[34]

Albeit for different reasons, the Stoics also shared this attitude of wonder at what appears and occurs in the present instant. For them, each instant and each present moment imply the entire universe, and the whole history of the world. Just as each instant presupposes the immensity of time, so does our body presuppose the whole universe. It is *within ourselves* that we can experience the coming-into-being of reality and the presence of being. By becoming conscious of one single instant of our lives, one single beat of our hearts, we can feel ourselves linked to the entire immensity of the cosmos, and to the wondrous fact of the world's existence. The whole universe is present in each part of reality. For the Stoics, this experience of the instant corresponds to their theory of the mutual interpenetration of the parts of the universe. Such an experience, however, is not necessarily linked to any theory. For example, we find it expressed in the following verses by Blake:

> To see a World in a Grain of Sand
> And a Heaven in a Wild Flower,
> Hold Infinity in the palm of your hand
> And Eternity in an hour.[35]

To see the world for the last time is the same thing as to see it for the first time, *tamquam spectator novus*.[36] This impression can be caused by the thought of death, which reveals to us the miraculous character of our relationship to the world: always in peril, always unforeseeable. Alternatively, it can be caused by the feeling of novelty brought about by concentrating one's attention on one instant, one moment of the world: the world then seems to come into being and be born before our eyes. We then perceive the world as a "nature" in the etymological sense of the world: *physis*, that movement of growth and birth by which things manifest themselves.[37] We experience ourselves as a moment or instant of this movement; this immense event which reaches beyond us, is always already there before us, and is always beyond us. We are born along with[38] the world. The feeling of existence of which Rousseau spoke is precisely this feeling of identity between universal being and our own existence.

6 The Sage and the World

Seneca was equally stupefied by the spectacle of the world (which he contemplated *tamquam spectator novus*), and by the spectacle of wisdom. By "wisdom," he meant the figure of the sage, as he saw it personified in the personality of the philosopher Sextus.

This is a very instructive parallel. There is in fact a strict analogy between the movement by which we accede to the vision of the world, and that by which we postulate the figure of the sage. In the first place, ever since Plato's *Symposium*, ancient philosophers considered the figure of the sage as an inaccessible role model, whom the *philo-sopher* (he who loves wisdom) strives to imitate, by means of an ever-renewed effort, practiced at each instant.[39] To contemplate wisdom as personified within a specific personality was thus to carry out a movement of the spirit in which, via the life of this personality, one was led toward the representation of absolute perfection, above and beyond all of its possible realizations. Similarly, in considering a partial aspect of the world, contemplation discovers the totality of the world, going beyond the landscape[40] glimpsed at a given moment, and transcending it on the way to a representation of totality which surpasses every visible object.

The contemplation mentioned by Seneca is, moreover, a kind of unitive contemplation. In order to *perceive* the world, we must, as it were, perceive our *unity with* the world, by means of an exercise of concentration on the present moment. Similarly, in order to recognize wisdom, we must, so to speak, go into training for wisdom. We can know a thing only by becoming similar to our object. Thus, by a total conversion, we can render ourselves open to the world and to wisdom. This is why Seneca was just as stupefied and filled with ecstasy by the spectacle of wisdom as he was by the spectacle of the world. For him, in both instances, it was a case of a discovery obtained by dint of an interior transformation and complete change in his way of seeing and living. In the final analysis, both the world as perceived in the consciousness of the sage, and the sage's consciousness itself, plunged in the totality of the world, are revealed to the lover of wisdom in one single, unique movement.

NOTES

1 B. Groethuysen, *Anthropologie philosophique*, Paris 1952, repr. 1980, p. 80.
2 Marcus Aurelius, *Meditations*, 4, 23.
3 Ibid 3, 2.
4 Seneca, *Letters to Lucilius*, 66, 6.
5 E. Hoffmann, "Epikur," in M. Dessoir, ed., *Die Geschichte der Philosophie*, vol. I, Wiesbaden 1925, p. 223.
6 Lucretius, *On the Nature of Things*, 3, 16–17, 28–30.

7 M. Merleau-Ponty, *La Phénoménologie de la perception*, Paris 1945, pp. ii–iii.

8 M. Merleau-Ponty, *Éloge de la philosophie et autres essais*, Paris 1953, pp. 285–6. Cf. E. Husserl, "Grundlegende Untersuchungen zum phänomenologiscen Ursprung der Räumlichkeit der Natur" (= Umsturz der Kopeinkanischen Lehre), in Marvin Faber, ed., *Philosophical Essays in Memory of E. Husserl*, Cambridge MA 1940, pp. 309–25.

9 Merleau-Ponty, *La Phénoménologie*, p. xvi.

10 H. Bergson, *La Pensée et le mouvant*, Paris 1946, pp. 152f.

11 [Cf. P. Hadot's important article "Conversion" in *Encyclopaedia Universalis*, pp. 979–81. – Trans.]

12 J. Ritter, *Subjectivität. Sechs Aufsätze*, Frankfurt 1974.

13 Cited in Ritter, *Subjektivität*, p. 155.

14 ["Logical truth" versus "aesthetic truth." – Trans.]

15 Immanuel Kant, *Critique of Judgement*, §29 (general remark).

16 ["Letters on Landscape-painting." They may be found in French translation in C.D. Friedrich and C.G. Carus, *De la peinture de paysage*, Paris 1988. – Trans.]

17 P. Klee, *Théorie de l'art moderne*, Paris 1964, repr. 1985, pp. 42–6.

18 ["*La nature naturante importe advantage au peintre que la nature naturée.*" I have translated *nature naturante* back into its Latin form, in which, issuing from Scholastic philosophy, it was made famous by Spinoza (cf. *Ethics*, I, 29). According to Lalande's *Vocabulaire technique et critique de la philosophie* (Paris 1988, 16th edn, p. 673), *natura naturans* traditionally designates God, insofar as he is creator and principle of all action; while *natura naturata* is "the totality of beings and laws he has created." Klee's meaning is that the artist is more interested in the dynamics of creative *processes* than in the visible world as end-result of these processes. – Trans.]

19 Cf. J. Gasquet, *Cézanne*, Paris 1988, p. 154.

20 R. Caillois, *Esthétique généralisée*, Paris 1962, p. 8.

21 M. Merleau-Ponty, "L'oeil et l'esprit," *Les Temps Modernes* 27 (1961), pp. 217, 219.

22 This idea was borrowed from Klee; cf. Klee, *Théorie*, p. 34.

23 Merleau-Ponty, *La Phénoménologie*, p. viii.

24 Seneca, *Letters to Lucilius*, 64, 6.

25 Lucretius, *On the Nature of Things*, 2, 1023–5, 1030–9. Similar remarks can be found in Cicero, *On the Nature of the Gods*, 3, 38, 96; Seneca, *Natural Questions*, 7, 1; Augustine, *On the Usefulness of Belief*, 16, 34.

26 Rainer Maina Rilke, *Duino Elegies*, Eighth Elegy.

27 ["Musings of a Solitary Stroller," written between 1776 and Rousseau's death in 1778. – Trans.]

28 J.-J. Rousseau 1964, 7th Promenade, p. 126.

29 Ibid, 5th Promenade, p. 102.

30 See above.

31 Marcus Aurelius, *Meditations*, 12, 3, 3–4; 7, 29, 3; 3, 12, 1.

32 Horace, *Epistle*, I, 4, 13.

33 M. Gigante, *Richerche Filodemee*, Naples 1983, pp. 181, 215–16.

34 Horace, *Odes*, 2, 16, 25.

35 William Blake, "Auguries of Innocence" in *Complete Writings with Variant Readings*, ed. Geoffrey Keynes, London 1972, p. 435, 1–5.

36 ["Like a new spectator." – Trans.]

37 [Cf. P. Hadot, "Remarques sur la notion de ≪physis≫ et de nature," in *Herméneutique et ontologie: Hommage à Pierre-Aubenque*, Paris 1990, pp. 1–15. – Trans.]

38 "Nous co-naissons au monde." The phrase is that of Paul Claudel, *Art Poétique*, Paris 1946, pp. 54ff.

39 Cf. above.

40 Cf. Ritter, *Subjektivität*, p. 151.

11

Philosophy as a Way of Life

Every person – whether Greek or Barbarian – who *is in training for wisdom*, leading a blameless, irreproachable life, chooses neither to commit injustice nor return it unto others, but to avoid the company of busybodies, and hold in contempt the places where they spend their time – courts, councils, marketplaces, assemblies – in short, every kind of meeting or reunion of thoughtless people. As their goal is a life of peace and serenity, they contemplate nature and everything found within her: they attentively explore the earth, the sea, the air, the sky, and every nature found therein. In thought, they accompany the moon, the sun, and the rotations of the other stars, whether fixed or wandering. Their bodies remain on earth, but they give wings to their souls, so that, rising into the ether, they may observe the powers which dwell there, as is fitting for those who have truly become citizens of the world. Such people consider the whole world as their city, and its citizens are the companions of wisdom; they have received their civic rights from virtue, which has been entrusted with presiding over the universal common-wealth. Thus, filled with every excellence, they are accustomed no longer to take account of physical discomforts or exterior evils, and they train themselves to be indifferent to indifferent things; they are armed against both pleasures and desires, and, in short, they always strive to keep themselves above passions . . . they do not give in under the blows of fate, because they have calculated its attacks in advance (for foresight makes easier to bear even the most difficult of the things that happen against our will; since then the mind no longer supposes what happens to be strange and novel, but its perception of them is dulled, as if it had to do with old and worn-out things). It is obvious that people such as these, who find their joy in virtue, celebrate a festival their whole life long. To be sure, there is only a small number of such people; they are like embers of wisdom kept smouldering in our cities, so that virtue may not be altogether snuffed out and disappear from our race. But if only people everywhere felt the same way as this small number, and became as nature meant for them to be: blameless, irreproachable, and *lovers of wisdom*, rejoicing in the beautiful just because it *is* beautiful, and considering that there is no other good besides it . . . then our cities would be brimful of happiness. They would know nothing of the things that cause grief and fear, but would be so filled with the causes of joy and well-being that there would be no single moment in which they would not lead a life full of joyful laughter; indeed, the whole cycle of the year would be a festival for them.[1]

In this passage from Philo of Alexandria, inspired by Stoicism, one of the fundamental aspects of philosophy in the Hellenistic and Roman eras comes clearly to the forefront. During this period, philosophy was a *way of life*. This is not only to say that it was a specific type of moral conduct; we can easily see the role played in the passage from Philo by the contemplation of nature. Rather, it means that philosophy was a mode of existing-in-the-world, which had to be practiced at each instant, and the goal of which was to transform the whole of the individual's life.

For the ancients, the mere word *philo-sophia* – the love of wisdom – was enough to express this conception of philosophy. In the *Symposium*, Plato had shown that Socrates, symbol of the philosopher, could be identified with Eros, the son of Poros (expedient) and of Penia (poverty). Eros lacked wisdom, but he did know how to acquire it.[2] Philosophy thus took on the form of an exercise of the thought, will, and the totality of one's being, the goal of which was to achieve a state practically inaccessible to mankind: wisdom. Philosophy was a method of spiritual progress which demanded a radical conversion and transformation of the individual's way of being.

Thus, philosophy was a way of life, both in its exercise and effort to achieve wisdom, and in its goal, wisdom itself. For real wisdom does not merely cause us to know: it makes us "be" in a different way. Both the grandeur and the paradox of ancient philosophy are that it was, at one and the same time, conscious of the fact that wisdom is inaccessible, and convinced of the necessity of pursuing spiritual progress. In the words of Quintillian: "We must . . . strive after that which is highest, as many of the ancients did. Even though they believed that no sage had ever yet been found, they nevertheless continued to teach the precepts of wisdom."[3] The ancients knew that they would never be able to realize wisdom within themselves as a stable, definitive state, but they at least hoped to accede to it in certain privileged moments, and wisdom was the transcendent norm which guided their action.

Wisdom, then, was a way of life which brought peace of mind (*ataraxia*), inner freedom (*autarkeia*), and a cosmic consciousness. First and foremost, philosophy presented itself as a therapeutic, intended to cure mankind's anguish. This concept is stated explicitly in Xenocrates,[4] and in Epicurus:[5] "We must not suppose that any other object is to be gained from the knowledge of the phenomena of the sky . . . than peace of mind and a sure confidence." This was also a prominent idea for the Stoics[6] and for the Skeptics, apropos of whom Sextus Empiricus[7] utilizes the following splendid image:

> Apelles, the famous painter, wished to reproduce the foam from a horse's mouth in a painting. He was not able to get it right, and decided to give up. So, he threw the sponge he used to wipe his brushes against the painting. When the sponge hit the painting, it produced nothing other than an imitation of a horse's foam. In the same way, the Skeptics start off like the other philosophers, seeking peace of mind in firmness and confidence in their judgments. When they do not achieve it, they suspend their judgment. No sooner do they they do this than, by pure chance, peace of mind accompanies the suspension of judgment, like a shadow follows a body.

Philosophy presented itself as a method for achieving independence and inner freedom (*autarkeia*), that state in which the ego depends only upon itself. We encounter this theme in Socrates,[8] among the Cynics, in Aristotle – for whom only the contemplative life is independent[9] – in Epicurus,[10] and among the Stoics.[11] Although their methodologies differ, we find in all philosophical schools the same awareness of the power of the human self to free itself from everything which is alien to it, even if, as in the case of the Skeptics, it does so via the mere refusal to make any decision.

In Epicureanism and in Stoicism, cosmic consciousness was added to these fundamental dispositions. By "cosmic consciousness," we mean the consciousness that we are a part of the cosmos, and the consequent dilation of our self throughout the infinity of universal nature. In the words of Epicurus' disciple Metrodorus: "Remember that, although you are mortal and have only a limited life-span, yet you have risen, through the contemplation of nature, to the infinity of space and time, and you have seen all the past and all the future."[12] According to Marcus Aurelius: "The rational soul . . . travels through the whole universe and the void that surrounds it . . . it reaches out into the boundless extent of infinity, and it examines and contemplates the periodic rebirth of all things."[13] At each instant, the ancient sage was conscious of living in the cosmos, and he placed himself in harmony with the cosmos.

In order better to understand in what way ancient philosophy could be a way of life, it is perhaps necessary to have recourse to the distinction proposed by the Stoics,[14] between *discourse about* philosophy and *philosophy itself*. For the Stoics, the parts of philosophy – physics, ethics, and logic – were not, in fact, parts of philosophy itself, but rather parts of philosophical *discourse*. By this they meant that when it comes to teaching philosophy, it is necessary to set forth a theory of logic, a theory of physics, and a theory of ethics. The exigencies of discourse, both logical and pedagogical, require that these distinctions be made. But philosophy itself – that is, the philosophical way of life – is no longer a theory divided into parts, but a unitary act, which consists in *living* logic, physics, and ethics. In this case, we no longer study logical theory – that is, the theory of speaking and thinking well – we simply think and speak well. We no longer engage in theory about the physical world, but we contemplate the cosmos. We no longer theorize about moral action, but we act in a correct and just way.

Discourse about philosophy is not the same thing as *philosophy*. Polemon, one of the heads of the Old Academy, used to say:

> we should exercise ourselves with realities, not with dialectical specula-
> tions, like a man who has devoured some textbook on harmonics, but
> has never put his knowledge into practice. Likewise, we must not be like
> those who can astonish their onlookers by their skill in syllogistic
> argumentation, but who, when it comes to their own lives, contradict
> their own teachings.[15]

Five centuries later, Epictetus echoed this view:

> A carpenter does not come up to you and say, "Listen to me discourse
> about the art of carpentry," but he makes a contract for a house and
> builds it. . . . Do the same thing yourself. Eat like a man, drink like a
> man . . . get married, have children, take part in civic life, learn how to
> put up with insults, and tolerate other people.[16]

We can immediately foresee the consequences of this distinction, formu-
lated by the Stoics but admitted by the majority of philosophers, concerning the relationship between theory and practice. An Epicurean saying puts it clearly: "Vain is the word of that philosopher which does not heal any suffering of man." [17] Philosophical theories are in the service of the philosoph-
ical life. That is why, in the Hellenistic and Roman periods, they were reduced to a theoretical, systematic, highly concentrated nucleus, capable of exercising a strong psychological effect, and easy enough to handle so that it might always be kept close at hand (*procheiron*).[18] Philosophical discourse was not systematic because it wanted to provide a total, systematic explanation of the whole of reality. Rather, it was systematic in order that it might provide the mind with a small number of principles, tightly linked together, which derived greater persuasive force and mnemonic effectiveness precisely from such systematization. Short sayings summed up, sometimes in striking form,

the essential dogmas, so that the student might easily relocate himself within the fundamental disposition in which he was to live.

Does the philosophical life, then, consist only in the application, at every moment, of well-studied theorems, in order to resolve life's problems? As a matter of fact, when we reflect on what the philosophical life implies, we realize that there is an abyss between philosophical theory and philosophizing as living action. To take a similar case: it may seem as though artists, in their creative activity, do nothing but apply rules, yet there is an immeasurable distance between artistic creation and the abstract theory of art. In philosophy, however, we are not dealing with the mere creation of a work of art: the goal is rather to transform *ourselves*. The act of living in a genuinely philosophical way thus corresponds to an order of reality totally different from that of philosophical discourse.

In Stoicism, as in Epicureanism, philosophizing was a continuous act, permanent and identical with life itself, which had to be renewed at each instant. For both schools, this act could be defined as an orientation of the attention.

In Stoicism, attention was oriented toward the purity of one's intentions. In other words, its objective was the conformity of our individual will with reason, or the will of universal nature. In Epicureanism, by contrast, attention was oriented toward pleasure, which is, in the last analysis, the pleasure of existing. In order to realize this state of attention, however, a number of exercises were necessary: intense meditation on fundamental dogmas, the ever-renewed awareness of the finitude of life, examination of one's conscience, and, above all, a specific attitude toward time.

Both the Stoics and the Epicureans advised us to live *in the present*, letting ourselves be neither troubled by the past, nor worried by the uncertainty of the future. For both these schools of thought, the present sufficed for happiness, because it was the only reality which belongs to us and depends on us. Stoics and Epicureans agreed in recognizing the infinite value of each instant: for them, wisdom is just as perfect and complete in one instant as it is throughout an eternity. In particular, for the Stoic sage, the totality of the cosmos is contained and implied in each instant. Moreover, we not only *can* but we *must* be happy *right now*. The matter is urgent, for the future is uncertain and death is a constant threat: "While we're waiting to live, life passes us by."[19] Such an attitude can only be understood if we assume that there was, in ancient philosophy, a sharp awareness of the infinite, incommensurable value of existence. Existing within the cosmos, in the unique reality of the cosmic event, was held to be infinitely precious.

Thus, as we have seen, philosophy in the Hellenistic and Greek period took on the form of a way of life, an art of living, and a way of being. This, however, was nothing new; ancient philosophy had had this character at least as far back as Socrates. There was a Socratic style of life (which the Cynics were to imitate), and the Socratic dialogue was an exercise which brought Socrates' interlocutor to put himself in question, to take care of himself, and to make his soul as beautiful and wise as possible.[20] Similarly, Plato defined philosophy as a training for death, and the philosopher as the person who does not fear death, because he contemplates the totality of time and of being.[21]

It is sometimes claimed that Aristotle was a pure theoretician, but for him, too, philosophy was incapable of being reduced to philosophical discourse, or to a body of knowledge. Rather, philosophy for Aristotle was a quality of the mind, the result of an inner transformation. The form of life preached by Aristotle was the life according to the mind.[22]

We must not, therefore, as is done all too often, imagine that philosophy was completely transformed during the Hellenistic period, whether after the Macedonian domination over the Greek cities, or during the imperial period. On the one hand, it is not the case, as tenacious, widely-held clichés would have us believe, that the Greek city-state died after 330 BC, and political life along with it. Above all, the conception of philosophy as an art and form of living is not linked to political circumstances, or to a need for escape mechanisms and inner liberty, in order to compensate for lost political freedom. Already for Socrates and his disciples, philosophy was a mode of life, and a technique of inner living. Philosophy did not change its essence throughout the entire course of its history in antiquity.

In general, historians of philosophy pay little attention to the fact that ancient philosophy was, first and foremost, a way of life. They consider philosophy as, above all, philosophical discourse. How can the origins of this prejudice be explained? I believe it is linked to the evolution of philosophy itself in the Middle Ages and in modern times.

Christianity played a considerable role in this phenomenon. From its very beginnings – that is, from the second century AD on – Christianity had presented itself as a philosophy: the Christian way of life.[23] Indeed, the very fact that Christianity was able to present itself as a philosophy confirms the assertion that philosophy was conceived in antiquity as a way of life. If to do philosophy was to live in conformity with the law of reason, so the argument went, the Christian was a philosopher, since he lived in conformity with the law of the Logos – divine reason.[24] In order to present itself as a philosophy, Christianity was obliged to integrate elements borrowed from ancient philosophy. It had to make the Logos of the gospel according to John coincide with Stoic cosmic reason, and subsequently also with the Aristotelian or Platonic intellect. It also had to integrate philosophical spiritual exercises into Christian life. The phenomenon of integration appears very clearly in Clement of Alexandria, and was intensely developed in the monastic movement, where we find the Stoico/Platonic exercises of attention to oneself (*prosoche*), meditation, examination of conscience, and the training for death. We also re-encounter the high value accorded to peace of mind and impassibility.

The Middle Ages was to inherit the conception of monastic life as Christian philosophy, that is, as a Christian way of life. As Dom Jean Leclerq has written: "As much as in antiquity, *philosophia* in the monastic Middle Ages designates not a theory or a way of knowing, but a lived wisdom, a way of living according to reason."[25] At the same time, however, the medieval universities witnessed the elimination of the confusion which had existed in primitive Christianity between theology, founded on the rule of faith, and traditional philosophy, founded on reason. Philosophy was now no longer the supreme science, but the "servant of theology;" it supplied the latter with the conceptual, logical, physical, and metaphysical materials it needed. The Faculty of Arts became no more than a preparation for the Faculty of Theology.

If we disregard, for the moment, the monastic usage of the word *philosophia*, we can say that philosophy in the Middle Ages had become a purely theoretical and abstract activity. It was no longer a way of life. Ancient spiritual exercises were no longer a part of philosophy, but found themselves integrated into Christian spirituality. It is in this form that we encounter them once again in the *Spiritual Exercises* of Saint Ignatius.[26] Neoplatonic mysticism was prolonged into Christian mysticism, especially among such Rhineland Dominicans as Meister Eckhardt.

Thus, the Middle Ages saw a radical change in the content of philosophy as compared to antiquity. Moreover, from the medieval period on, theology and philosophy were taught in those universities which had been creations of the medieval church. Even though attempts have been made to use the word "university" in reference to ancient educational institutions, it appears that neither the notion nor the reality of the university ever existed during antiquity, with the possible exception of the Orient near the end of the late antique period.

One of the characteristics of the university is that it is made up of professors who train professors, or professionals training professionals. Education was thus no longer directed toward people who were to be educated with a view to becoming fully developed human beings, but to specialists, in order that they might learn how to train other specialists. This is the danger of "Scholasticism," that philosophical tendency which began to be sketched at the end of antiquity, developed in the Middle Ages, and whose presence is still recognizable in philosophy today.

The scholastic university, dominated by theology, would continue to function up to the end of the eighteenth century, but from the sixteenth to the eighteenth centuries, genuinely creative philosophical activity would develop *outside* the university, in the persons of Descartes, Spinoza, Malebranche, and Leibniz. Philosophy thus reconquered its autonomy vis-à-vis theology, but this movement – born as a reaction against medieval Scholasticism – was situated on the same terrain as the latter. In opposition to one kind of theoretical philosophical discourse, there arose yet another theoretical discourse.

From the end of the eighteenth century onward, a new philosophy made its appearance within the university, in the persons of Wolff, Kant, Fichte, Schelling, and Hegel. From now on, with a few rare exceptions like Schopenhauer or Nietzsche, philosophy would be indissolubly linked to the university. We see this in the case of Bergson, Husserl, and Heidegger. This fact is not without importance. Philosophy – reduced, as we have seen, to philosophical discourse – develops from this point on in a different atmosphere and environment from that of ancient philosophy. In modern university philosophy, philosophy is obviously no longer a way of life or form of life – unless it be the form of life of a professor of philosophy. Nowadays, philosophy's element and vital milieu is the state educational institution; this has always been, and may still be, a danger for its independence. In the words of Schopenhauer:

> Generally speaking, university philosophy is mere fencing in front of a mirror. In the last analysis, its goal is to give students opinions which are to the liking of the minister who hands out the Chairs. . . . As a result, this state-financed philosophy makes a joke of philosophy. And yet, if there is one thing desirable in this world, it is to see a ray of light fall onto the darkness of our lives, shedding some kind of light on the mysterious enigma of our existence.[27]

Be this as it may, modern philosophy is first and foremost a discourse developed in the classroom, and then consigned to books. It is a text which requires exegesis.

This is not to say that modern philosophy has not rediscovered, by different paths, some of the existential aspects of ancient philosophy. Besides, it must be added that these aspects have never completely disappeared. For example, it was no accident that Descartes entitled one of his works *Meditations*. They are indeed meditations – *meditatio* in the sense of exercise – according to the spirit of the Christian philosophy of St Augustine, and Descartes recommends that they be practiced over a certain period of time. Beneath its systematic, geometrical form, Spinoza's *Ethics* corresponds rather well to what systematic philosophical discourse could mean for the Stoics. One could say that Spinoza's discourse, nourished on ancient philosophy, teaches man how to transform, radically and concretely, his own being, and how to accede to beatitude. The figure of the sage, moreover, appears in the final lines of the *Ethics*: "the sage, in so far as he is regarded as such, is scarcely at all disturbed in spirit, but, being conscious of himself, and of God, and of things, by a certain eternal necessity, never ceases to be, but always possesses true acquiescence of the spirit." [28] The philosophies of Nietzsche and of Schopenhauer are also invitations to radically transform our way of life. Both men were, moreover, thinkers steeped in the tradition of ancient philosophy.

According to the Hegelian model, human consciousness has a purely historical character; and the only lasting thing is the action of the spirit itself, as it constantly engenders new forms. Under the influence of Hegel's method, the idea arose among Marx and the young Hegelians that theory cannot be detached from practice, and that it is man's action upon the world which gives rise to his representations. In the twentieth century, the philosophy of Bergson and the phenomenology of Husserl appeared less as systems than as methods for transforming our perception of the world. Finally, the movement of thought inaugurated by Heidegger and carried on by existentialism seeks – in theory and in principle – to engage man's freedom and action in the philosophical process, although, in the last analysis, it too is primarily a philosophical discourse.

One could say that what differentiates ancient from modern philosophy is the fact that, in ancient philosophy, it was not only Chrysippus or Epicurus who, just because they had developed a philosophical discourse, were considered philosophers. Rather, every person who lived according to the precepts of Chrysippus or Epicurus was every bit as much of a philosopher as they. A politician like Cato of Utica was considered a philosopher and even a sage, even though he wrote and taught nothing, because his life was perfectly Stoic. The same was true of Roman statesmen like Rutilius Rufus and Quintus Mucius Scaevola Pontifex, who practiced Stoicism by showing an exemplary disinterestedness and humanity in the administration of the provinces entrusted to them. These men were not merely examples of morality, but men who lived the totality of Stoicism, speaking like Stoics (Cicero tells us explicitly[29] that they refused to use a certain type of rhetoric in the trials in which they testified), and looking at the world like Stoics; in other words, trying to live in accord with cosmic reason. They sought to realize the ideal of Stoic wisdom: a certain way of being human, of living according to reason, within the cosmos and along with other human beings. What constituted the object of their efforts was not merely ethics, but the human being as a whole.

Ancient philosophy proposed to mankind an art of living. By contrast, modern philosophy appears above all as the construction of a technical jargon reserved for specialists.

Everyone is free to define philosophy as he likes, to choose whatever philosophy he wishes, or to invent – if he can – whatever philosophy he may think valid. Descartes and Spinoza still remained faithful to the ancient definition: for them, philosophy was "the practice of wisdom." [30] If, following their example, we believe that it is essential for mankind to try to accede to the state of wisdom, we shall find in the ancient traditions of the various philosophical schools – Socratism, Platonism, Aristotelianism, Epicureanism, Stoicism, Cynicism, Skepticism – models of life, fundamental forms in accordance with which reason may be applied to human existence, and archetypes of the quest for wisdom. It is precisely this plurality of ancient schools that is precious. It allows us to compare the consequences of all the various possible fundamental attitudes of reason, and offers a privileged field for experimentation. This, of course, presupposes that we reduce these philosophies to their spirit and essence, detaching them from their outmoded cosmological or mythical elements, and disengaging from them the fundamental propositions that they themselves considered essential. This is not, by the way, a matter of choosing one or the other of these traditions to the exclusion of the others. Epicureanism and Stoicism, for example, correspond to two opposite but inseparable poles of our inner life: the demands of our moral conscience, and the flourishing of our joy in existing.[31]

Philosophy in antiquity was an exercise practiced at each instant. It invites us to concentrate on each instant of life, to become aware of the infinite value of each present moment, once we have replaced it within the perspective of the cosmos. The exercise of wisdom entails a cosmic dimension. Whereas the average person has lost touch with the world, and does not see the world qua world, but rather treats the world as a means of satisfying his desires, the sage never ceases to have the whole constantly present to mind. He thinks and acts within a cosmic perspective. He has the feeling of belonging to a whole which goes beyond the limits of his individuality. In antiquity, this cosmic consciousness was situated in a different perspective from that of the scientific knowledge of the universe that could be provided by, for instance, the science of astronomical phenomena. Scientific knowledge was objective and mathematical, whereas cosmic consciousness was the result of a spiritual exercise, which consisted in becoming aware of the place of one's individual existence within the great current of the cosmos and the perspective of the whole, *toti se inserens mundo*, in the words of Seneca.[32] This exercise was situated not in the absolute space of exact science, but in the lived experience of the concrete, living, and perceiving subject.

We have here to do with two radically different kinds of relationship to the world. We can understand the distinction between these two kinds by recalling the opposition pointed out by Husserl[33] between the rotation of the earth, affirmed and proved scientifically, and the earth's immobility, postulated both by our day-to-day experience and by transcendental/constitutive consciousness. For the latter, the earth is the immobile ground of our life, the reference point of our thought, or, as Merleau-Ponty put it, "the womb of our time and of our space."[34] In the same way, nature and the cosmos are, for our living perception, the infinite horizon of our lives, the enigma of our existence which, as Lucretius said, inspires us with *horror et divina voluptas*, a shudder and a divine pleasure. As Goethe put it in admirable verses:

> The best part of man is the shudder.
> However dearly the world makes him pay for this emotion,
> He is seized by amazement when he feels the Prodigious.[35]

Ancient philosophical traditions can provide guidance in our relationship to ourselves, to the cosmos, and to other human beings. In the mentality of modern historians, there is no cliché more firmly anchored, and more difficult to uproot, than the idea according to which ancient philosophy was an escape mechanism, an act of falling back upon oneself. In the case of the Platonists, it was an escape into the heaven of ideas, into the refusal of politics in the case of the Epicureans, into the submission to fate in the case of the Stoics. This way of looking at things is, in fact, doubly false. In the first place, ancient philosophy was always a philosophy practiced in a group, whether in the case of the Pythagorean communities, Platonic love, Epicurean friendship, or Stoic spiritual direction. Ancient philosophy required a common effort, community of research, mutual assistance, and spiritual support. Above all, philosophers – even, in the last analysis, the Epicureans – never gave up having an effect on their cities, transforming society, and serving their citizens, who frequently accorded them praise, the vestiges of which are preserved for us by inscriptions. Political ideas may have differed from school to school, but the concern for having an effect on city or state, king or emperor, always remained constant. This is particularly true of Stoicism, and can easily be seen in many of the texts of Marcus Aurelius. Of the three tasks which must be kept in mind at each instant, alongside vigilance over one's thoughts and consent to the events imposed by destiny, an essential place is accorded to the duty always to act in the service of the human community; that is, to act in accordance with justice. This last requirement is, moreover, intimately linked to the two others. It is one and the same wisdom which conforms itself to cosmic wisdom and to the reason in which human beings participate. This concern for living in the service of the human community, and for acting in accordance with justice, is an essential element of every philosophical life. In other words, the philosophical life normally entails a communitary engagement. This last is probably the hardest part to carry out. The trick is to maintain oneself on the level of reason, and not allow oneself to be blinded by political passions, anger, resentments, or prejudices. To be sure, there is an equilibrium – almost impossible to achieve – between the inner peace brought about by wisdom, and the passions to which the sight of the injustices, sufferings, and misery of mankind cannot help but give rise. Wisdom, however, consists in precisely such an equilibrium, and inner peace is indispensable for efficacious action.

Such is the lesson of ancient philosophy: an invitation to each human being to transform himself. Philosophy is a conversion, a transformation of one's way of being and living, and a quest for wisdom. This is not an easy matter. As Spinoza wrote at the end of the *Ethics*:

> If the way which I have pointed out as leading to this result seems exceedingly hard, it may nevertheless be discovered. It must indeed be hard, since it is so seldom found. How would it be possible, if salvation were easy to find, and could without great labour be found, that it should be neglected by almost everybody? But all excellent things are as difficult as they are rare.[36]

NOTES

1 Philo Judaeus, *On the Special Laws*, 2, 44–8.
2 Cf. above.
3 Quintillian, *Oratorical Institutions*, bk I, Preface, 19–20.
4 Xenocrates, fr. 4 Heinze.
5 Epicurus, *Letter to Pythocles*, §85.
6 Marcus Aurelius, *Meditations*, 9, 31.
7 Sextus Empiricus, *Outlines of Pyrrhonism*, I, 28.
8 Xenophon, *Memorabilia*, I, 2, 14.
9 Aristotle, *Nicomachean Ethics*, 10, 7, 1178b3.
10 Epicurus, *Gnomologicum Vaticanum*, §77.
11 Epictetus, *Discourses*, 3, 13, 7.
12 Cf. above.
13 Marcus Aurelius, *Meditations*, 11, 1.
14 E.g. Diogenes Laertius, *Lives of the Philosophers*, 7, 39.
15 Ibid, 4, 18.
16 Epictetus, *Discourses*, 3, 21, 4–6.
17 Cf. below.
18 On the concept of *procheiron*, see above.
19 Seneca, *Letters to Lucilius*, I, 1.
20 Plato, *Apology*, 29e1ff.
21 Plato, *Republic*, 486a.
22 Aristotle, *Nicomachean Ethics*, 10, 7, 1178aff.
23 Cf. below.
24 Justin, *Apology*, I, 46, 1–4.
25 J. Leclerq, "Pour l'histoire de l'expression 'philosophie chrétienne'," *Mélanges de Science Religieuse* 9 (1952), p. 221.
26 Cf. below.
27 A. Schopenhauer, *The World as Will and Representation*, trans. E.F.J. Payne, 2 vols, Indian Hills CO 1958, London/Toronto 1909, ch. 17, vol. 2, pp. 163–4.
28 Spinoza, *Ethics*, Part 5, Prop. 42, p. 270 Elwes.

29 Cicero, *On Oratory*, I, 229ff.
30 René Descartes, *Principii philosophiae*, Foreword to Picot.
31 See the references from Kant, Goethe, and Jaspers cited above.
32 "Plunging oneself into the totality of the world." Seneca, *Letters to Lucilius*, 66, 6.
33 E. Husserl, "Grundlegende Untersuchungen zum phänomenologiscen Urspung der Räumlichkeit der Natur" (= Umsturz der Kopernikanischen Lehre), in Marvin Faber, ed., *Philosophical Essays in Memory of E. Husserl*, Cambridge MA 1940, p. 132.
34 M. Merleau-Ponty, *Éloge de la philosophie et autres essais*, Paris 1953, p. 285.
35 Johann Wolfgang von Goethe, *Faust*, 6272ff.
36 Spinoza, *Ethics*, pp. 270–1.

Postscript: An Interview with Pierre Hadot

M.C. Pierre Hadot, you were born in Reims, France, in 1922. What were the earliest and strongest influences on your spiritual and intellectual development?

P.H. I received a very intense Catholic religious education. I gradually became detached from it, but it played a considerable role in my formation, both because of the first impressions it made upon me, and because of the problems it raised for me.

The first philosophy I came across was Thomism, which I encountered especially in the books of Jacques Maritain; thus it was a kind of Aristotelianism tinged with Neoplatonism. I think it was a good thing for me to have begun my philosophical studies with a highly systematic, structured philosophy, which was based on a long ancient and medieval tradition. It gave me a lasting distaste for philosophies which don't clearly define the vocabulary they use. Besides, it was thanks to Thomism, and especially to Étienne Gilson,[1] that I discovered very early on the fundamental distinction between essence and existence, which is dear to existentialism.

At the time, I was very much influenced by Newman's *Grammar of Assent*. Newman shows in this work that it's not the same thing to give one's assent to an affirmation which one understands in a purely abstract way, and to give one's assent while engaging one's entire being, and "realizing" – in the English sense of the word – with one's heart and one's imagination, just what this affirmation means for us. This distinction between real and notional assent underlies my research on spiritual exercises.

My religious education also made me come face to face with the phenomenon of mysticism, which I probably didn't understand at the time, but which has continued to fascinate me all my life.

We would need a very long discussion if we were seriously to approach the problem posed by the survival of Christianity in the modern world. From the point of view of my own personal experience, I can say that one of the great difficulties of Christianity – I'm thinking here of the textual criticism of the Bible – was what revealed to me a more general problem, which could be formulated in the following terms: is modern man still able to understand the texts of antiquity, and live according to them? Has there been a definitive break between the contemporary world and ancient tradition?

While studying at the Sorbonne in 1946 and 1947, I discovered Bergson, Marxism, and existentialism, three models which have had a strong influence on my conception of philosophy. Bergsonism was not an abstract, conceptual philosophy, but rather took the form of a new way of seeing the world, and of transforming one's perception. Existentialism – Heidegger, Sartre, Merleau-Ponty, Albert Camus; but also Gabriel Marcel – made me become aware of my simultaneous engagement in the world of experience, in perception, in the experience of my body, and in social and political life. Marxism, finally, proposed a theory of philosophy in which theory and praxis were intimately linked, and where daily life was never separated from theoretical reflection. I found this aspect of Marxism very seductive, but economic materialism was profoundly alien to me. I also had other influences: Montaigne, whom I have been reading since my adolescence, and the poet Rilke; for a while, I thought about writing my thesis on "The Relationship between Rilke and Heidegger."

M.C. Your career has always taken place more or less on the outskirts of the French intellectual "establishment." You took your diploma from the École Pratique des Hautes Études in 1961, and you then became director of studies at the same institution, where you remained from 1964 on. In 1982, you were elected to the chair of the History of Hellenistic and Roman Thought at the Collège de France. Now, in France, this is the most prestigious position which a historian of philosophy can obtain, and you arrived there without passing through the almost obligatory stage of the École Normale Supérieure, or any other of the so-called "great schools."

Did these somewhat unusual circumstances contribute anything to your conception of philosophy? I'm thinking in particular of your remarks on the negative influence which the university has exerted on philosophy.

P.H. My remarks on the negative influence which the university has exerted on philosophy have nothing to do with the fact that my career has taken place outside the university. Generally speaking, I admired the professors who taught me philosophy at the Sorbonne, from either an intellectual or a human point of view – or both. They devoted themselves to the task of teaching with exemplary dedication, and they had a highly-developed moral conscience. I'm thinking here of men like Émile Bréhier,[2] R. Bayer, Jean Wahl,[3] Paul Ricoeur, Maurice de Gandillac,[4] Jean Hyppolite,[5] R. Le Senne, Louis Lavelle, Maurice Merleau-Ponty, and J. Vuillemin.

The idea of a conflict between philosophy and the teaching of philosophy goes back to my youth. I think I came across it in Charles Péguy, who said: "Philosophy doesn't go to philosophy classes," and certainly in Jacques

Maritain, who wrote: "Thomist metaphysics is called 'Scholastic' after its most severe trial. Scholastic pedagogy is its own worst enemy: it always has to triumph over its intimate adversary, the professor." Ever since I started doing philosophy, I've always believed that philosophy was a concrete act, which changed our perception of the world, and our life: not the construction of a system. It is a life, not a discourse.

M.C. Your own philosophical trajectory is rather remarkable. To begin with, in the 1950s, you wrote reviews of Wittgenstein, Heidegger, and Berdiaev. At the same time, you were making a name for yourself on the one hand in Latin Patristics and textual criticism, and on the other as a specialist on Plotinus. In 1957, you presented a remarkable paper at the meeting of the Fondation Hardt devoted to Plotinus; this was followed, in 1963 by your first book, *Plotinus or the Simplicity of Vision*.[6] In 1961, in collaboration with Paul Henry, you had translated and given a copious commentary on the theological treatises of the Latin church Father Marius Victorinus. The year 1968 saw the publication of your monumental work *Porphyre et Victorinus*,[7] in which you gave a critical edition, with translation and commentary, of a commentary on Plato's *Parmenides*, which you attributed for the first time to Porphyry of Tyre. But this wasn't all; the work contained a summa of Neoplatonic metaphysics, in which you covered the immensely complex, hierarchic conceptual constructions of post-Plotinian metaphysics. After you were named to the Collège de France, you devoted your attention mainly to the seemingly more simple philosophies of Stoicism and Epicureanism, as well as continuing your study of Plotinus.

Perhaps your career could be summed up as follows: beginning with the bone-dry discipline of textual criticism, you then moved on to master the ontological complexities of Neoplatonism; surely among the most complicated creations of the human spirit. Then, however, it's as if you had turned back, in a way, to your point of departure: from this point on, it's no longer the great speculative edifices which occupy your attention, but those philosophers who teach us how to live: Marcus Aurelius, Epictetus, Lucretius, and, of course, your beloved Plotinus. Wouldn't you say that your own philosophical trajectory can serve as a paradigm for the "return to simplicity," the importance of which you have stressed in your teaching?

P.H. I'd be inclined to look at my intellectual and spiritual itinerary somewhat differently. From 1942 to 1946, I was only interested in metaphysics and in mysticism, in all their forms: Christian first and foremost, but also Arabic, Hindu, and Neoplatonist. It was my interest in mysticism that led me to Plotinus, and to the great Plotinian specialist Paul Henry. I went to see him in 1946, so that he could guide me in my Plotinian studies. He was interested, above all, in the influence of Plotinus on St Augustine, and on Christianity in general; he had written a book on the subject entitled *Plotin et l'Occident*.[8] He advised me to study Marius Victorinus, in the belief that I would find, in the almost incomprehensible Latin of this ecclesiastical author, some translated fragments of Plotinus. He suggested that we edit the theological works of Victorinus together, leaving the translation and the commentary up to me. Thus, he was the one who initiated me to textual criticism and philological studies; being a pure philosopher, I had had no preparation in either of these fields, and the only knowledge I had of Greek and Latin was what I had been taught by my secondary-school teachers.

All this was a long way from mysticism. I can say that I worked for twenty years on a subject that I had not chosen; I was interested in it, of course, but not fascinated by it. It was then that I learned how to read Latin manuscripts and, thanks to Paul Henry, how to prepare a critical edition. I also tried to understand, and explain as well as I could, the text of Victorinus. My book *Porphyre et Victorinus* was the result of this exegetical work, and in it I showed that Victorinus was the disciple of Porphyry rather than of Plotinus.

What attracted me in Wittgenstein – whom I first read around 1960 – was the problem of mysticism, which he mentions in the last pages of the *Tractatus*. My reading of Wittgenstein was very stimulating for me, and it brought about my lasting interest in the question of "language games," which are, he tells us, "forms of life." These ideas had a great deal of influence on my subsequent studies of ancient philosophy.

I returned to the mysticism of Plotinus in 1963, when Georges and Angèle de Radkowski asked me to write the little book entitled *Plotin ou la simplicité du regard*.

When, in 1964, I was elected to the Fifth Section of the École Pratique des Hautes Études,[9] my colleagues viewed me above all as the translator of Victorinus, and it was natural for me to have been elected to the chair of Latin Patristics. Among other factors, this explains how I came to publish an edition and translation of the *Apologia David* of Bishop Ambrose of Milan.[10] I must confess, however, that Latin Patristics didn't really interest me. Fortunately, my colleagues agreed to change the title of my chair, which became "Theologies and Mysticisms of Hellenistic Greece and of the End of Antiquity." Thus I was able to return to the mystical passages of Plotinus, on which I commented before my auditors for many years.

However, it was also at this time that my relationship with Plotinus began to become more complex, and that I arrived at my present position. On the one hand, I believe that this great author has yet to be explained in the detailed way he deserves, and that's why I have undertaken the translation with commentary of the totality of his works. Moreover, the phenomenon of mysticism, which is so striking in Plotinus, continues to intrigue me. Yet, as I grow older, Plotinus speaks to me less and less, if I may say so. I have become considerably detached from him. From 1970 on, I have felt very strongly that it was Epicureanism and Stoicism which could nourish the spiritual life of men and women of our times, as well as my own. That was how I came to write my book on spiritual exercises. Indeed, here at the end of the century – and no one is more surprised at this than myself – we are witnessing an increasing interest in these two philosophies on the part of the reading public. This is a remarkable phenomenon, hard to explain.

To sum up my inner evolution, I would say the following: in 1946, I naively believed that I, too, could relive the Plotinian mystical experience. But I later realized that this was an illusion. The conclusion of my book *Plotinus* already hinted that the idea of the "purely spiritual" is untenable. It is true that there is something ineffable in human existence, but this ineffable is *within* our very perception of the world, in the mystery of our existence and that of the cosmos. Still, it can lead to an experience which could be qualified as mystical.

M.C. What do the expressions "philosophy" and "living a philosophical life" signify for you?

P.H. For me, the word "philosophy" corresponds first of all to an historical phenomenon. In was the Greeks who created the word, probably in the sixth or fifth century BC, and it was Plato who gave it its strongest meaning: *philo-sophia*, "love of wisdom," the wisdom which one lacks. Since that time there has been an intellectual, spiritual, and social phenomenon, which has taken on a variety of forms, and which has been called philosophy. From this point of view, it is legitimate to ask whether there exists a "philosophy" outside of the Western tradition, or of the Arabic tradition, insofar as the latter is the inheritor of Greek philosophy.

Now, an historical phenomenon is in constant evolution. Contemporary "philosophy" is obviously very different from the "philosophy" of Socrates and Plato, just as contemporary Christianity is very different from the Evangelistic message. Is this evolution a good thing? Is it an evil? I won't go into that. I do think, however, that it is always legitimate to go back to the origins, in order better to understand the meaning of a phenomenon, and that is what I try to do.

I have tried to define what philosophy was for a person in antiquity. In my view, the essential characteristic of the phenomenon "philosophy" in antiquity was that at that time a philosopher was, above all, someone who lived in a philosophical way. In other words, the philosopher was someone whose life was guided by his or her reason, and who was a practitioner of the moral virtues. This is obvious, for example, from the portrait Alcibiades gives of Socrates at the end of Plato's *Symposium*. We can also observe it in Xenophon, where Hippias asks Socrates for a definition of justice. Socrates replies: "Instead of talking about it, I make it appear through my actions." Originally, then, philosophy is above all the choice of a form of life, to which philosophical discourse then gives justifications and theoretical foundations. Philosophical discourse is not the same thing as philosophy: the Stoics said so explicitly, and the other schools admitted it implicitly. True, there can be no philosophy without some discourse – either inner or outward – on the part of the philosopher. This can take the form of pedagogical activity carried out on others, of inner meditation, or of the discursive explanation of intuitive contemplation. But this discourse is not the essential part of philosophy, and it will have value only if it has a relationship with philosophical life. As an Epicurean sentence puts it: "The discourse of philosophers is in vain, unless it heals some passion of the soul."

M.C. Are spiritual exercises still possible today? They were thought up in the very distant past, as responses to specific social structures and material conditions, but our current living conditions bear very little resemblance to those of antiquity. The spiritual exercises of the Stoics and the Epicureans, for example, are the consequences of the basic hypotheses of each school: on the one hand, faith in the providential Logos; on the other, atomism, belief in chance, and denial of post-mortem existence. Nowadays, however, we may no longer believe in these hypotheses. Is it still possible to practice the spiritual exercises of antiquity, separating them from the systems of which they were a part, and substituting our own basic hypotheses for the outmoded ones of antiquity?

Let's take the example of injustice. One of the greatest sources of pain for modern man is, I would think, the suffering of innocent people. Every day, the media overwhelm us with images of this suffering, and we witness it every day in the streets of our cities. How can we avoid giving in to despair if we no longer believe, like Marcus Aurelius, in a divine providence, consubstantial with ourselves, which arranges everything for the best, and er.sures that injustices are only apparent?

P.H. To reply to your question, I refer you to the beginning of the chapter entitled "Spiritual exercises," where I quote the passage from the diary of Georges Friedmann which he quotes in his book *La Puissance et la Sagesse*:[11] "A 'spiritual exercise' every day – either alone or else in the company of someone who also wants to improve himself. . . . Step out of duration . . . try to get rid of your own passions." I think this testimony suffices to prove that spiritual exercises are still being practiced in our day and age.

Spiritual exercises do not correspond to specific social structures or material conditions. They have been, and continue to be, practiced in every age, in the most widely diverse milieus, and in widely different latitudes: China, Japan, India; among the Christians, Muslims, and Jews.

If one admits, as I do, that the various philosophical schools of antiquity were characterized above all by their choice of a form of life, which is then justified *after the fact* by a given systematic construction (for instance, Stoicism is the choice of an attitude of coherence with oneself, which is later justified by a general theory of the coherence of the universe with itself) – then it is easy to understand how one can can remain faithful to one's choice of a form of life without being obliged to adhere to the systematic construction which claims to found it. As Ruyer has written,[12] "Except for specialists, no one is very interested in the motives of Stoicism, taken over for the most part from Heraclitus, or in those of Epicurean ethics or Democritean atomism. Nevertheless, as attitudes, Stoicism and Epicureanism are still very much alive." As a matter of fact, ethics – that is to say, choosing the good – is not the consequence of metaphysics, but metaphysics is the consequence of ethics.

You give the example of injustice and the suffering of innocent people. For Marcus Aurelius, the fact that there is a providence (that is, simply, that there is coherence in the world), does not mean that injustice is only an appearance. It is quite real, and in his *Meditations* Marcus often expresses his anger against liars and the unjust. For him, the discipline of action consists precisely in acting in the service of the human community; in other words, in practicing justice oneself and in correcting injustices. Such an attitude is independent of any theory of providence. Besides, Marcus himself says: "Whether or not the world is ruled by reason (and thus by providence), don't *you* act unreasonably." He then goes on to add that if we *do* act according to reason, that proves that there is also reason in the world. This is proof that it is one's choice of life which precedes metaphysical theories, and that we can make our choice of life, whether or not we justify it by improved or entirely new arguments.

M.C. You often speak of "nature" or "universal nature" in the context of the triple discipline of the Stoics. For example, according to Marcus Aurelius we must learn "the ways and laws of nature." What is meant here by "nature"? Is it the "nature" in which we stroll and have picnics? The "nature" which "makes no leaps"?

P.H. For the Stoics, nature is at the same time the program in conformity with which the events which constitute the universe are necessarily linked to one another, and the programmed sequence which results from them. Thus, it is the rational order which presides over the evolution of the visible world. It is this programming and this rationality which give the world its coherence. To act according to nature is therefore to act in a programmed, rational manner, in full awareness of the fact that one is a part of the cosmic whole, as well as a part of the whole formed by the city of those beings which share in reason. On the one hand, then, it is to act in the service of the human community, and, on the other, to consent to the general movement of the universe. The Stoics were saying exactly the same thing as Einstein, when he denounced the optical illusion of a person who imagines himself to be a separate entity, while he is really a part of that whole which we call the universe. Einstein also declared that it is our duty to open our hearts to all living beings, and to all of nature in her magnificence.

M.C. The triple discipline of spiritual exercises is intended to lead me towards the inner transformation of my way of seeing, and eventually, to restore me as an integral and integrated part of the cosmos. According to this theory, my task is to discipline my desires, my inclinations, and my assent. The last two domains correspond respectively to ethics – I must observe my duties toward my fellow citizens – and to logic or epistemology: I must accept as true only that which is freed from my subjective prejudices.

All this seems feasible enough. But as far as the discipline of desire is concerned: it is surely true that the majority of our unhappiness comes from our unsatisfied desires; this was taught by the Buddha, among others. But is it really possible for me to discipline my desires; that is, to persuade myself by means of rational considerations no longer to desire a particular object? Let's take sexual desire as an example. If I feel desire for a woman, it is perfectly possible for me to tell myself that *I will not act according to my desire*; in other words, that I will not attempt to satisfy my desire. But can I really go further than that, and, in the presence of the desired object, *command myself not to desire it any longer*? I have difficulties with this point.

P.H. Can purely rational considerations be effective against passion or sexual desire? Here we return to the very idea of spiritual exercises.

What's interesting about the idea of spiritual exercises is precisely that it is not a matter of a purely rational consideration, but the putting in action of all kinds of means, intended to act upon one's self. Imagination and affectivity play a capital role here: we must represent to ourselves in vivid colors the dangers of such-and-such a passion, and use striking formulations of ideas in order to exhort ourselves. We must also create habits, and fortify ourselves by preparing ourselves against hardships in advance. In Epicurean communities, people help one another, admit their weaknesses to each other, and warn others of such-and-such a dangerous tendency which is beginning to manifest itself in them.

All these techniques can be useful in crisis situations. Yet we must not allow them to make us forget that what is most important is the profound orientation of our lives, the fundamental choice of a life, which engages us passionately. The problem is not so much to repress such-and-such a passion, as it is to learn to see things "from above," in the grandiose perspective of universal nature and of humanity, compared to which many passions may appear ridiculously insignificant. It is then that rational knowledge may become force and will, and thereby become extremely efficacious.

M.C. On May 22, 1991, you gave your last lecture at the Collège de France. After some three decades of teaching, the last words you pronounced in public were: "In the last analysis, we can scarcely talk about what is most important."

This seems paradoxical. After a lifetime devoted to humanistic studies, have you finally come to the conclusion of the Neoplatonist philosopher Damascius,[13] who wrote "What will be the limit of our discourse, if it is not an impotent silence, and the admission of our absolute lack of knowledge concerning those things about which we may never gain knowledge, since they are inaccessible"?

P.H. You're alluding to the last words of my last class: "In the final analysis, we can scarcely talk about what is most important." I was saying that about Plotinus, for whom the most important thing was not his teaching, but the unutterable experience of union with the One. For Plotinus, abstract teaching could allude to this experience, but could not lead to it. Only asceticism and a moral life could truly prepare the soul for such a union (and here again, we find the same opposition between philosophical discourse and the philosophical life).

Obviously, however, when I used this phrase, I was hinting at my own experience as a teacher and my experience of life. I wasn't only talking about the experience of the ineffable among the Neoplatonists, but about a more general experience.

Everything which is "technical" in the broad sense of the term, whether we are talking about the exact sciences or the humanistic sciences, is perfectly able to be communicated by teaching or conversation. But everything that touches the domain of the existential – which is what is most important for human beings – for instance, our feeling of existence, our impressions when faced by death, our perception of nature, our sensations, and a fortiori the mystical experience, is not directly communicable. The phrases we use to describe them are conventional and banal; we realize this when we try to console someone over the loss of a loved one. That's why it often happens that a poem or a biography are more philosophical than a philosophical treatise, simply because they allow us to glimpse this unsayable in an indirect way. Here again, we find the kind of mysticism evoked in Wittgenstein's *Tractatus*: "There is indeed the inexpressible. This shows itself; it is the mystical."

NOTES

[In April–May 1992, M. Hadot was kind enough to respond to some questions I had asked him during the course of the preparation of this translation. What follows is a translation of our exchange. All notes are my own. – Trans.]

1 [Étienne Gilson, author of many highly influential works on Medieval thought; cf. *History of Christian Philosophy in the Middle Ages*, New York 1955.]

2 [Émile Bréhier, the first modern editor and translator of Plotinus, also wrote important works on Stoicism, and a three-volume *History of Philosophy* which was, for many decades, the standard reference work on the subject in France.]

3 [Jean Wahl, expert on Existentialism, was the author of such works as *Études kierkegaardiennes* ("Studies on Kierkegaard"), 3rd edn, Paris 1967.]

4 [Maurice de Gandillac, a specialist on Neoplatonism, was author of important works on Plotinus (*La sagesse de Plotin*, Paris 1966), and Nicolas of Cusa, among others.]

5 [Jean Hyppolite was the translator and exegete of Hegel (*Genèse et Structure de la Phénoménologie de l'esprit de Hegel*, Paris 1946), who exercised a great influence on French Marxism.]

6 [3rd edn, Paris 1989. An English translation is in preparation.]

7 [2 vols, Paris 1968.]

8 [P. Henry, *Plotin et l'Occident. Firmicus Maternus, Marius Victorinus, Saint Augustin et Macrobe* (= Spicilegium sacrum Lovaniense, Études et Documents 15), Louvain 1934.]

9 [The Practical School of Higher Studies, of which the fifth section is the Section of Religious Sciences. Hadot had as his colleagues at this institution such eminent scholars as Claude Lévi-Strauss, Georges Dumézil, Henry Corbin, Henri-Charles Puech, and the great Hellenist André-Jean Festugière, to name but a few.]

10 [*Ambroise de Milan, Apologie de David*, intro. Latin text, notes and index Pierre Hadot, trans. Marius Cordier (= Sources Chrétiennes 239), Paris 1977.]

11 ["Power and Wisdom," Paris 1970.]

12 [R. Ruyer, *The Gnosis of Princeton*, p. 220.]

13 [*On the First Principles*, I, 7, p. 15, 22–5 Ruelle.]

Select Bibliography

ANTHOLOGIES

Von Arnim, H., ed., *Stoicorum Veterum Fragmenta*, 4 vols, Leipzig 1903 (abbreviated *SVF*).

Diels, H., and W. Kranz, eds, *Die Fragmente der Vorsokatiker*, 3 vols, Dublin/Zurich 1956, 8th edn, repr. 1974.

Long, A.A. and D.N. Sedley, *The Hellenistic Philosophers*, vol. 1: *Translations of the Principal Sources, with Philosophical Commentary*, vol. 2: *Greek and Latin Texts with Notes and Bibliography*, Cambridge 1987, repr. 1988.

Nauck, A., ed., *Tragicorum Graecorum Fragmenta*, Leipzig 1889, 2nd edn, repr. Hildesheim 1964.

ANCIENT AUTHORS

Apophthegmata Patrum (*The Sayings of the Fathers*), PG 65.

—— English trans.: *The Sayings of the Desert Fathers*, trans. Benedicta Ward, Mowbray 1975.

Aristophanes, *Nubes* (*Clouds*), ed. K.J. Dover, *Aristophanes' Clouds*, Oxford 1968, repr. 1970.

—— English trans.: *Aristophanes: The Acharnians, The Clouds, Lysistrata*, trans. and intro. Alan H. Sommerstein, Harmondsworth 1973, repr. 1985.

Aristotle, *Opera*, ed. I. Bekker, *Aristotelis opera*, 5 vols, Berlin 1831, repr. 1960.

—— English trans.: *The Complete Works of Aristotle*, Revised Oxford Translation, ed. Jonathan Barnes (= Bollingen Series 71.2), Princeton NJ 1984.

Aristotle, *Sophistici Elenchi* (*On Sophistical Refutations*), trans. W.A. Pickard-Cambridge.

Aristotle, *De partibus animalium* (*Parts of Animals*), trans. W. Ogle.

Aristotle, *Protrepticus*, ed. W.D. Ross, *Aristotelis Fragmenta Selecta*, Oxford 1955.
—— English trans.: J. Barnes and G. Lawrence in J. Barnes, ed., 1984, vol. 2.
—— German trans.: *Der Protreptikos des Aristoteles*, trans., intro. and commentary Ingemar Düring, Frankfurt 1969.
Athanasius, *Vita Antonii* (*Life of Antony*), PG 26, 835–976B.
—— English trans.: *Athanasius. The Life of Antony and the Letter to Marcellinus*, trans. and intro. Robert C. Gregg, preface William A. Clebsch (Classics of Western Spirituality), New York/Ramsey NY/Toronto 1980.
Augustine, *De Trinitate* (*On the Trinity*), PL 42, 819–1098.
Basil of Caesarea, *In Illud Attende tibi ipsi* (*Homily on the Words, "Give Heed to Thyself"*)
—— *L'homélie de Basile de Césarée sur le mot "observe-toi toi-même"*, ed. S.Y. Rudberg (= *Acta Universitatis Stockholmensis, Studia Graeca Stockholmensia* 2), Stockholm 1962.
—— English trans.: *Saint Basil: Ascetical Works*, trans. Sister M. Monica Wagner, CSC (= *FC* 9), Washington DC 1950, repr. 1970.
Basil of Caesarea, *Regulae fusius tractatae* (*The Long Rules*; otherwise known as *Asceticon magnum* or *Quaestiones*), PG 31, 901–1052.
—— English trans.: *Saint Basil: Ascetical Works*, trans. Sister M. Monica Wagner, CSC (= *FC* 9), Washington DC 1950, repr. 1970.
Clement of Alexandria, *Stromata*, eds O. Stählin, L. Früchtel and U. Treu, in *Clemens Alexandrinus* [= *GCS* 52 (15), 17], vol. 2, 3rd edn, Berlin 1960; vol. 3, 2nd edn, 1970.
—— English trans.: in *ANF* 2, trans. W.A. Wilson, Buffalo 1885, repr. Grand Rapids 1977.
Damascius, *Vita Isidori*, ed. C. Zinzten, *Life of Isidorus: Damascii vitae Isidori reliquiae* (= *Bibliotheca graeca et Latina suppletoria* I), Hildesheim 1967.
Diadochus of Photice, *Kephalaia Gnostica* (*Gnostic chapters*); *Capita centum de perfectione spirituali* (*One Hundred Chapters on Spiritual Perfection*), ed. Édouard des Places, SJ, in *Diadoque de Photicé, Oeuvres spirituelles* (= *SC* 5bis), Paris 1955, repr. with suppl. 1966.
Diogenes Laertius, *Vitae philosophorum* (*Lives of the Philosophers*), ed. R.D. Hicks, *Diogenes Laertius, Lives of Eminent Philosophers*, with English trans. R.D.H. (LCL), 2 vols, London/Cambridge MA 1925, repr. 1950.
Dorotheus of Gaza, *Didaskaliai* (*Instructions*), ed. with French trans., in *Oeuvres spirituelles*, eds L. Regnault and J. de Préville (= *SC* 92), Paris 1963.
—— English trans.: *Dorotheus of Gaza: Discourses and Sayings*, trans. E.P. Wheeler (= *Cistercian Studies* 33), Kalamazoo 1977.
Epictetus, *Opera*, ed. W.A. Oldfather, *Epictetus, The Discourses as reported by Arrian, the Manual, and the Fragments*, with English trans. W.A.O. (LCL), 2 vols, London/Cambridge MA 1928, repr. 1959.
Epicurus, *Opera*, ed. H. Usener, *Epicurea* (Sammlung Wissenschaftlicher Commentaren), Stuttgart 1887, repr. 1966.
—— ed. with English trans.: *Epicurus, The Extant Remains*, short critical apparatus, trans. and notes Cyril Bailey, Oxford 1926, repr. Hildesheim/New York, 1970.
—— ed. with Italian trans.: *Epicuro, Opere*, trans. Graziano Arrighetti (= *Bibliotheca di cultura filosofica* 41), Turin 1960; 2nd edn, 1973.

Eusebius, *Historia ecclesiastica* (*Ecclesiastical History*), ed. with French trans. G. Bardy, *Eusèbe de Césarée. Histoire ecclésiastique*, 3 vols (= *SC* 31, 45, 55), Paris 1952–8.

Evagrius of Pontus, *Praktikos*, ed. with French trans. A. and C. Guillaumont, *Évagre le Pontique: Traité pratique ou le moine*, vol. 2 (= *SC* 171), Paris 1971.

——English trans.: *Evagrius Ponticus. The Praktikos. Chapters on Prayer*, trans., intro. and notes John Eudes Bamberger (= *Cistercian Studies* 4), Kalamazoo 1978.

Galen, *De cognoscendis curandisque animi morbis* (*On Diagnosing and Curing the Illnesses of the Soul*), ed. Ioann. Marquardt (= *Claudii Galeni Pergameni scripta minora*, vol. I), Leipzig 1884.

——English trans: *Galen On the Passions and Errors of the Soul*, trans. P.W. Harkins, Columbus OH 1963.

Gregory Nazianzen, *Apologeticus de fuga* (*In Defense for his Flight to Pontus*), *PG* 35, 408–513.

Gregory Nazianzen, *Epistula 31*, trans. P. Gallay, in *Grégoire de Nazianze, Lettres théologiques* (= *SC* 208), Paris 1974. @BIB PLUS = Gregory Thaumaturgus, *In Origenem oratio panegyrica* (*Speech in Praise of Origen*), ed. H. Crouzel, *Grégoire le Thaumaturge. Remerciement à Origène suivi de la lettre d'Origène à Grégoire* (= *SC* 148), Paris 1969.

——English trans.: in *ANF* 6, trans. S.D.F. Salmond.

Homer, *Iliad*, English trans.: *The Iliad of Homer*, trans. and intro. Richmond Lattimore, London 1951, repr. 1961.

Homer, *Odyssey*, English trans.: *The Odyssey of Homer*, trans. Richmond Lattimore, New York 1965, repr. 1975.

Horace, *Horace, Satires, Epistles and Ars Poetica*, with English trans. H. Rushton Fairclough (LCL), London/Cambridge MA 1926, repr. 1947.

Horace, *Horace, the Odes and Epodes*, with English trans. C.E. Bennett (LCL), London/Cambridge MA 1914; 2nd edn, 1947.

Horace, *Odes*, English trans.: *Horace: The Complete Odes and Epodes with the Centennial Hymn*, trans. with notes W.G. Shepherd, Harmondsworth 1983.

John Cassian, *Collationes Sanctorum Patrum* (*Conferences of the Holy Fathers*).

——*Jean Cassien, Conférences*, ed. and French trans. E. Pichery, Paris, vol. 1 (= *SC* 42) 1966, vol. 2 (= *SC* 54) 1958, vol. 3 (= *SC* 64) 1959.

——English trans.: *John Cassian, Conferences*, trans. and preface Colin Luibheid, intro. Owen Chadwick (CWS), New York/Mahwah NJ/Toronto 1985.

John Chrysostom, *Adversus oppugnatores vitae monasticae* (*Against the Opponents of the Monastic Life*), *PG* 47, 319–86.

John Chrysostom, *Non esse ad gratiam concionandum* (*That One should not make Speeches intended to Please the Public*), *PG* 50, 653–62.

John of Salisbury, *Polycraticus*, ed. C.C.J. Webb, Oxford 1909, repr. 1965.

——partial English trans.: John Dickinson, *The Statesman's Book of John of Salisbury*, New York 1927.

——Joseph B. Pike, *Frivolities of Courtiers and Footsteps of Philosophers*, Oxford, 1938.

Flavius Josephus, *Antiquitates Iudaeorum* (*Antiquities of the Jews*), ed. B. Niese, *Flavii Iosephi opera*, 4 vols, Berlin 1887–90.

Justin, *Dialogus cum Tryphone* (*Dialogue with Trypho*), ed. E.J. Goodspeed, *Die ältesten Apologeten*, Göttingen 1915.

Justin, *Apologia* (*Apology*), ed. E.J. Goodspeed, *Die ältesten Apologeten*, Göttingen 1915.

Justin, *Apologia secunda* (*Second Apology*), ed. E.J. Goodspeed, *Die ältesten Apologeten*, Göttingen 1915.

Lactantius, *Divinae institutiones* (*Divine Institutes*), ed. and French trans. Pierre Monat [= *SC* 204 (1973); 205 (1973); 326 (1986); 337 (1987), etc.].

——English trans.: in *Lactantius, The Divine Institutes, Books I–VII*, trans. Sister Mary Francis McDonald (= *FC* 49), Washington DC 1964.

Leonidas of Tarentum, *Opera*, ed. W.R. Paton, in *The Greek Anthology*, with English trans. W.R.P. (LCL), 5 vols, London/Cambridge MA 1953.

Lucian, *Opera*, eds A.M. Harmon, K. Kilburn, et al., *Lucian with an English Translation* (LCL), 8 vols, London/Cambridge MA 1913ff.

Lucian, *Icaromennipus*, in *Opera*, eds Hamon et al., vol. 2, ed. Harmon, 1915, repr. 1960.

Lucian, *Charon sive contemplantes* (*Charon or the Overseers*), in *Opera*, eds Harmon et al., vol. 2, ed. Harmon, 1915, repr. 1960.

Lucian, *Dialogi mortuorum* (*Dialogues of the Dead*), in *Opera*, eds Harmon et al., vol. 7, ed. MacLeod, 1961.

Lucian, *Quomodo historia conscribenda sit* (*How One Should Write History*), in *Opera*, eds Harmon et al., vol. 6, ed. K. Kilburn, 1959, repr. 1968.

Lucretius, *De rerum natura* (*On the Nature of Things*), ed. W.H.D. Rouse, *Lucretius, De rerum natura*, revised with new text, introduction, notes, and index M.F. Smith (LCL), 2nd edn, London/Cambridge MA 1982.

Marcus Aurelius, *Opera*, ed. A.S.L. Farquharson, *The Meditations of the Emperor Marcus Aurelius*, ed., trans. and commentary A.S.L.F., vol. 1: Text and Translation; vol. 2: Greek Commentary, Oxford, 1944, repr. 1968.

Marcus Aurelius, *Marci Aurelii Antonini ad se ipsum libri XII*, ed. Joachim Dalfen, Leipzig 1979.

Maximus Confessor, Various writings, in *PG* 4; 19; 90–1.

Maximus Confessor, *Maximus Confessor: Selected Writings*, trans. and notes George C. Berthold, intro. Jaroslav Pelikan, preface Irénée-Henri Dalmais, O.P. (CWS), New York/Mahwah NJ/Toronto 1985.

Metrodorus, ed. A. Körte, "Metrodori epicurei fragmenta," *Jahrbücher für Classische Philologie*, Suppl. XVII (1890), pp. 529ff.

Olympiodorus, *In Alcibiadem*, ed. L.G. Westerink, *Commentary on the First Alcibiades of Plato*, critical text and indices L.G.W., Amsterdam 1956.

Origen, *Contra Celsum* (*Against Celsus*), ed. M. Borret, *Origène, Contre Celse*, 4 vols (= *SC* 132; 136; 147; 150), Paris 1967–9.

——English trans.: H.E. Chadwick, Cambridge 1965.

Origen, *In Canticum Canticorum* (*Commentary on the Song of Songs*), ed. W.A. Baehrens, *GCS* 33, Berlin 1925.

——English trans.: *Origen, The Song of Songs, Commentary and Homilies*, trans. and annotated R.P. Lawson (= *ACW* 26), London/Westminster MD 1957.

Ovid, *Metamorphoses*, with English trans. Frank Justus Miller (LCL), 2 vols, London 1916.

Philo Judaeus, *Opera*, eds L. Cohn and P. Wendland, 6 vols, Berlin 1896–1915.

Philo Judaeus, *De Specialibus legibus* (*On the Special Laws*), in *Opera*, eds Cohn and Wendland, vol. 5, ed. Cohn, 1906, repr. 1962.

—— Text and English trans.: F.H. Colson (LCL), vol. 7, London/Cambridge MA 1937, repr. 1958.

Philo Judaeus, *Vita Mosis* (*Life of Moses*), in *Opera*, eds Cohn and Wendland, vol. 4, Cohn, 1902, repr. 1962.

Philo Judaeus, *Legatio ad Gaium* (*The Legation to Gaius*), in *Opera*, eds Cohn and Wendland, vol. 6, eds Cohn and S. Reiter, 1915, repr. 1962.

Philo Judaeus, *De vita contemplativa* (*On the Contemplative Life*), in *Opera*, eds Cohn and Wendland, vol. 6, eds Cohn and S. Reiter, 1915, repr. 1962.Plato, *Opera*, ed. J. Burnett, Oxford 1900–7.

—— English trans.: *The Collected Dialogues of Plato, including the Letters*, eds Edith Hamilton and Huntington Cairns (= Bollingen Series 71), Princeton, NJ 1961; 2nd edn 1963.

Plato, *Apologia Socratis* (*Apology*), trans. H. Tredennick, in *Collected Dialogues*, eds Hamilton and Cairns.

Plato, *Laches*, trans. B. Jowett, in *Collected Dialogues*, eds Hamilton and Cairns.

Plato, *Phaedo*, trans. H. Tredennick, in *Collected Dialogues*, eds Hamilton and Cairns.

Plato, *Phaedrus*, trans. R. Hackforth, in *Collected Dialogues*, eds Hamilton and Cairns.

Plato, *Republic*, trans. P. Shorey, in *Collected Dialogues*, eds Hamilton and Cairns.

Plato, *Seventh Letter*, trans. A.L. Post, in *Collected Dialogues*, eds Hamilton and Cairns.

Plato, *Politicus* (*The Statesman*), trans. J.B. Skemp, in *Collected Dialogues*, eds Hamilton and Cairns.

Plato, *Symposium*, trans. M. Joyce, in *Collected Dialogues*, eds Hamilton and Cairns.

Plotinus, *Enneades*, eds P. Henry and H.-R. Schwyzer, *Plotini opera*, 3 vols, Leiden 1951–73.

—— English trans.: *Plotinus*, trans. Arthur Hilary Armstrong (LCL), 7 vols, Cambridge MA 1966–88.

Plutarch, *Moralia*, ed. and trans. F.C. Babbitt, *Plutarch's Moralia*, with English trans. (LCL), London/Cambridge MA.

Plutarch, *De communibus notitiis contra Stoicos* (*On Common Conceptions*), in *Moralia*, ed. Babbitt, vol. 13, pt. 2, ed. H. Cherniss, 1976.

Plutarch, *De defectu oraculorum* (*On the Obsolescence of Oracles*), in *Moralia*, ed. Babbitt, vol. 5, ed. F.C. Babbitt, 1957.

Plutarch, *De tranquillitate animi* (*On Peace of Mind*), in *Moralia*, ed. Babbitt, vol. 6, ed. W.C. Helmbold.

Plutarch, *Quaestiones conviviales* (*Table-talk*), in *Moralia*, ed. Babbitt, vol. 4, ed. C. Hubert, 1938, repr. 1971.

Plutarch, *Quomodo quis suos in virtute sentiat profectus* (*How One may Know One is Making Progress in Virtue*), in *Moralia*, ed. Babbitt, vol. 1, ed. F.C. Babbitt, 1927, repr. 1969.

Porphyry, *Ad Marcellam*, ed. W. Pötscher, *Porphyrios. προσ Μαρκελλαμ*, Leiden 1969.

—— English trans.: *Porphyry the Philosopher, To Marcella*, text, trans. intro. and notes by K. O'Brien Wicker (= Society of Biblical Literature, Texts and Translations 28, Graeco-Roman Religion Series 10), Atlanta 1987.

Porphyry, *De abstinentia* (*On Abstinence*), text and French trans., *Porphyre: De L'abstinence, Livre 1*, vol. 1, text and trans. Jean Bouffartigue, Paris 1977.

—— *Livres 2 et 3*, vol. 2, text Jean Bouffartigue, trans. Jean Bouffartigue and Michel Patillon, Paris 1979.

—— English trans.: *Select Works of Porphyry . . . Translated from the Greek*, trans. Thomas Taylor, London 1823, repr. Ann Arbor 1965.

Porphyry, *Sententiae* (*Sentences*), ed. E. Lamberz: *Porphyrius, Sententiae ad Intelligibilia Ducentes*, Leipzig 1975.

—— English trans.: *Select Works of Porphyry . . . Translated from the Greek*, trans. Thomas Taylor, London 1823, repr. Ann Arbor 1965.

Proclus, *In Alcibiadem* (*Commentary on Plato's First Alcibiades*), text and French trans., *Proclus: Sur le Premier Alcibiade de Platon*, text and trans. A. Ph. Segonds, 2 vols, Paris 1985–6.

Quintillian, *Institiutio Oratorica* (*Oratorical Institutions*), text and English trans. ed. H.E. Butler (LCL), 2 vols, 1921–2.

Rufinus, *Historia Monachorum* (*History of the Monks*), *PL* 21.

Sallustius, *De diis et mundo*, text and English trans., *Sallustius: Concerning the Gods and the Universe*, ed., prolegomena and trans. A.D. Nock, Cambridge 1926.

Seneca, *Opera*, ed. and English trans. Thomas H. Corcoran (LCL), 10 vols, London/Cambridge MA.

Seneca, *Ad Lucilium epistulae morales* (*Letters to Lucilius*), ed. and English trans. Richard C. Gummere, 3 vols, London/Cambridge MA, 1934.

Seneca, *De beneficiis* (*On Benefits*) in *Seneca: Moral Essays*, with English trans. John. W. Basore (LCL), 3 vols, London/Cambridge MA 1935, repr. 1958.

Seneca, *Questiones naturales* (*Natural Questions*), in *Opera*, ed. Corcoran, vol. 7, London/Cambridge MA 1971.

Septuagint, ed. A. Rahlfs, *Septuaginta, Id est Vetus Testamentum graece iuxta LXX interpretes*, Stuttgart 1935.

Sextus Empiricus, *Opera*, ed. and English trans. R.G. Bury, *Sextus Empiricus* (LCL), 4 vols, London/Cambridge MA 1933–49.

Tatian, *Oratio ad Graecos* (*Address to the Greeks*), ed. E.J. Goodspeed, *Die ältesten Apologeten*, Göttingen 1915.

Theodoret of Cyrrhus, *Historia Religiosa* (= *Philotheus*) (*History of the Monks of Syria*), ed. and French trans. P. Canivet and A. Leroy-Molinghen, *Théodoret de Cyr. L'histoire des moines de Syrie*, 2 vols (= *SC* 234; 257), Paris 1977–9.

Xenophon, *Memorabilia*, ed. E.C. Marchant, *Xenophontis opera omnia*, vol. 2, 2nd edn, Oxford 1921, repr. 1971.

—— English trans.: H. Tredennick and R. Waterfield, in *Xenophon: Conversations of Socrates*, Harmondsworth 1990.

MODERN AUTHORS

Adnès, P., "Garde du coeur," *Dictionnaire de Spiritualité*, vol. 6, col. 108.

Africa, T.W., "The opium addiction of Marcus Aurelius," *Journal of the History of Ideas* (Jan.–Mar. 1961), pp. 97–102.

Alexandre, M., "Le travail de la sentence chez Marc Aurèle: philosophie et rhétorique," in *Formes brèves* (= Publications de la Faculté des Lettres et des Langues de l'Université de Poitiers 3), Poitiers 1979.

Andresen, C., *Logos und Nomos*, Berlin 1955.

Apelt, O., *Platonische Aufsätze*, Berlin 1912.

Association Guillaume Budé, *Actes du VIIIᵉ Congrès* (Paris, 5–10 April 1968), Paris 1969.

Bacon, Helen H., "Socrates crowned," *The Virginia Quarterly Review* 35 (1959), pp. 415–30.

Bergson, Henri, *L'Énergie spirituelle*, 14th edn, Paris 1930.

—— *La Pensée et le mouvant*, Paris 1946.

—— English trans.: *The Creative Mind*, trans. Mabelle L. Andison, New York 1946.

Bertram, E., *Nietzsche. Versuch einer Mythologie*, Berlin 1918, repr. Bonn, 8th edn, 1965.

Blake, William, *Complete Writings, with Variant Readings*, ed. Geoffrey Keynes, London 1972.

Blumenberg, Hans, *Die Legitimität der Neuzeit*, Frankfurt 1966.

Blumenthal, Henry, "Soul, world-soul, and individual soul in Plotinus," in *Le Néoplatonisme*, 1971.

Bohlin, T., *S. Kierkegaards Leben und Werden*, 1925.

Böhm, B., *Sokrates im achtzehnten Jahrhundert. Studien zum Werdegang des modernen Persönlichkeitsbewusstseins*, Leipzig 1929.

Bonitz, H., *Index aristotelicus*, Berlin 1870, repr. Graz 1955.

Borinski, K., *Die Antike in Poetik und Kunsttheorie*, vol. I, Leipzig 1914.

Bruns, I., *De schola Epicteti*, Kiel 1897.

Caillois, R., *Esthétique généralisée*, Paris 1962.

Carus, C.G., *Symbolik der menschlichen Gestalt*, 1858, repr. Hildesheim/Darmstadt 1962.

Chadwick, H., *The Sentences of Sextus*, Cambridge 1959.

Chenu, M.-D., *Introduction à l'étude de saint Thomas d'Aquin*, Paris 1954.

Courcelle, Pierre, *La Consolation de Philosophie dans la tradition littéraire*, Paris 1967.

Courcelle, Pierre, *Connais-toi toi-même. De Socrate à saint Bernard*, 3 vols, Paris 1974–5.

Dailly, R., and H. van Effenterre, "Le cas Marc Aurèle. Essai de psychosomatique historique," *Revue des Études Anciennes* 56 (1954), pp. 347–65.

Delcourt, Marie, "Utrumque-neutrum," in *Mélanges H.-Ch. Puech*, Paris 1974.

Delorme, J., *Gymnasion*, Paris 1960.

Descartes, R., *Discourse on the Method of Rightly Conducting the Reason and Seeking for the Truth in the Sciences*, English trans. in *Descartes: Selections*, ed. Ralph M. Eaton, New York 1927.

Détienne, M., *De la pensée religieuse à la pensée philosophique. La notion de Daimon dans le pythagorisme ancien*, Paris 1963.

Détienne, M., *Les maîtres de vérité dans la Grèce archaïque*, Paris 1967.

Détienne, M., and J.-P. Vernant, *Les ruses de l'intelligence. La mètis des Grecs*, Paris 1974.

Dirlmeier, F., "Vom Monolog der Dichtung zum 'inneren' Logos bei Platon und Aristoteles," in *Augewählte Schriften zu Dichtung und Philosophie der Griechen*, Heidelberg 1970.

Dodds, E.R., *The Greeks and the Irrational* (= Sather Classical Lectures 25), 3rd edn, Berkeley/London 1963.

Dodds, E.R., *Pagan and Christian in an Age of Anxiety*, Cambridge 1965.

Düring, I., "Aristotle and the heritage from Plato," *Eranos* 62 (1964), pp. 84–99.

Düring, I., *Aristoteles. Darstellung und Interpretation seines Denkens*, Heidelberg 1966.

Düring, I., "Von Aristoteles bis Leibniz. Einige Hauptlinien in der Geschichte des Aristotelismus," in P. Moraux, ed., *Aristoteles in der neueren Forschung* (= Wege der Forschung 61), Darmstadt 1968.

Eckermann, J.P., *Gespräche mit Goethe*, Wiesbaden 1955.

Emrich, W., *Die Symbolik von Faust II*, Frankfurt 1957.

Festugière, A.-J., *Épicure et ses dieux*, Paris 1946.

Festugière, A.-J., *La révélation d'Hermès Trismégiste*, vol. 2, Paris 1949.

Festugière, A.-J., *Contemplation et vie contemplative selon Platon*, 2nd edn, Paris 1950.Foucault, M., "L'écriture de soi," *Corps écrit* 5 (1983), pp. 3–23.

Foucault, M., *Histoire de la sexualité*, vol. 2: *L'Usage des plaisirs*, Paris 1984.

Foucault, M., *Histoire de la sexualité*, vol. 3: *Le Souci de soi*, Paris 1984.

——English trans.: *The Care of the Self* (= *History of Sexuality*, vol. 2), trans. Robert Hurley, New York 1986.

Frank, K.S., ed., *Askese und Mönchtum in der alten Kirche* (= Wege der Forschung 409), Darmstadt 1975.

Friedländer, P., *Plato: An Introduction* (= Bollingen Series 59.1), trans. H. Meyerhoff, vol. 1, 2nd edn, Princeton NJ 1969.

Friedmann, G., *La Puissance et la Sagesse*, Paris 1970.

Friedmann, G., "Le Sage et notre siècle," *Revue de Synthèse* 99 (1978).

Friedrich, C.D., and C.G. Carus, *De la peinture de paysage*, Paris 1988.

Gaiser, K., *Protreptik und Paränese bei Platon. Untersuchungen zur Form des platonischen Dialogs*, Stuttgart 1959.

Gaiser, K., *Platons ungeschriebene Lehre. Studien zur systematischen und geschichtlichen Begründung der Wissenschaften in der platonischen Schule*, Stuttgart 1963, 2nd edn, 1968.

Gaiser, K., *Platone come scrittore filosofico*, Naples 1984.

Gasquet, J., *Cézanne*, Paris 1988.

Gerhard, G.A., *Phoinix von Kolophon*, Leipzig 1909.

Gernet, L., *Anthropologie de la Grèce antique*, Paris 1968.

Van Geytenbeek, A.C., *Musonius Rufus and Greek Diatribes*, Assen 1963.

Gigante, M., "Philodème: Sur la liberté de la parole," *Actes du VIIIᵉ Congrès Budé*, Paris 1969.

Gigante, M., *Ricerche Filodemee*, Naples 1983.

von Goethe, Johann Wolfgang, *Goethes Gespräche mit Eckermann*, ed. Franz Deibel, 2 vols, Leipzig 1908.

——English trans.: *Conversations with Eckermann*, trans. John Oxenford, 2 vols, 1850.von Goethe, Johann Wolfgang, *Wilhelm Meisters Lehrjahre*.

——English trans.: *Wilhelm Meister's Apprenticeship and Travels, From the German of Goethe*, trans. Thomas Carlyle, 2 vols, 2nd edn, 1839.

Goldschmidt, V., "Sur le problème du 'système de Platon'," *Rivista critica di storia della filosofia* 5 (1959), pp. 169–78.

Goldschmidt, V., *Les dialogues de Platon. Structure et méthode dialectique* (= Bibliothèque de philosophie contemporaine, Histoire de la Philosophie et Philosophie générale), 2nd edn, Paris 1963.

Goldschmidt, V., *Le système stoïcien et l'idée de temps*, 4th edn, Paris 1985.

Gould, Thomas, *Platonic Love*, London 1963.

Goulet-Cazé, M.-O., *L'Ascèse cynique. Un commentaire de Diogène Laërce, VI, 70, 71*, Paris 1986.

Groethuysen, B., *Anthropologie philosophique*, Paris 1952, repr. 1980. [First German edn 1928–31.]

De Guibert, J., "Ascèse," in *Dictionnaire de Spiritualité*, vol. 1, cols 936–1010.

Guyau, J.M., *La morale d'Épicure*, Paris 1927.

Hadot, I., *Seneca und die griechisch-römische Tradition der Seelenleitung*, Berlin 1969.

Hadot, I., "Épicure et l'enseignement philosophique hellénistique et romain," in *Actes du VIIIᵉ Congrès Budé*, Paris 1969.

Hadot, I., "Tradition stoïcienne et idées politiques au temps des Gracques," *Revue des Études Latines* 48 (1970), pp. 133–79.

Hadot, I., "Le système théologique de Simplicius dans son commentaire sur le Manuel d'Épictète," in *Le Néoplatonisme*, 1971.

Hadot, I., *Le problème du néoplatonisme alexandrin, Hiéroclès et Simplicus*, Paris 1978.

Hadot, P., "Epistrophè et metanoia dans l'histoire de la philosophie," in *Actes du XIeme congrès international de philosophie* XII, Amsterdam 1953.

Hadot, P., "La distinction de l'être et de l'étant dans le 'De Hebdomadibus' de Boèce," in *Miscellanea Mediaevalia*, vol. 2, Berlin 1963. Hadot, P., "La métaphysique de Porphyre," in *Porphyre* (= Entretiens Hardt sur l'Antiquité Classique 12), Vandoeuvres/Geneva 1966.

Hadot, P., *Porphyre et Victorinus*, 2 vols, Paris 1968.

Hadot, P., "Zur Vorgeschichte des Begriffs Existenz," *Archiv für Begriffsgeschichte* 13 (1969).

Hadot, P., "Conversio," in *Historisches Wörterbuch der Philosophie*, vol. 1, cols 1033–6, 1971.

Hadot, P., "Les divisions des parties de la philosophie dans l'Antiquité," *Museum Helveticum* 36 (1979), pp. 201–23.

Hamann, J.G., *Sokratische Denkwürdigkeiten*, erklärt von F. Blanke, Gütersloh 1959.

—— English trans.: *Hamann's Socratic Memorabilia, A Translation and Commentary*, trans. James C. O'Flaherty, Baltimore 1967.

Happ, H., *Hyle*, Berlin 1971.

Hasse, H., *Das Problem des Sokrates bei F. Nietzsche*, Leipzig 1918.

Hauser, R., and G. Lanczkowski, "Askese," in *Historisches Wörterbuch der Philosophie*, vol. I, cols 538–41, 1971.

Hegel, G.W.F., *Vorlesungen über die Geschichte der Philosophie*.

—— English trans.: E.S. Haldane, *Hegel's Lectures on the History of Philosophy*, 3 vols, London 1892, repr. London 1955.

Henry, P., *Plotin et l'Occident. Firmicus Maternus, Marius Victorinus, Saint Augustin et Macrobe* (= Spicilegium sacrum Lovaniense, Études et Documents 15), Louvain 1934.

Heussi, K., *Der Ursprung des Mönchtums*, Tübingen 1936.

Hijmans, B.-L., Jr, ΑΣΚΗΣΙΣ, *Notes on Epictetus' Educational System*, Assen 1959.

Hildebrandt, K., *Nietzsches Wettkampf mit Sokrates und Platon*, Dresden 1922.

Hillman, J., "On psychological creativity," *Eranos-Jahrbuch* 35 (1966), pp. 370–98.

Himmelstrup, J., S. *Kierkegaards Sokrates-Auffassung*, Neumünster 1927.

Hintikka, J., *Time and Necessity*, Oxford 1973.

Hoffmann, E., "Epikur," in M. Dessoir, ed., *Die Geschichte der Philosophie*, vol. I, Wiesbaden 1925.

Hölderlin, Friedrich, *Gedichte*, English trans.: *Friedrich Hölderlin, Poems and Fragments*, trans. Michael Hamburger, London 1966.

Husserl, E., "Grundlegende Untersuchungen zum phänomenologiscen Ursprung der Räumlichkeit der Natur" (= Umsturz der Kopernikanischen Lehre), in Marvin Faber, ed., *Philosophical Essays in Memory of E. Husserl*, Cambridge MA 1940.

Ingenkamp, H.-G., *Plutarchs Schriften über die Heilung der Seele*, Göttingen 1971.

von Ivánka, E., "Kephalaia," *Byzantinische Zeitschrift* 47 (1954), pp. 285–91.

Jaeger, Werner, *Paideia*, vol. 2, Berlin 1954.

Jankélévitch, Vladimir, *L'Ironie*, Paris 1964.

Jaspers, K., "Epikur," in *Weltbewohner und Weimarianer (Festschrift E. Beutler)*, Zurich 1960.

Joly, H., *Le renversement platonicien*, Paris 1974.

Jung, C.G., *Von den Wurzeln des Bewusstseins*, Zurich 1954.

Kant, Immanuel, *Immanuel Kant's Werke*, ed. Ernst Cassirer, Berlin 1916.

Kant, Immanuel, *Die Metaphysik der Sitten* (1797), *Ethische Methodenlehre, Zwieter Abschnitt. Die ethische Asketik*, in *Werke*, ed. Cassirer vol. 7.

—— English trans.: *The Metaphysical Principles of Virtue: Part II of the Metaphysics of Morals*, trans. James Ellington, 1964.

Kaufmann, Walter, *Nietzsche. Philosopher, Psychologist, Antichrist*, 4th edn, Princeton NJ 1974.

Kierkegaard, Søren, *Gesammelte Werke*, Düsseldorf/Cologne 1961 (abbreviated *GW*).

Kierkegaard, Søren, *Tägebücher (Diaries)*, Düsseldorf/Cologne 1982.

Kierkegaard, Søren, *Der Gesichtspunkt für meine Wirksamkeit als Schriftsteller*, in *GW 33*.

—— English trans.: *Søren Kierkegaard, The Point of View for my Work as an Author, A Report to History, and Related Writings*, trans., intro. and notes Walter Lowrie, New York 1962, 1st edn 1939.

Kierkegaard, Søren, *Abschliessende unwissenschaftliche Nachschrift*, in *GW* 16.

—— English trans.: *Søren Kierkegaard, Concluding Unscientific Postscript*, trans. David F. Swenson and Walter Lowrie, Princeton NJ 1941, repr. 1974.

Kierkegaard, Søren, *Der Augenblick (The Instant)*, in *GW* 34.

Kierkegaard, Søren, *Christliche Reden (Christian Speeches)*, in *GW* 20.

Kierkegaard, Søren, *Philosophische (Philosophical Fragments)*, in *GW* 10.

Kierkegaard, Søren, *Über den Begriff der Ironie mit ständiger Rücksicht auf Socrates*, in *GW* 31.

—— English trans.: *The Concept of Irony with Constant Reference to Socrates*, trans., intro. and notes Lee M. Capel, New York 1965.

Klauser, T., "Apophthegma," *Reallexikon für Antike und Christentum* I (1950), pp. 545–50.

Klee, P., *Théorie de l'art moderne*, Paris 1964, repr. 1985.

Krämer, H.-J., *Arete bei Platon und Aristoteles. Zum Wesen und zur Geschichte der platonischen Ontologie*, Heidelberg 1959; 2nd edn, Amsterdam 1967.

Krämer, H.-J., *Platonismus und hellenistische Philosophie*, Berlin/New York 1971.

Kretschmar, G., "Der Ursprung der frühchristlichen Askese," *Zeitschrift für Theologie und Kirche* 61 (1964), pp. 27–67.

Laín Entralgo, P., "Die platonische Rationalisierung der Besprechung (ἐπῳδή) und die Erfindung der Psychotherapie durch das Wort," *Hermes* 68 (1958), pp. 298–323.

Lain Entralgo, P., *The Therapy of the Word in Classical Antiquity*, New Haven 1970.

Landmann, M., *Elenktik und Maieutik*, Bonn 1950.

Lausberg, H., *Handbuch der literarischen Rhetorik*, Munich 1960.

Leclerq, J., "Pour l'histoire de l'expression 'philosophie chrétienne'," *Mélanges de Science Religieuse* 9 (1952), pp. 221–6.

Lemke, D., *Die Theologie Epikurs*, Munich 1973.

Leo, F., "Der Monolog im Drama," *Abhandlungen der Götting. Gesellschaft der Wissenschaft.*, NF 10, 5 (1908).

van Lieshout, H., *La théorie plotinienne de la vertu. Essai sur la genèse d'un article de la Somme Théologique de saint Thomas*, Fribourg 1926.

Lohse, B., *Askese und Mönchtum in der Antike und in der alten Kirche*, Munich/Vienna 1969.

Long, A.A., "Heracleitus and Stoicism," in *Philosophia* (Academy of Athens) 5–6 (1975–6).

Malingrey, A.N., *"Philosophia." Étude d'un groupe de mots dans la littérature grecque, des Présocratiques au IVe siècle ap. J.-C.*, Paris 1961.

Marrou, H.-I., *Saint Augustin et la fin de la culture antique*, Paris 1938.

Marrou, H.-I., *Histoire de l'éducation dans l'Antiquité*, 6th edn, Paris 1971.

Méautis, G., *L'âme hellénique*, Paris 1932.

Merlan, P., *Monopsychism, Mysticism, Metaconsciousness. Problems of the Soul in the Neoaristotelian and Neoplatonic Tradition* (= Archives internationaux d'Histoire des idées 2), The Hague 1963.

Merleau-Ponty, M., *La Phénoménologie de la perception*, Paris 1945.

——English trans.: *The Phenomenology of Perception*, trans. Colin Smith, London/New York 1962.

Merleau-Ponty, M., *Éloge de la philosophie et autres essais*, Paris 1953.

——English trans.: *Maurice Merleau-Ponty, In Praise of Philosophy and Other Essays*, trans. John Wild and James Edie, Evanston IL 1988.

Merleau-Ponty, M., "L'oeil et l'esprit," *Les Temps Modernes* 27 (1961).

Misch, G., *Geschichte der Autobiographie*, vol. I, Bern 1949.

Montaigne, *Essays*, eds P. Villey and V.-L. Saulnier, *Les Essais de Michel de Montaigne*, 3rd edn, Paris 1978.

——English trans.: *The Essays of Michel de Montaigne*, trans. and notes George B. Ives, intro. André Gide, comments Grace Norton, 3 vols, New York 1946.

Moraux, P., "La joute dialectique d'après le huitième livre des Topiques," in G.E.L. Owens, ed., *Aristotle on Dialectic* (= Proceedings of the Third Symposium Aristotelicum), Oxford 1968.

Morenz, S., *Die Zauberflöte*, Münster 1952.

Nagel, P., *Die Motivierung der Askese in der alten Kirche und der Ursprung des*

Mönchtums (= Texte und Untersuchungen zur Geschichte der altchristlichen Literatur 95), Berlin 1966.

Nietzsche, Friedrich, *Friedrich Nietzsche, Sämtliche Werke*, eds. G. Colli and M. Montinari, 15 vols, Berlin 1980.

Nietzsche, Friedrich, *Die Geburt der Tragödie*, in *Sämtliche Werke*, eds Colli and Montinari, vol. 1.

——English trans.: *The Birth of Tragedy and the Case of Wagner, by Friedrich Nietzsche*, trans. with commentary Walter Kaufmann, New York 1967.

Nietzsche, Friedrich, *Götzen-Dämmerung*, in *Sämtliche Werke*, eds Colli and Montinari, vol. 6.

——English trans.: *Twilight of the Idols*, in *The Portable Nietzsche*, trans., intro., preface and notes Walter Kaufmann (= Viking Portable Library 62), New York 1954, repr. 1968.

Nietzsche, Friedrich, *Ecce Homo, Die Unzeitgemässen*, in *Sämtliche Werke*, eds Colli and Montinari, vol. 6.

——English trans.: *Ecce Homo*, trans. Walter Kaufmann, in *Friedrich Nietzsche, On the Genealogy of Morals*, trans. Walter Kaufmann and R.J. Hollingdale, New York 1969.

Nietzsche, Friedrich, *Jenseits von Gut und Böse*, in *Sämtliche Werke*, eds Colli and Montinari, vol. 5.

——English trans.: *Beyond Good and Evil, Prelude to a Philosophy of the Future, by Friedrich Nietzsche*, trans. with commentary Walter Kaufmann, New York 1966.

Nietzsche, Friedrich, English trans.: *Friedrich Nietzsche: The Will to Power*, trans. Walter Kaufmann and R.J. Hollingdale, ed. with commentary Walter Kaufmann, New York 1968.

Nietzsche, Friedrich, *Menschliches, Allzumenschliches II, Der Wanderer und sein Schatten*, in *Sämtliche Werke*, eds Colli and Montinari, vol. 2.

——English trans.: *Friedrich Nietzsche: Human, All Too Human, A Book for Free Spirits* (= Texts in German Philosophy), trans. R.J. Hollingdale, Cambridge 1986.

Nietzsche, Friedrich, *Morgenröte*, in *Sämtliche Werke*, eds Colli and Montinari, vol. 3.

——English trans.: Extracts in *Portable Nietzsche*, trans. Kaufmann.

Nietzsche, Friedrich, *Unzeitgemäße Betrachtungen*, in *Sämtliche Werke*, eds Colli and Montinari, vol. 1.

——English trans.: *Friedrich Nietzsche; Untimely Meditations*, trans. R.J. Hollingdale, intro. J.P. Stern, Cambridge 1983, repr. 1990.

Nietzsche, Friedrich, *Die fröhliche Wissenschaft*, in *Sämtliche Werke*, eds Colli and Montinari, vol. 3.

——English trans.: *Friedrich Nietzsche, The Gay Science, with a Prelude in Rhymes and an Appendix of Songs*, trans. Walter Kaufmann, New York 1974.

Nock, Arthur Darby, *Conversion*, Oxford 1933.

Norden, E., "Beiträge zur Geschichte der griechischen Philosophie," *Jahrbücher für classische Philologie*, supplementary vol. 19, Leipzig 1893.

Pascal, Blaise, *Pensées*, ed. L. Brunschvicg, Paris 1971.

Patzer, Andreas, ed., *Der historische Socrates* (= Wege der Forschung 585), Darmstadt 1987.

Pivcevic, E., *Ironie als Daseinsform bei Sören Kierkegaard*, Gütersloh 1960.

Pohlenz, M., *Die Stoa. Geschichte einer geistigen Bewegung*, Göttingen 1948–9; 5th edn, 2 vols, Göttingen 1978–80.

De Quincey, Thomas, *Confessions of an English Opium-eater*, 1st edn in *London Magazine*, Sept./Oct. 1821–Dec. 1822, repr. New York 1950.

Rabbow, Paul, *Seelenführung. Methodik der Exerzitien in der Antike*, Munich 1954.

Ravaisson, F., *Essai sur la Métaphysique d'Aristote*, Paris 1846, repr. Hildesheim 1963.

Refoulé, F., "Rêves et vie spirituelle d'après Évagre le Pontique," *Supplément de la Vie Spirituelle* 59 (1961), pp. 470–516.

Renan, Ernest, *Marc Aurèle ou la fin du monde antique*, preface Yves Bonello, Paris 1984.

Richard, M.-D., *L'Enseignement oral de Platon, une nouvelle interprétation du platonisme*, preface Pierre Hadot, Paris 1986.

Rilke, Rainer Maria, English trans.: *Rainer Maria Rilke, Duino Elegies*, trans. David Young, New York 1978.

Ritter, J., *Subjektivität. Sechs Aufsätze*, Frankfurt 1974.

Robin, Léon, *La théorie platonicienne de l'amour*, Paris 1933.

Robin, Léon, "Introduction," in *Platon, Le Banquet* (Budé), Paris 1951.

Rodis-Lewis, G., *Épicure et son école*, Paris 1975.

Rutherford, R.B., *The Meditations of Marcus Aurelius: A Study*, Oxford 1989.

Sandvoss, E., *Sokrates und Nietzsche*, Leiden 1966.

Schadewelt, Wolfgang, *Monolog und Selbstgespräch. Untersuchungen zur Formgeschichte der griechischen Tragödie*, Berlin 1926.

Schadewelt, Wolfgang, *Goethestudien*, Zurich 1963.

Schaerer, René, "Le mécanisme de l'ironie dans ses rapports avec la dialectique," *Revue de Métaphysique et de Morale* 49 (1941), pp. 181ff.

Schaerer, René, *La Question platonicienne. Études sur les rapports de la pensée et de l'expression dans les Dialogues* (= Mémoires de l'Université de Neuchâtel 10), 2nd edn with postscript, Neuchâtel 1969.

Schissel von Fleschenberg, O., *Marinos von Neapolis und die neuplatonischen Tugendgrade*, Athens 1928.

Schmid, W., "Das Sokratesbild der Wolken," *Philologus* 97 (1948), pp. 209–28.

Schmid, W., "Epikur," in *Reallexikon für Antike und Christentum*, vol. 5, 1962, cols 735–40.

Schmid, W., *Die Geburt der Philosophie im Garten der Lüste*, Frankfurt 1987.

Schmidt, H.J., *Nietzsche und Sokrates*, Meisenheim 1969.

Schmitz, H., *Goethes Altersdenken*, Bonn 1959. Schneider, K., *Die schweigenden Götter*, Hildesheim 1966.

Schopenhauer, Arthur, English trans.: *The World as Will and Representation by Arthur Schopenhauer*, trans. E.F.J. Payne, 2 vols, Indian Hills CO 1958, repr. London/Toronto 1969.

Schrijvers, P.-H., *Horror ac Divina Voluptas. Études sur la poétique et la poésie de Lucrèce*, Amsterdam 1970.

Schuhl, P.-M., and P. Hadot, eds, *Le Néoplatonisme* (= Colloques Internationaux du Centre National de la Recherche Scientifique, Sciences Humaines, Royaumont 1969), Paris 1971.

Schweingruber, F., "Sokrates und Epiktet," *Hermes* 78 (1943), pp. 52–79.

Seebeck, H.-G., *Das Sokratesbild vom 19. Jahrhundert*, Göttingen 1947.

Spengler, O., *Der Untergang des Abendlandes*, Munich 1923.

——English trans.: *The Decline of the West, by Oswald Spengler*, trans. C.H. Atkinson, 2 vols, New York 1946.

Spiegelberg, H., *The Socratic Enigma*, New York 1964.

Spies, A., *Militat omnis amans. Ein Beitrag zur Bildersprache der antiken Erotik*, Tübingen 1930.

Spinoza, Benedict de, *On the Improvement of the Understanding, The Ethics, Correspondence*, trans. and intro. R.H.M. Elwes, New York 1955.

Spoerri, W., "Gnome," in *Der kleine Pauly*, vol. 2, 1967, cols 822–9.

Sudhaus, S., "Epikur als Beichtvater," *Archiv für Religionswissenschaft* 14 (1911), pp. 647ff.

Taylor, A.E., *Varia Socratica*, Oxford 1911.

Thurot, Charles, *Extraits de . . . manuscrits latins pour servir à l'histoire des doctrines grammaticales*, Paris 1869.

Vauvenargues, *Introduction à la connoissance de l'esprit humain, suivie de Réflexions et Maximes*, 1746.

——English trans.: F.G. Stevens, 1940.

Vernant, J.-P., *Mythe et pensée chez les Grecs*, Paris 1971.

Vööbus, A., *A History of Asceticism in the Syrian Orient* (= CSCO vol. 184, Subsidia 14; vol. 197, Subsidia 17), Louvain 1958–60.

de Waelhens, A., *La philosophie de Martin Heidegger* (= Bibliothèque Philosophique de Louvain 2), 4th edn, Louvain 1955.

Wahl, J., *Études kierkegaardiennes*, 3rd edn, Paris 1967.

Weil, E., "La place de la logique dans la pensée aristotélicienne," *Revue de Métaphysique et de Morale* 56 (1951), pp. 283–315.

——English trans.: As ch. 6 in J. Barnes, M. Schofield and R. Sorabji, eds, *Articles on Aristotle, vol. I: Science*, London 1975.

Wendland, P., *Anaximenes von Lampsakos*, Berlin 1905.

Wild, J., "Kierkegaard and classic philology," *Philosophical Review* 49 (1940), pp. 536–7.

Wippern, J., ed., *Das Problem der ungeschriebenen Lehre Platons* (= Wege der Forschung 186), Darmstadt 1972.

Index

Abelard 33
abstraction, and oral tradition of philosophy 20
Academicians 60
aesthetics
  Aristotle 190
  Marcus Aurelius 189–90, 251
  perception 254–6
Africa, Thomas W. 180, 181–2
Agathon 166, 169
Alexander Severus 4
Ambrose
  Philo's text, use of 65
  translation of Plotinus 3, 51
Andronicus of Rhodes 72
Antisthenes 91
Antoninus Pious 57
Antony, St
  attention to oneself 131, 133, 139
  conscience, examination of 135
  conversion 131
  writing, therapeutic value 135, 209, 211
Apelles 266
Apologists 128
Apophthegmata 133
Aristophanes 90–1, 166, 169
Aristotelianism
  absorption into Platonism 56
  exegetical phase 5
  life, conduct of 58
  physics 97
  scholasticism 63
  theory and practice, relationship between 60
Aristotle
  aesthetics 190

Boethius' translation 51
  dialogue 21, 22, 105–6
  discourse 28
  exegesis 71, 72, 75
  philosophy as a way of life 266, 269
  on Socrates 153
  theory 29
Arrian of Nicomedia 191, 195, 199, 200
artists 254, 255, 256
asceticism 128
Asianism 67
assent *see* judgment
Athanasius 131, 135
attention to oneself
  Christianity 130–6
  displacement of 254
  Marcus Aurelius 198
  Stoic spiritual exercises 84–5, 130
Augustine
  confessions in *Confessions* 186
  Confessions, inspiration of 68
  conversion 51–2
  exegesis 16–17
  Husserl's adaptation 65
  mistranslations 3, 66, 75
  physics, logic, and ethics 26
  rules of discourse 13
  self, mystery of 15–17: original sin 16, 52
  structure of work for spiritual progress 64
  Trinity 107
Aulus Gellius 190, 191, 199
authentic texts 73–4

Barth, Casper 10
Barthes, Roland 56

Basil of Caesarea
   attention to oneself   130–1, 134, 139
   watch of the heart   132
Baudelaire, Charles   248
Baumgarten   254
being
   as infinitive   5–6, 75
   negative theology of   6
   as participle   5–6, 75
Bergson, Henri   253–4, 257, 258, 272, 278
Bernard, Paul   54
Bernard of Clairvaux   129
biographies of philosophers   30
Blake, William   260
Boethius
   esse and *id quod est*, distinction
      between   6, 76
   translation of Aristotelian
      commentator   51
brevity of existence   185–6

Caillois, Roger   256
Cambiano, Giuseppe   30
Carus, G. G.   255
Casaubon, Meric   179
Cato of Utico   272
Celsus   74
Cézanne, Paul   255–6, 257
Chastel, André   243
Chenu, M.-D.   73
Christianity
   Hadot, influence on   277–8
   historical evolution of philosophy   32,
      107, 269–70
   Kierkegaard's views   157
   and paganism   4–5, 74–5
   as a philosophy   128–30
   spiritual exercises   127–40
Chrysippus   123–4n
   happiness and wisdom   228
   lost works   53
   and Marcus Aurelius   188, 190
   philosopher, concept of   30, 272
   Stoic dogmas   61
   wine in the sea   229
Cicero, Marcus Tullius
   flight of the soul   240
   infinity   184
   philosophers   272
   self-mastery   135
   on Socrates   152

Clearchus of Soloi   241
Clement of Alexandria   74, 128
   attention to oneself   130
   integration   269
   spiritual perfection   138
Cleonymus of Athens   74, 128, 241
   attention to oneself   130
   integration   269
   spiritual perfection   138
conscience, examination of   131, 134–5,
   139
consolations   22–3
contamination of paganism and
      Christianity   4–5
Copernican revolution   253
cosmic consciousness   266, 273
Courcelle, Jeanne   52
Courcelle, Pierre   50–2
Crantor   72
creative misunderstandings   6–7
cryptography, mystical   10–11
Cynicism
   flight of the soul   245–7
   life, conduct of   58, 103–4
   philosophy as a way of life   266, 269

Dailly, R.   180
Damascius   104, 284
Dead Poets' Society   187
death
   awareness of: Antony   131; Epictetus
      131; Marcus Aurelius   131
   Christianity   138, 139
   Epicureanism   222, 225–6
   and flight of the soul   240–1
   Lucretius' views   187
   Marcus Aurelius' views   187
   philosophy as a training for   242
   preparation for   68–9: consolations
      22–3; Epicurus   68, 95; Heidegger
      96; Maximus Confessor   138;
      meditation   59; Plato   22, 28, 68,
      95, 96–7, 241, 269; Socrates   94;
      spiritual exercises   93–101;
      Stoicism   68, 96, 229
Delphic oracle   65
Democritus   186, 241
demonic   164–5
Descartes, René
   philosophy as way of life   272
   spiritual exercises   33, 271

desire 11
  Epictetus 193, 194
  Hadot on 284
  Marcus Aurelius 195–7, 198, 201
  and physics 12, 194
  tyranny of 95
Diadochus of Photice
  attention to God and oneself 132–3
  dreams 135
dialectic and persuasion 92–3
dialogue
  learning to 20, 89–93
  philosophical work as 105
diatribe 63
Dio Cassius 180
Diogenes Laertius 118n, 123n
Diogenes the Cynic 98, 161
discourse 26–8, 31–2
Dodds, E. R. 180
Domitian 191
Dorotheus of Gaza
  attention to oneself 131
  conscience, examination of 134–5
  meditation 134
  obedience 140
  peace of mind 138
  self-mastery 135
  sin 139
  spiritual perfection 136
dreams
  Christianity 135
  and flight of the soul 241
  tyranny of desire revealed in 95
  Zeno's beliefs 113n
Düring, I. 105–6
duties 193

Eckhardt, Meister 270
eclecticism 210
Effenterre, H. van 180
Einstein, Albert 283
Eleusis 28
Epaphroditus 191
ephemerality of human life 185–6
Epictetus 191–5
  death, awareness of 131
  discourse 27, 267
  exegesis 108
  and Marcus Aurelius 195–202
  objective representation 188
  philosophical *topoi* 12–13, 193–5

philosophy as a way of life 267
  physical vision of human reality 187
  physics 97
  serenity 136
  on Socrates 152
  Socratic style 116 n
Epicureanism
  cosmic consciousness 266, 267, 268
  ethics 208–9
  exegetical phase 5
  features 34, 35
  flight of the soul 243, 245
  Hadot's interest in 280–1
  library find 53–4
  life, conduct of 57, 58
  meditation 59
  present, value of 69, 88, 209–10, 212,
    222–6, 259–60, 268
  sage 252
  self-control 59
  spiritual exercises 126: happiness
    103; learning to die 95; learning to
    live 87–9
Epicurus
  death, philosophy as exercise for 68
  discourse 27
  dogmas, disagreements 61
  flight of the soul 243
  meditation, dogmas for 60
  philosopher concept 30, 272
  philosophy as a way of life 266
  theory and practice, relationship
    between 60
  wisdom 57
Erasmus 33
Eros 160–5
  wisdom 265
erotic irony 158–65
escapism, ancient philosophy as 274
ethics 137
  Epicurean 208–9
  Foucault 24–5, 206–7
  and inclinations 12
  spiritual exercises 23–5, 126–7
  Stoicism 25–6
Euclid 64, 68
Eusebius of Caesarea 4
Evagrius Ponticus
  dreams 135
  self-mastery 135
  spiritual exercises 133

Evagrius Ponticus (*cont.*)
  spiritual perfection 136–7, 138
exegetical philosophy 5–7, 71–6
  Augustine 16–17
  scholasticism 63–4
existentialism 277, 278

Ficino, Marsilio 69
Flavius Josephus 129
flight of the soul 238–48
Foucault, Michel
  care of the self 206–12
  enthusiasm for Hadot 1, 206
  ethics and spiritual exercises 24–5,
    206–7
Friedmann, Georges 70, 81, 97, 108, 282
  power and wisdom 235
  spiritual exercises 82: learning to live
    83, 86
friendship, Epicurean attitudes 88–9
Fronto 200

Galen 180–1
Gataker, Thomas 179
Gesner, Andreas 179
Gilson, Étienne 277
Glaucos 102–3
Goethe, Johann Wolfgang von 176n
  on demonic 164–5
  dialogue 217–21
  erotic pedagogy 164
  eternity 233–4
  existence, joy of 234–5
  flight of the soul 238–9, 244–5
  horror 115n, 274
  poetry 239, 244–5
  present, value of 69, 217, 220–1, 222,
    230–4
  on reading 109
  and Socrates 164
gratitude, Epicurean piety 87
Greek literature 50–1
Gregory Nazianzen 138
Gregory Thaumaturgus 163–4
Groethuysen, Bernard 251
Guarducci, Margherita 8–9
Guyau, J. M. 224

Hadot, Ilsetraut 22–3
Hamann, J. G. 150
happiness

spiritual exercises 102
  Stoicism 227, 228
healing, Epicureanism 87
Hegel, Georg Wilhelm Friedrich 272
Heidegger, Martin 272
  death, philosophy as training for 96
Henry, Paul 51, 279–80
Heraclitus 68
Herod Atticus 199
hierarchy, Christianity and paganism 5
Hippocrates 186
historical psychology
  Augustine 16, 17
  dangers 15
Hölderlin, Friedrich
  erotic pedagogy 164
  and Socrates 167, 168
Holzmann, Wilhelm 10
Homer
  dialogue 118–19, 195
  flight of the soul 238–9, 240, 247
Horace
  carpe diem 88, 224–5
  dialogue 118n
  present, value of 69, 224
Husserl, Edmund
  Delphic oracle, adaptation of 65
  "know thyself" tradition 66
  perceptions of the world 272, 273
  world of science and world of
    perception 253
hypomnemata 11, 179, 209–10

Ignatius of Loyola 82, 126, 127, 270
inclinations 11
  Epictetus 193
  and ethics 12
  Marcus Aurelius 195, 198, 201
indifference to indifferent things 86, 197
indirect communication 151, 156
infinity 184
  Marcus Aurelius on 183, 184
investigation, as spiritual exercise 86
irony, Socratic
  dialectical 149–58
  erotic 158–65

Jesus Christ 10–11
John of Salisbury 129
judgment 11
  Epictetus 193, 194

and logic 12, 194
Marcus Aurelius 195, 198
Julian 4
jurists 57
Justin 74, 128

kairos 221
Kant, Immanuel
aesthetic perception 255
ancient representation of philosophy 33
virtue, practice of 124n
Kephalaia 173
Kierkegaard, Søren
Christianity 157
existence, seriousness of 156
pseudonymy 150–1
on Socrates 157, 158: erotic irony 159
Klee, Paul 255, 256, 257
"know thyself" maxim 20
Husserl 66
Socrates 20, 90

landscape-painting 255
Leclerq, Jean 129, 130, 270
Leonidas of Tarentum 182
listening, as spiritual exercise 86
live, learning to 82–9
logic
and judgment 12, 194
spiritual exercises 24–5
Stoicism 25–6
logoi sokratikoi 149
love, and Socrates 158–64
Lucian 57
flight of the soul 245–6, 247
Lucretius
anxiety 186
on death 187
flight of the soul 243, 245
physics 97
Plato's model 68
poetic meter 62
rules of discourse 13
sage 252
universalism 226
world 257–8, 274

Marcus Aurelius
aesthetics 189–90, 251
banality of life 185
cosmic consciousness 266

cultivation of the self 207, 212
death, awareness of 131
divine providence 282, 283
and Epictetus 195–202
flight of the soul 244, 245
Meditations: as spiritual exercise
179–91; style 133; underlying
structure 10–11, 12–15
parensis 107
peace of mind 229
physics as spiritual exercise 98, 99
political ideas 274
present, attention to 132, 226–8
rhetoric 60
sage 251
Maritain, Jacques 277, 278–9
Marius Victorinus 279–80
Marx, Karl 272
Marxism 278
Maximus Confessor 138
Maximus of Tyre 184
meditation 59–60
Christian spiritual exercises 133–4
Epicurean spiritual exercises 87, 88
Socrates's disciples 91
Stoic spiritual exercises 85–6
by writing 195
memorization
monastic spiritual exercises 133
Stoic spiritual exercises 85–6
Merleau-Ponty, M. 253, 254, 256, 257, 273
meteorologia 243
Metrodorus 208–9, 226, 266
Meyer, C. F. 166
mistranslations 3, 66, 75
misunderstandings 6–7
monasticism 269–70
as a philosophy 129
spiritual exercises 131, 132, 133, 138,
140: passions 135
monotheism 5
Montaigne, Michel de 33
death, views on 96
Hadot, influence on 278
Montgolfier brothers 239
Morenz, Siegfried 221
Moses 74
Musonius Rufus 191

names, Marcus Aurelius' views 186
nature

nature (*cont.*)
  Marcus Aurelius on 189–90
  Hadot on 283
  see also physics
Neoplatonism
  being as infinitive and being as
    participle, distinction between 5–6
  emergence 56
  exegesis 75
  new meanings of earlier works 66
  spiritual exercises 99, 100
  Stoic ethics, integration of 136
Newman 277
Nietzsche, Friedrich Wilhelm
  ancient philosophy tradition 272
  erotic pedagogy 164
  genius of the heart 170
  indirect communication 151
  present, focus on 212, 235
  and Socrates 148, 151–2, 156, 167–70:
    seductive powers 165–6; style
    155–6

obedience 139–40
objective representation 187–9
opium, and Marcus Aurelius 180–1
oral tradition of philosophy 19–22, 23,
  61–3
Origen
  Ambrose's translations 3
  Christianity as a philosophy 129
  on Chrysippus 123–4n
  conscience, examination of 134
  dogmas, disagreements 61
  exegesis 72
  Gregory Thaumaturgus' praise 163–4
Ovid
  flight of the soul 245
  time as a river 182

paganism 4–5, 74–5
Parain, Brice 93
parenesis 106–7
Pascal, Blaise 184
Paul, St 66
peace of mind 138
  Marcus Aurelius 229
  Seneca 229
Péguy, Charles 278
penitence 139
perception

aesthetic 254–6
  everyday 252–4
persuasion 92
Peter, St 8–9
Petrarch 33
Philo Judaeus
  exegesis 72
  Platonic formulae, use of 65
Philo of Alexandria
  flight of the soul 240, 243–4
  Judaism as a philosophy 129
  philosophy as a way of life 265
  set speeches 69
  spiritual exercises 84, 86, 97–8
  universalism 184
Philodemus 225
philosopher, concepts of 30–4, 272
physics 137–8
  and desire 12, 194
  flight of the soul 242–3
  Marcus Aurelius 197
  spiritual exercises 24–5
  Stoicism 25–6
  study, as spiritual exercise 87–8, 97–9
Plato
  being as infinite and being as participle,
    distinction between 5–6, 75
  death, philosophy as training for 22,
    28, 68, 95, 96–7, 241, 269
  dialogue 20, 21, 62, 90, 91–3, 105:
    methodology 106
  discourse 28
  exegesis 71, 72, 73, 75
  flight of the soul 240–2, 243
  and Moses 74
  river of Heraclitus 182
  on Socrates 148, 149–50, 153: erotic
    irony 158, 160, 161, 163
  Timaeus, as model 68
  universalism 184
  wisdom, nature of 57
Platonism
  Academy 106
  adaptations 65
  exegetical phase 5
  flight of the soul 242–3
  Glaucos 102–3
  life, conduct of 58–9
  philosophical death 242
  river 182
  Scholasticism 63–4

Socrates' death 94
spiritual exercises 99
spiritual progress 64
Stoicism and Aristotelianism,
    absorption of 56
theory and practice, relationship
    between 60
pleasure, Epicurean attitudes 88–9,
    222–6, 268
Plotinus
    Ambrose's translations 3, 51
    dialogue 2, 22
    discourse 28–9
    exegesis 72, 73, 74
    Hadot's interest in 279, 280, 281, 285
    methodology 106
    Plato's text, use of 65
    spiritual exercises 99, 100, 101, 102, 107
    structure of work for spiritual
        progress 64
    theory and practice, relationship
        between 60
Plutarch
    flight of the soul 241
    spiritual exercises 59: curiosity, cure
        for 136; learning to live 86;
        physics 97–8
Polemon 267
Porphyry
    attention to God and oneself 132
    being as infinitive and being as
        participle, distinction between 6, 75
    exegesis 73
    influence on late Christian thought 51
    nature and soul 144n
    on Plotinus 72, 106
    spiritual progress 99–100, 137
    style 133
    theory and practice, distinction
        between 60
present, value of 69, 221–2, 259–60
    Christians 131–2
    Epicureans 69, 88, 209–10, 212,
        222–6, 259–60, 268
    Goethe 69, 217, 220–1, 222, 230–4
    Marcus Aurelius 132, 226–8
    Nietzsche 212, 235
    Seneca 228, 229
    Stoics 69, 84–5, 212, 222, 226–30, 260,
        268
Priscianus 73–4

Proclus 61
    Euclid's model 64, 68
    flight of the soul 241
    treatises 64
Pythagoreans 9

Quincey, Thomas De 181–2, 183, 184
Quintillian 265
Quintus Mucius Scaevola Pontifex 272

Rabbow, Paul 126
Ramus, Petrus 49, 52
reading, as spiritual exercise 86, 101–9
relaxation, Epicureans 88
Renan, Ernest 179–80, 247
research, as spiritual exercise 86
Revelations 72
rhetoric 21
    and persuasion 92
    and spiritual exercises 127
Rilke, Rainer Maria 258, 278
Ritter, J. 254
Robin, Léon 226
Rogatianus 57
Rousseau, Jean-Jacques 259, 260
Rufus, Musonius 111n
Rusticus, Quintus Iunius 199–200
Rutilus Rufus 272
Ruyer, R. 282–3

sage
    nature of 57–8, 147, 226
    and the world 251–61
Sallustius 104
Scholasticism 72–3, 107, 270–1
Schopenhauer, Arthur 271, 272
science, world of 252–4
self-control 59
self-mastery, as spiritual exercise 86,
    135
Seneca
    belonging to the whole 208
    eclecticism 210
    Epicureanism 124n
    flight of the soul 240, 245
    joy 207, 225
    objective representation 189
    peace of mind 229
    present, value of 228, 229
    river of being 182, 183
    sage's life 58

Seneca (*contd*)
  spiritual exercises: learning to die
    96; learning to live 86, 130;
  physics as 98–9
    universalism 230
    wisdom 261
    world 257, 261, 273
serenity
  Epictetus 136
  Epicureans 88, 225
  present, value of 221, 222
Sextus 261, 266
Sileni 148, 161, 162
Simplicius 27–8
Skepticism
  life, conduct of 56–7, 104
  philosophy as a way of life 266
  theory and practice, relationship
    between 60
Socrates
  death 93–4, 166–7, 168–70
  dialogue 20, 23, 89–91, 92–3, 149
  figure of 147: *daimon* 164; dialectical
    irony 149–58; Dionysos 169–70;
    erotic irony 158–65; and Nietzsche
    165–70;
  physical appearance 147–8; seductive
    powers 165–6
  "know thyself" maxim 20, 90
  Logos, faithfulness to 93
  philosophy as a way of life 266, 269,
    281
  unclassifiability 57
  wisdom 235, 265
soul
  flight of 238–48
  immateriality and immortality 100–1
Spinoza, Benedict de 271–2
  Euclid's model 68
  philosophy as a way of life 272, 275
  spiritual exercises 33
Stoicism
  absorption into Platonism 56
  cosmic consciousness 266
  death, exercise for 68
  dogmas, disagreements 61
  Epictetus 191–2
  exegetical phase 5
  features 34, 35

flight of the soul 242–3
Hadot's interest in 280–1
life, conduct of 57, 58–9
and Marcus Aurelius: aesthetics
  190; objective representation
  187–8, 189; river of being 182,
  183; spiritual exercises 13, 14
meditation 59
new meanings of earlier works 65–6
philosophical death 242
philosophical discourse 25–6
philosophy as a way of life 266–7,
  268
pleasure and joy 207
political ideas 274
premeditation on future evils 23
present, value of 69, 84–5, 212,
  222, 226–30, 260, 268
sage 251, 252
self-control 59
spiritual exercises 126: happiness
  103; learning to die 96; learning
  to live 82–7
spiritual perfection 136

teaching, texts written for 63
theology 137–8
theoretical discourse 29
theoretical life 29
Therapeutae 129
theriac and Marcus Aurelius 180–1
theses 63
Thomism 27
Thoreau 33
Thurot, Charles 73–4
treatises 64
truth
  authentic texts 73–4
  pagan and Christian conceptions 4

Ulpian 57
universities, nature of 32, 270–1, 278–9

Veyne, Paul 25
view from above 238–48
Voltaire 250n
wisdom

love of 265
nature of 57, 58, 103, 228, 261
Wittgenstein, Ludwig Josef Johann 17, 18, 280, 285
worry, Epicureans' attitudes 88
writing, therapeutic values 209–11
  Antony 135, 209, 211
  Foucault 209–10
  Marcus Aurelius 195

Xenocrates 266
Xenophon 117n
  flight of the soul 240
  on Socrates 23, 155, 158, 167
Xylander 10

Zeno 113n
Zopyrus 148